Global
Health Systems

Comparing Strategies for Delivering Health Services

Margie Lovett-Scott, EdD, RN, FNP-BC
Associate Professor
Department of Nursing
The College at Brockport, State University of New York

Faith Prather, PhD
Associate Professor
Department of Public Administration
The College at Brockport, State University of New York

JONES & BARTLETT
LEARNING

World Headquarters
Jones & Bartlett Learning
5 Wall Street
Burlington, MA 01803
978-443-5000
info@jblearning.com
www.jblearning.com

Jones & Bartlett Learning books and products are available through most bookstores and online booksellers. To contact Jones & Bartlett Learning directly, call 800-832-0034, fax 978-443-8000, or visit our website, www.jblearning.com.

Substantial discounts on bulk quantities of Jones & Bartlett Learning publications are available to corporations, professional associations, and other qualified organizations. For details and specific discount information, contact the special sales department at Jones & Bartlett Learning via the above contact information or send an email to specialsales@jblearning.com.

Production Credits
Publisher: Michael Brown
Managing Editor: Maro Gartside
Associate Production Editor: Rebekah Linga
Senior Marketing Manager: Sophie Fleck Teague
Manufacturing and Inventory Control Supervisor: Amy Bacus
Composition: Laserwords Private Limited, Chennai, India
Cover Design: Michael O'Donnell
Rights and Photo Reasearch Associate: Amy Rathburn
Cover Image: © Juan Manuel Ordóñez/ShutterStock, Inc.
Printing and Binding: Edwards Brothers Malloy
Cover Printing: Edwards Brothers Malloy

Library of Congress Cataloging-in-Publication Data
Lovett-Scott, Margie.
 Global health systems : comparing strategies for delivering health services / Margie Lovett-Scott and Faith Prather.
  p. ; cm.
 Includes bibliographical references and index.
 ISBN 978-1-4496-1899-5 (pbk.) — ISBN 1-4496-1899-5 (pbk.)
 I. Prather, Faith. II. Title.
 [DNLM: 1. Delivery of Health Care—organization & administration. 2. Cross-Cultural Comparison. 3. Developed Countries. 4. Developing Countries. W 84.1]
 362.109172'4—dc23
                                                                              2012015797

6048

Printed in the United States of America
16 15 14 13 10 9 8 7 6 5 4 3 2

Dedication

First and foremost, we dedicate this book to all of the consumers around the world who have not yet realized *true access* to health care.

—Margie Lovett-Scott and Faith Prather

I personally dedicate this book to my family, especially my children Cassandra, Matthew, Johnny, Terri, Joanne, and Debbie, for their patience and support. Special thanks to my grandson, Bernard (BJ) Lewis, for his creative and inspirational ideas for the book. Additionally, I wish to thank my friends and colleagues—Dr. Elizabeth Heavey for her ongoing support and encouragement; Dr. Katherine Detherage for her reviews and edits; my department chair, Dr. Kathleen Peterson; and our department secretary, Ms. Laurie Allen—for their unrelenting encouragement and support from beginning to end.

—Margie Lovett-Scott

Table of Contents

List of Figures and Tables

Preface

No matter where we choose to reside, we live, work, and play in a global society. The healthcare world is changing. Healthcare systems are striving to become transparent while promising to uphold quality standards, execute seamless processes, and contain costs. In light of this, healthcare professionals are expected to demonstrate outcomes-based performance as they respond to consumer needs. As discussions unfolded in class each year about the major challenges and disparities in the United States healthcare system, our interest in writing this book mounted, particularly as it was clear that the challenges outweighed the opportunities.

This text is written for undergraduate and beginning graduate students, professors, healthcare administrators, public health clinicians and administrators, anyone studying for, or preparing to enter, healthcare administration, and those actively involved in teaching, planning, or improving healthcare systems. The text provides a useful tool for educators in igniting interaction in the classroom. A key feature of the text is the richness and diversity of the case scenarios, which challenge students to think critically and encourage reflective and timely application of the information presented in the text. The scenarios provide limitless opportunities for the professor to engage learners and assess their level of knowledge. Discussion questions can easily be converted to more formal tests of knowledge gained. The Eight Factor Model provides a clear, user-friendly framework from which to assess each country discussed in the text in attempting to determine the extent to which countries provide *true access* to health care and services. Learners are encouraged to conceptualize the information described in the model to assist them in creating their own framework for action in addressing such things as healthcare quality, costs, and true access. Readability is enhanced by this organizing framework. The text presents an overview and synthesis of health care in 11 countries, and challenges and opportunities for transforming systems and maximizing outcomes through vision and leadership. The authors have strived to accurately represent the countries discussed, and believe the text is a valuable resource for any professor teaching about global health care.

The text is divided into four parts. Part I contains three chapters and provides an overview of and introduction to health challenges in the United States which provided the impetus and motivation for writing the text. Among the greatest challenges in the U.S. healthcare system is the high cost of care and health disparities. Part I also includes an introduction to the Eight Factor Model, the organizing framework for the discussion of the 11 countries presented in the text. The six countries discussed in Part II of the text are industrialized (developed) countries, and the five countries discussed in Part III are developing countries. Part IV discusses specific challenges and opportunities, such as those devoted to behavioral health care. It also summarizes comparative data by country. Emphasis is placed on what the managers of one system might learn from the managers of the others, conveying that even wealthier, better informed, industrialized (developed) countries can learn from smaller, more vulnerable, developing countries. This section culminates in a discussion about what is required of 21st century leaders in order to transform healthcare systems.

Foreword

Global Health Systems: Comparing Strategies for Delivering Health Services is an excellent text that is timely, comprehensive, and relevant in today's economy when many countries, especially the United States, are concerned about the financing and delivery of health care. Many of the countries are investigating healthcare reform.

It is often stated that if individuals have good health, then they are rich; good health being the norm of being able to work, play, and lead a productive life. How health care is provided to the citizens of the world is determined by the country in which they live. Some countries may be very involved in ensuring their people are recipients of quality health care, while other countries may be less involved. The age-old question of whether the provision of health care is a right or a privilege is one that is difficult to answer, and may have ethical and moral undertones. How a country treats and provides for the health of its citizens may provide a clue as to the moral fiber of its leadership and populace.

Health care is delivered within a system or systems that are often complex, bureaucratized, and difficult for the average consumer to maneuver. The knowledge and understanding of how health care is delivered and paid for should not simply be known to the leaders and the workers within the systems—all citizens of the world should know how health systems work, how they are organized, and how they are funded. This knowledge is essential to recognizing how healthcare dollars are spent and where, and more importantly, to gaining a better understanding of the system and being an informed consumer in such complex systems. In addition, knowledge of healthcare systems may provide a greater understanding of what norms and standards are in practice and also the quality of care that should be provided within the systems.

Global Health Systems: Comparing Strategies for Delivering Health Services is a comprehensive work that will provide the necessary information for scholars, students, and others interested in and concerned about the provision of health care in multiple countries. It is a comprehensive description of how healthcare systems are organized and delivered. The authors have provided a great service to the readers by compiling this important body of information in one text. The introduction of the Eight Factor Model for evaluating true access is a valuable tool for students and scholars to use in comparing and contrasting countries' healthcare delivery systems. In addition, the model is an excellent tool to use as a framework for researchers interested in studying these systems. This model may help to organize data in a more meaningful and organized way, thereby providing standard data to assist in understanding and guiding decision making.

As a professor who has taught healthcare systems for many years, and who is now approaching the end of my distinguished teaching career, I only wish this book were available during my tenure in the academy.

The authors have provided us with a body of work that is unsurpassed in its comprehensiveness.

Katherine S. Detherage, PhD, RN
Associate Professor of Nursing
Interim Chair, Department of Nursing
Nazareth College
Rochester, NY

Part

I

Overview of Health Care: Addressing True Access

CHAPTER 1

Introduction

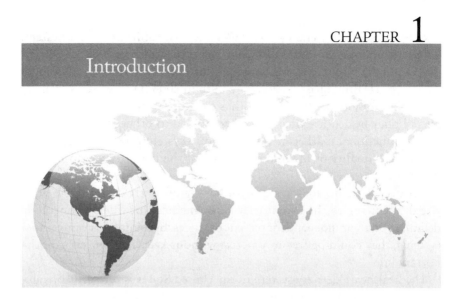

Do not follow where the path may lead. Go instead where there is no path and leave a trail.

—Ralph Waldo Emerson

KEY CONCEPTS

Behavioral

Behavioral health

Developed country

Developing country

Mental health

Disparities

The true measure of a nation's worth is not merely inherent in its wealth, resources, and power, but in how it responds to the health of its people. Yet, America, the wealthiest nation in the world and global leader in a business sense, has allowed its healthcare system to lag behind every other industrialized (developed) country in the world. The United States healthcare system ranks 37th in the industrialized world. In 2006, the United States was number one in terms of healthcare spending per capita but ranked 43rd for adult female mortality, 42nd for adult male mortality, and 36th for life expectancy (Doe, WHO Statistical Information System, 2009). Its ranking for infant mortality went from 28th in 1998, to 29th in 2004, the latest year for which data are available for all countries (National Center for Health Statistics, 2007), to 39th in 2006 (Doe, WHO Statistical Information System, 2009). It still has the lowest life expectancy, and an overall poor healthcare track record compared to other global powers. It is a dysfunctional market-driven healthcare system that has managed to disrupt the quality of life and well-being of the majority of those living in America.

For over three decades, the system has significantly changed the practice of medicine to the extent that many medical providers deliberately defaulted on their independent patient practices. By joining large integrated systems, they could be free to practice without keeping their eyes on the bottom line.

The healthcare delivery system in the United States is primarily private-sector financed and operated. It has been criticized for being highly politicized and influenced, and even bought off by big business. The pharmaceutical industry and other special interest groups are so adamantly opposed to comprehensive healthcare reform that they will resort to any means necessary to prevent it.

According to Nardi and Rooda (2004), the world is shrinking. "We now live and work in an ever-shrinking global village, in which all parts of the globe and its peoples, from Antarctica to Iceland, are not only accessible, but interact with and influence each other in a transactional dance of cross-cultural behaviors, values, views, and beliefs" (Nardi & Rooda, 2004, p. 87). The race and ethnic profile in the United States is changing; the white majority is shrinking as the population ages while the underrepresented ethnic and racial groups are younger and growing in numbers (Spector, 2002). The United States as a nation is becoming a mosaic of many cultures. The long-standing homogeneous communities in which we once lived are a figment of the past (Purnell & Paulanka, 2003). Health professionals in the United States must conduct business differently if they are to improve health outcomes nationally. Health professionals, especially leaders, must be committed to effectively addressing health problems never before witnessed in this country, and it must be done expeditiously and with fiscal savvy.

This text discusses health care in 11 countries, of which six are industrialized (developed) and five are developing (once referred to as Third World). In distinguishing between countries that are developed and developing, the authors use international criteria. Although experts do not entirely agree on what makes a country developed or developing, many agree on some strong distinguishing characteristics. The strongest distinguishing support is that *developed countries* (industrialized) have high incomes per capita, high gross domestic products per capita, industrial dominance, and the most recent criterion is that they have a high United Nations Human Development Index (HDI). In addition to the first three criteria, this Index factors in life expectancy and education. In other words, how a country converts its income and resources to develop people educationally and provide opportunities for them to enjoy good health (United Nations, 2010) is an important consideration in determining whether a country makes the developed list. Countries with HDIs of 0.788 and greater are considered by the International Monetary Fund (IMF) and the CIA as advanced (CIA, 2009), qualifying them as developed countries. In the opinion of Kofi Annan, former Secretary General of the United Nations, a developed country is "a country that allows all its citizens to enjoy a free and healthy life in a safe environment," (Kofi Annan, 2008). *Developing countries* (non-industrialized, once referred to as underdeveloped or Third World) are those countries that lack the characteristics of developed countries in that they are still struggling with their economies, are not major exporters of commodities, and/ or have poorer overall life expectancy and health outcomes.

The United Kingdom was the first country to earn the distinction of developed, followed by Belgium, then the United States. The countries discussed in Chapters 4–14 of this book that are accredited with being developed countries are the United Kingdom, the United States, Canada, Japan, France, and Italy. The countries considered developing countries are Brazil, Cuba, India, the Russian Federation, and Ghana. Although there are inconsistencies in the criteria applied to determine whether a country falls into the developed or developing category, it is often expected that the more economically and fiscally secure developed countries should have better economic, education, and health outcomes.

The major rationale for the selection of countries was author interest. Each of the 11 systems of health care is examined within the framework of a true *access* model developed by the authors. The motivation for the book emerged from annual class discussions about the problems in the United States Health Care Delivery System (USHCDS) including major disparities in care, and similarities to and differences among other systems of care. The Institute of Medicine and *Healthy People 2010* have identified the elimination of health disparities as priority initiatives for health professionals to address. As a consequence, a special chapter in the book is devoted to a discussion of disparities in the USHCDS with age- and race-based case scenarios.

The text builds on the premise that the current system of healthcare delivery in the United States is in need of major transformation. In attempting to fix the United States system, much can be learned from healthcare systems around the world. It also demonstrates how imperative it is for healthcare leaders to shift their focus from management to leadership.

Perhaps the most compelling reason for writing *Global Health Systems: Comparing Strategies for Delivering Health Services* is to make an appeal to the reader to consider new ways of conducting healthcare business. The text's comparative perspectives are discussed in Chapter 16 with a brief overview of global perspectives in general and a summarizing discussion of the 11 systems addressed in the book. The U.S. healthcare system has been so busy managing that it has managed its way into disrepair. In the words of Warren Bennis, "managers are people who do things right, while leaders are people who do the right thing" (Bennis, 2009, p. 1). True leaders must be visionaries prepared to delegate the responsibility for managing to those capable of handling the day-to-day system operations. This will allow leaders to shift their attention to proactively planning for a brighter healthcare future. If they fail to do so, the system loses much more than could ever be imagined.

Developing countries are challenged daily because they lack the necessary resources to meet the healthcare needs of their people. For example, India, despite already lacking resources to address its healthcare challenges, must now contend with the problems created by new slums that emerged during the 20th century. The Russian Federation, with its extremely high death rate, is committing new financial resources in an attempt to reverse this devastating trend.

What makes this text different from other health systems books is that it offers a novel view of systems globally and suggests what the managers of one system can learn from those of another. *Global Health Systems: Comparing Strategies for Delivering Health Services* challenges healthcare leaders around the world to approach their healthcare delivery in new ways, by taking innovative measures. In the United States for example, healthcare leaders must suspend their exhaustive, time-consuming national healthcare debate, engage in civil, across the aisle collaboration, and seize control of an out-of-control system. Working together to closely examine what is wrong, might finally result in implementing the necessary processes to fix the system and eliminate *health disparities* defined by the Institute of Medicine as "racial or ethnic differences in the quality of health care that are not due to access-related factors such as, insurance coverage, or clinical needs, preferences, and appropriateness of intervention" (Smedley, Stith, & Nelson, 2002, p. 5).

An Eight Factor Model for striving to achieve *"true access"* is introduced (in Chapter 3) and defined by the authors as being able to get to and from services, having the ability to pay for the services, and getting your needs met once in the system. Far too often, when discussions occur regarding access to health care there is no consideration given to the quality of the service consumers receive once in the system. The premise of true access suggests that even when a patient is able to make it to and from healthcare services, and have the ability to pay, they have been denied access if they leave that encounter without receiving what they needed.

The Eight Factor Model derives from extensive discussions with consumers and healthcare providers about the true meaning of *access, health disparities,* and the relatively poor outcomes achieved in the United States healthcare delivery system. The model provides a framework for examining each of the 11 healthcare systems introduced in the book. Healthcare leaders and policymakers are encouraged to consider these eight foundational factors when attempting to determine the extent to which a system is providing *true access* to health care. All eight factors depicted in the model must be assessed before a final decision is made about access. The fundamental assumption behind utilizing this model is that it will inform health policy decisions. When informed about what prevents a system from providing access, policymakers are better positioned to implement corrective strategies. The model is presented in detail in Chapter 3.

Objectives and key concepts introduced at the beginning of each chapter are of particular relevance to the healthcare system being discussed, and are significant complements to the book. Discussion questions at the end of each chapter, designed to stimulate critical thinking about healthcare delivery, are an added feature of the text. A list of references at the end of each chapter affords readers an opportunity to retrieve citations easily and engage in enrichment reading if desired. The final feature of the text is a glossary of terms, and an easy to use index catalogued by topic.

The text is divided into four parts and 17 chapters. Part I includes three sections and provides the motivation for writing the text. This motivation, fueled by an extensive examination of the delivery of health care in the United States and the major role health disparities played in catapulting the country toward reform, suggested the importance of including a section in the text exclusively devoted to disparities in the U.S. health system. The introductory discussion (Chapter 1) provides some background and an overview of the healthcare system in the United States and how it is ranked among other countries in the world. It also discusses the transcultural nature of health, challenges to be addressed, and opportunities for change. "Disparities in Health Care: Race and Age Matters" (Chapter 2) focuses on major health disparities seen in the United States. As Marmot and colleagues advise:

> George Orwell notwithstanding, all people are not born equal. Individual differences in genetic endowment may well control differences in life-expectancy. Even if all individuals are subject to the same environmental influences they would not flourish, age, and die at the same rate (Marmot, Bobak, & Smith, 1995, p. 174).

"The Eight Factor Model for Evaluating True Access" (Chapter 3) introduces the reader to the Eight Factor Model, a framework for assessing the strengths and weaknesses of systems in order to determine the extent to which a system is providing what the authors refer to as true access. The eight factors in the model are 1) historical, 2) structure, 3) financing, 4) interventional, 5) preventive, 6) resources, 7) major health issues, and 8) health disparities.

"Health Care in Industrialized (Developed) Countries" (Part II, which comprises Chapters 4–9 of the text) discusses health delivery in six systems: the United States, Canada, France, Japan, the United Kingdom, and Italy. The remaining five countries, Brazil, Cuba, Ghana, India, and the Russian Federation are discussed in Part III of the text. Starting with the United States health system, discussions regarding each country's provision for long-term care and care of older adults are presented from a comparative viewpoint. The intent is to bring clarity and understanding to these care options. Behavioral healthcare costs and challenges are integrated into a separate discussion (see Chapter 15).

"The Healthcare System in the United States" (Chapter 4) provides an in-depth look at the system of healthcare delivery in the United States during the critical period from 1984 to 2010. It also discusses the challenges as the country emerged cyclically from primary care being provided in emergency departments thirty years ago, to receiving care in Community/Migrant Health Centers (C/MHCs) during the late eighties and nineties, and today where patients once again are seeking primary care in emergency departments.

After a brief introduction and overview, the historical perspectives of each country are discussed, followed by a country-by-country examination of performance based on achievement of the remaining seven factors in the model. Again, the emphasis is on what one country might learn from another. For example, one might wrongfully assume that the wealthier the country, the better the health outcomes. However, a country that has historically lacked the fiscal capacity and infrastructure to support a well-qualified staff, with uniquely different ways of providing services, may have better outcomes and greater success in providing true access than a country rich in fiscal and human resources.

In examining major health issues, financing priorities, and serious system challenges such as health disparities, the discussions within each of the 11 countries (Chapters 4–14) offer enriching case scenarios with commentaries designed to bring collaborative excitement to the learning experience. Discussion questions are included to emphasize, with clarity, the extent to which disparities in health occur. The questions should also stimulate discussion about ways in which disparities might be eliminated. These scenarios provide the learner with opportunities to thoroughly discuss health issues with special attention to identifying solutions.

The fourth and final part of the text presents discussions in three chapters (15, 16, and 17). "Prevalence and Management of Behavioral Health Care" (Chapter 15) is devoted to a discussion about the prevalence and management of behavioral health problems in the 11 countries presented in Parts II and III of the text. Behavioral health is, in some countries, the overarching umbrella under which community-based psychiatric mental health services are often grouped. However, it is important to note that many countries make reference only to psychiatric/mental health problems with no mention of behavioral health. When discussing behavioral health in this text, the NIH definition of *behavioral* as overt actions to underlying psychological processes such as cognition, emotion, temperament, and motivation, and bio-behavioral interactions is used. The Office of Behavioral and Social Research of the NIH (2010) agreed on this definition for the purpose of engaging in research to predict or influence health outcomes or health risk factors. *Behavioral health* places emphasis on maintaining health and function and preventing illness (Matarazzo, 1980), as well as hospitalization by focusing on actions that can be managed or changed.

"Comparative Health Systems" (Chapter 16) is a culminating discussion about comparative perspectives on health. It provides a focused discussion about the health challenges internationally, the leading causes of death worldwide, common diseases of each country, the similarities and differences between Western and non-Western delivery systems, and a brief discussion about health disparities in and among countries from a comparative perspective. It appeals to the reader to utilize information without criticizing systems; rather, learning from each.

"Conclusion and Future Leadership" (Chapter 17) focuses on the future of health care globally and the leadership needed to move the healthcare agenda into the 21st century. It also reemphasizes the importance of what one country might learn from another. This discussion encourages learners to remain optimistic as they consider the future of health care. As healthcare policymakers, administrators, and providers make informed health policy decisions, they position themselves to prepare for a brighter future in health care.

REFERENCES

Annan, K. (2008). Retrieved February 23, 2011 from http://www.unescap.org/unis /press/G_05_00.htm

Bennis, W. (2009). *On becoming a leader: The leadership classic.* New York: Random Century.

Central Intelligence Agency (CIA). (2009). The world fact book. Retrieved on 11/23/2010 from https://www.cia.gov/library/publications/the world-factbook /rankorder/2102rank.html

Doe, J. (2009). WHO Statistical Information System (WHOSIS). Geneva: World Health Organization, September.

Marmot, M., Bobak, M., & Smith, G. D. (1995). Explanations for social inequalities in health. In Benjamin C. Amick, Sol Levine, Alvin R. Tarlov, and Diana Chapman Walsh, *Society and Health* (p. 174). New York: Oxford University Press.

Matarazzo, J. D. (1980). Behavioral health and behavioral medicine: Frontiers for new health psychology. *American Psychologist 35,* 807–817.

McGraw-Hill Medical Dictionary of Allied Health. Mental health. (2002). New York: McGraw-Hill Companies, Inc.

Nardi, D. A & Rooda, L. A. (2004). Diversity and patient care in a shrinking world. *Advances in Renal Replacement Therapy, 11*(1), 87–91.

National Center for Health Statistics. (2007). *Health, United States, 2007 with chartbook on trends in the health of Americans.* Hyattsville, MD.

National Institute of Health (NIH). (2010). *Behavioral and social sciences (BSSR) definition.* The Office of Behavioral and Social Research. Retrieved February 13, 2012 from http://www.obssr. od.nih.gov/about_ obssr/BSSR_CC/BSSR_definition /definition.aspx

Purnell, L & Paulanka, B. (2003). *Transcultural health care: A culturally competent approach.* Philadelphia: F.A. Davis Company.

Smedley, B. D., Stith, A. Y., & Nelson, A. R. (2002). *Unequal treatment: Confronting racial and ethnic disparities in health care.* Institute of Medicine. Committee on understanding and eliminating racial and ethnic disparities in health care, Board on Health Policy, Institute of Medicine. Washington, DC: The National Academies Press.

Spector, R. (2002). Cultural diversity. In S. Janes and Karen Spucier Lundy, *Essentials in Community Based Nursing* (p. 122). Sudbury, MA: Jones and Bartlett Publishers.

United Nations (UN). (2010). Human development report. Retrieved February 23, 2010 from http://www.hdr.undp.org/en/media/HDR_2010_complete_reprint .pdf

CHAPTER 2

Disparities in Health Care: Race and Age Matters

Nearly all men can stand adversity, but if you want to test a man's character, give him power.

—Abraham Lincoln

BEHAVIORAL OBJECTIVES

At the end of this chapter the learner will be able to:

1. Examine the concept of access and the extent to which it is addressed.
2. Discuss at least three race-based disparities in health.
3. Discuss at least two age-based disparities in health.

KEY CONCEPTS

EPIC

Metabolic syndrome

Prevalence

INTRODUCTION

America has always been referred to as "the land of the free and home of the brave," the most powerful country in the world, rich in human and fiscal resources, and world leader in the advancement of scientific knowledge. Despite its wealth and position globally, health care is so unevenly distributed in the United States that a quick assessment reveals some individuals receive fewer services than others. Being an older adult and disenfranchised can greatly influence care received and overall health outcomes. The United States is one of only two countries in the industrialized world without a universal system of health care. In fact, the healthcare delivery system in the United States has a rather embarrassing track record, with disparities in health care being an important underlying factor. Although limited progress has been made in passing a healthcare bill, the newly drafted legislation lacks a "public option" and falls short of providing coverage for everyone in need. Even when the healthcare plan is fully implemented, it will not eliminate disparities. It is imperative that health providers acknowledge the imperfections in the system's care delivery, and clearly conceptualize the true meaning of access to quality health care, so that policies and procedures might be implemented to address these serious matters.

This chapter raises five questions that require serious attention by health providers if true access and elimination of disparities are to be addressed. What is all the disparity fuss about? Is access adequately defined, or is the concept outdated and in need of redefinition? Is lack of access perceived or real? How do providers determine quality outcomes? Finally, how if at all, can compliance be better addressed? These are not new topics but are discussed in such a way as to assist providers to better understand and address disparate care in their practices.

WHAT IS ALL THE DISPARITY FUSS ABOUT?

Since 2002, when the Institute of Medicine released its report on ethnic and racial disparities in health care, the topic has been prevalent in the literature. Many have documented unequal diagnosis and treatment of underrepresented cultural groups in the United States (Schneider, Zaslavsky, and Epstein, 2002; Smedley, Stith, Nelson, 2002; Petersen et al., 2002; Hill, Shipp, and Wilson, 2002; Clegg et al., 2002; and Margolis et al., 2003).

Although cardiovascular disease is the leading cause of death in the United States for all races and ethnicities, African Americans are 50% more likely to develop heart disease, have a 43% greater incidence of death from heart disease, and tend to die earlier as compared to European Americans. Additionally, African American women have a 25% higher chance of dying within a year of diagnosis, as compared to men (Patlak, 2001).

In a large study using Medicare data from more than 294 plans, Schneider et al. (2002) found that African American patients received fewer appropriate medical services such as mammography, diabetic retinal examinations, beta blockers at discharge after a heart attack, and follow up for mental illness, than white patients, leading the authors to conclude that access is not the only driver of racial and ethnic healthcare disparities.

It is common knowledge that African American patients receive far fewer invasive cardiac procedures than white patients (Conigliaro et al., 2000; Peterson et al., 1994; and Whittle et al., 1993). However, African American patients in one study, although considered ideal candidates, were 42% less likely than whites to receive life-saving thrombolytic therapy upon arrival at the Veterans Health Administration Hospital, a facility considered an equal-access care system. African American patients were also less likely to receive bypass surgery, but more likely to receive aspirin at discharge (Petersen et al., 2002). Racial disparities in the use of medications, angiography, and angioplasty among veterans with acute myocardial infarction (heart attack) were not observed.

African American women are in double jeopardy, facing differential treatment as a result of being black and female. They are more likely to die of a heart attack before ever reaching the hospital and less likely to be recommended for, or actually receive, therapeutic surgical procedures. The reasonable explanation is that physician differential treatment of women directly and indirectly influences their health outcomes (Hill, Shipp, and Wilson, 2002). Hill, Shipp, and Wilson (2002, p. 3) indicate "from our research, we have found that there is differential treatment of African American females with heart disease and that there are disparities in outcomes among African American females with heart disease due to differential treatment on the part of the physician in proposing invasive treatment plans or prescribing particular medicines."

ACCESS DEFINED: OUTDATED OR IN NEED OF REDEFINITION?

Most health professionals define access to health care as typically having insurance, or the ability to pay out of pocket for quality health care, and having transportation to get to and from healthcare services. Therefore, in the eyes of the provider, insurance coverage and transportation equates to access. Access so narrowly defined creates a dilemma for most of the nation's disenfranchised. True access, in our view, goes beyond getting to and from the service and having the ability to pay. Rather, *true access includes patients getting their needs met once they enter the system.*

In a study of adolescents attending a clinic, Pope and John (1999) found that patients were often labeled before even being seen, and interventions were clearly negatively skewed during provider interactions with minority patients as compared to majority patients. When this occurs, access to care is impossible. Because the typical health provider honestly believes that the system is fair, and that people living in the United States generally have equal access to health services, they are puzzled by, and at times react defensively to, the mere suggestion that physicians and nurses would intentionally give better care and treatment to some patients over others. However, it happens more often than most would like to think.

The discussion about disparities is an age-old topic among the health-care community. It is time, however, to move the disparity agenda from the boardroom to the action-oriented workplace, particularly as hypertension and chronic respiratory problems such as reactive airway disease, diabetes mellitus, renal failure, metabolic syndrome, and multiple organ dysfunction with its debilitating complications are raising havoc in the African American and Latino American communities even when access is not a factor (Prussian, Barksdale-Brown, and Dieckmann, 2007). Each of these preventable problems disproportionately affects racial and ethnic minorities. Some racial and ethnic minorities have much higher percentages of metabolic syndrome than general population estimates. For example, Latinos have a prevalence rate of 32%, African Americans have a 22% prevalence rate, and women have a much higher prevalence rate than men (American Heart Association, 2005). *Prevalence* is the total number of cases at a particular point in time.

Metabolic syndrome is defined as a set of health factors that are associated with an increased chance of developing heart disease, stroke, diabetes, or a combination of these problems and it is strongly linked to insulin resistance. Several factors contribute to developing metabolic syndrome, including being overweight, physical inactivity, and genetics (Prussian, Barksdale-Brown, Dieckmann, 2007). Prussian et al. (2007) suggest that African Americans have high rates of hypertension even without considering metabolic syndrome, and may be at more disease risk than other populations. Hispanics have an increased risk of diabetes associated with metabolic syndrome.

These examples illustrate the importance of moving the disparity topic from discussant roundtables to implementation of healthcare policies that can be fully operationalized. Otherwise, we lose the battle against quality of life for many who we claim to serve. The foundational basis for these health problems are threefold: 1) lack of true access, 2) inability to pay for prescribed medications, and 3) inadequate patient and family teaching to enhance compliance. Not one of these problems is new but if they are to effectively addressed, then they must be examined in a new way.

Decades after the implementation of federal initiatives such as Medicaid and EPIC (a prescription plan for the elderly), and years after Child Health

Plus (health insurance for infants and children), racial and age disparities still exist in this country. Once the problem is acknowledged, health providers must push for an agenda for change—a call for action. Much of the world's population is dying from illnesses and conditions that are well within the realm of prevention.

Redefining access is perhaps long overdue. In addition to getting to and from services and having the ability to pay, we propose that true access to health care is also defined as *when individuals enter the healthcare system and leave having had their needs met.* This might include routine visits to primary care offices, clinics, health centers, or specialty offices; visits to the emergency room or urgent care centers; or even stays in hospitals or other healthcare facilities. When patients attempt to access these services and perceive they have been insulted, offended, disrespected, labeled, or even ignored, they have been denied access.

It has been well documented in the literature that African American patients are more likely to report distrust of the healthcare system, to report being treated with disrespect during healthcare visits, and to report feeling that they might be better served by a nonwhite physician (Kaplan, Gandek, Greenfield, Rogers, & Ware, 1995; Cooper-Patrick et al., 1999; Saha, Komaromy, Koepsell, Bidman, 1999; Doescher, Saver, Franks, Fiscella, 2000). Patients often share stories of visiting the same primary care provider (PCP) for over 20 years and being poorly received, repeatedly labeled, misunderstood, and/or misjudged by the first person who greets them in the office or with whom they speak on the telephone. In these cases, even if patients are received well by the PCP, true access in this office is still a problem.

Much of the problem results from what we describe as "the front desk syndrome," the receptionist or secretary consistently oversteps their boundaries and speaks for, or intervenes on behalf of, the provider. This behavior is often pervasive and damaging. It sometimes occurs with the full knowledge of the busy provider, resulting in some patients dropping from the practice without explanation. An easy fix might be to consider sensitizing staff to respond better to the needs of clients from various cultural backgrounds. This would help to maximize provider–patient interactions. Another strategy might be to carefully review and revise hiring goals to include persons reflecting the racial and ethnic backgrounds of the clients seen by the provider. This good faith initiative is important, especially as patients report never seeing an employee who even remotely resembles their age, race, or ethnicity except in cleaning positions. A more culturally representative staff might model appropriate behaviors and encourage staff competency in communicating across cultures.

A classic example of ineffective communication across cultures is dismissing the verbal and non-verbal cues conveyed by patients who report they are in serious pain and instead labeling them as "drug seeking." Pain is subjective, it must be thoroughly assessed and is not to be undermined or minimized. Another example is taking a patient's response to assessment questions literally without consideration for their age or culture. For example, when a provider in the emergency department seems annoyed or openly makes statements such as, "This is the third patient I've seen today claiming their problems just started. If I see one more patient today who tells me he has had his symptoms 'for a minute,' and yet, showed up in this ED, I'm going to scream." The physician's frustration with the patient who responds he has had his symptoms "for a minute" shows lack of cultural knowledge. For many, especially younger persons, the phrase "for a minute" means they have been sick for a long time. This provider is demonstrating age and cultural insensitivity.

In many instances, although dissatisfied with support staff and/or their provider, patients feel trapped, and remain with a practice because they feel they lack other options. A final example of failure to communicate across cultures involves depression, especially in Asian women. Asian women who complain of pain in their head, heart, and stomach for three years or who present in the ED with complaints of their heart hurting might receive a battery of diagnostic cardiac tests, but depression might be the problem. Being initially assessed by a provider without regard for the patient's culture leads to a cardiac workup instead of tests for depression (Estin, 1999). Settling in America can often lead to a dramatic role change for Asian women. This example demonstrates how important it is for health professionals to educate themselves about the health beliefs and practices of the ethnic groups most prevalent in their practice areas (Estin, 1999).

LACK OF ACCESS TO CARE: PERCEPTION OR REALITY?

Is lack of access to care in the eyes of the patient or is it real? Lack of access needs a critical new look. As explained earlier in this chapter, lack of access is typically viewed as the patient's inability to see the provider, or to pay for services. With regard to transportation, many providers, partly due to the availability of Medicaid transport services, would argue that very few of their patients have legitimate excuses for not getting to their provider's offices. While getting to the provider's office may not be a problem, in reality, true access goes beyond just making it to the appointment. In many cases, although the patient gets to see the provider, some report later that they leave without having their health concerns addressed. The next section highlights three specific patients who were actually seen by their providers yet still lacked true access.

QUALITY HEALTH OUTCOMES: THE PROVIDER'S PERSPECTIVE

Part of what makes the discussion of true access so vibrant in regard to achieving quality health outcomes is what occurs in practice settings after patients arrive. Three situations illustrating patient attempts at accessing quality care and getting their needs met are described in the following scenarios.

A Latino patient who lives within walking distance of the provider's office arrives at the practice without difficulty. This patient may be considered to have great access. Yet the provider, after spending 15 or 20 minutes with the patient, misses the real message being conveyed during the visit and the patient leaves feeling his needs were unmet. Missing critical cues during an encounter with a patient may happen just because the provider knows nothing about the patient's culture. The provider may be culturally insensitive or simply providing disparate treatment. In other words, the provider may have let the patient's race negatively influence the care decisions. However, if asked, providers may be unaware that patients in their offices are treated differently.

Another example of denied access can be seen in the case of an older adult, European American diabetic patient who comes in for a routine visit and is dehydrated (e.g., lips cracked and skin tenting). This patient needs more than a routine encounter. During the encounter it seems obvious that the patient is probably not taking his medication. He did not bring his glucometer to the visit but says his sugar checks have been okay at home. In spite of this, the patient gets a flu shot, has his feet checked, and leaves with an appointment for a four week follow-up visit. There is other information needed, and diagnostic tests are indicated. Yet, not even a fingerstick blood glucose is obtained during the encounter. When later questioned, the provider seemed honestly surprised that an office glucose check was not done, the need for increasing fluids was not discussed, and the patient was not sent for labs.

Another lack of access example is seen in the intervention with an African American hypertension patient who is being currently treated with Vaseretic 10-25. The patient's blood pressure is 196/100. She is either not taking her medication, or in need of a medication adjustment, although she does not complain of any particular ill feelings except her usual chronic headache.

She also leaves with a one month follow-up appointment after being reprimanded by her provider for "gaining three pounds since her last visit, poor BP control, and being non-compliant." The patient reported that no one rechecked her blood pressure during the visit or before leaving.

When later discussing this scenario with two uninvolved providers they agreed the patient was clearly non-compliant but someone should have rechecked the blood pressure. Neither made mention of the fact that a more thorough assessment of the patient's neurological status should have been done because of her headaches. Also, perhaps Vaseretic (a combination drug containing enalapril, an ACE inhibitor, and hydrochlorothiazide, a thiazide diuretic) may not have been the best medication for this patient. ACE inhibitors are generally less effective in African Americans (Exner et al., 2001). In one study of black and white patients with left ventricular dysfunction, white patients showed significant reduction in blood pressure after being treated for 1 year with enalapril, black patients did not; the black patients also had higher rates of hospitalization and death (Burroughs et al., 2002; Exner et al., 2001). Furthermore, although the JNC VII guidelines, recommend thiazide diuretics as the first line of treatment for hypertension, because it has an adverse effect of increasing the blood sugar (NPPR, 2008, p. 24) it may also not have been the best diuretic choice for a patient already at risk for diabetes mellitus type II. Kudzma (1992) and Munoz and Hilgenberg (2005) encourage health providers to be more selective when prescribing medications for their patients, suggesting that medications, although effective in treating one group of individuals, may not be the right choice for a different group of individuals.

On the surface, each patient appears to have had access to health care because they each completed their visits with their primary providers, the one person who knew them better than anyone else in the practice. However, despite being seen by competent providers that day at least two of the patients are in serious trouble. Not one of the three had true access. For whatever reason, obvious signs and symptoms were missed, ignored, dismissed, or considered as something to be addressed during the next visit.

Listening with your eyes, ears, and a caring attitude to what patients are really trying to convey, or even conceal for fear of being labeled non-compliant, or to a drug seeker, uncaring or not responsible for his or her own health status, is essential to providing true access to health care. Being in sync with every patient's health need and concern is no easy task but is required if a provider is to address true access to care.

Another common problem impacting access is that the Medicaid system is so structured that when patients present with multiple across-service problems, they can only have one problem addressed on any given visit. This prevents a health center patient who keeps an important appointment with the primary care provider (PCP) from seeing a dentist in the health center on the same day. Even if the PCP discovers that the patient is in need of immediate dental care, Medicaid will not pay for a second visit on the same day. Once the encounter has started, the PCP must suspend that visit, not document it, and send the patient across the hall for an emergency dental visit instead. Providers must make difficult decisions based on how the patient presents, about the most important intervention needed, and follow-up visits. The flu shot or pneumonia vaccine might have to wait for a few days until after a dental visit.

LACK OF RESOURCES FOR PRESCRIPTIONS

A problem of particular concern that results in disparities is that some clients lack the ability to pay for medications. Despite the fact that the medication they need may be stockpiled in a storeroom at the practice site, some patients are never offered samples by the provider. This is particularly reported to be true of the working poor and older adults who are on fixed incomes. They leave with the prescription sometimes knowing in advance they have no money to fill it, but pride prevents them from revealing this information. Consequently, their condition worsens, and they return either to the ED or present to their provider's office at a later date with a now, significantly more complicated problem which is more costly to treat. Sometimes out of pride, or maybe even fear of being labeled poor, not a hint of this is shared with the provider.

A child, then, with reactive airway disease (asthma) who does not get asthma maintenance medication will repeatedly return to the emergency department for rescue treatments when the acute attack, which is certain to happen, occurs. The parent in this case might be openly criticized for not filling the prescriptions but also allowed to leave without samples, a social work referral, or intervention, only to have the emergency cycle repeat itself.

There is even inequity in terms of which patients actually get the drug samples to tide them over until getting the prescription filled; this boils down to how the person is viewed by the provider. Unfortunately, the decision is sometimes race-based. It is essential that providers monitor the dissemination of samples and ensure that they go to the patients most in need.

TEACHING FOR IMPROVED COMPLIANCE

It has been well established that often people of African descent will not go on antihypertensive medications. They share a common notion that "once on it, you're on it for life." Somehow, they have gotten the inaccurate notion that the problem will improve without the medication. They negotiate a personal bargain, "If I just start eating right, avoid the extra salt, and lose a few pounds the blood pressure will come down." Although weight reduction and diet will help, by the time medications are needed the problem won't be resolved with diet and weight control alone. Patients need to be given all the necessary information to make decisions about management of their health and if the decision is contrary to the providers, they will learn to deal with it.

I recall recently taking a client's blood pressure at church because she was complaining of a terrible headache. One glance in her eyes revealed broken capillaries leading me to believe it prudent to do so. I knew her blood pressure was elevated, even before taking it, and suspected she knew she had hypertension. I said, "I can tell you haven't been taking your blood pressure medicine." She replied, "I was given a prescription five weeks ago but never filled it because someone told me once you start taking blood pressure pills, you can't stop, you're on them for life." Her blood pressure was 200/110. I told her daughter to take her mom directly to the ED. I explained that without medicine she was at risk for having a massive stroke and dying, but with medication she could control her blood pressure and headaches and still lead a long, quality life.

This was not likely her first time hearing this information but her response was, "Oh my God, my mother and aunt both died from a stroke, I'm going to get the prescription filled today." She made a point of following up with me during our many church encounters and she reports her blood pressure is now well controlled, as are her headaches. She has also worked out a weight reduction plan and exercise program with her PCP and is beginning to read food labels to increase her awareness of especially high sodium and fat content.

A casual informative session with a person who isn't even responsible for her health care probably made a strong enough impact on her to lower her risk of target organ damage and preserve her life. Even if she reaches a point at which she no longer complies with the regimen developed by her PCP, she has all the necessary information to improve her compliance, if she so desires. When patients understand their illness and the importance of following specific regimens they are more likely to comply. Although scare tactics were not the intent during the church encounter with this individual, being candid with patients sometimes helps them to put the situation in perspective, which might result in them taking action.

SUMMARY

Researchers often take differing positions on the causes of disparities and the solutions needed to address them. However, many would agree that resolving the disparity problem is a multidisciplinary effort. Healthy People 2010 placed eliminating health disparities among its most important goals (USDHHS, 2006). Long, Chang, Ibrahim, and Asch (2004, p. 811) suggest that "the elimination of hypertension, HIV infection, diabetes, and homicide would contribute the greatest to eliminating racial disparities in mortality" (Long et al., 2004, p. 811), an accurate, but unrealistic achievement. Improving the health of all people is achievable when everyone comes together to collaborate on putting forth the best efforts in creating an environment of health equity and change. The nation's healthcare leaders must ensure that 21st century practices are better than those of the previous era.

The final pages of this chapter present case scenarios that call attention to disparities in health, evidenced by differential practices and access to care issues. The cases can be used to facilitate discussions in class and training forums.

CASE STUDIES

As this chapter on disparities so vividly points out, diversity issues are uncomfortable; they take us outside our realm of understanding. The following scenarios are designed to stimulate candid discussion about disparities in health care, and to help staff identify best practices for building a climate of cultural competence. Each scenario draws on a real-life experience. The cases demonstrate how seriously cultural differences, when unattended and not addressed explicitly, can impact workplace relations, staff performance, supervision, administrative policy, and ultimately, the quality of patient care.

The letters of the scenarios spell out the phrase "ASK ME." Interpreting the meaning of this title could be an effective warm-up activity in this series. We believe it is worthwhile to ask participants what they think the title means. Some staff may suggest that "ASK ME" means never to forget the patient in the treatment situation—we must work *with,* rather than around, the patient. We must talk *to,* rather than *about* the patient. We should remember to listen to patients, ask for clarification, and re-state their concerns and feelings.

Another interpretation of "ASK ME," and one that falls in line with facilitating this exercise, is that we should recognize the people who do the work. In the sensitive context of diversity, health practitioners not only follow policies and procedures, they must manage a number of situations with few rules and precedents. The scenarios ask staff to talk about their encounters with culturally different patients. The lessons of cultural competence are embedded in their stories. The scenarios establish a forum for staff to discuss what they know, what they find perplexing or difficult, and how they have finessed potentially explosive situations. Over a busy work day, this kind of discussion and the valuable insights that surface may get passed around at the proverbial water cooler but they are rarely written down. This exercise provides a structured opportunity to turn this situation around.

Facilitating the Scenarios

The scenarios are intended as discussion starters and therefore do not prescribe a "right" answer. This exercise is flexible. For example, the facilitator can work with one case or the whole set of scenarios. The context for the scenarios can be a formal training session or an informal small group meeting. The aim of the discussion is to produce strategies that support the development of cultural competence. The dialogue should be a vibrant exchange of ideas for developing a culturally competent workplace: What are we doing well? What needs work? Participants' comments should be recorded on flipcharts or whiteboards. This approach validates and reinforces the importance of each person's contribution to the discussion.

The scenarios include three key questions for participants followed by discussion points the facilitator can utilize for further exploration of the topic.

Diversity discussions typically evoke strong emotions and should be carefully planned. For example, who should facilitate the discussions—someone within the agency or an outside consultant? Who should attend these discussions? Should we have a mix of administrators and staff or conduct separate sessions for each group? All too often the good intentions of diversity discussions break down because these critical issues are not thoroughly considered.

A Case Study #1

INSTRUCTIONS

Critique the case and analyze the situation. Ask yourself the following questions:

1. Did this patient have access to care? If your answer is "No," why not? If your answer is "Yes," why?
2. What, if anything, should the provider do?
3. Is there anything the patient can do?

Mr. Andersen is a 68-year-old, African American male who recently recovered from a Trans Ischemic Attack (TIA) commonly known as a mini stroke. He has a history of hypertension and takes Metoprolol 50 mg and hydrochlorothiazide 25 mg once a day. He is just completing his follow-up visit with his primary care provider. As the visit is winding down the physician writes a prescription for Plavix 75 mg (a 90-day supply) with directions to take one tablet every day. He also tells him to take 1 baby aspirin a day. As the physician proceeds to write the prescription he stresses repeatedly the importance of taking both medications without fail in order to "prevent another TIA."

Unknown to Mr. Andersen, having a first TIA puts him at great risk of having a second one. Mr. Andersen works his way through the packed waiting room to the front desk. The receptionist glances down as she is scheduling Mr. Andersen's next appointment. Seeing the prescription Mr. Andersen is holding, she buzzes the physician over the intercom stating, "the patient has no insurance so he will have to pay out-of-pocket for the Plavix, what do you want him to do?" Out comes the physician who, as he rips up the prescription, tells Mr. Andersen to just take the aspirin, assuring him he would be just fine.

DISCUSSION POINTS

1. What prompted the physician to make such a dramatic turnaround in his advice to Mr. Andersen?
2. What message is the doctor sending to Mr. Andersen?
3. Identify the medical issues that require attention.
4. Explain the receptionist's behavior in this situation. How do you think Mr. Andersen felt when she announced his lack of insurance over the intercom? What happened to patient confidentiality in this situation?

S Case Study #2

INSTRUCTIONS

Critique the case and analyze the situation. Ask yourself the following questions:

1. Did this patient have access to care? If your answer is "No," why not? If your answer is "Yes," why?
2. What, if anything, should the provider do?
3. Is there anything the patient can do?

Mr. Smith, a 52-year-old, African American male lives down the street from a prominent health center. He enters complaining of a chronic, dry cough for 3 months. He offers to the doctor, "I think it's all these medicines you have me on. How do you expect a person to get better taking all this junk anyway?" His BP is 170/98, pulse 64, and he has gained 10 pounds since his last visit 6 months ago when he was placed on an ACE inhibitor and told to stop smoking cigarettes. The doctor responds to Mr. Smith's statement with, "You are obviously not taking your medications. You need to stop smoking and lose 20 pounds." He quickly examines Mr. Smith and gives him a follow-up appointment stating, "On the next visit you must convince me that you are serious about following the plan I prescribed for you. Otherwise, you are just not going to get better."

DISCUSSION POINTS

1. Mr. Smith asks the doctor: "How do you expect a person to get better taking all this junk anyway?" What is Mr. Smith getting at? What is he feeling?
2. Identify the medical issues that require attention.
3. How would you characterize the doctor's approach to Mr. Smith (e.g., straightforward, helpful, punitive)?

K Case Study #3

INSTRUCTIONS

Critique the case and analyze the situation. Ask yourself the following questions:

1. Did this patient have access to care? If your answer is "No," why not? If your answer is "Yes," why?
2. What, if anything, should the provider do?
3. Is there anything the patient can do?

Ms. Kirk is an African American women's health nurse practitioner who, after witnessing an interaction between another nurse practitioner (European American) and a 30-year-old woman, intervenes. The 30-year-old, Latina mother of three entered a prominent health center with the primary complaint of severe lower abdomen pain. She walked in slumped over, holding her abdomen, tears rolling down her cheeks, with her children ages 6, 4, and 3, walking hand in hand and appearing frightened. She was dropped off by her boyfriend who was already late for work. Before leaving, the boyfriend instructed her to phone him when she was ready to be picked up.

The European American triage nurse insisted, "either call the boyfriend back, call someone else to watch the children, or reschedule your appointment, otherwise I will have to call the social worker." The triage nurse further explained to the patient that she was going to need a pelvic exam and there was no way that could be accomplished with her children present.

Ms. Kirk, the nurse practitioner who witnessed the encounter, ushered teary-eyed mom and children into an examining room while reassuring her that it would be just fine. She positioned the children close to mom's head, put the 6-year-old in charge of the 3-year-old giving them all coloring books to distract them and proceeded to perform the pelvic exam without the children's awareness of what was going on. In less than an hour mom was on the way to the emergency room to be prepared for surgery for a ruptured appendix and her children were in the care of their grandmother.

DISCUSSION POINTS

1. The most obvious concern in this case is: How is it that the two nurses responded in such markedly different ways to this situation?
2. Once things were settled and the young mother was off to the emergency room for treatment, what do you think transpired between Ms. Kirk and the triage nurse ?
   a. Did they argue about the way things were handled?
   b. Did the triage nurse claim there was a breach in health center policy?
   c. Does Ms. Kirk's ethnicity (African American) have anything to do with how she managed this issue?
3. Conflict is inevitable in the workplace. Do we have skills for working things through in difficult situations?
4. It could be argued that experience rather than race was the driving factor in how things played out in this situation. What do you think?
5. How do you think health center administrators responded to the way Ms. Kirk handled this situation?

6. Under what circumstances is it appropriate to exercise creative approaches to solving problems, and when should we enforce strict adherence to policy?
7. Identify what might have happened if the rules had been followed and the mother had not received treatment.
8. Did the ethnicity of the patient have anything to do with the triage nurse's response in this situation? Did any stereotyping take place?
9. Should the patient have insisted that her boyfriend stay with her?

M Case Study #4

INSTRUCTIONS

Critique the case and analyze the situation. Ask yourself the following questions:

1. Did this patient have access to care? If your answer is "No," why not? If your answer is "Yes," why?
2. What, if anything, should the provider do?
3. Is there anything the patient can do?

Ms. Ming, a 90-year-old, Asian female, accompanied by her 65-year-old daughter, presents to the emergency department with complaints of nausea, projectile vomiting for several hours, and constipation for two weeks. She speaks only Chinese but the daughter is fluent in Chinese and English. The patient complains that her body has been out of balance for several weeks. She feared she would become very ill when none of her normal remedies restored her balance.

A CT scan of the abdomen reveals a major bowel obstruction. The surgeon informs the patient, with the daughter translating, that she will need immediate surgery. The daughter translates this to her mother who consents to the surgery and willingly signs the permission form. Within a half hour the patient's 68-year-old son arrives in the emergency department, speaks with his mother and sister, and the patient changes her mind about the surgery. The surgeon (European American) returns to speak with the family and attempts to convince them that without the surgery their mother will get sicker and eventually die. The family still refuses. They leave the hospital against medical advice.

DISCUSSION POINTS

1. Would things be different if an Asian doctor advised the family?
2. What does the patient attribute to her illness?
3. Why did the patient change her mind about the surgery?

E Case Study #5

INSTRUCTIONS

Critique the case and analyze the situation. Ask yourself the following questions:

1. Did this patient have access to care? If your answer is "No," why not? If your answer is "Yes," why?
2. What, if anything, should the provider do?
3. Is there anything the patient can do?

Angel Eber, a 20-year-old, European American female arrives in her doctor's office for a routine sports physical. During her last office visit, two years ago, she was seen by the nurse practitioner for a college physical. Except for being treated during her mid-teens for severe acne, she is healthy, physically active, and has no complaints.

The doctor greets her as he enters, "Hello Angel. I haven't seen you for a long time. How's everything? You've grown up to be a beautiful young lady. The boys are probably in hot pursuit!" Angel frowns and looks away.

Near the end of the exam, the doctor asks Angel if they should be discussing birth control. She firmly replies, "No." Smiling, the doctor begins writing out a prescription, saying, "Trust me, an attractive young lady like you needs to be on birth control. You can't be too careful." Passing the prescription to Angel, he continues to advise, "If you're not sexually active now you soon will be; take this and read the directions carefully before using." Angel hangs her head quietly, and for the remainder of the visit she answers the doctor's questions with "yes" and "no" answers. As she leaves the office she rips up the prescription and disposes it in the trash basket.

DISCUSSION POINTS

1. What do you believe accounts for Angel's behavior?
2. What assumptions may be influencing the doctor's approach to Angel?
3. What non-verbal cues did the doctor miss? Why is this important?
4. In what way could the doctor have altered his approach to be more responsive to Angel's needs? For example, would the doctor have made more headway with Angel if he had brought up "safer sex"?

REFERENCES

American Heart Association. (2005). Metabolic syndrome. Retrieved July 8, 2006. http\\www.americanheart.org/presenter.jhtml?identifier=4756

Burroughs, V. J., et al. (2002). Racial and ethnic differences in response to medicines: Towards individualized pharmaceutical treatment. *Journal of the National Medical Association, 94*:10, 1–26.

Clegg, L. X., Li, F. P., Hankey, B. F., Chu, K., & Edwards, B. K. (2002). Cancer survival among US whites and minorities: A SEER (Surveillance, Epidemiology, and End Results): Program population-based study. *Archives of Internal Medicine. 162*:1985–1993 [PMID:12230422]

Conigliaro, J., Whittle, J., Good, C. B., Hanusa, B. H., Passman, L. J., Lofgren, R. P., et al. (2000). Understanding racial variation in the use of coronary revascularization procedures: The role of clinical factors. *Archives of Internal Medicine, 160*:1329–1335. [PMID: 10809037]

Cooper-Patrick, L., Gallo, J. J., Gonzales J. J., Vu, H. T., Powe, N. R., Nelson, C., et al. (1999). Race, gender and partnership in the patient-physician relationship. *JAMA, 282*: 583–589 [PMID: 10450723]

Doescher, M. P., Saver, B. G., Franks, P., & Fiscella, K. (2000). Racial and ethnic disparities in perceptions of physician style and trust. *Archives of Family Medicine, 9*:1156–1163. [PMID: 11115223]

Estin, P. J. (1999) Spotting depression in Asian patients. *RN, 62*(4), 39–41.

Exner, D. V., et al. (2001). Lesser response to angiotensin-converting-enzyme inhibitor therapy in black as compared with white patients with left ventricular dysfunction. *New England Journal of Medicine, 344*:18, 1351–1357.

Hill, M., Shipp, S., & Wilson, J. (2002). Listen to your heart: The effects of differential treatment by physicians in heart disease management among African American women. Retrieved September 16, 2004 from http:www.Stanford.edu/classe297c /war_ peace/ structures of poverty_in_the_african_am

Kaplan, S. H., Gandek, B., Greenfield, S., Rogers, W., & Ware, J. E. (1995). Patient and visit characteristics related to physicians' participatory decision-making style. Results from the Medical Outcomes Study. *Medical Care, 33*:11, 1176–1197. [PMID:7500658]

Kudzma, E. C. (1992). Drug response: All bodies are not created equal. *American Journal of Nursing, 92*(12), 48–50.

Long, J. A., Chang, V. W., Ibrahim, S. A., & Asch, D. A. (2004). Update on the health disparities literature. *Annals of Internal Medicine, 141*:10, 805–812.

Margolis, M. L., Christie, J. D., Silvestri, G. A., et al. (2003). Racial differences pertaining to a belief about lung cancer surgery: Results of a multi-center survey. *Annals of Internal Medicine, 139*:558–563. [PMID: 14530226]

Munoz, C. & Hilgenberg, C. (2005). Ethnopharmacology: Understanding how ethnicity can affect drug response is essential to providing culturally competent care. *American Journal of Nursing, 105*:8 40–48.

Nurse Practitioners' Prescribing Reference (NPPR). (2008, Fall). Haymarket Media Publication. 24.

Patlak, M. (2001). *Women and heart disease*. Food and Drug Administration.

Petersen, L. A., Wright, S. M., Peterson, E. D., Daly, J., & Thibault, G. E. (2002). Impact of race on cardiac care and outcomes in veterans with acute myocardial infarction. *Medical Care*, 86–96. [PMID: 11789635]

Peterson, E. D., Wright, S. M., Daly, J., & Thibault, G. E. (1994). Racial variation in cardiac procedure use and survival following acute myocardial infarction in the Department of Veterans Affairs. *JAMA, 271*:1175–1180. [PMID: 8151875]

Pope, C. & John, A. M. (1999). Interview with C. Pope, April 23, 1999, Rochester, New York.

Prussian, K. H., Barksdale-Brown, D., & Dieckmann, J. (2007). Racial and ethnic differences in the presentation of metabolic syndrome. *The Journal for Nurse Practitioners.* Retrieved February 18, 2008 from http:www.npjournal.org

Saha, S., Komaromy, M., Koepsell, T. D., & Bidman, A. B. (1999). Patient-physician racial concordance and the perceived quality and use of health care. *Archives of Internal Medicine. 159*:997–1004. [PMID: 10326942]

Schneider, E. C., Zaslavsky, A. M., & Epstein, A. M. (2002). Racial disparities in the quality of care for enrollees in Medicare managed care. *JAMA, 287*:188–194. [PMID: 11886329]

Smedley, B. D., Stith, A. Y., & Nelson, A. R. (Eds.). (2002). *Unequal treatment: Confronting racial and ethnic disparities in health care.* Washington, DC: National Academies Press.

United States Department of Health and Human Services. (2006, Dec.). Healthy People 2010: Midcourse Review. Washington, DC: Office of Disease Prevention & Health Promotion.

Whittle, J., Conigliaro, J., Good, C. B., & Lofgren, R. P. (1993). Racial differences in the use of invasive cardiovascular procedures in the Department of Veteran Affairs medical system. *New England Journal of Medicine, 329*:621–627. [PMID: 8341338]

CHAPTER **3**

The Eight Factor Model for Evaluating True Access

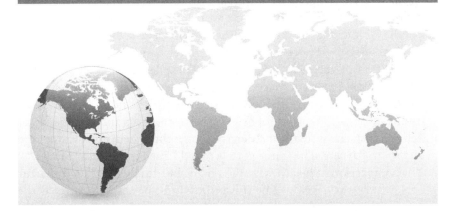

Getting your needs met, once in the system, is a must.

—Lovett-Scott & Prather

BEHAVIORAL OBJECTIVES

At the end of this chapter the students will be able to:

1. Discuss the Eight Factor Model as a framework in determining true access.
2. Determine whether true access exists in selective healthcare systems.
3. Identify ways in which they might utilize the Eight Factor Model in their practices.

KEY CONCEPTS

Primary care

True access

Restorative

Third party payer

Primary health care

Disparity

Social determinants

INTRODUCTION

When the health community makes reference to patients having access to care, the reference is generally limited. The concept of access is too often described as individuals getting to and from health services and having the ability to pay for the services either by virtue of a third party or out-of-pocket. We believe access to be much more than this and suggest that a redefinition of access is long overdue. *True access* means being able to get to and from health services, having the ability to pay for the services needed, and getting your needs met once you enter the health system. This text introduces a framework for assessing the strengths and weaknesses of selective healthcare systems, and determining if the system is providing true access to health care. The framework is called "The Eight Factor Model."

The comparison of health systems is made by utilizing The Eight Factor Model, which was developed by the authors, and has "true access" as the driving value. As illustrated in **Figure 3-1**, the model has true access at its core, and eight surrounding factors that are important for health systems to demonstrate in order to provide that true access. A solid directional arrow from the factor to the core depicts a system that has demonstrated evidence to support that it is providing true access. A broken directional arrow from the core to the factor suggests the system is not providing true access, and much work must be done to achieve it. **Table 3-1** (a format for assessing true access) provides a template for learners to formulate their own opinions about the extent to which countries discussed in this text provide true access. **Table 7** in Chapter 16, The Eight Factor Model for True Access, summarizes author observations regarding the extent to which each of the 11 countries discussed in the "Health Care in Industrialized (Developed) Countries and "Health Care in Developing Countries" sections of this text have addressed true access. This will hopefully enable the learner to briefly review it against the Eight Factor Model illustrated in Figure 3-1. Table 7, The Eight Factor Model for True Access, which appears at the end of Chapter 16 (Comparative health perspectives) should be fully reviewed as the learner approaches the end of the text.

In describing comparatively what systems are doing globally, we apply this model which allows for a thorough and critical analysis of each healthcare system solely for the purpose of promoting what the users of one system might learn from the users of another rather than focusing on a system's shortcomings. The eight factors depicted by the model are: 1) historical 2) structure, 3) financing, 4) interventional, 5) preventive, 6) resources, 7) major health issues, and 8) health disparities.

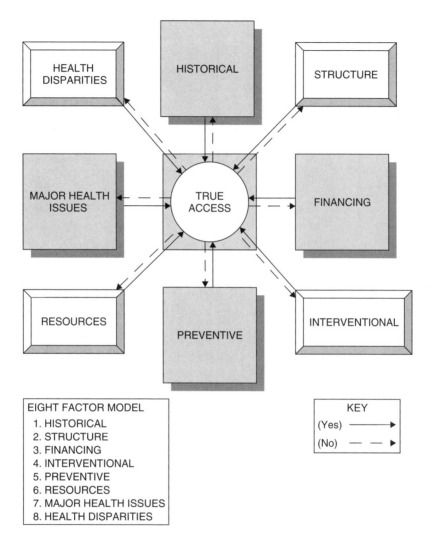

Figure 3-1 The Eight Factor Model

HISTORICAL

The first factor, historical, describes the health of each nation and explores how health and access to health services have been historically defined by the nation discussed. This includes how the health system emerged, and the role of emergency departments, community-based health centers, and clinics in providing health care.

Table 3-1 The Eight Factor Model for true access.

United States	Canada	Japan	United Kingdom	France	Cuba	India	Ghana	Italy	Brazil	Russian Federation
HISTORICAL (Determine access & barriers)										
STRUCTURE (Infrastructure, policies, staff needs, roles, & responsibilities)										
FINANCING (Cost & funding priorities)										
INTERVENTIONAL (Care: primary, acute, & restorative)										
PREVENTIVE (Success with promoting health, & preventing disease)										
RESOURCES (Human & fiscal)										
MAJOR HEALTH ISSUES (Top 10 diseases)										
HEALTH DISPARITIES (Race/ethnicity, age, & income based)										

STRUCTURE

The second factor in the model examines the structure of healthcare delivery. This structure includes whether it is a national healthcare system, the health system's infrastructure, health policies, interdisciplinary roles and responsibilities, staffing patterns and needs (supply vs. demand), physician providers, nurses, advanced practice nurses, other health professionals, and related outcomes. For example, in regard to interdisciplinary roles, responsibilities, and outcomes, physicians around the globe are proficient at diagnosing and treating illnesses. Some even instruct their patients on how to prevent illness and stay healthy. However, no matter where you are in the world, nurses are generally found in the trenches striving to make the communities in which they work and live more viable and healthy. In many cases advanced practice nurses are bridging the physician gap and are advocating for patients and families to get true access once in the healthcare system. It is very difficult, if not impossible, for any system to provide true access without embracing an interdisciplinary approach to care and services.

This factor also examines the presence of structural barriers that exist that could prevent or impede access to care, or it could identify structures in place to facilitate access to care and services. These include such things as the location of services, government policies and procedures, and various health policies and legislation.

FINANCING

The third factor, financing, is perhaps one of the most difficult factors to address in discussing true access in that much reliance is placed on a nation's ability to fund health care. This factor describes the nation's fiscal responsibilities and financing priorities, and helps to determine where the majority of the healthcare budget goes. Particular attention is given to long-term and older adult care, maternal child care, technology, research, and the emphasis a system places on curative. How health care is funded and where the funds come from (private or public) are important considerations of factor three. The government's role in administering and overseeing health care, and provider compensation is also examined.

INTERVENTIONAL

The importance of service quality is critical, especially in today's healthcare environment, and is the focus of factor four, interventional. This factor calls attention to whether the delivery focus is on primary care, primary health care, acute care, or restorative care, in relation to outcomes. An important measure of a healthcare system's effort in preserving health and preventing illness is how the system is structured. In the case of a *primary healthcare* system, the majority of its services are community-based rather than hospital-based, making services more accessible to everyone in the system. Examples of primary healthcare systems are Cuba and Brazil. Another measure is whether the system offers primary care, perhaps best exemplified by the healthcare systems in the United States and Canada. *Primary care* focuses on health promotion, disease prevention, early intervention, cure, and care. From the perspective of one notable expert, primary care is:

> ... care that is coordinated, comprehensive, and personal and available on first encounter and continuous thereafter. It involves such tasks as, medical and psychological diagnosis and treatment; personal support of patients of all backgrounds, in all stages of their illness; communication of information about diagnosis, treatment, prevention, and prognosis; maintenance of patients with chronic illness; and prevention of disability and disease through detection, education, behavioral change and preventive treatment (Stoeckle, 2000, p. 1).

Despite the type of system offered, the focus, or the approach to care, there are often similarities in outcomes. As individuals age, if the healthcare focus is not on maximizing physical, mental, and spiritual function, there will likely be a decline in functioning and in achievement of quality outcomes. In a system such as the United States, achieving desired outcomes may very well determine whether a *third party payer* reimburses a healthcare system for the care provided. For example, if a patient develops a major preventable complications, such as skin ulcerations, while hospitalized, in many cases insurance companies in the United States will refuse to reimburse the hospital for care. In other countries, reimbursement for services may not be an issue.

When care is evaluated in any system it is important to consider care outcomes. Outcomes are typically evidenced by patient and staff satisfaction with the health services provided. The overall patient/family experience since entering the healthcare system is a good measure of service quality. Met and unmet needs of patients and families are very important considerations. For example, part of quality care delivery includes making a determination about whether care received or services provided are congruent with the patient's culture (Leininger, 2004; Purnell & Paulanka, 2008). When care is consistently incongruent with the individual's culture it will be ill-received, sometimes openly challenged, and might result in individuals separating from a practice without notice.

The extent to which health professionals include patients and families in the health decisions may be evidenced by such questions as, "How would you feel about this procedure or this method of treatment?" "What would you like us to do?" And in deciding about actions to take, raising questions such as, "What makes your problem worse, or better?" "What do you do other than take a prescribed or over-the-counter medicine to feel better, or get better when this problem occurs?" Asking questions of the primary caregiver prior to the patient entering the system should include, "In your opinion, what seems to work best?" Such questions could be a key indicator of the desire to provide quality care and services. Inclusion of essential "others" in the interventional plan, especially when they are close family members, is key to providing service quality.

PREVENTIVE

The fifth factor provides an evaluation of preventive measures. It includes making a determination about the extent to which the system is maintaining and preserving the physical, emotional/mental, and social health of its people. Environmental health and safety (tobacco and substance use and abuse), traditional health practices, religion, family, long-term care, women's health, child and adolescent health, and adult and older adult care and services are important considerations of factor five.

RESOURCES

The sixth factor, resources, does not consider fiscal resources. Rather, it evaluates the availability and adequacy of human resources and social and spiritual resources. These include licensed and unlicensed professional staff, trained and untrained workers, traditional healers, unpaid volunteers, family (extended and nuclear), community, and other support systems. This factor considers the extent to which these types of resources are available in each healthcare system discussed.

MAJOR HEALTH ISSUES

Factor seven, major health issues, describes specific social determinants of health such as illiteracy (generally and as it pertains to health), poverty, culture, race, and gender. It also describes public health challenges and initiatives, the top ten diseases for each nation, the nature of the diseases, and the similarities and differences among nations in their approaches to treating diseases. These include the incidence rates and prevalence of diseases, chronic illnesses, vulnerable populations, familial and genetic illness tendencies, and how people are coping in regard to their level of independence or dependence in carrying out their daily care activities.

HEALTH DISPARITIES

Factor eight, the final factor for evaluating true access, concentrates on health disparities, or unequal treatment. It reports the top three diseases that disparately affect the particular country's population based on such social determinants as race/ethnicity, age, and income. For example, in some nations heart disease leads the way as the major cause of death, in other nations it is infection. Both are preventable yet deadly, and often the poor outcome is tied to income, age, or race (Long, Chang, Ibrahim, & Asch, 2004; Burroughs et al., 2002; Exner et al., 2001).

SUMMARY

The model introduced in this chapter, if consistently applied, provides a great opportunity for assessing the strengths and weaknesses of a healthcare delivery system. Utilization of the model will be beneficial in identifying countries that not only provide its residents true access to health care, but determine the extent to which access is provided. It could possibly be a catalyst to changing initiatives in countries searching for new directional approaches to addressing gross inequities in their systems.

Discussion Questions

1. Why is it useful to examine the concept of access from the framework of the Eight Factor Model?

2. How does the Eight Factor Model affect your understanding about providing the best possible access to patients? Which factors are familiar to you? What factors are new to you or provide you with a different way of thinking about access?

3. To what extent does your work setting reflect true access as defined by the Eight Factor Model? What factors would you say are effectively addressed? What factors represent ongoing challenges?

4. Do you know of a healthcare setting that practices (demonstrates) true access? Utilizing the Eight Factor Model, describe how this organization

achieves this outcome. What factors stand out? What happens in this healthcare setting that could be replicated in your own workplace?

5. As a health practitioner or administrator, what aspects of the Eight Factor Model do you feel you can manage on your own? What factors require teamwork? In your opinion, are there factors in the model that represent issues outside of your control? If so, explain your point of view.

REFERENCES

Burroughs, V. J., et al. (2002). Racial and ethnic differences in response to medicines: Towards individualized pharmaceutical treatment. *Journal of the National Medical Association, 94*:10, 1–26.

Exner, D. V., et al. (2001). Lesser response to angiotensin-converting-enzyme inhibitor therapy in black as compared with white patients with left ventricular dysfunction. *New England Journal of Medicine, 344*:18, 1351–1357.

Leininger, M. M. (2004). Culture care diversity and universality. *Nursing Science Quarterly, 1*(4) 152–160. Sage journals online. Retrieved from nursing.jbpub .com. doi:10.1177108941988318488001004408.sitzman/ih.15.pdf.pdf

Long, J. A., Chang, V. W., Ibrahim, S. A., & Asch, D. A. (2004). Update on the health disparities literature. *Annals of Internal Medicine, 139*:558–563. [PMID: 14530226]

Purnell, L. & Paulanka, B. (2008). *Transcultural health care: A culturally competent approach* (4th ed.). Philadelphia: F.A. Davis Company.

Stoeckle, J. D. (2000). The tasks of primary care. In Goroll, A. H. & Mulley, A. G. *Primary care medicine: Office evaluation and management of the adult patient* (4th ed., p. 1). Philadelphia: Lippincott Williams & Wilkins.

Part II

Health Care in Industrialized (Developed) Countries

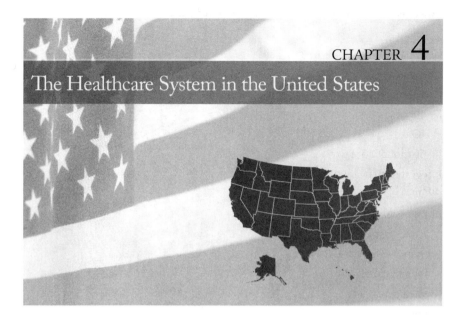

The Healthcare System in the United States

And miles to go before I sleep.

—Robert Frost, 1923

BEHAVIORAL OBJECTIVES

At the end of this chapter the students will be able to:

1. Describe the emergence of healthcare delivery in the United States from a historical perspective, emphasizing the past 25 years.
2. Discuss healthcare financing and delivery initiatives, priorities, and challenges.
3. Describe the government's role in healthcare delivery.
4. Discuss the incidence, prevalence, and treatment of disease.
5. Discuss the emergence of healthcare reform and its potential impact on health delivery.

KEY CONCEPTS

Affordable Care Act

Medigap

Capitation

COBRA

Co-payments

Cultural competence

Deductibles

HMO

Institutional core

Integrated delivery systems

PPO

Primary care

Magnet hospital

Primary health care

Managed care

Medicaid

Medicare

Push and pull factor

Social security

State exchanges

INTRODUCTION

The United States of America (USA) covers 3,717,727 square miles and is made up of 50 states (Infoplease, 2010). The USA's population in 2004 was 293,027,571 (U.S. Census, 2004). In 2010 the population reached over 307 million. The proportion of the population that is under 15 years old in the United States (U.S.) is 21%, and the over-60 population proportion is 16% (UNO, 2004). Slightly more than 12.4% of the population were 65 years and older of which 1,557,800 (4.5%) were living in nursing homes (U.S. Census, 2010). The primary languages spoken in the United States are English and Spanish. The largest ethnic groups are European American (75%). African American and Latino groups each constitute approximately one-eighth of the population. The largest religious groups are Protestant (over 50%) and Roman Catholic (25%).

The United States is the largest, most powerful nation in the industrialized (developed) world, and it has a high literacy rate. However, in 2006, while it led the world in healthcare spending per capita, it ranked 39th for infant mortality, 43rd for adult female mortality, 42nd for adult male mortality, and 36th in life expectancy, earning an overall ranking of 37th in the industrialized world in healthcare performance (Murray & Frenk, 2010, p. 1).

Life expectancy in the United States is 80 years of age for European American women, 75.9 for African American women, 75.3 for European American men, and 68.9 for African American men. The life expectancy rate for the United States is among the lowest for the industrialized world, and infant mortality is among the highest. Americans consider quality, affordable health care a birthright, an expectation. Yet, unlike other world powers, the U.S. government plays a small role in ensuring that everyone has equal access to quality health care and services.

Although the United States is envied for its wealth, high technological capabilities, and research savvy, historically it has not kept pace with other industrialized nations in the area of healthcare delivery. This is reflected by its poor outcomes in infant mortality and life expectancy. The healthcare system is also overwhelmed by disparities and inequities in care and lack of access (except for the most affluent and informed), and cost that has outpaced care. Despite an international reputation as an advocator for human rights, a nation which has openly shown intolerance of non-Western countries charged with violating the human rights of their citizenry, the United States is a system plagued with its own injustices. Though a commodity to some, many believe health care is a birthright. Primary care is of major importance to maximizing health outcomes. The Institute of Medicine (Starfield, 1994) describes primary care as care on first contact, comprehensive care, coordinated or integrated care, and care that is longitudinal rather than episodic.

Three decades ago many in the United States overutilized emergency departments for routine, non-acute care. To reverse this trend, the healthcare system began focusing more on primary care and prevention. By allowing patients to see the same provider on each wellness and illness visit, many individuals stopped seeking routine care in emergency rooms. Rather, they began utilizing physician's offices and community and migrant health centers (C/MHCs) where the focus was, and still is, on maintaining health and wellness. Health providers enrolled patients to their maximum capacity in these centers and private offices. Years later, as providers stopped taking new patients and began denying services to those on *Medicaid* (a government funded insurance plan for the poor and disabled funded under Title XIX of the Social Security Act), there was a cyclical trend of consumers migrating back to emergency departments for primary care, in numbers not seen for more than thirty years. Many attribute this to the downturn in the U.S. economy resulting in a historically high unemployment rate. Today the only *primary care* (preventive and illness care provided by the same health provider) that many people receive is in the emergency departments.

Some of the barriers that limit access to care are financial, structural, and personal. Financial barriers include not having health insurance, not having enough health insurance to cover needed services, or not having the financial capacity to cover services not paid for by a specific health plan or insurance. Structural barriers include the lack of primary care providers, medical specialists, or other healthcare professionals to meet special needs, or the lack of healthcare facilities (USDHHS, Healthy People 2010).

HISTORICAL

The first operation performed in the United States was an excision of a tumor from a patient's neck. During an address before the American Medical Association, John Collins Warren confirmed that he performed the world's first surgical procedure on October 16, 1846 in a Boston, Massachusetts hospital, using sulphuric ether anesthesia (Cincinnati, Ohio, May 8, 1850). Over 20 years later, the United States is the only country in the industrialized world that does not have a National Health Care program. In the decades leading up to the seventies, health care was provided almost exclusively in outpatient clinics or general practice/family practice offices. The 1970s witnessed the emergence of primary care as we know it.

Approximately 30 years ago the United States healthcare system was medically dominated. Physicians ruled. The diagnostic tests, procedures, and referrals made, and length of hospital stays of patients were based on physician's unscrutinized decisions. During the past twenty-five years the United States has moved from physician dominance, where physicians were autonomous decision-makers, to insurance companies and business dominance. Other systems, such as the United Kingdom and Ghana, still place physicians in powerful autonomous roles.

In the early 1990s, President Clinton proposed healthcare reform to provide universal coverage but this effort failed and the current system, though widely criticized, prevails. In 2009, President Barack Obama proposed an "Insurance Mandate Plan," called the *Affordable Care Act*, designed to ensure that everyone with the ability to do so, purchases insurance coverage.

The Affordable Care Act

The status of health care in the United States has posed critical problems for individuals, families, older adults, state budgets, and the U.S. economy. Prior attempts at healthcare reform in the United States have failed.

In 2007, the United States spent approximately $2.2 trillion ($7,421 per person) or 16.2% of the GDP on health care (Office of the Actuary, 2007). By 2009, healthcare spending escalated to $2.5 trillion (an increase of $134 million) and reached a record estimate of 17.3% of the U.S. economy

(OECD, 2008; Orszag, 2008). Long-term projections suggest that aging will play a critical role in healthcare spending with Medicare and Medicaid taking up a significant proportion of the healthcare budget. If the projections hold true, healthcare spending could rise to 25% of the federal budget by 2025 and, more ominously, to nearly half (49%) of the budget by 2082 (Orszag, 2008). In the wake of the economic crisis of 2007, increasing numbers of Americans are uninsured or they have inadequate health coverage.

According to the U.S. Census Bureau, the number of uninsured increased from 46.3 million in 2008 to 50.7 million in 2009 (DeNovas-Walt, Proctor, & Smith, 2010). "Because uninsured persons often postpone seeking care, have difficulty obtaining care when they ultimately seek it, and must bear the full brunt of healthcare costs, prolonged periods of uninsurance (no insurance coverage for over a year) can have a particularly serious impact on a person's health and stability. Over time, the cumulative consequences of being uninsured compound, resulting in a population at particular risk for suboptimal health care and health status" (Agency for Healthcare Research and Quality (AHRQ), 2007, p. 118).

The 2008 National Scorecard on U.S. Health System Performance observed that the quality of health care in the United States is "uneven" and falls short of what is expected given its resources. Across 37 indicators, the United States achieved an overall score of 65 out of a possible 100. "Performance measures of health system efficiency remain especially low, with the United States scoring 53 out of 100 on measures gauging inappropriate, wasteful, or fragmented care; avoidable hospitalizations; variation in quality and costs; administrative costs; and use of information technology. Lowering administrative costs alone could save up to $100 billion a year at the lowest country rates" (The Commonwealth Fund Commission, 2008, p. 10). Eight in ten Americans are dissatisfied with the prohibitive costs of health care (Gallup Poll, 2007); and many are likely to forgo healthcare services altogether (Healthreform.gov, 2011).

Ideas and strategies to improve health care in the United States have been enmeshed in heated political debates for over two decades. However, the country has taken more definitive steps to build a comprehensive healthcare plan. On March 23, 2010, the Patient Protection and Affordable Care Act (PPAC), more commonly referred to as the Affordable Care Act, was signed into law by President Barack Obama. The new health reform intends to ensure that all Americans have access to quality, affordable health care. "A major goal of the Affordable Care Act is to put American consumers back in charge of their health coverage and care" (Healthcare.gov, 2010, Provisions: Patient's bill of rights). The PPAC is particularly aimed at low- to moderate-income groups, and vulnerable populations including children and low-income childless adults. A statement by the U.S. Secretary of Labor captures the essential expectations of the legislation.

> A new day is finally dawning for every American family that has seen its wages and dreams eroded by a healthcare system that has worked only for insurance companies—and at the expense of regular people. Last night's historic vote in the U.S. House of Representative clears the path for Americans to gain coverage and financial stability that they both need and deserve. More than 32 million people now will be covered by health insurance and pre-existing conditions cannot be the basis to deny aid to those who need it most (U.S. Secretary of Labor Hilda L. Solis, March 22, 2010).

In order to achieve the goal of affordable health care, the PPAC has created a number of provisions to hold the insurance industry accountable, especially in terms of driving down costly premiums, limiting out-of-pocket expenses, and preventing discriminatory practices such as denying coverage to people with pre-existing conditions. Under the new law, it is illegal for insurance companies to rescind coverage due to a mistake in paperwork. The new regulations also prohibit the use of lifetime limits on coverage as well as annual dollar limits, i.e., what the insurance company will pay (Healthcare.gov, 2010, Provisions: Patient's bill of rights). The Affordable Care Act extends coverage up to age 26 and requires coverage of preventive services and immunizations. The new regulations protect consumers' rights to choose their physicians, or keep the ones they have. This is based on the premise that, "people who have a regular primary care provider are more than twice as likely to receive recommended preventive care; are less likely to be hospitalized; are more satisfied with the healthcare system, and have lower costs. Yet, insurance companies do not always make it easy to see the provider you choose" (Healthcare.gov, 2010, Provisions: Patient's bill of rights). This protection extends to emergency care and protects the consumer from being charged higher co-payments.

As part of its strategy to lower costs and make coverage more accessible, the PPAC calls for building a more competitive private health insurance market through American Health Benefit Exchanges, sometimes referred to as State Exchanges. Exchanges offer a choice of health plans that meet certain benefits and cost standards. Health benefits offered through an Exchange must include a uniform package of essential health benefits. There are federal government-sponsored grants available to states to facilitate the implementation of health benefit packages. **Table 4-1** provides information on the health benefits offered through a State Exchange. The Exchanges

Table 4-1 Health benefits offered through the Exchange.

Levels of Coverage: In general, qualified health plans must offer various plans based on the portion of the healthcare costs that would be covered by the plan.

· Bronze: 60% of actuarial value
· Silver: 70% of actuarial value
· Gold: 80% of actuarial value
· Platinum: 90% of actuarial value

Catastrophic Plan: A plan covering all of the essential benefits and a minimum of three primary care visits for individuals under the age of 30 (as well as establishing certain individuals exempt from the individual mandate) once a certain level of cost sharing is reached.

Child-Only Plan: Any qualified health plan offered under the Exchange must also be available as a plan only to individuals who have not attained the age of 21.

Annual Cap: May not exceed the cost sharing for high-deductible health plans in the individual market in 2014 (currently $5,950 per individual/$11,900 per family). The limitation on cost-sharing is indexed to the rate of average premium growth.

Deductibles: For plans in the small group market deductibles are limited to $2,000 for individual/$4,000 for a family, indexed to average premium growth.

Uniform Benefits Package: Qualified health plans are required to offer a uniform benefits package as defined by the secretary of the federal Department of Health and Human Services. At a minimum, the package must include the following "essential health benefits":

· Ambulatory patient services
· Emergency services
· Hospitalization
· Maternity and newborn care
· Mental health benefits
· Substance use disorder services
· Prescription drugs
· Rehabilitative and habilitative services and devices
· Laboratory devices
· Preventive and wellness services
· Chronic disease management
· Pediatric services, including oral and vision care

Source: Taylor, M. (2010) *LAO: The Patient Protection and Affordable Care Act: An Overview of its Potential Impact on State Health Programs,* May 13, 2010, p. 8.

will provide a "One-Stop Shop" for comparing benefits, pricing, and quality (Healthcare.gov 2010, Provisions: Patient's bill of rights). American citizens and legal immigrants who do not have coverage can obtain it directly through an affordable insurance Exchange. The Exchange is available to small businesses (fewer than 100 employees) who wish to obtain coverage for their employees (Taylor, 2010). Consumers and small businesses that use the Exchanges may qualify for tax credits.

As part of the plan to make health care more accessible, the Affordable Care Act includes an individual mandate that requires U.S. citizens and legal residents to obtain coverage or pay a penalty. Several components of the new health reform focus on the needs of the older adults including free preventive care (e.g., annual wellness visits); a community care transitions program designed to avoid unnecessary readmissions; and 50% drug discounts for seniors who reach the "donut hole" or coverage gap when buying Medicare Part D brand name or generic drugs.

The Affordable Care Act is a massive reform and may take as long as ten years to become fully implemented. Proponents of the new healthcare reform anticipate several positive outcomes including a more stable economy with a reduction in government overspending by more than $100 billion over the next decade (Healthcare.gov, 2010, Provisions: About the law); enhanced work productivity, better informed consumers, an increased sense of responsibility for personal health, and the development of a more efficient, coordinated system of health care.

Although a far cry from universal health care as proposed under the Clinton plan, and considered by many as a step in the right direction, it is currently being argued in the courts for repeal. Those opposing reform reportedly fear too much government involvement, cost escalation, and tampering with Medicare benefits in order to fund reform. The country's healthcare flaws have become such an embarrassing legacy that the government feels compelled to take action to improve health delivery. Hence, many continue to rally for the country to pass healthcare reform.

STRUCTURE

Healthcare delivery in the United States is highly fragmented and decentralized with much collaboration among local clinics, C/MHCs, and hospitals. Many hospitals in and near large metropolitan cities are highly specialized, such as hospitals for women and children; orthopedics; eye, ear, nose and throat; spinal cord injuries; and special surgeries. Specialty care within hospitals is prescribed by the complexity of the services required. According to the American Hospital Association (AHA, 2010), there are a total of 5,795 hospitals in the United States. The majority (3,011) are urban community hospitals, and 1,997 are rural community hospitals. Of these, 2,918 are not-for-profit; 1,092 are state and local government owned; 211 are federal government owned, 998 are investor-owned, for-profit hospitals, and 117 are non-federal, long-term care hospitals. Community hospitals are defined as all non-federal, short-term general, and other special hospitals (AHA, 2010). Acute care hospitals are highly technological and specialized. They are well staffed and include specializations in burns; brain and other trauma; hemodialysis; neonatal, and pediatric intensive care; high risk maternity; and palliative care.

The United States relies on physicians and other clinical specialists to routinely care for patients, even those experiencing complications. Most of the care delivery in the United States is hospital-based with an upward trend toward community-based, primary care that encourages patients to access their primary care provider practices (private physician offices, community health centers, and clinics) before seeking care in more costly emergency departments. Private, for-profit hospitals must operate in what Americans refer to as the "black" (making a profit) in order to fully function. As smaller, more financially vulnerable hospitals' financial statements approach the "red" as a result of low cash flow from accumulating more debt than profit, they seek creative ways to remain afloat. The most recent approach to addressing financial fluidity for many smaller hospitals across the country is to merge with larger, more financially stable ones, and, upon merger, create an *integrated delivery system*. This provides them with the financial cushion needed to remain viable.

Many well-educated healthcare professionals make up the healthcare workforce in the United States. In regard to interdisciplinary roles, responsibilities, and outcomes, there is a tremendously large demand for healthcare services in the United States. During the last two decades, the shortage of healthcare professionals, especially registered nurses, has become a national crisis. Numerous reports by organizations such as the American Association of Colleges of Nursing (AACN), the American Nurses Association (ANA), and the New York State Labor-Health Industry Task Force on Health Personnel have reported that this shortage will become more pronounced as the effects of declining enrollments and increased retirements are felt by the healthcare community. The shortage of minority nurses (those of African, Latino, Asian, and Native/Alaskan descents) is most noticeable.

Prior to the downturn in the United States economy in 2008, vacant budgeted nursing positions in hospitals more than doubled. In 2008, vacancy rates in hospitals nationally were at an all-time high. The AACN reported that the downturn in the economy resulted in a short-term stabilizing of the nursing workforce in some parts of the country (AACN, 2009). Despite the current shortage of registered nurses in the United States, Buerhaus, Staiger, and Auerbach (2009) suggest that the United States should brace itself for a worsening of the shortage, and predict that the RN shortage could reach as high as 500,000 by 2025.

This is partly attributed to the large number of baby boomer nurses (born between 1944 and 1960) expected to retire in the next five to ten years. The latest projections from the U.S Bureau of Labor Statistics (BLS), predict more than one million new and replacement nurses will be needed by 2016, creating more than 587,000 new nursing positions, making nursing the nation's top profession in terms of projected growth (United States Department of Labor, 2007).

The majority of the nurses entering the profession in the United States do so by completing a two year Associate's Degree in Nursing rather than a four year baccalaureate degree in nursing (BSN). Although hospital-based diploma programs still exist is in the United States, there are relatively few. Also, there is extensive documented evidence that patient outcomes are better with BSN-prepared nurses at the bedside (AACN, 2009; Tourangeau, et al., 2007; Aiken, et al., 2008; Aiken, et al., 2002; Smedley, et al., 2003; Needleman, et al., 2002; American Nurses Association, 2000) resulting in an American Nurses Association (ANA) initiative to increase educational requirements for entry level into professional practice to the baccalaureate level. Called "BSN in 10," the legislation further standardized the nursing profession.

In 2008 there were 3,063,163 licensed registered nurses (RNs) living in the United States. Of this number, 2,596,599 (84.8%) were employed in various settings; however, hospitals were the largest employers of RNs, employing 62.2%. Of the total, 5.6% of RNs practicing in the United States received their initial education in another country or a U.S. territory. The majority of these nurses, approximately 48.7%, are from the Philippines, 11.5% are Canadians, and 9.3% are from India. During the past fifty years, the United States has regularly imported nurses to ease the nursing shortage. This demand-driven U.S. nurse shortage is referred to by Brush, Sochalski, and Berger (2004) as the migratory *push and pull factor*. Nurses throughout the world feel *pushed* out of their home countries because of low pay and poor employment conditions, and *pulled* into industrialized countries because of better pay, and other perks. This factor is credited with stimulating the growth of for-profit organizations that serve as brokers to ease the way for nurses to emigrate (Brush et al., 2004). The major push and pull factors associated with international nursing recruitment are listed in **Table 4-2**.

In 2001, Filipino nurses represented more than half of the foreign graduates taking the licensing examination. Nurses from Canada, the United Kingdom, India, Korea, and Nigeria collectively accounted for an additional 25% (NCSBN, 2004). Nurses are enticed to leave their home countries by promises of better pay and working conditions; improved learning and practice opportunities; and free travel, licensure, and room

Table 4-2 Main push and pull factors in international nursing recruitment.

Push Factors	Pull Factors
Low pay (absolute and relative)	Higher pay and opportunities for remittance
Poor working conditions	Better working conditions
Lack of resources to work effectively	Better resourced health systems
Limited career opportunities	Career opportunities
Limited educational opportunities	Provisions of post-basic education
Impact HIV/AIDS	Political stability
Unstable/dangerous work environment	Travel opportunities
Economic instability	Aid work

Source: Buchan, Parkin, & Sochalski, WHO, 2003. International nurse mobility: Trends and role implications; WHO_eip_osd_2003.3pdf

and board (Buchan, Parkin, & Sochalski, 2003). For example, in 2004 the U.S. Department of Labor reported the median annual earnings for RNs as $48,090. Average earnings for RNs working in hospitals were $49,190, and those working in nursing homes were $43,850 (USDL, BLS 2004–2005). These wages contrast sharply with the annual wages of $2,000–$2,400 earned during the same year in the Philippines (Sison, 2002). **Table 4-3** presents destination countries of many of the foreign nurses recruited to practice in countries other than their home countries. Although the

Table 4-3 Destination countries: total number of nurses and main source of international recruitment.

Country	Number of Nurses	Main Source of International Recruitment
Australia	149,202	UK and New Zealand
Ireland	61,629	UK, Philippines, So. Africa
Norway	45,133	Other Scandinavian countries, Germany, Philippines
United Kingdom (UK)	640,000 (580,000)	Philippines, So. Africa, Australia
United States (US)	2,238,800	Philippines, Canada, Africa (mainly So. Africa & Nigeria)

Note: Data from OECD Health Data (CD-ROM, 2001b), reported as full time equivalent (FTE) practicing nurses in some countries. This figure appears to be the number of nurses on the registry, some of whom are inactive. OECD data for the United Kingdom (UK) is incorrect so bracketed figure is the actual number of registrants in the UK.

Source: Buchan, Parkin, & Sochalski, 2003, WHO, 2003. International nurse mobility: Trends and role implications, WHO_eip_osd_2003.3.pdf

percentage of foreign nurses working in hospitals has steadily declined in the past ten years, their numbers in public/community health and ambulatory settings have grown (Brush et al., 2004). Foreign nurse representation in nursing homes has risen from 7.4% to 9.3% (National Sample Survey of Registered Nurses, 2000).

There is a two-step process for obtaining an RN license in the United States. This process is separate from the process necessary for obtaining a work visa. Foreign nurses wishing to practice in the United States are prescreened by the Commission on Graduates of Foreign Nursing Schools (CGFNS). This commission reviews the educational background, licensure in the home country, English language proficiency testing, and a predictor exam that provides an indication of the nurse's ability to pass the U.S. nursing licensing examination (NCLEX). In many cases, foreign educated nurses, other than those from Canada, must successfully pass the NCLEX licensing exam in the United States before being permitted to practice. However, because each state has its own board of nursing and operates independently, some states may have additional requirements, and a few states may directly endorse foreign educated nurses who have not taken the NCLEX (Buchan et al., 2003).

The scope of a nurse's practice in the United States is governed by the nurse's educational preparation and experience. Currently, a nurse who is newly graduated can enter general practice and work in various settings in the United States by two methods—by earning a two year associate's degree (ADN) or a four year baccalaureate degree (BSN). Hospital-based diploma programs that were very popular during the fifties and sixties are almost non-existent today. Nurses can earn national certification in a number of specialty areas through highly recognized professional nursing organizations such as the American Nurses Association's (ANA's) American Nursing Credentialing Center (ANCC).

Advanced practice nurses (APN) have expanded scopes of practice. The scope of practice, and practice privilege parameters, for advanced practice nurses such as nurse practitioners (NPs) and clinical nurse specialists (CNS) are defined by each state. APNs are nurses who have earned a master's degree. These nurses have successfully completed advanced course work in pathophysiology, pharmacology, health assessment, research, and case management. Furthermore, they have gained expertise in particular specialty careers such as clinical nurse specialist, nurse practitioner, nurse midwife, and nurse anesthetist. Most recently, nurses have become experts in nurse informatics, integrating nursing information and technology to develop structures needed to build systems that better document and support nurses' actions and clinical decisions; and forensics nursing that addresses

sexual assault, abuse, domestic violence and death investigations (*see* www
.nursecredentialing.org). Some states require NPs to have a collaborating
agreement with an approved physician in order to practice. NPs have, for
many years, rallied for states to expand their scopes of practice. In 2008,
22 states had expanded scopes of practice for NPs in all specialty areas.
Despite the critical need for more community-based mental health providers,
some physicians in psychiatric mental health practice object to the autonomy given nurse practitioners, arguing that only psychiatrists, not NPs, are
qualified to practice independently (Ginsberg, Taylor, & Barr, 2009).

The RN workforce is aging. The average age of RNs practicing in the
United States is 46.8 years. Additionally, 16.2% of RNs in the U.S. workforce
are between 50 and 54 years old. This raises significant concerns among
individuals who fear that the aging trends and future retirements could
substantially reduce the size of the U.S. nursing workforce. Further, because
the general population and the proportion of older adults in the population is growing, there will be an even greater future need for healthcare and
nursing services across the nation (USDHHS, HRSA, 2004). The average
annual earnings for RNs in 2008 were $57,785.

Nurses with master's or doctorate degrees rose to 376,901, an increase
of 37% from the year 2000 (USDHHS, HRSA, 2004). Advanced practice
nurses have met educational and clinical practice requirements beyond
their initial nursing education, and are educated at minimally the master's
level. Most advanced practice nurses have advanced credentialing and certification by each state and a nationally recognized accrediting body. In 2008
there were approximately 250,527 advanced practice nurses, of which nurse
practitioners were the majority (63.2%). The median nurse practitioner's
salary was $89,845. Like physicians, nurses certified as anesthetists and
those in specialty care make considerably more.

New APN guidelines by the American Association for Colleges of Nursing
(AACN) recommend that new masters programs be developed in order
to prepare clinical nurse leaders who are clinicians with evidenced-based
application expertise, and practice doctorates (DNP) a new terminal degree
for clinical experts similar to doctorates in medicine (MD), doctorates
in dentistry (DDS and DMD), doctorates in pharmacy (PharmD), and
doctorates in physical therapy (DPT). The AACN believes that such
advanced degrees are particularly needed in complex healthcare areas in
order to strengthen overall healthcare delivery and practice (AACN, n.d.).
Many of the most recent initiatives in planning to improve the nursing
profession grew out of the Institute of Medicine's (IOM) initiated research
that revealed that an enormous number of patients (44,000 to 98,000) die
annually due to preventable medical errors. The Joint Commission on the

Accreditation of Healthcare Organizations (JCAHO) responded with its National Patient Safety Goals. Approximately four years after reporting their initial findings, the IOM followed up by commissioning a task force to examine the educational preparation of healthcare professionals specifically in an attempt to determine if new graduates were adequately prepared to practice. The task force recommended that the curricula in all programs be revised, giving rise to a greater focus on increasing the entry level into nursing and advanced practice.

In addition to RNs there were 596,355 Licensed Practical/Vocational Nurses in the U.S. workforce. Licensed Practical/Vocational Nurses complete an approved program in 10–12 months. LPNs/LVNs are slightly older on average than the RN workforce, fewer are foreign born, they work in long-term care, C/MHCs, clinics, primary care offices, and males make up a relatively small percentage of both RN and LPN/LVN workforces (USDHHS, HRSA, 2004). Well-trained patient care technicians and nurse assistants work closely together in hospitals, nursing homes, and primary care settings assisting with care delivery.

In many areas in the United States there is no longer a shortage of nurses. When the economy declined during 2008, many retired nurses returned to work and those approaching retirement continued to work. For the first time in decades new graduates were having difficulty landing their first graduate nursing position.

According to the Health Policy Institute, in 15 years the United States will have a physician shortage of 200,000. A shortage of physicians, and until recently, also nurses, resulted in the demand for care exceeding the supply, triggering the growth of what is called mid-level providers. To compensate for the shortage of physicians in the United States, professionals such as advanced practice nurses who are mostly certified nurse practitioners and clinical nurse specialists have tremendously helped to bridge the physician gap. Both are typically educated at, minimally, the Masters level. These nurse experts are employed by hospitals, C/MHCs, clinics, urgent care centers, and independent practices. Physician's assistants, also considered mid-level providers, are employed directly by physicians or hospitals. In addition to advanced practice nurses, registered professional nurses manage and supervise the overall care of patients in a variety of roles and settings, including hospitals and nursing homes.

Physicians in the United States are well educated. After completing four years of pre-professional baccalaureate education, they complete four years of medical school, and four to seven years residency in their chosen specialty, such as family medicine, obstetrics/gynecology, orthopedics, or pediatrics. After the residency, the physician is eligible to become board certified in their selected specialty. According to the American Medical Association (nd) physicians who attended medical school outside the United States or Canada must first be certified to practice by the Educational Commission for Foreign Medical Graduates (ECFMG). All international medical graduates (IMGs) must complete residency training in the United States before they can obtain a license to practice medicine even if they were fully trained, licensed, and practicing in another country. Most physicians in the United States are board certified. It is relatively easy for employers to utilize government sponsored waivers to sponsor foreign born students who complete medical residency or fellowship programs in the United States. Siskind and Siskind (nd) describe three basic visa categories: J-1, requiring physicians to return to their home country for at least two years after their medical training before being eligible to apply for a work visa or green card; H-1B, that does not require the physician to work in under-served communities; and IGA, or interested government agency, where a government entity or state health department writes a letter of sponsorship stating that it is in the best interest of the public for the physician to remain in the United States.

Professional licensing is administered through each state's Education Department, Division of Professional Licensing. The number of employed providers per 100,000 persons in the population is data used to measure the rate of growth of the provider workforce relative to the growth of the overall U.S. population. The USDHHS, HRSA (2001) reports that in 2000, the physician workforce in the United States included 737,504 actively practicing physicians, equating to 263.8 practicing physicians per 100,000 persons in the population. Of this number, 238,734 were primary care physicians (85.4/100,000 population), 154,300 had surgical specialties (55.2/100,000 population) 101,353 (36.3/100,000) were in internal medicine, 86,315 (30.9/100,000) were general/family practice physicians, 51,066 (18.3/100,000) were in pediatrics, and 40,241 (14.4/100,000) were in obstetrics and gynecology. With the exception of endocrinologists, there are considerably more medical specialists than general practice (primary care) physicians. There are few endocrinologists, demonstrating the need for primary care physicians to play an active role in the management of diabetes care and other endocrine problems.

The average net annual income for all physicians was $205,700. Surgeons had the highest average income at $274,700, obstetrics/gynecologist earned $227,000, internal medicine at $196,000, general/family practice physicians at $144,700, and pediatricians at $137,800 (American Medical Association, 2004–2005). Physicians in specialty practices, such as cardiology, oncology, orthopedics, and anesthesiology tend to earn considerably higher salaries.

FINANCING

The United States spends 19.3 percent of its budget for health care ($6,714) per capita, considerably higher than Canada, France, and the United Kingdom (OECD, 2008). Sources of funding for healthcare services in the United States include direct pay by the individual using the services where the consumer privately pays out-of- pocket, sometimes according to a sliding fee scale; charity/welfare which is written off; Medicare and Medicaid for which the government pays; and insurance, which is almost exclusively through *Health Maintenance Organizations (HMOs)*, managed care in an attempt to lower costs. Under the HMO plan patients choose a primary care physician (PCP) within a network. That physician takes care of all their medical needs including referrals to specialists. The *Preferred Provider Organization (PPO)* is similar to the HMO but patients choose a provider or specialist from a network, and if they are seen by anyone other than a PPO provider, payment for services provided by the non-PPO provider are typically lower, and may even be withheld. In 1996, Medicap surfaced in an attempt to contain costs by capping payments made to hospitals and health providers at a preset fixed rate for services. This was replaced by managed care.

The direct-out-of-pocket payment, direct reimbursement models include "Contract" models, such as Independent Preferred Provider, Integrated models, and HMOs. Modes of payment to providers include hospital reimbursements using *diagnostic related groupings (DRGs)*, setting fees by grouping similar health problems, a negotiated fee-for-service, per diem, and *capitation,* a set limit on the amount that providers are reimbursed for services. Physicians are paid a standard fee for services. This fee is set by a HMO and paid directly to the physician. Consumers are responsible for a *co-payment* when they visit their providers or specialists. The co-payment is an out-of-pocket payment that is a fraction of the actual cost of care. The rigors of cost controls are many. Financing of health care overall has always been within the realm of insurance companies.

Shi and Singh (2004) describe the healthcare system in America as characteristically in disarray, plagued with a multiplicity of social and economic constraints that have resulted in a severely compromised three tier system relegated to Medicare for older adults, Medicaid for those lacking the ability to pay, and private insurance for everyone else. These authors paint a rather grim picture of the United States healthcare system fraught with a malady of problems. Although major improvements have been made in regard to professional standards of practice and quality in-hospital indices evidenced by many hospitals reaching magnet status during the past decade, the financing and the *institutional core* is still missing, that is, many hospitals lack well-coordinated, integrated systems of care, and their technology is outdated.

The cost of health care in the United States escalated out of control during the last twenty years. Managed care and Health Maintenance Organizations (HMOs) have not been the answer. This is partly because there must be better solutions to the healthcare problem that preserves the health and quality of lives without pitting one important initiative against another. Many were disappointed that the Clinton Health Care Reform Bill could not garner enough support to work out a legitimate compromise. The pharmaceutical companies were blamed for paying off key players that squashed any hopes of survival for the bill.

In examining the role of government in financing health care it is important to discuss its reliance on *Medicare* for those 65 and older, and *Medicaid*, health coverage for the poor, which is covered by the Federal Social Security Act, 1966, and is funded through taxes. Management of both is decentralized to the state and local governments. The Federal Social Security Act was later amended to fund Social Security disability, providing health care for those who have conditions that prevent them from being employed. The United States also provides health care to American Indians and Alaskan Natives through the Indian Health Services (IHS) and comprehensive medical and psychiatric care to veterans through its federal-government-operated Veterans Administration.

According to the most current Department of Health and Human Services (2012) publication of *"Medicare and You,"* Medicare provides coverage in four different parts, Parts A, B, C and D. Medicare is health insurance for people 65 and over, people under 65 with certain disabilities, and people of any age with end-stage renal disease which is permanent kidney failure that requires either dialysis or kidney transplant to live. It does not cover long-term care or custodial care. Also, individuals are often responsible for co-payments, deductibles, and coinsurance. A *co-payment* is the person's share of the cost for services such as $10.00–$40.00; a *deductible* is the amount the person pays before Medicare, the prescription drug plan, or other insurance begins to pay; and *coinsurance* is a preset percentage of the cost of the service such as 20% after deductibles.

The 2012 *Medicare & You Handbook* further describes what is covered by Parts A through D. Part A is generally referred to as hospital insurance. However, hospitalization helps cover a skilled nursing facility, such as rehabilitation, hospice, and home health care. Part B is known as medical insurance. It helps cover provider services such as physicians, outpatient care, durable medical equipment such as wheelchairs, walkers, and hospital beds, and it covers home health care and some home preventive services to help maintain health and prevent complications. When persons retire they become eligible for Medicare Part B. The health plan they were previously under while working requires them to enroll in Medicare Part B within an eight month window that begins one month after employment ends. Those failing to do so will probably pay a penalty and will be forced to wait until the next annual, general enrollment period to sign up, which is usually between the months of October and December. If they need Part B services during this waiting period, they must pay for the services out-of-pocket. These services include such things as diagnostic laboratory tests and procedures such as CT scans, MRIs, colorectal cancer screenings, immunizations, kidney dialysis, ambulatory surgical center procedures, and a variety of other services such as what is considered to be medically necessary transportation by ambulance to a hospital or skilled nursing facility. Part C, also referred to as Medicare Advantage, is a supplemental plan for retirees for which the individual pays extra. This plan covers any gaps in coverage and provides the individual with service upgrades. For example, individuals who have Part C would qualify for a higher quality placement in a rehabilitation facility after surgery than individuals without a supplemental advantage plan. Some popular Medicare Advantage plans include Medicare Blue, MVP Gold, Humana, and the American Association of Retired People (AARP)-recommended advantage plan through United Health Care. Part C is similar to an HMO or PPO. Medicare Part D covers prescription drugs. Part D is run by a Medicare-approved private insurance company.

When a person turns age 65, if that person is already receiving social security or railroad retirement benefits, he or she will, in most cases, automatically get Part A and B effective the first day of the month in which they turn 65. Persons who are under 65 but disabled, and receiving social security disability benefits, also automatically get Medicare Part A and B. If a person is not receiving social security or railroad retirement board benefits, as would be the case if the person was still working, the person can sign up for both A and B but if they are not eligible for free premiums they will have to pay out-of-pocket for Part A and B.

The IHS, located on or near reservations, provides acute and chronic care to American Indians.

Veteran services (outpatient and inpatient) are totally paid for by the government. The U.S. healthcare insurance plan covering active duty and retired military service workers is called TRICARE. This plan covers outpatient visits, hospitalization, preventive services, maternity care, immunizations, mental/behavioral health for active and retired service members and their families. There is also dental coverage. The basic TRICARE health plans are Prime, Standard, and Extra. TRICARE Standard and Extra provide the most flexibility in regard to visiting authorized providers in or outside the network, scheduling appointments, the need for referrals, and the percentage paid of the total cost, known as a cost-shares. TRICARE Prime is only available to members on active duty and command-sponsored family members. Referrals are required by all three plans for approval to see specialists. **Table 4-4** provides an overview of TRICARE health plan options.

The struggle to provide affordable, equitable quality health care in this country resulted in an out-of-control national debate about the feasibility of a government led fixable plan. Many question the ability of the government to offer a fiscally sound plan, arguably doubting that the government is in a position to effectively manage health care using management problems of *Medicaid* and *Medicare* as examples of irresponsibility. Medicare, a health insurance for individuals 65 and older, disabled individuals who are entitled to Social Security benefits, and those with end stage renal disease has long been criticized as falling short of its goal. Care of the older adult is funded through Medicare and coinsurance called *Medigap* to cover gaps between what Medicare covers after a person reaches 65, is chronically ill, or is disabled. Despite Medigap, Americans still are often bankrupted because of the extremely high cost of medical care either because they have insufficient Medigap coverage or no coverage at all beyond Medicare.

Long-term care in the United States is definitely an area in need of serious consideration. With the exception of Medicaid, long-term care coverage, such as for nursing home stays, is not covered by U.S. government financing. People sometimes become so desperate for solutions that they resort to

Table 4-4 TRICARE: an overview of beneficiary costs.

Active duty service members	· No enrollment fees or co-payments for any plan
	· $0 at military treatment facilities
Active duty family members	· No enrollment fees or co-payments when enrolled in TRICARE Prime
	· Low cost-shares when using TRICARE Standard and Extra
	· $0 at military treatment facilities
Retired service members and families	· Low annual enrollment fees for TRICARE Prime ($260/individual or $520/family)
	· Minimal network co-payments (ranges from $12–$30)
	· Low cost shares when using TRICARE Standard and Extra

Source: TRICARE: military health insurance at: www.tricare.mil/mybenefit/profile filter;do.sessionid=PrKXmx8Xl58,56n0pQzLKDKvg1YFlwyTOBgGcw1PvhfmRFQGf Tyw!-1368627664? Last updated March 6, 2012.

uncustomary methods of meeting their chronic care needs. Paying for long-term care out of pocket costs approximately $70,000 per year. Unless the individual has considerable financial resources this is not a feasible option. Medicaid rather than Medicare pays most nursing home costs for people with limited income and assets. The best option, for most middle-income earners, is to purchase long-term care insurance for approximately $2,000 per year, well in advance of needing it. If purchased later in life, premiums can be considerably higher.

Medicaid will cover the nursing home care for those without means to pay, but their nursing home choices are limited, waiting times are lengthy, the facilities and care are less than optimal, and outcomes are poorer. To be eligible for Medicaid, the person has to first spend all their savings, including retirement assets, leaving no opportunity to leave their assets to their heirs. Under these circumstances, a long-term illness can be financially devastating.

The United States healthcare system has an extremely high reliance on technology, resulting in more money being spent at the tertiary level of care. Funding priorities are acute hospital care which is more draining on the healthcare budget.

The role of payers in the United States system is threefold. It includes government, employers, and individuals, whereas employers have little or no role in most other healthcare systems worldwide. The role of insurers in the United States system is extensive and involves, in part, Health Maintenance Organizations (HMO) open enrollment, and fees based on *individual experience ratings*, based on how often a person utilizes the system and the complexity of their health problems. An individual hospitalized with an acute illness who has several comorbidities, for example, will be more costly to treat with each hospital or primary care encounter than an individual who is relatively healthy. This person's individual insurance rate will be higher than a healthy individual. *Group insurance ratings* that are based on an overall healthier aggregate are considerably lower. There is little or no centralization of health care in the United States system.

INTERVENTIONAL

Interventions in the U.S. system are highly scrutinized by insurance companies, a practice that is considered by many Americans to be extremely controlling and restrictive. Referrals for diagnostic testing are often denied even when an experienced physician deems the test or referral is necessary. The following scenario depicting the problems primary providers experience when attempting to manage a traumatic injury effectively and expediently, exemplifies the problem:

> X-Rays have ruled out a fracture but Mr. Jey, a 52-year-old male is still complaining of severe pain on weight bearing. His physician highly suspects a soft tissue injury which cannot be detected by a CT scan. Despite the fact that the gold standard test is an MRI, his insurance company insisted that a CT scan be done first, and only if negative would they then approve the MRI. Although a CT scan will not reveal the highly suspected soft tissue injury which, if untreated, can cause impingement on nerves, unrelieved pain, and serious damage to surrounding organs, an MRI cannot be ordered first. The patient was reluctantly sent for a CT scan which was negative; he then had the MRI which, as suspected, revealed severe contusions and a tendon tear that required surgical repair.

This apparently insensitive, and fiscally unsound, insurance company practice slowed the diagnostic process and disregarded the patient and the physician's knowledge. The time spent with the problem unresolved was significantly longer, and ultimately the insurance company paid for both diagnostic tests. In this case where were the cost savings? To their credit, some physicians send patients for MRIs despite insurance company directives and fight with them later for payment.

Americans often voice concerns that insurance companies should not interfere in the practice of medicine. Rather they should develop institutional processes and execute claims more efficiently and effectively. This would, in the minds of many, allow physicians to practice medicine. Also, politicians are criticized for pitting one program against another for their own political gains rather than making decisions that are in the best interest of the American people.

PREVENTIVE

Government regulation of practice licensure, food, and drugs is evidence of its attempt to ensure the quality and safety of patients in the United States. In fact, the U.S. government is often accused of overlegislating and overregulating medications. Preventive measures must consider, among other things, the culture and traditional practices of its people. It also considers how well the country handles such environmental problems as tobacco use and substance use and abuse; which may include funding for programs to address health and safety programs. It is a particular challenge for the United

States to address these problems when smoking and drinking alcohol are socially accepted, and using illicit mood-altering drugs is common.

Prevention is very much evidenced in care received in community/migrant health centers (C/MHCs) although it is severely underfunded. The mission of these health centers has always been to provide comprehensive primary care services to community residents regardless of the individual's ability to pay (Plaska & Vieth, 1995). Centers located in health professional shortage areas are partially funded by a grant from the Department of Health and Human Services, United States Public Services Section 329/330. The focus of the C/MHC's care is to promote health and prevent illness, keeping people out of the hospital. In the mid-60s, C/MHCs served an estimated 7 million people, and in 2010, they served more than 20 million of the nation's most vulnerable residents, including a large number of migrant/seasonal farm workers, and one million homeless patients, at over 8,000 sites (Whelan, 2010). Yet, C/MHCs continually face financial challenges because of the nationwide movement toward managed care. A major goal of managed care is to decrease cost by paying greater attention to productivity, and better management of human and fiscal resources.

Culture is a major consideration when planning for, and implementing, patient care in and out of the hospital. Health seeking beliefs and practices emanate from an individual's culture. How patients perceive, or accept, the care being provided them is contingent on their culture, for it reflects who they are. Experienced medical and nursing providers with *cultural competence,* that is, those who strive to incorporate treatment and care plans embracing of the person's culture, will model behaviors that underscore the importance of providing culturally congruent care. These providers are more likely than incompetent providers to influence the practices of novice providers by modeling and coaching the right behaviors.

Despite the diverse culture of the people it serves, the United States' standard of health and medical deliveries are generally Eurocentric. Family, culture, religion, and social health, the very elements of importance to preventing illness are often disregarded when a person enters the healthcare system. Preventing illness and maintaining healthy lifestyles are imperative to longevity. This is especially important because in the United States, life expectancy is lower than other industrialized nations and infant mortality is among the highest.

Just as no two persons are the same, no two cultural groups respond the same way to a provider's recommended treatment. A clear example of this is the way in which the significance of food for some cultures is overlooked when health providers make attempts to convince patients to modify their diets in order to improve their health. Although it is relatively easy for providers to inform their patients that they must absolutely reduce their fat or salt intake, this advice is ineffective if culture is not addressed. Patients' cultural backgrounds may be deeply rooted in not only the food they eat but the specifics on how the food is prepared. If the approach taken does not include culturally acceptable alternatives, patients' eating habits are not likely to change, their blood pressures are not likely to decrease, and as a consequence, the heart attack or stroke the provider may have been attempting to prevent may not be successfully averted.

There are many barriers to healthcare access in the United States resulting in health disparities (see Chapter 14). This further illustrates the magnitude of the problem of addressing disease prevention. When there is a widened gap between health and culture, and the poor and wealthy maintaining health and preventing illness is a great challenge.

RESOURCES

Community support is very important as the strength or weakness of an individual's immediate community often reflects the strength of individuals and families residing in it. The safety of the environment might determine how often children are allowed to play and exercise outdoors, get fresh air, or even if environmental hazards and contaminants keep them confined to their homes. When residents share a sense of community and belonging this could contribute to a sense of comfort and well-being.

Family support provided to the ill spans generations and cultural groups. Family traditions and values often influence how an individual defines health, and the specific health seeking beliefs and practices. Grandparents and godparents often share in the upbringing of children. Family, in America, is defined as nuclear or extended, depending on the cultural group. European Americans tend to be more nuclear in their family orientation than other cultural groups in the United States (Purnell & Paulanka, 2004). Many men and women are raising families as single parents and depend on the support of family and friends to succeed. Some cultural groups rely on women to care for children, parents, even in-laws when ill. During the past 25 years there has been a major trend toward eldercare in America, pressuring many to balance multiple roles of job/career, immediate family, care of their parents, and, during especially tough economic times, supplementing their parents' fixed incomes.

Spirituality and religion is a source of strength for many living in America. Religious freedom and choice, with the exception of a few extremists, is embraced in the United States. People are permitted to formally and informally openly practice their religion peacefully. Numerous cultural groups wear religious symbols without fear of discrimination. Immigrants often come to America in search of religious freedom.

Religion and spirituality also play a major role in death and dying across cultures. Many health providers consider a good death as spending the end-of-life in a hospital, hospice, or nursing home surrounded by experts who are needed to guide everyone through the process and loved ones for additional support (Long, 2003). Americans consider death as a natural process when it occurs during old age, or when the person is chronically ill. Funerals and memorial activities are ways of validating the lives of the deceased but often strengthen the lives of those left behind (Walsh and Burke, 2006). During times of loss and grief, financial, physical, and emotional comfort and support are often critical in assisting families through some of their most challenging times.

MAJOR HEALTH ISSUES

Historically, America as a nation has been accused of being a country where, with the exception of exercise, everything is done in excess. Americans eat, drink, and smoke too much, and many Americans drive wherever they go, even when traveling a few blocks. This accounts for heart-related diseases leading the list of health problems affecting the United States.

There are multiple barriers to individuals seeking health care in the United States. Personal barriers include cultural or spiritual differences and language, particularly for non-English speaking immigrants. It also includes not knowing what to do or when to seek care, and includes concerns about confidentiality or discrimination (USDHHS, *Healthy People 2010*).

Strengthening C/MHCs might be the way to go in addressing access and decreasing some of the barriers discussed in *Healthy People 2010*. Expanding funding to these centers may be a good way to compensate for the under-funded preventive care in the United States. Wilensky and Roby (2005) suggest that C/MHCs play a vital role regardless of the type of insurance system in place because they reduce barriers to care and provide quality, culturally competent care to vulnerable populations. The current private employer-based U.S. healthcare system does not create incentives for providers to care for low-income and vulnerable populations. Even in countries with universal health coverage, health centers increase access to care and improve health outcomes.

The Top Ten Leading Causes of Death in the United States

The ten leading causes of death in the United States for all ages, races, and genders disproportionately affect some groups as compared to others, and

Table 4-5 Top 10 causes of death (all ages) in the United States, 2002, with the number and percent of years of life lost by disease.

Disease Deaths	Number	Percent	Years of Life Lost %
All causes	2420	100	100
1. Ischemic heart disease	514	21	15
2. Cerebrovascular disease (stroke)	163	7	4
3. Trachea, bronchus, lung cancers	157	7	7
4. Chronic obstructive pulmonary disease	128	5	4
5. Alzheimer and other dementias	93	4	1
6. Diabetes mellitus	76	3	3
7. Colon & rectal cancers	64	3	3
8. Lower respiratory infections	59	3	2
9. Breast cancer	45	2	2
10. Road traffic accidents	45	2	6

Data From: Death and DALY estimates by cause, 2002. http://www.who.int/entity/healthinfo/statistics/bodgbddeathdalyestimates.xls

are among some of the most fiscally and pathologically challenging problems to combat. These problems, ranked from the cause affecting the greatest number of people to the least number of people, are listed in **Table 4-5.**

DISPARITIES

Globally, countries are in a quest for healthcare systems that provide quality, and are not costly but efficient. In 1997, approximately 37 million persons in America were without health insurance (Clinton, 2003). Healthy People 2010 indicates that health insurance provides access to health care; persons with health insurance are more likely to have a primary care provider, receive appropriate preventive care such as Pap tests, immunizations, or early prenatal care. Additionally, adults with health insurance are twice as likely to receive routine check-ups than adults without health insurance. Further, about one-third of adults under age 65 years who were below the poverty level were uninsured. Approximately one in three persons of Latino descent was without health insurance coverage in 1997. Mexican Americans had one of the highest uninsured rates, at 40%. Today, approximately 40 million persons in the United States are uninsured (USDHHS, *Healthy People, 2010*).

In the United States, heart disease leads the way for mortality followed by cancer and stroke. These top three diseases, heart disease, cancer, and stroke, account for the overwhelming majority of deaths in the United States. However, people of African and Latino descents are more likely to die than individuals of European descent. Women in general, and those 65 and older, are more likely to die than men (National Institutes of Health, 2006). Malignant neoplasms, with which, again, the over 65 year old group is more affected and cerebrovascular disease (stroke) have devastatingly poorer outcomes. Unintentional injury ranks as the number one cause of death in the United States for the 1–44 age group, third for ages 45–54, and fifth for ages 55–64. Prevention is key to improving outcomes. For example, educating individuals in safeproofing their homes is of paramount importance if there are older adults and small children in the home. Basic measures such as the use of seat belts when in automobiles, smoke detectors, and carbon monoxide detectors can also be lifesaving. Nine of the ten leading causes of death are preventable. Table 4-5 lists the top ten causes of death in the United States. Despite these alarming statistics, a relatively small portion of the nation's healthcare budget is appropriated to promotion of health and prevention of disease.

During the decade of the 1990s, the Clinton administration, under the leadership of first lady Hillary Clinton, introduced a Health Care Reform bill called, *Clinton: American Health Choices Plan.* Clinton writes,

> There were compelling reasons to push ahead. By the time Bill became President, 37 million Americans, most of them working people and their children, were uninsured. They weren't getting access to care until they were in a medical crisis. Even for common medical concerns they wound up in an emergency room, where care was most expensive, or they went broke trying to pay for medical emergencies on their own. In the early 1990s, one hundred thousand Americans were losing coverage each month, and two million were without coverage temporarily as they changed jobs. Small businesses were unable to offer coverage for their employees because of the exploding cost of healthcare premiums. And the quality of medical care was suffering, too. In an effort to control costs, insurance companies often denied or delayed treatment prescribed by doctors in deference to their corporate bottom lines. Rising healthcare costs were sapping the nation's economy, undermining American competitiveness, eroding workers' wages, increasing personal bankruptcies and inflating the national deficit (Clinton, 2003, p. 144).

The Clinton plan would have allowed people to keep their existing insurance if they were satisfied. If they were not, they had an option to choose a plan similar to the plan afforded to Congress or to choose a government option similar to Medicare (Clinton HC Plan). Tactics by those in opposition to the bill and pharmaceutical companies that paid off key supporters of this bill are credited with the demise of a plan that could have proven to be what the country needed.

The healthcare system is currently out of sync with anything that even remotely resembles fairness and reason. Ironically, of all the industrialized nations in the world, the United States is the only one without a national health insurance plan. Also, prescription medications around the world are a fraction of the cost of the same medications in America. Insurance companies are out of control and people are dying every day while awaiting approval for a lifesaving treatment, surgery, or diagnostic procedure that requires prior authorization. Others are outright denied coverage due to preexisting problems, and are illegally unenrolled. For some patients, the co-payment for an essential medication is so high that they do without it. Eventually they need a much more expensive intervention for a complication that may have been prevented had they been able to afford the medication. Still others die while awaiting treatment approval or after having been denied treatment.

If individuals lose their jobs in this country, most can continue their healthcare insurance for eighteen months by paying out-of-pocket to the tune of $800 or $900 a month, for what is called the Consolidated Omnibus Budget Reconciliation Act (COBRA). *COBRA* is available for workers and their dependent children if they lose their jobs, only if they were employed in a workforce with at least 20 employees. They are entitled to continue their coverage under their former employer for 18 months, and, if disabled, for up to 29 months (*Consumer Reports*, p. 85). When persons are out of work and paying premiums this high there is little left over for rent or mortgage, utilities, food, and medication; that is, if they are fortunate enough to be receiving unemployment benefits in the first place. Immediately upon reaching the 18-month COBRA deadline, individuals have to pay 2 or 3 times the COBRA amount to continue insurance coverage, which very few have the means to do.

Some breathe a sigh of relief when they reach age 65 because they qualify for Medicare. However, even if individuals make it to Medicare age they are likely to be required to pay for additional health insurance, such as Medigap or HMO Medicare coverage, for services not covered by Medicare. A final disparity perspective comes from guest essayist Penelope Frontuto, who relates her personal experience with the healthcare system and the need for reform:

> After being laid off from my job at the Visiting Nurse Service of Rochester and Monroe County, I continued family coverage under

> COBRA for $900 per month. When COBRA ran out I paid $2,200 a month. As I reached Medicare eligibility, my husband and I qualified for an HMO-based Advantage Plan which went from an initial monthly $94.50, to $165.00 in addition to co-pays for medications all totaling over $400 a month. However, my daughter became uninsured. While one senator in the spotlight for writing healthcare reform was reported to have received $1.5 million in re-election funds from the pharmaceutical industry . . . We have to fix this . . . We have to stop politicizing healthcare reform (Frontuto, 2009, p. 21A).

Almost overnight individuals are relegated to second-class citizenry; at a time when they should be retiring and living the good life, they lose their health, their homes, and their dignity almost simultaneously. As a nurse practitioner, this is a common scenario I have observed repeatedly, and feel powerless to change. Very little can be done apart from giving samples whenever possible, encouraging patients to appeal insurance company decisions, and to not give up hope.

Insurance company tactics such as instituting a physician grading system based on the number of referrals made and diagnostic tests ordered often dissuade health providers from making referrals to specialists, or ordering expensive diagnostic procedures. If not for the highly publicized actions of a few who deliberately disrupted town hall meetings throughout the country, healthcare reform would, without question, be much further along. However, ready or not, much needed healthcare reform is on the horizon. The system will eventually get the long awaited overhaul that is needed.

SUMMARY

Approximately 25 years ago, the United States healthcare system was medical dominated and physicians ruled. The diagnostic tests, procedures, referrals, and length of hospital stays were based on physician's unscrutinized decisions. For the last twenty-five years however, health care has been moving from physician dominance to business dominance. In effect, insurance companies now rule. More focus must be placed on cost containment and achieving clear measurable outcomes.

By tracing over two decades of health care in the United States, this chapter has provided insight on how health care is financed, the role of the health centers in providing affordable, comprehensive care, and practice challenges experienced by providers and consumers. This has all led to health reform. Healthcare reform, a response to controlling escalating healthcare costs, preserving a patient's right to choose their health provider, and assuring that all Americans have access to affordable, high quality care will likely be further debated and challenged before finalized. With a particular focus on patient safety, quality of care, preserving wellness, preventing insurance companies from unenrolling patients and cancelling their coverage when they become ill, health outcomes will probably be improved. Those in opposition to changing the healthcare system reportedly fear too much government involvement, cost escalation, and tampering with Medicare benefits in order to fund reform. This chapter has also presented some convincing arguments in support of healthcare reform. In the words of guest essayist Frontuto, "the United States healthcare problem is fixable and must be fixed now!"

Discussion Questions

1. Where are people most likely to receive primary care today, and why?
2. Describe the changes in specializations over the past 30 years. How have these changes affected the primary provider and the consumer?
3. Explain why Managed Care and HMOs are not "the answer" to healthcare issues in the United States.
4. Explain why Community and Migrant Health Centers are viable alternatives to emergency care.
5. Identify arguments for and against healthcare reform.
6. Describe three strengths or barriers that facilitate or limit access to health care and give examples of each.

Case Scenario for the United States

Mr. Samuels' Long-Term Care Service Options

Mr. Samuels, a 93-year-old severely hard of hearing male, slipped on the ice, suffered severe contusions and sprains of his left lower leg, and was hospitalized for three days before being transferred to a nearby nursing home for rehabilitation. His hearing aid was misplaced somewhere between the hospital and the nursing home; however, no one ever claimed responsibility for it. Prior to being hospitalized, Mr. Samuels lived independently in his own home in the New York City area. He never complained about his care at the nursing home where he spent most of his time in bed or sitting for extended periods in a chair, but he repeatedly begged his niece, who lived almost 600 miles away, to take him out of the nursing home. Once assured by Medicare that, with the exception of a wheelchair, her uncle would receive full home care services, the niece had him discharged after five months in the nursing home, and he was to continue rehabbing at her home in upstate NY. Upon discharge, Mr. Samuels had lower extremity weakness, could not take more than a few steps without his knees buckling, and he needed to be bathed. Despite a home care referral being submitted by his new primary care physician, for the first six weeks no one visited from the local home care agency. When services did begin around the 7th week, physical therapy and occupational therapy services abruptly ended after 4 visits, and the home health aide services provided two hours a day, ended after 40 hours. Although the niece made several appeals for continuation of services, no one from Medicare contacted her to clarify the numerous questions she had about the change in services or to explain why the services were halted.

DISCUSSION POINTS

There are several quality of life issues for Mr. Samuels as he moves through various stages of care. Let's address his situation at each phase.

1. Mr. Samuels lived on his own for a long time. Identify the qualities it takes for an older adult to do that.
2. Recognizing these characteristics, what could have been done to make sure Mr. Samuels' time in the nursing home involved more than staying in bed or sitting around? What could have been done immediately? What could have been done over his five month stay?
3. Instead of getting better, Mr. Samuels' health steadily declined in the nursing home. How does this happen? As an administrator or as a health practitioner, what could have been done to ensure that Mr. Samuels was healing properly?
4. Imagine life for the niece the first six weeks without healthcare assistance for her uncle. How do you think she felt? How do you think she managed Mr. Samuels' care?
5. Mr. Samuels is aware of the problems surrounding support for his health care. How do you think he feels about depending on his niece?
6. In view of the problems and confusion with Medicare, where does the niece go from here?
7. What can the niece do to obtain uninterrupted healthcare services from Medicare? Are there steps she missed? How can health practitioners assist families through the maze of Medicare?

REFERENCES

Agency for Healthcare Research and Quality (AHRQ). *2007 National Healthcare Disparities Report*. Rockville, MD: U.S. Department of Health and Human Services, Agency for Healthcare Research and Quality, February 2008. AHRQ Pub No. 08-0041.

Aiken, L. H., Clarke, S. P., Sloane, D. M., Lake, T. L., & Cheney, T. (2008). The effects of hospital care environment on patient mortality and nurse outcomes. *Journal of Nursing Administration, 38*(5), 223–229.

Aiken, L. H., Clarke, S. P., Sloane, D. M., Sochalski, J., & Silber, J. H. (2002). Educational levels of hospital nurses and surgical patient mortality. *JAMA 290*:1617–1623.

American Association of Colleges of Nursing. (2009). Nursing shortage resource. Retrieved November 22, 2009 from http://www.aacn.nche.edu/media/shortaberesource.htm

American Association for Colleges of Nursing. (n.d.). DNP Programs. Retrieved February 3, 2011 from http://www.aacn. nche.edu/DNP/index.htm

American Association of Colleges of Nursing. (n.d.). DNP Programs. Retrieved December 22, 2011 from http://www.aacn.nche.edu/dnp/index.htm

American Hospital Association. (2010). Fast facts on U.S. hospitals. Retrieved March 14, 2011 from http://unv.ah.org/aha/resources-center/statistics-and-studies/fast-facts

American Medical Association. (n.d.). *Physician education licensure and certification*. Retrieved November 15, 2011 from http://www.ama-assn.org/aps/physred.htm/#foreign

American Nurses Association. (2000). Nurse staffing and patient outcomes in the in-patient hospital setting. Washington, DC: American Nurses Publishing.

Brush, B. L., Sochalski, J., & Berger, A. M. (2004). Imported care: Recruiting foreign nurses to US healthcare facilities. *Health Affair, 23*(3). 78-87. Doi:10.1377/hlthaff.23.3.78.

Buchan, J., Parkin, T., & Sochalski, J. (2003). *International nurse mobility: Trends and policy implications*. Royal College of Nursing/World Health Organization/International Council of Nurses. WHO Geneva, Switzerland. www.icn.ch/int_nurse_mobility%20final.pdf.

Buerhaus, P. I., Staiger, D. O., & Auerbach, D. I. (2009). The future of the nursing workforce in the United States: Data, trends and implications. Sudbury, MA: Jones and Bartlett Publishers.

Clinton, H. R. (2003). *Living history: Hillary Rodham Clinton*. New York: Simon & Schuster, p.144.

Consumer Reports. Health insurance for the unemployed. Retrieved October 23, 2010 from http://www.ConsumerReports.org.

DeNovas-Walt, C., Proctor, B. D., & Smith, J. C. (2010). *U.S. Census Bureau, Current Population Reports, P60-236, Income, Poverty, and Health Insurance Coverage in the United States: 2009*. U.S. Government Printing Office, Washington D.C.

Department of Health and Human Services. (2012). *Medicare and You: The official U.S. government Medicare handbook*. Centers for Medicare and Medicaid Services.

Frontuto, P. (October 18, 2009). Reform Needs to Lower Costs. *Democrat and Chronicle*. Guest Essayist, p. 21A.

Gallup Poll. Nov. 11–14, 2007. http://www.pollingreport.com/health3.htm

Ginsberg, J., Taylor, T., & Barr, M. (2009). Nurse practitioners in primary care (Monograph) American College of Physicians. Philadelphia, PA.

Healthcare.gov. (2010). Provisions: About the law. Retrieved November 15, 2011 from http://www.healthcare.gov/law/about/index.html.

Healthcare.gov. (2010). Provisions: Patient's bill of rights. Retrieved November 15, 2011 from www.familiesusa2.org/assets/pdfs/health-reform/patients-bill-of-rights.pdf. The Bill of Rights appears on page 5 of the Health Reform document.

Healthreform.gov. (2011). Protecting families and putting more money in your pocket: How health insurance reform will lower costs and increase choices. Retrieved November 15, from: http://www.healthreform.gov

Infoplease. (2010). A profile of the world fact book, geography age: 4.55 billion years old. Retrieved November 10, 2010 from http://www.infoplease. com/ipa/A0762380.html

Long, S. O. (2003). Becoming a cucumber: Culture, nature, and the good death in Japan and the United States. *The Journal of Japanese Culture, 29*:1.

Murray, C. J. L. & Frenk, J. (2010). Ranking 37th—measuring the performance of the U.S. healthcare system. *New England Journal of Medicine*. Retrieved February 17, 2011 from http://www.healthpolicyandreform.nejm.org/?p=2610

National Center for Health Statistics. (1999). *Health, United States, 1999 with health and aging chartbook*. Department of Health and Human Services. Hyattsville, MD.

National Commission of State Boards of Nursing. (2001). Licensure and examination statistics.

National Commission of State Boards of Nursing. (2004, February). NCLEX. www.ncsbn.org/

Needleman, J., Buerhaus, P., Mattke, S., Stewart, M., & Zelevinsky, K. (2002). Nurse staffing levels and the quality of care in hospitals. *New England Journal of Medicine, 346*:22, 1715–1722.

Office of the Actuary, Centers for Medicare and Medicaid Services, National Health Expenditure 2. Data for 2007. U.S. Department of Health and Human Services, retrieved 10/15/10 from http: www.cms.hhs.gov/NationalHealthExpendData/02_National Health AccountsHistorical.asp#TopOfPage

Organization for Economic Cooperation and Development (OECD). (2008). Health Data.

Orszag, P. R. (2008). Growth in Health Care Costs: Statement Before the Committee on the Budget, 4. United States Senate, (Washington, DC: Congressional Budget Office, Jan 31 2008). Available at http://www.cbo.gov/doc.cfm?index=8948

Plaska, M. & Vieth, E. (1995, October). The community health center: An enduring model for the past and future. *Journal of Ambulatory Care Management, 18*:2 Lippincott, Williams & Wilkins, Inc.

Purnell, L. & Paulanka, B. (2004). *Transcultural health care: A culturally competent approach*. 2nd ed. Philadelphia: F. A. Davis Company.

Shi, L. & Singh, D. A. (2004). Delivering Health Care in America: A Systems Approach (3rd ed.). Sudbury, MA: Jones and Bartlett Publishers.

Sison, M. (2002, May). Exodus of nurses grows: Health system feels effect. *CyberDyaryo*. Retrieved December 10, 2010 from www.cyberdyaryo.com/features /f2002_0508_04.htm

Smedley, B. D., Stith, A. Y., & Nelson, A. R. (Eds.). (2002). Unequal treatment: Confronting racial and ethnic disparities in health care. Washington, DC: National Academies Press.

Starfield, B. (1994). Is primary care essential? Institute of Medicine. *The Lancet*, 2:8930.

Solis, H. (2010). US Secretary of Labor, in a news release statement on the House of Representative passage of health care reform. Retrieved November 22, 2011 from http://www.dol.gov/opa/ media/press/opa/opa20100370.htm

Siskind, G. & Siskind, S. B. (2008). Immigration options for hiring international physicians. Retrieved December 22, 2010 from www.visalaw.com/Bloomberg .pdf

Taylor, M. (2010). *The patient protection and affordable care act: An overview of its potential impact on state health programs. Congressional Research Services.* Washington, DC: Legislative Analyst's Office.

The Commonwealth Fund Commission. (July, 2008). *Why Not the Best? Results from the National Scorecard on U.S. Health System Performance, 2008.* Commonwealth Fund Pub. no. 1150. Available at: commonwealthfund.org

Tourangeau, A. E., Giovannetti, M., & Tu, J. V. (2007). The impact of hospital nursing care on 30 day mortality for acute medical patients. *Journal of Advanced Nursing*, 57(1) 32–44.

TRICARE (2012). *My benefits.* Retrieved from: Tricare.mil/mybenefit/profilefilter .do.jsessioid=

United States Census Bureau. Bureau of Labor Statistics. (2010). Monthly labor review. November. In: AACN (2009) p. 2. Retrieved November 22, 2009 from aacn.nche.edu/media/shortageresource.htm

United States Census Bureau. Bureau of Labor Statistics. (2007). Monthly labor review. November. In: AACN (2009) p. 2. Retrieved November 22, 2009 from aacn.nche.edu/media/shortageresource.htm

United States Census Bureau. Bureau of Labor Statistics. (2004). Monthly labor review. November. In: AACN (2009) p. 2. Retrieved November 22, 2009 from aacn.nche.edu/media/shortageresource.htm

United States Department of Health and Human Services. (2006). Healthy people 2010: Midcourse review. Washington, DC: Office of Disease Prevention and Health Promotion.

United States Department of Health and Human Services. (2004). The nurse workforce in the United States. HRSA, Washington, DC: Office of Disease Prevention and Health Promotion.

United States Department of Health and Human Services. (2006). Health disparities. Retrieved August 15, 2009 from http://nih.gov/aboutresearchforthepublic

United States Department of Labor. Bureau of Labor Statistics (2004–2005). Occupational outlook handbook. Retrieved on February 23, 2010 from www .bls.gov/oco/home.htm

UNO (2004). Retrieved October 10, 2010 from Un.org/esa/population/publications /WorldPop.pdf

Walsh-Burke, K. (2006). The Handbook of Grief and Loss. Chapter 5, Grief and loss: Theories for helping professionals. Boston: Pearson Education. Retrieved October 10, 2010 from http://www.pearsonhighered.com/samplechapter/0205398812.pdf

Whelan, E. M. (2010, August). The importance of community health centers: Engines of economic activity and job creation. Center for American Progress.

Wilensky, S. & Roby, D. H. (2005). Health centers and health insurance: Complements, not alternatives. *Journal of Ambulatory Care Management, 28*:4, 348–356.

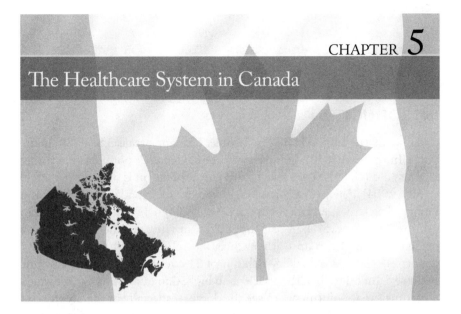

CHAPTER 5

The Healthcare System in Canada

Knowledge is power, information is liberating and education is the premise of progress.

—Kofi Annan

BEHAVIORAL OBJECTIVES

At the end of this chapter the learner will be able to:

1. Discuss how Canada's healthcare system emerged.
2. Discuss the incidence and prevalence of disease.
3. Discuss the top three diseases and how they are treated.
4. Determine how health care is structured, financed, and accessed.
5. Identify funding priorities, initiatives, and challenges.
6. Describe health practices that are commonly used to maintain and restore health.
7. Explain how social determinants affect health seeking beliefs and practices.

KEY CONCEPTS

Universal health coverage
Single payer
Disparities

Self-harm

Portable

INTRODUCTION

Canada's population is 33 million people. The land area is 3,854,082 square miles (Infoplease, 2010). Eighteen percent of Canada's population is under 15 years old (UNO, 2004), and 17% of the population is over the age of 60 (WHO, 2004). The primary languages spoken in Canada are English and French. The largest ethnic groups are British, French, and other European groups. The largest religious groups are Roman Catholic with a strong presence of Anglican and other Christian religions (who.intl/profiles_ countries). Canada is ranked 25th out of 31 countries in the literacy rate. Because demand for health services is so high, Canadians often must wait a long time for appointments to see the doctor, especially in the province of Quebec. In the words of Frogue (2001, p. 10), "everything is free but nothing is readily available."

HISTORICAL

Dating back to 1867 Canada's Constitution assigned most of the healthcare responsibilities to its ten provinces and three sparsely populated northern territories. These provinces vary widely by size and fiscal capacity. For example, in 2001, Prince Edward Island had a population of 135,000 while Ontario had 11.4 million.

Canada, unlike the United States, provides universal health coverage, a national health insurance program provided by the Medical Care Insurance Act of 1966. Universal coverage provides health care to all members of its society, combining mechanisms for health financing and service provision (WHO, 2008). Health care in Canada is funded through general taxes and Medicare. The National Medical Care Insurance Act operates on the basis of four principles: 1) it is comprehensive, covering all medically necessary services provided by physicians, 2) universal coverage is available to all legal and illegal residents, 3) it is publicly administered, either directly by provincial government or by an authority directly responsible to it, and 4) it is portable.

The Canada Health Act, passed in 1984, established a fifth core principle, accessibility, which sought to force provinces to forbid extra billing and cost sharing. It called for the Canadian government to deduct the amount of such charges from its payments to any province.

During the early 1990s there were growing concerns about the perceived notion that the country was approaching physician saturation, even the potential for a surplus. This led to policy decisions such as enacting a 10% cut in first year medical school admissions, contributing to a drop in physician supply.

STRUCTURE

Canada has a readily available supply of physicians, and less availability of nurses. Levels of nurses practicing in Canada are comparable to those in the United States and include registered nurses, nurse practitioners, nurse midwives, and LPNs. However, nurse practitioners and physicians assistants are relatively new to Canada and are not yet widely utilized. Other health professionals in Canada include dentists, pharmacists, medical and radiology technicians, chiropractors, and physiotherapists.

In 2004, workforce aging became a significant challenge in that health professionals were aging more rapidly than the Canadian population with the average physician being 49 and the average RN being 45. Between 1990 and 2005, the number of nurses practicing in Canada decreased from 11.1 to 10 nurses per 1,000 population, with the lowest point occurring in 2003, at 9.6 per 1,000 (OECD Health Data, 2007). Also, increasing numbers of women are entering the medical workforce.

According to OECD (2007) data, 24% of Canadians live in rural areas, yet only nine percent of the physician workforce practices in rural Canada. Although Canada has a stable supply of physicians, in 2008 approximately 14% (5 million) of Canadian adults did not have a family physician. Between 2002 and 2006, permanent migration of physicians to other countries tripled and temporary migration increased over 10%. Permanent migration of nurses increased by 40%, and temporary migration increased by 35%. In 2006, 9% of all nurses and 19% of physicians born in Canada were working in other OECD countries. Physicians also move freely among provinces, in fact 62.3% of the physicians in Canada are concentrated in the two provinces of Ontario and Quebec. Although the number of male registered nurses almost tripled from 1985 to 2006, from 5,000 to 14,000, they make up only 6% of Canada's nursing workforce and more than half the male nurses in Canada practice in Quebec. Physicians from South Africa, and nurses from the Philippines also are part of the Canadian workforce (OECD, 2007). Many of the nurses working in the United States in the travelling nurse program were Canadians.

Canada regulates physician supply, physician and hospital budgets, and technology. The government also coordinates financing, insurance, and payment function. Unlike the American healthcare system, because the Canadian healthcare system is government run there is no need for employer involvement in health care except, of course, for supplemental catastrophic additional coverage. The role of payers is limited to the government and individuals. The role of insurers in Canada is minimal.

In the Canadian healthcare system the physicians, through their medical associations, have a great deal of autonomy. Medical associations negotiate with provinces for fee schedules. There is centralization at the province level although activities vary among provinces. There are more general practitioners than specialists demonstrating the emphasis on promoting healthy communities and preventing disease. Generally, medical specialists earn more than family practice physicians with the largest variance being in Ontario, where specialists earn on average 1.68 times more than family physicians, whereas in Quebec the variance is smaller, amounting to 1.22 times more. Major differences in nurse salaries differ among provinces. Most nurses work on union contracts negotiated by the Canadian Federation of Nurses Association. The maximum wage ranges between 70,000 Canadian dollars (C$) in Ontario, 51,000 C$ in Quebec, and the minimum ranges from 53,000 in Manitoba and 34,000 in Quebec. However, some nurses in Canada make over 500,000 C$ (OECD, 2007).

FINANCING

During the 1970s physicians commonly billed patients for additional costs that were already covered by the government plan. In 1984, the passing of the Canada Health Act prevented medical providers from billing patients for services if they had also billed the public insurance system. A reaffirmation of the government's stance that they were committed to health care that was, "comprehensive, universal, portable, publically administered, and accessible," was issued by the Prime Minister in 1999. *Portable* means coverage continues when patients travel or move between provinces.

Single payer is used to primarily describe a system that is government funded and controlled. Canada has a single payer system, complemented by insurance and direct out-of-pocket payments. There are global budgets for hospitals and physicians, negotiated fees for services, and consumer co-payments. Hospitals and physicians must operate within a set budget with which they must strictly adhere. In order to finance Canadian health care, provincial funds are gathered from a mix of federal transfers that favor poorer provinces, general provincial revenues, employer payroll taxes, and insurance premiums.

In provinces like Alberta and British Columbia where premiums exist, there are special provisions for assistance to people with low incomes. Residents of each province receive insurance cards, which they present when being seen in a hospital or physician office. They must produce this card for care because benefits vary slightly among provinces. There is typically no general dental coverage, but most provinces provide some pediatric dentistry, and all provinces cover in-hospital oral surgery as part of hospital coverage. Many provinces provide limited optometric, chiropractic, and physical therapy coverage. Financial support for pharmaceutical expenses is included in separate programs, generally for seniors and other categories of the needy. Contraception is available to all women in Canada free of charge as birth control is also covered under the public insurance plan. Every provincial plan insures all medically necessary physician and hospital care.

Private insurance is allowed for what is referred to as non-core services. Private insurance plans are prohibited from billing patients for core services, or any service covered by the standard public insurance plan. An estimated 80% of Canada's population has supplementary coverage for items such as private rooms, dental care, and other non-core services (Irvine, Ferguson and Cackett, 2002, p. 17). This is financed primarily through employers, and, as in the United States, is treated as a business expense for tax purposes.

INTERVENTIONAL

The social and economic conditions experienced by a people have a definite influence on their health status. Any proposed interventions must be geared toward addressing health issues within the realm of these conditions.

Despite problems with access, and language challenges that are closely related to cultures other than French, there is a high user satisfaction with health care in Canada. Canada places less reliance on technology and there is greater access to health providers in urban settings. However, there are often long waits for appointments and services. In 2005, on average, Canadians waited 12.3 weeks for an MRI, 5.5 weeks for a CT scan and 3.4 weeks for an ultrasound (Fraser Institute, 2005). Almost half of the Canadian public, when surveyed by Pollara polling in 2005, reported their willingness to pay out-of- pocket for faster access to services (Irvine et al., 2005, p. 59). Absenteeism and turnover rates for nurses are also high. For example, absenteeism rates for full time RNs was 83% higher than it was for the general labor market. The Canadian government paid 962 million C$ in absentee, overtime, and replacement wages among nurses in 2007 (Drebit, 2010).

Health care for older adults in Canada is plagued by major long-term care challenges, lengthy waits to gain admission into nursing homes, and poor quality of care.

PREVENTIVE

Approaches to addressing health promotion and disease prevention in Canada are perhaps as diverse as the population. Indigenous to Canadian society are the Francophones that include the Mètis, Native American and European descendants, and the Acadians, descendants of the early French colonists. Canada, with its multiethnic, multilingual, and cultural mosaic is a melting pot of diversity (Coutu-Wakulczyk, Moreau, and Beckingham, 2003, p. 160).

Despite Canada's nearly perfect literacy rate (approximately 99%), illiteracy is high among the Francophones and the elderly. In fact, in some communities, Canada's high school drop-out rates exceed 40%, highest in poor and rural areas, especially for Aboriginals and Francophones, and among boys (Office of Francophone Affairs of Ontario, 2000). Another problem is obesity and obesity related hypertension especially among women. Pausova et al. (2000) believe these are attributed in great part to the TNF-α gene locus.

There has been a steep decline among Francophones in fertility rates from 4.95 children for the period 1956–1961, to 1.57 from 1991–1996 leading to the concern about long-term viability of Francophones outside Quebec especially since they have very little access to healthcare services where providers speak French (Office of Francophones Affairs of Ontario, 2001, Chung, 2009). Ansen (2000) found among Francophone women, the more educated the women the lower the fertility rate. Edwards and Rootman (1993) reported the responses of Canadians aged 15 and older who were asked about practices for improving health. In order of importance they identified smoking cessation 81%, increased relaxation 69%, exercise 65%, income security 45%, quantity of time spent with family 45%, weight loss 42%, better dental care 27%, job changes 22%, reduced drinking 16%, moving 14%, and reduced drug use 9%.

Canada's government-focused initiatives to address promotion of health and prevention of disease include specific programs to address obesity and the dissemination of health information via hard copy and online, keeping in mind that if the information is not disseminated in minimally English and French it will not likely be beneficial. Education always appears to be a key indicator in preventing illness.

RESOURCES

Men appear to be the hallmark of the Canadian society. They are typically viewed as the moral authority, and the one responsible for providing for, and protecting the family. Women, on the other hand, are charged with responsibility for running the household, child care, and caring for family members when ill (Langelier, 1996). For childbearing women, midwives and maternity centers are commonly used.

In some segments of Canada's population, family, extended family, and clergy are particularly supportive in the care of persons at or nearing the end-of-life. For example, African Canadians account for more than half (52%) of Nova Scotia's visible minorities (Statistics Canada, 2003). According to Clairmont and Magill (1970), years of poor living conditions, racism, hostile treatment, and a widespread lack of acceptance and integration into Nova Scotia society has led to the creation of a Black community that has been oppressed. Rather than seeking help from the healthcare system, many persons of African descent draw heavily on each other for support when challenged by an illness. Crawley et al. (2000) describe the rich religious tradition among African Americans in explaining some of the behaviors of African Canadians. The authors explain that in considering the omnipotence of God, if they do not receive a healing miracle, they often welcome death as a "home going."

MAJOR HEALTH ISSUES

Canadians are plagued by troubling diseases that often result in death, with cancer leading the way. Although the incidence of smoking is trending down, lung cancer is still the leading cancer killer in Canada for men and women (The Canadian Cancer Society, 2007). Heart disease and stroke rank as the second and third leading causes of death in Canada. The WHO (2010) record of the top ten diseases causing death in Canada are as listed in **Table 5-1**.

DISPARITIES

The top three diseases, cancer, heart disease, and stroke, in Canada are treated similarly to the United States. There are many similarities and

Table 5-1 Top 10 causes of death (all ages) in Canada, 2002, with the number and percent of years of life lost by disease.

Disease Deaths	Number	Percent	Years of Life Lost %
All causes	222	100	100
1. Ischemic heart disease	43	19	15
2. Trachea, bronchus, lung cancers	17	8	9
3. Cerebrovascular disease	15	7	4
4. Alzheimer and other dementias	10	5	2
5. Chronic obstructive pulmonary disease	10	5	3
6. Colon and rectal cancers	7	4	4
7. Diabetes mellitus	7	3	3
8. Lower respiratory infections	5	3	1
9. Breast cancer	5	3	3
10. Lymphoma, multiple myeloma	4	2	2

Source: Death and DALY estimates by cause, 2002.

http://www.who.int/entity/healthinfo/statistics/bodgbddeathdalyestimates.xls

differences in treatment approaches among Canadian provinces. Whether health outcomes are positive or negative they are influenced by social determinants such as population, poverty, age, race/ethnicity, and gender.

SUMMARY

There are many more strengths in the urban healthcare area than rural among Canadian provinces. It is important for Canada to build a workforce that is more sustainable and effective at meeting the needs of its residents both rural and urban. Recruitment and retention incentives may be effective ways to address these two important workforce issues.

Discussion Questions

1. Technology is not a major part of Canada's approach to health care. In your opinion, how does the limited application of technology impact the quality of patient care? Describe how technology affects patient care in your work setting. What technological interventions are critical to service delivery? What technology does your work setting need? Explain why this technology is important.

2. Edwards and Rootman (1993) identify a prioritized list of health issues Canadians are attempting to address. How does this list compare to your

own observations of health problems in the community you serve? What are the similarities? What are the differences? How would you rank order the list of health concerns that require preventive measures and health promotion in your community? What preventive activities are taking place in your community to address these health issues?

3. For some segments of Canada's population, family, particularly women, serve in important caregiver roles, and religion is a strong therapeutic element of support in healthcare situations. Describe what you have observed along these lines. In your opinion, what are the advantages of family as participants in the cycle of care, and what might be some drawbacks. As greater numbers of women join the workforce, how do you think the caregiver role of the family will change? What are the implications for healthcare providers? Discuss your views of religion in relation to health care? In your opinion, to what extent does a person's religious beliefs help or detract from efforts to improve a patient's health status?

4. Canada has more GPs than specialists. Discuss the advantages of this situation in relation to providing quality health care? Are there any drawbacks?

5. Education is an important determinant of health. Considering Canada's high school drop-out rate, particularly in the poor rural areas, what preventive and health promotion strategies should be undertaken to ensure positive health outcomes for the drop-out segment of the population? How would you approach this challenge? Are you facing similar issues in your work setting? What are the most frequent health issues of this population? What interventions are in place to address their health issues?

6. Canada is facing challenging staffing issues in terms of high absenteeism and turnover rates of nursing staff. What might account for this situation? Have you observed similar staffing problems in your workplace or are you aware of this issue in other healthcare settings? How does nursing turnover and absenteeism impact healthcare delivery (e.g., continuity of care, staff relations, healthcare costs)? What can be done to reduce the incidence of high turnover and absenteeism among nursing staff?

Case Scenario

Mrs. Carisse: Crossing the Border

Mrs. Carisse, a 48-year-old married mother of three, is recovering from brain surgery after suffering a major bleed in a vessel in her head. She is on a medication that costs over $400 a month. She has been unable to work for almost four years, as she is unsteady on her feet and at risk for falls. Her husband, Peter, has just learned he is losing his job and insurance benefits due to major profit losses at the small company where he works. The Carisses' are both concerned because without insurance they will be unable to pay for her medications. If she skips the medication for one day she will experience serious side effects and her health will rapidly decline. Peter has a co-worker who travels to Canada to purchase pain relievers because he can get them cheaper and without a prescription. He has convinced him to try to get the medication his wife needs in Canada.

DISCUSSION POINTS

1. It looks as if Peter has found a win-win solution. Do you agree? Should he cross the border to get the medications for his wife?
2. If you found yourself in Peter's situation would you seek help across the border? How does being a health practitioner or administrator influence your decision one way or the other?
3. Do you know people who go to Canada for medications? What observations have you made? Are there practices in Canada that we should replicate in America?
4. What type of advice would you give to people who crossed the border for medications?

REFERENCES

Ansen, J. (2000). Nationalism and fertility in Francophone Montreal: The majority as a minority. *Canadian Studies in Population, 27*(2), 377–400.

Canadian Cancer Society. (2007). Smoking rates dropping, but lung cancer deaths still leading cause of cancer death. Retrieved November 11, 2011 from http://www.cancer.ca/canada-wide/about us/media center/cw-media releases/cw-2007 /smoking rates dropping but lung cancer deaths still leading cause of cancer

Chung, A. (2009). Quebec tackles high school drop-out crisis. *The Toronto Star News.* www.thestar.com/news/canada/article/600889-quebec-tackles-high-school -dropout-crisis, March 12.

Clairmont, D. H. & Magill, D. W. (1970). *Novia Scotia Blacks: An historical and structural overview* (Publication No. 83). Halifax, Nova Scotia, Canada: Institute of Public Affairs, Dalhousie University.

Coutu-Wakulczyk, G., Moreau, D., & Beckingham, A. C. (2003). People of French Canadian Heritage. In: Larry Purnell and Betty Paulanka. *Transcultural health care: A culturally competent approach* (p. 161). Philadephia: F.A. Davis Company.

Crawley, L., Payne, R., Bolden, J., Payne, T., Washington, P., & Williams, S. (2000). Palliative and end of life care in the African American community. *Journal of the American Medical Association, 284,* 2518–2521.

Drebit, S. (2010). Trends and costs of overtime among nurses in Canada. *Health Policy, 9*(1), 28–35.

Edwards, P., & Rootman, I. (1993). Supports for health. In: Purnell, L. & Paulanka, B. (2004). *Transcultural health care: A culturally competent approach* (p,161). Philadephia: F.A. Davis Company.

Esmail, N., & Walker, M. (2005). Waiting your turn: Hospital waiting lists in Canada. (15th ed). Toronto, Canada: Fraser Institute. Chart 16, p. 30.

Frogue, T., Gratzer, D., Evans, T., & Testie, R. (2001). Buyer beware: The failure of single payer health care. The Heritage Foundation. Washington, DC: Heritage Lectures. No 02.

Infoplease. (2010). A profile of the world source: The world factbook, geography age: 4.55 billion years old. Retrieved November 10, 2010 from website: http://www.infoplease.com/ipa/A0762380.html

Irvine, B., Ferguson, S., & Cackett, B. (2002). *Background briefing: The Canadian health care system*. Based on a report written by Stephen Pollard, 2002, updated 2005.

Langelier, R. & Langelier, P. (1996). French Canadian families. In: M. McGoldrick, J. K. Pearce, & J. Giordano (Eds.). *Ethnicity and family therapy*. (2nd ed. pp. 477–495.). New York: Guilford Press.

OECD. (2007). Health Data. Public information. French language services. Retrieved, October 10, 2010 from ofa.gov.on.ca

Office of Francophone Affairs of Ontario. (2000*). French language services: A historical overview*. Retrieved February 16, 2011 from http://www.ofa.gov.on.ca

Office of Francophone Affairs of Ontario. (2001*). French language services: A historical overview*. Retrieved February 16, 2011 from http://www.ofa.gov.on.ca

Pausova, Z., Deslauriers, B., Gaudet, D., Tremblay, J., Koetchen, T. A., Larochelle, P. et al. (2000). Role of tumor necrosis factor-α gene locus in obesity and obesity-associated hypertension in French Canadians. *Hypertension, 36*(1), 14–19.

Pollara Poll. Retrieved February 10, 2011 from http://www.pollara.ca/Library/Reports/HCIC8.pdf. 58-59 http://www.cancer.ca/canada-wide/about us/media center/cw-media releases/cw-2007/smoking rates dropping lung cancer deaths still leads cancer

Statistics Canada. (2003). 2001 Census: Analysis series: Canada's ethnocultural portrait: The changing mosaic (Catalogue No. 96F0030XIE2001008). Ottawa, Ontario, Canada: Statistics Canada Census Operations Division.

UNO. (2004). Un.org/esa/population/publications/WorldPopulation.pdf

WHO. (2008). Decentralized health systems in transition. Based on a presentation to the 14th Annual Conference of the RHN in 2006 by Vaida Bankuaskaite, Scientific Project Officer, Public Health Executive Agency, European Commission.

WHO. (2010). *World health statistics 2010*. Geneva: World Health Organization, 2010. http://www.who.int/whosis/whostat/EN_WHS10_Full.pdf

CHAPTER 6

The Healthcare System in Japan

Philosophize upon alternative medicine, Japan holds true to the saying you can't achieve anything without risking something.

—B. J. Lewis

BEHAVIORAL OBJECTIVES

At the end of this chapter the learner will be able to:

1. Discuss how Japan's healthcare system emerged.
2. Discuss the incidence and prevalence of disease.
3. Identify the top ten diseases and related challenges.
4. Determine how health care is structured, financed, and accessed.
5. Identify funding priorities, initiatives, and challenges.
6. Describe health practices that are commonly used to maintain and restore health.
7. Explain how social determinants affect healthseeking beliefs and practices.

KEY CONCEPTS

Acupuncture

CAM

Care houses

Coining

Datura

Dokudami

Feverfew

Gennoshoko

Gold Plan

Health service facilities

Reflexology

Respite care

Shiatsu

Ukon

INTRODUCTION

In 2005 the population of Japan was 128 million. The land area is 377, 914 square kilometers, the equivalence in size to Montana. There is a low infant and neonatal mortality rate which has steadily declined over the past 50 years. In fact, Japan's infant mortality rates are among the lowest in the world. According to WHO, the infant mortality rate for 1000 live births for boys is 4:1,000, and for girls, 3:1,000, with an overall rate of 3.6 per 1,000. The total fertility rate, (the average number of children a woman gives birth to in her lifetime) is low, just 1.43 (CIA World Factbook, 2006; Kaneko, 2008). Adult mortality for men is 92:1,000 and for women 45:1000 (WHO Health Statistics, 2006). The proportion of Japan's under 15 year old age group is 14%, and the over 60 year old age group is 24% (UNO, 2004; Kaneko, 2008). The primary language spoken in Japan is Japanese and it is the largest ethnic group. Shintoism and Buddhism are the largest religious groups (WHO, 2004). Japan has one of the highest literacy rates in the world and is the third highest economic power. Japan is known as the "aging society" and it is predicted that by 2030 one in every three people will be 65+ years old and one in five people will be 75+ (Muramatsu & Akiyama, 2011). According to the WHO (2011), Japan has the highest proportion of older adults in the world, with a life expectancy for women of 86 and men 80.

The Huffington Post reporters Alabuster, Yamaguchi, Tomoko, Kageyana, and Kageyama (2011, March 11) described the biggest natural disaster to hit Japan since the late 1800s and its potential to raise havoc on Japan's public health. The 8.9 disastrous earthquake, triggering a near 30 foot tsunami and a nightmarish aftermath of repeated aftershocks, oil spills, and explosions, have become an unexpected financial and public health problem. In addition, a failed cooling of the nuclear reactor at the Fukushima Nuclear Power Plant, contamination of the water supply, and cities that were instantly converted to "junk yards," has served a severe blow to Japan's economy. Despite help from the Red Cross and tremendous assistance received from numerous other volunteers, it also has the potential to disrupt its health care system.

HISTORICAL

Reportedly, the first operation performed under general anesthesia using *datura*, a narcosis eliciting plant, was in 1804 by a Japanese physician called Hanaoka Seishu. One of the most challenging health problems of the 19th century was poor sanitation, partly due to cross contamination of plants from a poorly draining sewage system, a system that was greatly improved by William Burton, a Scotsman who redesigned Japan's crumbling water supply system in an attempt to decrease communicable disease (Hays 2009, p. 3).

The evolution of national health insurance began in 1905 when Japanese industries began providing limited health care to its employees. In 1922, legislation inspired by the German system, mandating coverage by enterprises, was enacted. By 1927 multiple companies followed this lead covering more and more employees. In 1938 health insurance was extended to farmers, fisherman, foresters, and other groups not covered by the 1922 legislation. By WWII, approximately 70% of Japanese were covered. After the war, in an effort to rebuild Japan, the national healthcare insurance plan was expanded and by 1958, 100% of residents in Japan had universal coverage. Three years later, the plan was further revised with improved access for everyone (Rodwin, 1993). The Japanese government's Ministry of Health, Labor and Welfare sets all health insurance policies standardizing medical charges countrywide.

STRUCTURE

Graziano (2009) provides a great overview of the Japanese healthcare system structure and organization. Japan is a publicly administered healthcare system that is financed in numerous ways. Healthcare delivery is highly fragmented and decentralized with much integration among local clinics and specialized hospitals. Most of the care delivery is in the medical private sector. Of the 8,943 hospitals 18% are publicly operated, and 5% of the 98,609 clinics are public. Specialty care is described by the complexity of the services required. There are 8.4 acute care hospital beds per 1,000 population.

In regard to interdisciplinary roles, responsibilities, and outcomes, there is a huge demand for healthcare services in Japan that is provided essentially by doctors and nurses. There are no mid-level professionals such as nurse practitioners, physician assistants, or clinical nurse specialists. The physician workforce in 2006 included 263,540 actively practicing physicians, equating to two practicing physicians per 1,000 persons in the population, of which 49% were primary care physicians practicing in internal medicine, pediatrics, and gynecology. The average hospital physician earned 14,100,000 yen (145,565 USD). Physicians who operate solo clinic practices earned considerably more, averaging 25,300,000 yen (261,178 USD). There is a shortage of obstetricians, anesthesiologists, and emergency medicine physicians (Harden, 2009)

Of the 896,724 registered professional nurses (RNs) in Japan during 2005, 46,764 worked in public health, 27,047 were nurse midwives, and 822,913 were registered nurses working in various specialty areas. The average RN salary was 4,561,800 yen (47,095 USD). In addition to RNs there were an additional 411,685 Licensed Practical Nurses in the Japanese workforce. Including LPNs, there are 10.3 total nurses per 1,000 population in the Japanese workforce.

Physicians are well educated, but relatively few in number. Medical school is six years combined undergraduate and professional school with board certifications and other credentialing of physicians, nurses, and other providers are earned through specialty societies. Licensing is administered through the Ministry of Health.

FINANCING

All Japanese have essentially the same healthcare coverage. Physicians and hospitals are generally paid a fee for services. Physicians typically work long hours and extensive periods without days off. Revisions to the fee structure are politically negotiated between the government and providers, usually biennially. There is a strong relationship between the National Medical Expenditure (NME) and the Gross Domestic Product (GDP); both grew at the same rate from 1980 to 1989 but the healthcare share of the economy grew out of proportion to the GDP in 1999 (Ikegami & Campbell, 2004, p. 27). Economic stagnation led to greater pressures to contain expenditures within the existing healthcare framework, but it also added fuel to long-standing proposals for more radical reforms advocating for a change in how health services are reimbursed (Ikegami & Campbell, 2004).

There are two basic types of medical insurance in Japan—employee's health insurance, covering employees and their families, and national health insurance for self-employed and unemployed individuals and their families. Subscribers pay insurance premiums calculated according to their annual income which equates to approximately 10% of their income. In other words, consumers of health care pay based on their financial ability to do so.

Medical coverage is pretty comprehensive but varies by income and appreciates with age. Two-year-olds and younger are 80% covered, favoring a healthy start. Individuals who are three years to 69 are 70% covered and 70 and older are 90% covered except for those with very high incomes. In this case, they receive 80% health coverage. Individuals who pay out-of-pocket for medical expenses exceeding $600.00 per month are fully reimbursed by the government. Homes for the elderly, home care assistance and services, respite care (short-term care programs) and similar services have been covered since 1963 from funds from taxes of the central and local governments under the Welfare Law for the Elderly. The Health Service for the Elderly, enacted in 1982, covers all of the medical services necessary including hospital admissions, extended rehabilitation in extended care facilities, in-home rehabilitation, home visits for nursing care, and day care programs. The Gold Plan of 1986, and revised New Gold Plan of 1994 expanded service targets for home care aides, respite care, day care, home nursing visits, special nursing homes for the elderly, health service facilities for the elderly (providing rehabilitation in long-term care facilities) and assisted living facilities referred to as care houses (Ministry of Health and Welfare, 1998).

Japan has a National Health Insurance Program. The employer also provides insurance for its workers and pays, in addition, 10% of medical costs. The government sets healthcare and physician fees so they are relatively low.

INTERVENTIONAL

Although Japan has one of the lowest physician-to-population ratios among Organization for Economic Cooperation and Development (OECD) countries, they have the highest number of physician contact per capita, more than twice the American rate, although their typical patient encounter is 6.9 minutes compared to over 20 minutes for United States physicians (Rodwin, 1993).

In regard to service quality, primary versus acute, and restorative care, like most industrialized countries, Japan utilizes high technology medical care. However, physicians have a definite preference for non-invasive procedures and the approach to care emphasizes ambulatory, over in-patient care. In fact, Japan prides itself on its low rate of hospital admissions (Rodwin, 1993, Harden, 2009) demonstrating the emphasis on primary care over acute care. Their low cost and high quality are considered a birthright of the Japanese.

In regard to long-term care in Japan, the Japanese healthcare system promotes longevity, which is demonstrated by its higher life-expectancy and decline in the live birthrate. The number of infirm elderly in Japan needing care increased 50% from 1993 to 2009. It is predicted to increase 60% by 2025. The number of older adults who are bedridden, have dementia, or have other problems requiring assistance with their activities of daily living is expected to increase from 2.8 million in 2000 to 5.2 million by 2025 (Ministry of Health and Welfare, 1998).

As advances in medical care rise these numbers will likely show a further associated increase. Irrespective of whether the Japanese are in need of acute, sub-acute, rehabilitative, long-term, or community-based care, it is covered by insurance.

Since 1983, Japan has had health insurance for the older adults aged 70 and over, as well as coverage for disabled persons aged 65–69. Seventy percent of the total cost for services is covered by what is known as 'all sickness funds,' of which 20% is financed by the national government and 10% by local governments. The proportion borne by local government is considerably lower, reflecting the importance placed on long-term care for the elderly (Fukawa, 2002).

PREVENTIVE

The medical insurance system is universal coverage for individuals of all ages, which includes a government managed mandatory long-term care insurance for citizens over 40 years old, and a special medical insurance program for people 75 years of age and older.

Community health services focus on disease prevention and health promotion. The government sets public health policy and legislation. Public health centers in each prefecture treat, among other problems, infectious diseases, mental health, environmental problems, sanitation, and hygiene. Public health nurses provide maternal child health and elderly care. Pregnant women receive impeccable care. They receive a maternal child health handbook, and receive post-partum home visits from public health nurses. All newborns and high risk pregnant women receive routine health checkups. Annual health checkups for those over 30 are also provided for a nominal fee. Women receive screenings for breast and uterine cancer, and everyone gets screened for cancer of the stomach, lungs, colon, and rectum.

Japanese pride themselves on maintaining traditional practices such as folk and herbal medications similar to the Chinese practices, and use of complementary and alternative medicine *(CAM)*. The use of such herbal medicines as ginseng, sesame, and ginger oils, rubbed on the forehead to cure headache are common remedies. The Yin and Yang practice is important, especially during pregnancy and disease. Among the traditional Japanese medicines are *gennoshoko* (Japanese germanism), an effective treatment for diarrhea and digestive infections; *dokudami*, a low creeping plant with white flowers and a nasty smell used to treat heart problems and counteract poisons; *ukon* (turmeric), attributed to helping the liver and fighting bacteria; and *feverfew* (bachelor's button, or *natsushirogiku*) a popular relief for migraine headaches. Also a popular Chinese herbal called *kampo* is widely used in Japan to treat diabetes, hepatitis, asthma, and menopausal and digestive disorders (Facts and Details, 2002).

When it comes to maintaining beauty and health, Japanese are firm believers in the use of massage, acupuncture, and Shiatsu, a type of needle-less acupuncture using the fingers to place pressure on the meridians. *Reflexology*, or foot massage has become almost synonymous with relaxation and stress reduction (Hays, 2009 p.8). Prevention is key as is evidenced by all children being immunized, and children receive mandatory medical and dental care. Every age is protected against disease.

RESOURCES

Perhaps some of the most significant demonstrations of human resource support was seen during the aftermaths of some of the most devastating natural disasters known to humankind. Although these disasters had profound physical, emotional, and economic implications, they revealed positive aspects of Japanese society, older adults' wisdom and resilience for survival and coping, active social and labor participation at older ages, and strengths of social relationships (Muramatsu & Akiyama, 2011).

It is common in Japan for a daughter or a daughter-in-law to care for older adult family. Japanese consider it to be the woman's responsibility to take care of her parents or her husband's parents in their old age; to not do so is considered abandonment, which brings shame to the entire family. Partly for this reason, cohabitation is higher in Japan than in other industrialized (developed) countries. Japanese women typically assume the role of caregiver for others as well. They look after and anticipate and protect the needs of children, their husbands, and other close relatives. Children are cherished and highly desired, especially the first born male, but children are usually limited to two. Men are the decisionmakers.

Japanese, like most cultural groups, find strength in organized religion. Shintoism, Buddhism, and Confucianism are among the most widely practiced religions in Japan. Temples and shrines are used for prayer and healing. Death is accepted as a natural occurring process and is handled with confidence and strength.

MAJOR HEALTH ISSUES

From 1950 to the mid 1960s, tuberculosis was the most common illness in Japan. However, today, geriatric diseases such as chronic hypertensive disease, cerebrovascular disease, heart disease, and malignant neoplasms are dominant. In fact, as is illustrated in **Table 6-1**, 21 percent of the illnesses plaguing Japanese appear as some form of cancerous lesions. This table lists the top ten medical problems in Japan by number, percent, and years of life lost.

The aftermath of the largest natural disaster to hit Japan since the late 1800s has severely challenged Japan's public health. The disease-ridden

Table 6-1 Top 10 causes of death (all ages) in Japan, 2002, with the number and percent of years of life lost by disease.

Disease Deaths	Number	Percent	Years of Life Lost %
1. Cerebrovascular disease (stroke)	133	14	10
2. Ischemic heart disease	93	10	8
3. Lower respiratory infection	91	9	5
4. Trachea, bronchus, lung cancer	56	6	6
5. Stomach cancer	50	5	6
6. Colon and rectal cancer	39	4	4
7. Liver cancer	34	4	4
8. Self-inflicted injuries	31	3	9
9. Nephritis and nephrosis	21	2	1
10. Pancreatic cancer	20	2	2

Data From: Death and DALY estimates by cause, 2002.

http://www.who.int/entity/healthinfo/statistics/bodgbddeathdalyestimates.xls

conditions of contaminated water, massive debris throughout major cities, and radioactive debris around the Fukushima Nuclear Plant could eventually result in increased outbreaks of communicable diseases. The horrific conditions, with which those in communities most affected by the earthquake and tsunami must contend, could likely have far-reaching, longer-term effects than ever imaginable; potentially putting at risk the health of entire communities of people for years to come.

DISPARITIES

Health standards, costs, and fairness in the Japanese health system by many accounts make access to care non-problematic. The weakest part of the Japanese system is the lack of professional accountability, putting consumers at a disadvantage when seeking care. Another weakness is that doctors overprescribe medications because their salaries are linked to how many pills they dish out (Facts and Details, 2002). Enforced budget restraints for care of the elderly have resulted in financing challenges for long-term care of that group.

The top three diseases causing death in Japan are stroke, heart disease, and lower respiratory infection. There is considerably more use of CAM in the treatment of diseases in Japan than in Western countries.

SUMMARY

Although there are unforeseen consequences of the March 11, 2011 earthquake and tsunami, Japan is a strong, resilient country with the ability to overcome most challenges. A major strength of the Japanese system of health care is its emphasis on prevention and promotion. There is universal coverage for all and progressive premium rates based on ability to pay with tremendous access to services.

Major weaknesses in the system are inherent in the increased numbers of elderly. Obviously, with longevity come chronic illness, greater demand for long-term care services, and a strain on Japanese families, and on Japan's national budget.

Discussion Questions

1. Japan is known as "the aging society." Identify three factors that you think account for this reputation. Do you observe these same factors in your own life situation? If not, do you believe that these factors are critical to living

longer? Explain your point of view. What can healthcare providers do to ensure longevity of the people they serve?

2. The Japanese pride themselves on maintaining several traditional practices. Are you familiar with these practices and are they a part of your own health regimen? As a healthcare provider, would you recommend acupuncture or shiatsu to patients? Why or why not?

3. What preventive measures in Japan stand out for you? For example, how does the care for pregnant women compare to your observations or experiences with pre-natal care?

4. Japan's healthcare structure does not include mid-level professionals. In your opinion, what are the advantages and disadvantages of this structure? How is the quality of health care affected? If you had a say in staffing a healthcare facility, would you follow Japan's design? Explain your point of view.

5. What are your thoughts regarding the expectations of Japanese women as caregivers for elderly family members? Have you observed these expectations for women as a healthcare provider? To what extent is the caregiver role considered in treatment plans for women patients?

6. In view of Japan's high literacy rate and excellent preparation of physicians, why do you think there is such a low physician-to-population ratio? Does your work setting have enough physicians? If not, how is health care managed?

7. Describe healthcare coverage in Japan, including their approach to coverage of pharmaceuticals. What aspects of Japan's healthcare coverage do you find particularly impressive? Explain your point of view. How would Japan's healthcare coverage apply to you or your family? Do you know patients who would benefit from Japan's healthcare coverage? In what way?

8. Discuss the potential impact of the March, 2011 earthquake and tsunami on Japan's health outcomes. What, in your opinion, are the projected epidemiological communicable and non-communicable disease trends likely to occur as a consequence?

Case Scenario

Mika Takashi

In the following scenario, a healthcare practitioner talks about her experience with Mika Takashi, a Japanese patient. Here, she presents a time line of events and healthcare provider actions that led to a number of unintended consequences for Mika. As you move through her account, what sounds familiar and what would have happened differently if you were the healthcare provider?

MIKA TAKASHI

A few years ago, I conducted a history and physical examination for a 42-year-old Japanese patient who was new to my practice. After her husband was killed in an automobile accident, Mika Takashi came to the United States with her two small children (ages 2 and 5) to live with her sister and her family. She was 32 years old. Upon her arrival she spoke very little English. However, in our encounter, she spoke and understood English very well. Mika was switching primary care physicians after three years in another practice where she was dissatisfied with her care. A review of her record from the previous office revealed that soon after entering the practice, Mika complained of her heart "hurting," resulting in a full cardiac workup; the findings were normal. She was prescribed antacids and advised to exercise more.

After taking a brief history, and questioning her about her current health status, I asked if she continued to have either pain or sadness in her heart. She slowly nodded and replied, "Sad, very sad!" Her facial expression immediately changed from engaging with full eye contact, to dejection, and avoidance of my eyes. In follow up I asked, "How long have you felt sad, Mika?" She replied, "A long time," which I later learned was for nine years. She had taken the death of her husband very hard which made her depression worse. To further complicate the situation, when her then 7-year-old son was sent to the school nurse after vomiting in class one day, the nurse, finding welts completely covering the child's body, asked the child, "Who did this to you?" The child responded, "Mommy." Consequently, Mika was accused of child abuse. Despite clarification by the family of the harmless *Coining* practice, in which warm coins are rubbed across the body for medicinal purposes, Mika was being accused of deliberately harming her child. A lengthy investigation resulted, and Mika became even more severely depressed. The Office of Child Protective Services became involved, and their lives were disrupted for three years before she was finally exonerated.

I prescribed an antidepressant with the fewest side effects, and referred Mika to a clinical psychologist. She is currently doing very well.

DISCUSSION POINTS

1. When it became obvious that Mika was not "hurting" physically, why didn't someone work at clarifying what she meant? What questions might have helped Mika address her emotional issues?
2. It can be argued that Mika could have spoken up or found some way to be clearer about her problem. What do you think?

3. Did the school nurse respond appropriately to the situation presented by Mika's 7-year-old? Did she rush to judgment?
4. Suppose the school nurse knew about the Coining practice, would she still have been obligated to report the welts?
5. Mika's problems dragged on for approximately 6 years after arriving in the United States. Is it fair to blame the healthcare system for her troubles?

References

Alabuster, J., Yamaguchi, M., Tomoko, A., Kageyama, H., & Kageyama, Y. (2011, March 11). Earthquake in Japan. Huffington Post. Huffingtonpost.com

CIA World Factbook, United States Department of State, Handbook of the US Library of Congress. (2008). Retrieved October 22, 2010 from http://www.cia.gov/cia /publications/factbook/index.html

Facts and Details. (2002). Health care in Japan. Retrieved, January 10, 2011 from http://www. factsanddetails.com/japan.php?itemid=8397catid=237subcatid =151

Fukawa, T. (2002). Public health insurance in Japan. *The International Bank for Reconstruction and Development/The World Bank.* Washington, DC: 6–15.

Graziano, C. (2009). Japanese health care system structure and organization. Retrieved on December 10, 2010 from http://dmaa.pbworks.com/w/page/17960778/Care ContinuumAllianceJapan-Healthcaresystem.htm

Harden, B. (2009, September 7). Health care in Japan: Low cost for now. Washington Post Foreign Services. Retrieved March 11, 2011 from http://star. com.jo/main /index.php?option=com_content&view=article&id=15722

Hays, J. (2009). Health care in Japan. Retrieved on December 10, 2010 at http:// factsanddetails.com/japan.php?itemid=839&catid=23&subcatid=151

Ikegami, N. & Campbell, J. C. (2004). Japan's health care system: Containing costs and attempting reform. *Health Affairs, 23:*3, 26–36.

Kaneko, R., Ishikawa, A., Ishii, F., Sasai, T., Iwasawa, M., Mita, F., and Moriizumi, R. (2008). Population projections for Japan: 2006 – 2055 outline of results, methods, and, assumptions. *Japanese Journal of Population,* 6:1.

Ministry of Health and Welfare. (2002). Japan's long-term care insurance programs. www.mhlw.go.jp/english/topics/elderly/care/index.html

Muramatsu, N. & Akiyama, H. (2011). Japan: Super-aging society preparing for the future. *The Gerontologist, 51*(4), 425–432. doi:10.1093/geront/gnr/0671

Rodwin, V. (1993). Japan's universal and affordable health care: Lessons for the United States. Retrieved March 11, 2011 from website: http://www.nyu.edu/projects /rodwin/lessons.html

UNO. (2004). Retrieved November 12, 2010 from Un.org/esa/population/publications /WorldPop.pdf

World Health Organization (WHO). (2006). Health statistics. Retrieved November 12, 2010 from who.int/whosis/database/core/core_select_process.cfm

World Health Organization (WHO). (2004). Health statistics. Retrieved November 12, 2010 from who.int/whosis/database/core/core _select_process.cfm

World Health Organization (WHO). World Health Statistics (2011). Retrieved, November 12, 2010 from http://www.who.int/whosis/whostat/EN_WHS2011 _Full.pdf

CHAPTER 7

The Healthcare System in the United Kingdom

Even though the old man is strong and hearty, he will not live forever.

—Ashanti proverb

BEHAVIORAL OBJECTIVES

At the end of this chapter the learner will be able to:

1. Discuss how the United Kingdom's healthcare system emerged.
2. Discuss the incidence and prevalence of disease.
3. Discuss the top three diseases and related challenges.
4. Determine how health care is structured, financed, and accessed.
5. Identify funding priorities, initiatives, and challenges.
6. Describe health practices that are commonly used to maintain and restore health.
7. Explain how social determinants affect health-seeking beliefs and practices.

KEY CONCEPTS

Agenda for change

Levels of nurses

Nurse specialists

Advanced practice nurses

INTRODUCTION

The United Kingdom (UK) was the first country in the world to earn the distinguished OECD's industrialized status. Every country in the United Kingdom (England, Northern Ireland, Scotland, and Wales) has a national health service (NHS) that provides free, public health care to all permanent residents. However, each has a uniqueness in its system and a variety of different policies and priorities that guide healthcare practices. Complementary and alternative medicines and holistic treatment for illness is prevalent throughout the United Kingdom (NHS, 2008a). The NHS is funded through taxes. Private healthcare companies successfully exist alongside the public system.

The current population in the United Kingdom (UK) exceeds 63 million (CIA World Fact Book, 2012a). The land area is 241,590 square km (CIA World Fact Book, 2012b). According to WHO (2007), the infant and neonatal mortality rate is 4:1,000; the under-five mortality rate for 1,000 live births for boys is 6:1,000, and for girls is 5:1,000, with an overall under-5 mortality rate of 6.0 per 1,000. The total fertility rate, (the average number of children a woman gives birth to in her lifetime) is low (WHO, 2007). Adult mortality for men is 102:1,000 and for women 63:1,000 (WHO, 2007). The UK has a high literacy rate, and is a strong economic power. Life expectancy is 81 years for women and 76 years for men. The under 15-year-old population in the UK is 18% (UNO, 2004) and the over 60-year-old population is 21% (WHO, 2004). The major languages spoken are English, Welsh, Scottish, Gaelic, and South Asian. The largest ethnic groups in the UK are English, individuals of Scottish descent, Irish, Welsh, African Caribbean, and South Asian. The major religions of the UK are Anglican, Roman Catholic, and Muslim (WHO, 2005).

HISTORICAL

One of the most intriguing observations of the healthcare system in the UK is that it is the home of Florence Nightingale, the first nurse researcher and educator. As many are probably aware that Florence Nightingale founded and operated the first nursing training school located at St. Thomas Hospital in London, England.

The national health insurance began in 1948 as a universal system standardizing health care across Europe. The UK's Ministry of Health, Labor and Welfare sets all health insurance policies, but today there are four different systems in the four countries making up the UK, all sharing the same underlying values (news.bbc, 2005).

In 1976 the Department of Health restructured its budget allocation to regions of the National Health service on the basis of need which was measured by standardized mortality ratios (SMRs)(Ministry of Health, Labor and Welfare, 2004).

The UK has a diverse population of native born ethnic groups and immigrants. There is a particularly large number of African Caribbeans and Filipinos among the population. The rights of all residents in the UK are protected under The Equality and Human Rights Commission that was established under the Equality Act 2006, merging the Equal Opportunities Commission, the Commission for Racial Equality, and the Disability Rights Commission (Equality and Human Rights Commission, 2006).

STRUCTURE

The healthcare structure and function in any system is only as strong as the number and quality of its workforce. The UK has a publicly administered healthcare system that is financed in numerous ways. Of the four countries making up the UK there are distinct differences that have created considerable resentment among patients who are envious of the services provided in other UK countries. England is a NHS market-driven system, where hospitals and community services must compete with the private sector for patients; patients consequently have the ability to shop around for services. This resulted in a major drop in waiting times. Patients pay for prescriptions in England whereas in Wales, Scotland, and Northern Ireland they are free. Scotland's NHS that is similar to the 1948 structure gives physicians more of a voice in services with limited private sector involvement. There is a level of cooperation and coordination of services. Patients enjoy free personal care, unlike the means-tested systems in place elsewhere and there is less tension between doctors and managers. In Wales, the NHS and local government work closely, focusing on innovation and public health. However, there is less emphasis placed on attempting to reduce waiting times. The Northern Ireland healthcare system, although sometimes referred to as the NHS, really is not. Health care is Northern Ireland is provided by a system called Health and Social Care. There is good integration between social care and the NHS in Northern Ireland. Envy occurs among patients not in systems where waiting is not a problem and prescriptions are free (news.bbc, 2005).

In regard to interdisciplinary roles, responsibilities, and outcomes, there is a huge demand for healthcare services in the UK provided, essentially, by doctors and professional nurses. Specialty care is described by the complexity of the services required. Nurses and midwives are central to health care in the UK. Operating on the premise that better educated nurses deliver higher quality care (Aiken, Clarke, Cheung, Sloane, & Silber, 2003), entry level into professional nursing practice in Wales is the baccalaureate degree in nursing. A report commissioned by the prime minister on the future of nursing and midwifery in England recommends the move to a baccalaureate degree-level registration by 2013, for all newly qualified nurses. All currently registered nurse and midwives must be fully supported if they wish to obtain a relevant degree, defined as the bachelor's. Therefore such considerations must be given to financial support and more flexible work schedules. A relevant degree must become a requirement for all nurses in leadership and specialist practice roles by 2020 (Commission on the Future of Nursing and Midwifery in England, 2010).

Registered professional nurses are currently categorized according to levels in the UK health system. Of the approximate 400,000 nurses in the UK workforce in 2007, the majority were level one nurses. *Level one nurses* include registered general nurses (RGN), registered sick children's nurses (RSCN), registered mental health handicapped (RNMH) nurses, registered nurses in mental health, and registered fever nurses (RFN). Although there are no longer level two nurse programs in the UK, these state-enrolled nurses are still legally able to practice in England and Wales. Most *level two nurses* have basic nursing training and have either retired or transitioned into level one programs. *Specialist nurses* or *level three nurses* are those nurses who have many years of experience in a particular area in which they have completed extra education. Nurse practitioners, also known as *Advanced Practice Nurses,* practice collaboratively with physicians and are equivalent to the roles and responsibilities of nurse practitioners in the United States. They also practice in public health as consultants and as lecturers. The *fourth level of nurse* is the senior manager. Some nurses have earned doctorate degrees. Wales is the only country in the UK that now requires a baccalaureate degree in nursing to enter professional nursing practice. Nurses already in practice were grandfathered. England is now planning to upgrade their entry level to a baccalaureate degree.

Of the practicing nurses in the UK, there are a large number of Caribbeans and Filipinos, more than 25,000 are nurse midwives, and ten percent are men (Buchan, Parkin & Sochalski, 2006). Nurses wishing to practice in the UK must first register with The Nursing Midwifery Council (NMC), the professional regulatory authority. Nurses with general nursing qualifications from other countries of the European Union (EU/EEA) have the right to practice in the UK due to mutual recognition of qualifications across EU countries. Nurses from countries outside of the EU must apply to the NMC for verification of their qualifications before being admitted to the Register. Most will also apply for, and be granted, a work permit to practice. Nurses from countries other than Australia, Canada, New Zealand, and the United States may be required to work for a specified period of supervised clinical practice, orientation, and assessment at an approved site before being approved for work (NCSBN, 2002).

Much can be learned from Wales about improving the nursing profession as Wales has required a BSN for new nurses entering practice for several years. Wales, for example, was the first country in the United Kingdom to increase the entry level to the BSN for individuals seeking to enter nursing. Also, Wales not only has the best retention rate for student nurses (13%), but there students are recruited from some of the poorest communities then helped to them find jobs in their home communities after graduation. The attrition rate in Wales is the lowest for nursing programs in the UK. England's attrition rate is approximately 27% and Scotland's attrition rate is 29%. The nursing education model in Wales stresses keeping people at home whenever possible and for as long as possible, thus shifting care from hospital-based to community-based. Maintaining a balanced health workforce is valued in Wales. It is believed that too many professionals waste money, and too few compromises the quality of care delivered. Having a skilled professional mix that showcases various levels of expertise such as nurses, midwives, and allied health professionals is important in Wales (Wales CYNGOR CYMRU, 2011).

Similar to other countries in the UK, many of the healthcare services in and outside the National Health System (NHS) are led by nurses and midwives. These include nurse- and midwife–owned-and-operated clinics and birthing centers (Frontline Care, 2010, p. 83). In both cases, patients are rapidly assessed and receive access to the right level of less costly care, because follow-up care will be, whenever possible, managed at home with support. According to Caird et al. (2010) midwives who deliver care for low-risk women have improved range of outcomes, reduced number of procedures, and improved satisfaction. In contrast, in the United States, health services are predominately physician led; relatively few professional nurses in the U.S. own or operate clinics and birthing centers. Many countries seeking to improve their healthcare outcomes and access to care could benefit from adopting approaches utilized in Wales.

In following the example of Wales, England will require all new nurses entering the nursing profession to have a BSN by 2013. They have adopted specific steps for reassuring and supporting the existing nursing workforce while providing opportunities for those wishing to earn the degree to do so (Frontline Care, 2010, p. 91).

Nurses in the UK typically work for the National Health Service (NHS). It was predicted in 2007 that an additional 4,000 nurses would be needed by 2012 to meet the nation's service demands. Most nurses in England and Wales are employed under the newly negotiated *Agenda for Change* gradated salary structure of 2010–2011. This salary structure promises "equal pay for work of equal value." All available information under the Agenda for Change structure reported nurse salaries in categories referred to as Bands that ranged from 2–9. Although it can be assumed that a Band 1 exists, it could not be clearly determined by reviewing the literature. Nurses falling in the Band 2 salary range earn £13,653–16,753. Bands 2–4, representing primarily unregistered nurses, were the lowest reported salaries. Those nurses in the Band 9 category earned salaries ranging from £77,079–97,478. Band 9 is reserved for the most senior members of nursing management, and was the highest (Royal College of Nursing, 2010/2011).

Each NHS system uses general practitioners (GPs) to provide primary care. Hospitals provide specialist services including emergency medical services and care for persons with psychiatric problems. Pharmacies outside the hospital setting are privately owned and operated. According to OECD (2009), in 2008 the UK had approximately 243,770 licensed, practicing physicians. Included in the physician workforce are generalists (GPs, also called family doctors) who are expected to be in short supply in the next 4 years, and a variety of specialists, among which are medical specialists who are in the greatest demand but are in the shortest supply. There were also physicians specializing in surgery, emergency medicine, anesthesia, radiology, obstetrics/gynecology, and pediatrics. There is a major shortage of pediatricians and neonatologists in the UK. Radiologists and physicians specializing in emergency medicine are among the highest paid at £58,975–161,000 and £52,000–159,875, respectively (Empire-Locums, 2010–2011). A shortage of Physicians, especially GPs and nurses, is predicted to worsen as the NHS has extensively cut jobs in an effort to save money to compensate for budgetary shortfalls. Mullan suggests, that there is substantial migration of physicians from the U.K., and their destination countries are Australia, Canada and the U.S. (2008). Davies, of the Royal College of Nursing (2007, p. 45) also suggests the UK exhibits "a yo-yo attitude toward workforce planning."

There is an array of other healthcare professionals and services including dentists; dental assistants and technicians; pharmacists; pharmaceutical assistants and technicians; laboratory scientists, assistants, and technicians; radiographers; environmental and public health officers, and technicians; sanitarians; and hygienists.

Community health workers are also integral to the healthcare workforce in the UK and include such individuals as traditional medicine practitioners, faith healers, health-educators, family health workers, personal care workers and traditional birth attendants. A large number of occupations such as dieticians and nutritionists, medical assistants, occupational therapists, optometrists and opticians, physiotherapists, podiatrists, prosthetic engineers, psychologists, respiratory therapists, speech pathologists, medical trainees, and interns also make up the full and part time workforce as well as health workers on temporary and long- and short-term contracts in the UK.

FINANCING

There are significant inequalities in allocation of financial resources to various regions and districts in the UK. Scotland, Wales, and Northern Ireland have enjoyed higher levels of funding per capita than England; England has fewer doctors, nurses, and managers per population. Of the four countries in the UK, England is the only one that still has prescription charges. Approximately £7.40 per prescription is charged (Funding and performance of healthcare systems, 2010).

INTERVENTIONAL

Preventing illness and promoting health; early interventions; treatment and effective, efficient management of health are all critical elements of health care. Interventions including medical, high technology, and the use of complementary and alternative medicine are important in the healthcare industry in the UK. Stroke is the third leading cause of death in that country. Techniques to improve interventions within the narrow, three hour early treatment window are crucial to saving lives, and preventing long-term debilitating disability. Jenkinson (2006) describes a stroke improvement program that uses mobile and wireless methods of assessing patients during video conferencing and remotely reviewing brain scans allowing experts from around the world to consult, make a speedy diagnosis so that clot busting drugs can be prescribed more quickly, thereby saving lives and money.

Free ambulance services assist in getting patients into the system when they need emergency care. Free prescription coverage is significant in maximizing care compliance. Health management and support workers assist in the implementation of care at all service levels, and are essential

to achieving quality outcomes. Managers contend with the daily operations of clinics and hospital facilities. Gardeners keep hospital grounds
aesthetic, and administrative staff stress focusing on achieving overall
better outcomes.

A variety of interventions are directed at protecting the mentally ill,
curbing relationship violence, and intervening early. These initiatives are
protected by a 2007 Mental Health Act amending the Mental Health Act of
1983, the Mental Capacity Act of 2005, and the Domestic Violence, Crime
and Victims Act of 2004 (dh.gov, 2007).

Providers in the UK strive to offer equitable care to all residents irre-
spective of their race or disability status. These rights are protected under
The Equality and Human Rights Commission that was established under
the Equality Act 2006, merging the Equal Opportunities Commission, the
Commission for Racial Equality, and the Disability Rights Commission
(Equality and Human Rights Commission, 2006).

PREVENTIVE

The age-old adage, "an ounce of prevention is worth a pound of cure," is
reality in that one method of addressing prevention in the UK is through
educating the public. NHS Choices is a web-based service providing easily
accessible health and healthcare information that can be personalized for
different patients, using material from existing NHS websites and links
to other reputable national and local health and social care organizations
(national health service.uk, 2009b).

There is a high suicide rate in the UK, so in 2007 The National Public
Health Service for Wales published its goal to reduce the suicide rate from
12.3 per 100,000 in 1995 to 11.1 per 100,000 by 2012 (national health
service.uk, 2009b).

RESOURCES

Family support is essential for overcoming chronic health challenges in the
United Kingdom. Home-based eldercare is common, especially among close
families, particularly near the end-of-life. Elders are often cared for in the
home of one of their children until it becomes too difficult to do so, or too
financially draining.

The Barnardos organization, one of the leading charities in the United
Kingdom, provides emotional and mental health and support for families
and children by focusing on each family's strength while at the same time

addressing the vulnerabilities. They offer early intervention initiatives such as counseling and peer support, and during crises like incidences of sexual exploitation of children. This organization has structured programs for parents with learning disabilities to assist them with their parenting skills and to help ensure that parents are better able to meet the needs of their children. For example, one home-based one-to-one teaching program utilizes electronic dolls to mimic skills needed to care for real babies (Evans & Fowler, 2008).

MAJOR HEALTH ISSUES

The top ten diseases causing death in the United Kingdom and the years of life lost are listed in **Table 7-1**. Very typical of most developed countries, ischemic heart disease and cerebrovascular disease are at the top list.

DISPARITIES

There is a disparity in the allocation of financial resources to some regions for health services. Also, stroke care is almost too costly to treat. Many argue that the NHS provides insufficient emergency and acute stroke care, and it provides too few rehabilitative services after discharge

Table 7-1 Top 10 causes of death (all ages) in the United Kingdom, 2002, with the number and percent of years of life lost by disease.

Disease Deaths	Number	Percent	Years of Life Lost %
All causes	599	100	100
1. Ischemic heart disease	120	20	17
2. Lower respiratory infection	65	11	6
3. Cerebrovascular disease (stroke)	59	10	7
4. Trachea, bronchus, lung cancer	33	6	6
5. Chronic obstructive pulmonary disease	28	5	4
6. Colon and rectal cancer	19	3	3
7. Breast cancer	14	3	4
8. Alzheimer and other dementias	13	2	1
9. Prostate cancer	10	2	1
10. Lymphomas, multiple myeloma	8	1	2

Data From: Death and DALY estimates by cause, 2002.

http://www.who.int/entity/healthinfo/statistics/bodgbddeathdalyestimates.xls

(The Stroke Association, 2005). Stroke care costs the NHS £2.8 billion a year in direct costs and £1.8 billion in lost productivity and disability (Rothwell et al., 2005). Thrombolytic therapy is highly effective in selected patients when administered within the first 3 hours of having a stroke (Wardlaw, del Zoppo, Yamaguchi, & Berge, 2003). The Stroke Research Network in the UK has developed an infrastructure for research in stroke prevention, primary care, acute care, and rehabilitation. With an allocation from the Department of Health of £20 million over 5 years, and a campaign slogan, "Stroke is a Medical Emergency" outcomes are improving (Jenkinson, 2006). Bringing emergency stroke care to the patient more quickly should be beneficial in addressing care disparities in the third leading cause of death in the UK.

SUMMARY

The UK has made tremendous progress in many important healthcare areas: resource-based advances in stroke care, programs directed at preventing exploitation of children, and protection for the mentally ill, to name a few. With greater attention toward interventions to address the relatively high suicide rate, this trend could be reversed. As the UK forges ahead with future healthcare initiatives it might benefit from better workforce planning, allocation of more resources for the purpose of retraining and retention of level two nurses, and improved utilization of advanced practice nurses.

Discussion Questions

1. The UK has given considerable attention to providing mental health services. Describe how mental health is addressed in your work setting? What more can be done?

2. Based on the extensive services provided in the UK, how would you characterize their definition of public health? For example in what ways is it broadly defined? In what ways is it innovative?

3. Discuss the relationship of ethnic diversity and access to care in the UK. What are the challenges and how are they being addressed? What similarities do you observe regarding racial challenges in your work setting? Are the issues addressed appropriately? What more can be done?

4. In your opinion, why is complementary/alternative medicine (CAM) a more accepted practice in the UK than other countries? In what way is CAM supported in your work setting?

Case Scenario

Hello doctor, hello nurse, it's me, Mrs. Anna!

Mrs. Anna, an 82-year-old female, fell on her kitchen floor injuring her right side and chest. Accompanied by her daughter, she was taken by ambulance to the hospital nearest her home, as is expected under the National Health Plan in the United Kingdom. Because there were no beds in the emergency department, Mrs. Anna remained on a gurney for six hours while being evaluated. As she waited for a bed, she tied up the ambulance gurney as well as the EMS workers as they could not leave for another call until the gurney was free and the hospital does not have loaners.

Mrs. Anna was most uncomfortable during her stay in the emergency department. She complained of intense pain in her chest and ribs for which she was given narcotic pain medication. She had x-rays and blood work and was told, after six hours, she was fine and could go home. In less than three hours, the daughter received a call from the hospital insisting that she return her mother to the hospital because her potassium level was dangerously high; to which the daughter responded, "That is not surprising since she is on dialysis. Her next treatment is tomorrow and I am sure her potassium level will decrease after her treatment." However, the doctor convinced the daughter to return to the hospital with her mother who continually complained of pain, for which she continued to receive narcotic pain medicine. The next day, because there were no dialysis services at that hospital, and the Health Plan did not provide for transportation, her daughter transported her mother to her dialysis treatment outside the hospital. Because Mrs. Anna was so short of breath and continually complained of pain, her three hour dialysis treatment was stopped after 1½ hours.

They returned to the hospital where Mrs. Anna remained for 4 days. Mrs. Anna did not appear to be improving and was now complaining of severe abdominal pain; her abdomen appeared impregnated and hard. The daughter, now joined by the granddaughter, kept advocating on Mrs. Anna's behalf that more be done to determine the problem. The family overheard one of the doctors say, "she has no bowel sounds." The grand-daughter, a prominent nurse, intervened, insisting that her grandmother be checked for a bowel obstruction. She was told that was not an option; families do not make such decisions and because of Mrs. Anna's age, the physicians would not support such an aggressive treatment plan. The family was outraged; their mother and grandmother was a very happy, active, and productive family member who could not simply be dismissed. They continued appealing to the doctors and nurses to do the right thing. A few hours later the daughter overhead a nurse speaking with a physician about the situation saying, "I don't know what we are going to do with this family, and one of them is an American!" The family removed Mrs. Anna from that hospital, and she was admitted to a private hospital where the daughter paid out-of-pocket for her care. Five days after her fall she was diagnosed with five broken ribs, and a perforated bowel that the family suspected was narcotic-induced.

DISCUSSION POINTS

1. If Mrs. Anna is tying up the only available gurney for six hours, how many other people may be at risk for emergency service? Would this situation happen in your work setting? How many calls for emergency service occur per hour in your area? Would you say your health setting is well-equipped and responds effectively to emergency situations? What does Mrs. Anna's situation suggest about access to emergency care under the National Health Plan?

2. The hospital seems to be very thorough and deliberate with follow-through regarding Mrs. Anna's blood work but the x-rays did not pick up on her five broken ribs. Explain this discrepancy in care. Would this happen in a private hospital? Is what happened to Mrs. Anna an unfortunate incident or is her situation an example of what can go wrong in a socialized system of health care?

3. The daughter's explanation for Mrs. Anna's high potassium levels falls on deaf ears. Why didn't the hospital take her information more seriously? Was the hospital right to insist on Mrs. Anna's return? Why or why not? As a health professional, would you welcome the daughter's input? Would you have supported her decision to wait another day? Where would you draw the line? Should family caretakers be viewed as partners in the care of the patient? Describe your ideal conception of the relationship between the health practitioner and the family caregiver.

4. The National Health Plan does not cover transportation to Mrs. Anna's dialysis treatment or coverage for care in a non-public hospital. How do you think Mrs. Anna would survive without her daughter's help in these areas? As you consider these two critical aspects of Mrs. Anna's care, what is your opinion of the Health Plan? What are the benefits? What are the problems?

5. Mrs. Anna's age played into the doctor's decision not to perform surgery to treat her bowel obstruction. Do you agree with his reasoning? Why or why not? As a health practitioner, do you

believe there is a "cutoff" or a particular age group for "aggressive" treatments? How do you think age affects cost considerations for the National Health Plan?

6. Why wasn't the granddaughter's expertise as a health practitioner respected in this situation?

7. As the rift between the family and the hospital grew more intense, a nurse emphasized that one of Mrs. Anna's family members was American. What was she getting at? Why would she point out this cultural difference?

REFERENCES

Aiken, L., Clarke, S., Cheung, R., Sloane, D., & Silber, J. (2003). Educational levels of hospital nurses and surgical patient mortality. *Journal of the American Medical Association, 290*(12), 617-623. Retrieved December 11, 2010 from http://www.ncbi.nlm.nih.gov/pubmed/14506121.

BBC. (n.d.). Health policies for four countries. Retrieved December 11, 2010 from http://news.bbc. co.uk/2/hi/health/7925167.stm. p 3

BBC. (n.d.). Envy grows among patients. Retrieved December 11, 2010 from http://news.bbc.co.uk/2health/7925167.stm. p. 5

Buchan, J., Parkin, T., & Sochalski, J. (2005). International nurse mobility: Trends and policy implications. WHO/EP/OSD/2003.3

Caird, J., Rees, R., Kavanagh, J., Sutcliffe, K., Oliver, K., Dickson, K., Woodman, J., Barnett-Page, E., & Thomas, J. (2010). The socioeconomic value of nursing and Midwifery: A rapid systematic review of reviews. Eppi Centre report 1801. London, EPPI Centre, Social Science Research Unit. Institute of Education and University of London.

CIA World Fact Book. (2012a). Retrieved July 12, 2012 from http://www.theodora.com/wfbcurrent/united_kingdom/united_kingdom_people.html

CIA World Fact Book. (2012b). Retrieved July 12, 2012 from http://www.theodora.com/wfbcurrent/united_kingdom/united_kingdom_geography.html

Commission on the Future of Nursing and Midwifery in England. (2010). Front line care: Report by the Prime Minister's Commission.1-113.

Davies, J. (2007). Two levels of practice: Meeting professional or workforce needs. *Nursing Standard, 21*(27) 44-47.

Empire-Locums. (2010-2011). co.uk.nhs-hospitals.asp

Evans, J. & Fowler, K. (2008). Family minded: Support for children in families affected by mental illness. www.barnardos.org.uk/resources. family_minded_report.pdf .p19

Frontline Care. (2010). *Report by the Prime Minister's Commission on the Future of Nursing and Midwifery in England,* 15-112.

Nuffield Trust. (20 January 2010.). Funding and performance of healthcare systems in the four countries of the UK before and after devolution. Retrieved from http://www.nuffieldtrust.org.uk/publications/detail.aspx/ id=145&PRid+675

Infoplease. (2010). A profile of the world source: The world factbook, geography age: 4.55 billion years old. Retrieved November 10, 2010 from http://www .infoplease.com/ipa/A0762380.html

Jenkinson, D. (2006). Research and development in stroke services is taking off in the United Kingdom. *British Medical Journal, 332*(7537). 318.doi:10.1136 /bmj.332.7537.318

Ministry of Health, Labor, and Welfare. (2004). NHS on standardized mortality ratios. Retrieved December 11, 2010 from http://www.kaigo.gr.uk/hp.htm

Mullan, F., Frehywot, S., & Jolley, L. J. (2008). Aging primary care and care and self sufficiency: Health care workforce challenges ahead. *Journal of Law and Ethics, 36*(4), 703-08.

Department of Health. (2008). Health is global: A UK government strategy 2008-2013. Retrieved December 10, 2010 from http://www.dh.gov.uk/health/category /policy-areas/nhs/

National Council of State Boards of Nursing. (2002). International nurse workforce. NCSBN: Chicago.

National Health Service (NHS). (2009a). Educating the public in prevention. Retrieved December 10, 2010 from http://www.uk1/hi/health/7149423.stm

National Health Service (NHS). (2008b). NHS 'now four different systems.' Retrieved January 2, 2008 from http://news.bbc.co.uk/1/hi/health/7149423.stm

OECD. (2011). Comparing health statistics across OECD countries. Retrieved June 5, 2012 from oecd.org/documents/57/0,3746,en_21571361_44315775_43

Rothwell, P. M., Coull, A. J., Silver, L. E., Farhead, J. F., Giles, M. F., Lovelock, C. S., et al. (2005). Population based study of event-rate, incidence case fatality and mortality for all acute vascular events in all arterial territories: Oxford vascular study. *Lancet, 2005*(366), 1773–83.

Royal College of Nursing. (2010). NHS Agenda for change in pay rates 2010/11. Retrieved December 11, 2010 from http://www.rcn.org.uk/__data/assets/pdf _file/0018/233901/003303.pdf

The Stroke Association. (2005). Stroke is a medical emergency. www.stroke.org.uk /campaigns/latestcampaign/stroke is a medical emergency

UNO. (2004). Un.org/esa/population/publications/WorldPop.pdf

Wales CYNGOR CYMRU. (2011, May). *Improving care now: Investing for the future. Nursing, midwifery and allied health professions.* A briefing for candidates in the National Assembly election.

Wardlaw, J. M., del Zoppo, G., Yamaguchi, T., & Berge, E. (2003). Thrombolysis for acute ischemic stroke. *Cochrane Databases Systematic Review, 2003*(3): CD000213.

WHO. (2004). who.int/whosis/database/core/core_select_process.cfm

WHO. (2005). United Kingdom Country Profile. who.int.profiles_ countries. uk_s_u .2005

WHO. (2007). World Health Statistics. Mortality. Retrieved November 11, 2010 from http:// www. who.int/whosis/whostat2007-1mortality.pdf

Equality and Human Rights Commission. (2006). Equality Act 2006. Retrieved November 11, 2010 from http://www.equalityhumanrights.com/

United Kingdom Government Legislation. (2005). Disability Discrimination Act 2005. Retrieved from http://www.legislation.gov.uk/ukpga/2005/13/contents

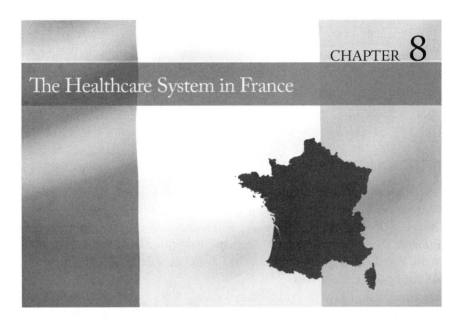

CHAPTER **8**

The Healthcare System in France

Prejudices are what fools use for reason.

—Voltaire

BEHAVIORAL OBJECTIVES

At the end of this chapter the learner will be able to:

1. Discuss how France's healthcare system emerged.
2. Discuss the incidence and prevalence of disease.
3. Discuss the top three diseases and how they are treated.
4. Determine how health care is structured, financed, and accessed.
5. Identify funding priorities, initiatives, and challenges.
6. Describe health practices that are commonly used to maintain and restore health.
7. Explain how social determinants affect health-seeking beliefs and practices.

KEY CONCEPTS

Amenable mortality

ANAES

Copayments

Deductibles

Docteur

SAMU

INTRODUCTION

France, a leader among European countries, is a developed (industrialized) world power that has a good healthcare system and a strong economy. This Western European land area of 545,630 square km is nestled among six countries: The United Kingdom, Germany, Belgium, Switzerland, Italy, and Spain, and three major waterways: the Bay of Biscay, the English Channel, and the Mediterranean Sea.

According to the CIA World Factbook (CIA, 2009), in 2001 France's population was approximately 59,551,227, of whom 65.19% were between the ages of 15 and 64. Slightly more than 16% of the population was 65 years and older. The majority of France's residents are natives of France. However, France is home to some immigrants and has a particularly strong African and Southeast Asian presence. The proportion of France's under 15-year-old age groups is 18% (UNO, 2004), and the over 60 population is 20% (WHO, 2004). The predominant language spoken in France is French. The largest ethnic groups are Celtic, Latin, and Teutonic. Other ethnic groups are Slavic, Northern African, and South East Asian. The largest religious group in France is Roman Catholic (WHO, n.d.). Overall life expectancy in France is 78.9 years, 83.01 years for women, and 75.01 for men. Total fertility rate is 1.75 children born per woman. The infant and neonatal mortality rate was estimated to be 4.46 deaths/1,000 live births and this number has steadily decreased over the years. France's literacy rate is 99% for men and women. Women are well educated and are very competitive.

Like most other industrialized countries, French residents enjoy a universal healthcare system that is largely financed through national healthcare insurance and is ranked among the best healthcare systems in the world (WHO, 2000).

HISTORICAL

France, priding itself on its promise to take good care of its entire population, has had a form of National Health Care since 1945. The country has always had a threefold goal; to provide a single health insurer, make it compulsory for all employers and workers to pay premiums based on their salaries, and allow patients to choose their own doctors. However, doctors are permitted to charge additional fees and prescribe therapies, diagnostic procedures, and medications as they see fit, without interference from the national health insurance. Unlike some healthcare systems that offer universal health there are no long waiting periods to schedule elective surgery or see specialists in France.

Legislation in 1999 further refined the national health insurance plan mandating that anyone with a regular residence permit was entitled to health benefits without strings attached. This legislation also clarified that illegal residents would be managed by giving them full coverage if they could prove they lived in a French territory for more than three months and had no financial means to pay for health care (Gauthier-Villars). In a 2000 WHO ranking of the best healthcare systems worldwide, France was ranked number one. It has, over the past 30 years, been forced to reduce its healthcare coverage and incrementally increase its healthcare taxes. However, consumers still give France high marks for its healthcare delivery and quality.

STRUCTURE

Healthcare administration and oversight is provided by the Minister of Health and Solidarity. This cabinet position oversees the healthcare public services and the health insurance part of Social Security

The government pays for medical school for those seeking to pursue medicine as a career. Once licensed, most physicians work in private practice but their fees-for-services are paid by publically-funded insurance companies. General practitioners, commonly referred to as *docteurs*, are responsible for all aspects of care, including acute and chronic. They are key in providing treatment of diseases not requiring a specialist and they provide preventive services. General practitioners can be summoned by the *samu*, the emergency medical services to assist with emergency care.

Physicians make a modest net average annual salary of approximately €40,000 (Tanner, 2008), the equivalent of $51,243. This is approximately one-third that of physicians in the United States. Because French physicians charge relatively low fees for services, many earn more by increasing their patient load, or by prescribing more diagnostic tests and procedures—a technique, also popular in the United States, that inflates healthcare costs (Capell, July 2007, p. 12). Once physicians have practiced in a hospital for at least four years it is permissible for them to charge extra fees for consultations (Capell, July 2007). This is another way in which the salary can be increased. Approximately 90% of France's general practitioners have an agreement with Assurance Maladie, the country's largest buyer of medical services that prevents them from charging more than €22 ($32.00) for a consultation, and an additional €3.50 if they make a house call (Gauthier-Villars, 2009). Gauthier-Villars, quotes nurse practitioner Lanfranchi, as saying, "If you are in medical care for the money, you'd better change jobs" (p. 4).

Nurses in France receive professional training for three years to gain the basic entry level into practice. Advanced practice nurses are not included in the French model for nursing practice. In 2004, there were approximately 6.7 practicing nurses per 1,000 people in the population as compared to 3.37 physicians (OECD, 2008).

FINANCING

France, like the United States, relies on both private insurance and government insurance which is generally obtained through the person's employer. Everyone pays compulsory health insurance to non-profit agencies that participate in annual fee-setting negotiations with the state. There are three main funds that, when combined, provide coverage for approximately 96% of the population. The compulsory premium is automatically deducted from all employees' pay. The 2001 Social Security Funding Act sets the rates for health insurance covering the statutory healthcare plan at 5.25% on earned income, capital, and winnings from gambling, and at 3.95% on pension benefits and other allowances (WHO, 2000).

France spends approximately 11 percent of its GDP on health care. Health care is funded through taxes proportionate to the person's income which funds Assurance Maladie, a state health insurer that has operated in the red since 1989. Budgetary shortfalls are predicted to exceed €9 bill ($13 billion) in 2011 (Gauthier-Villars, p.2). When a person visits a doctor in France, 70% of the bill is covered by the national insurance program. The remaining 30% is covered by supplemental private insurance, which literally everyone has because it is affordable, and in almost all cases is paid for by employers. The entire cost of care is paid by the national insurance program for persons with long-term chronic illnesses, diabetes, cancer, and heart diseases. Also 100% of major surgeries are covered.

Approximately 65% of hospital beds in France are publically operated, 15% are private non-profit, and approximately 20% are privately run for-profit hospitals (WHO, 2000). There are also private and public funded clinics, doctor offices, and special centers called Protection Maternelle et Infantile (PMI) discussed under the Preventive section.

INTERVENTIONAL

There are emergency services, an abundance of emergency vehicles, and acute care provided in all three types of hospitals (public, non-profit, and for-profit). According to Aiken and colleagues (Aiken et al., 2001), as hospital workloads increase, so does mortality, and as nursing education increases mortality decreases. This has led many to advocate for a minimum of a college/university earned baccalaureate degree to become a professional nurse. In an investigation into nursing education in 19 European countries, it was found that nurses in France receive three years of professional training (RN 4 cast, 2009–2011).

Fundamentally, all health providers (medical, nursing, and other health professionals) should focus on achieving the very best outcomes for their patients. However, the French government pays a role in attempting to maximize provider practices. In an attempt to ensure quality services ANAES (Agence Nationale d' Accreditation et d'Evaluation en Santè) translated as The National Agency for Accreditation and Health Care Evaluation, is a government body that issues recommendations and practice guidelines in an attempt to ensure that provider practices reflect quality healthcare services. In fact, ANAES publishes practice guidelines.

Ambulatory care is provided basically by general practitioners, over 60% of them work in solo independent practices. This care is provided in a variety of settings including the home. France has a collaborative agreement with Canada directed at nursing practice outcomes with an emphasis on access as the foundation of this collaboration.

PREVENTIVE

Prevention of illness is a key factor in the economic growth, development, and productivity of any nation. France is no different; with its quality outcomes and longevity as a measure of its healthcare system, France is a leader in prevention. Some researchers consider another factor in determining longevity. This factor is called *amenable mortality*, more simply put, a measure of deaths that could have been prevented with good health. The health challenges are many and resources are scarce but France's preventive initiatives are admirable. France ranks number one on disease prevention, the United States ranks last (Shapiro, 2008). General practitioners are essential to providing preventive services. They make home visits when patients cannot come to their offices, and are especially responsive to the needs of children and older adults. They also engage in epidemiological surveying of diseases to predict outbreaks and to contain diseases.

Other significant preventive measures include a track record of excellence for their attention to prenatal and childhood care. There are thousands of healthcare facilities strategically located in some of the poorest communities in France as well as in communities largely inhabited by immigrants. These facilities, called Protection Maternelle et Infantile (PMI) focus on ensuring that every mother and child in the country receives basic preventive care, in other words, promoting health and preventing illness. Children are evaluated by a team of private practice pediatricians, nurses, midwives, psychologists, and social workers. A social worker pays a visit to the home when children do not show up for follow-up visits. Incentives are also given to pregnant mothers for attending pre- and postnatal visits. Again, the focus is on keeping children healthy and preventing illness. General practitioners also make home visits especially to follow up on children.

In spite of these prevention initiatives there are a number of specific challenges that threaten preventive efforts in France. There is a lack of initiatives to standardize sewage (waste) and preserve the quality of the water supply and sanitation. Although among other European countries France has the lowest incidence of obesity and the healthiest dietary practices, there has been a recent rise in obesity (Freeman, 2010). There is also a 0.44% prevalence rate of HIV/AIDS affecting a significant portion of the population. There were an estimated 130,000 persons living with HIV/AIDS in 1999 and an additional 2,000 HIV/AIDS related deaths (CIA, 2001).

Over the years, France has become a transshipment point for, and consumer of, South American cocaine, Southwest Asian heroin, and synthetic drugs made in Europe. As a consequence, the battle against illegal distribution and abuse of illicit drugs has presented a notable problem that threatens the public health of its people (CIA, 2001).

RESOURCES

In addition to such supportive professional initiatives as PMI focusing on decreasing pre- and postnatal risks and thereby maximizing perinatal maternal child outcomes, the most obvious resources are reflected during care of individuals at, or nearing, the ends of their lives. For example, extraordinary efforts are directed toward providing palliative care that directs attention to affirming the life of the dying individual and relieving pain and other signs and symptoms experienced during death and dying.

MAJOR HEALTH ISSUES

Despite France achieving relatively overall great health outcomes, and being ranked number one in the world, they do experience major health issues. The top ten leading causes of death and years of life lost in France are listed in **Table 8-1**.

DISPARITIES

The top three causes of death in France, coronary heart disease, stroke, and lung cancer, are identical to the top three causes of death in Germany. Although life expectancy statistics are calculated the same way irrespective of the country, what people die from and why they die can vary tremendously from one country to the next. For example many people die around the world from infections because of the unavailability of antibiotics, whereas in countries where antibiotics are readily available, people may die because of resistance to antibiotics of choice or they lack access to care.

SUMMARY

France is touted as one of the most admired healthcare systems in the world. This is because of its overall good outcomes, its strong emphasis

Table 8-1 Top 10 causes of death (all ages) in France, 2002, with the number and percent of years of life lost by disease.

Disease Deaths	Number	Percent	Years of Life Lost %
All causes	499	100	100
1. Ischemic heart disease	45	9	7
2. Cerebrovascular disease	37	8	5
3. Trachea, bronchus, lung cancer	26	5	7
4. Lower respiratory infections	19	4	2
5. Colon and rectal cancer	17	4	3
6. Alzheimer & other dementias	16	3	1
7. Chronic obstructive pulmonary disease	16	3	2
8. Breast cancer	12	2	4
9. Diabetes mellitus	11	2	2
10. Falls	10	2	1

Data From: Death and DALY estimates by cause, 2002.

http://www.who.int/entity/healthinfo/statistics/bodgbddeathdalyestimates.xls

on prevention, and its demonstrated excellence in the care of infants and children. As the government explores new ways to contain costs for health services provided while improving the pay structure of physicians, the outcomes will likely be further improved, and more appreciated by everyone, including those the system serves.

Discussion Questions

1. France has notably become one of the world leaders in providing quality health outcomes. What are the areas in need of further consideration?

2. Because of the modest salaries of physicians in France, many seek others ways to increase their incomes. What do you think of the initiatives physicians take to increase their income? In what ways could advanced practice nurses be utilized in France?

3. To what extent is an address of salary inequities in a healthcare system the role and responsibility of administration? In what ways can employees share responsibility for addressing salary? Describe how salary inequities are addressed in your work setting?

4. How would you characterize France's attention to maternal and child health? Compare and contrast the maternal child health priorities and practices in France with the practices in your work setting. What more can be done?

Case Scenario

Mr. Petit: There's nothing wrong with me

Mr. Petit recently had a battery of tests to rule out cardiovascular problems after experiencing a rise in his serum cholesterol level and shortness of breath. His primary doctor planned to refer him to follow up with a cardiologist on his next visit. Mr. Petit never returned for his follow-up appointment with his primary provider (a general practitioner) at the community-based clinic in his neighborhood. After his second missed appointment, his primary doctor made a home visit. He questioned Mr. Petit about his missed appointments, reviewed the results of his diagnostic tests, and completed a quick examination. Mr. Petit, feeling tremendously improved since adding an extra glass of red wine to his diet every day, feels no need to be seen so often at the clinic. He calls the wine a protection against a heart attack and believes it is a waste of time to see a cardiologist as he has no pain.

DISCUSSION POINTS

1. Why would Mr. Petit believe there is no danger of having a heart attack?
2. What advice do you think the doctor gave Mr. Petit, and why?
3. France has National Health Care so why is Mr. Petit so reluctant to see a cardiologist?
4. What strategies might the physician use to convince Mr. Petit to regularly follow up with his doctor and the cardiologist?

REFERENCES

Aiken, L., Havens, D., Clarke, S. P., Sloane, D. M., Sochalski, J. A., Busse, R., Clarke, H., Giovannetti, P., Hunt, J., Rafferty, A. M., & Shamian, J. (2001, May/June). Nurses' reports on hospital care in five countries. *Health Affairs, 20*(3), 43–53.

Capell, K. (2007, July 9). The French lesson in health care. The nation's system isn't quite as superb as 'Sicko' maintains, but it's pretty good. Bloomberg Businessweek.

Central Intelligence Agency (CIA). (2001). *The world factbook* – France. Retrieved August 22, 2010 from http://www.apiguide.net/05science/02eco/france-cia.html

Central Intelligence Agency (CIA). (2001). *The world factbook* – France. HIV/AIDS Adult prevalence. Retrieved August 22, 2010 from http://www.apiguide.net/05science/02eco/france-cia.html

Central Intelligence Agency (CIA). (2009). *The world factbook* – France. Retrieved from http://www.cia.goc/library/publications/the-world-factbook/geos/france.html

Freeman, S. (2010, December 14). Obesity still eating away at health of the nation. Retrieved from http://www.yorkshirepost.co.uk/features/obesity-still-eating-at.6660925.jp

Gauthier-Villars, D. (2009, August). France fights universal care's high costs. Retrieved August 24, 2010 from http://www.who.int/entity/healthinfo/statistics/bodgbddeathdalyestimates.xls

Organization for Economic Cooperation & Development (OECD). (2008). *Comparing health outcomes.* OECD, Paris.

RN 4 cast. (2009–2011). Nurse forecasting in Europe. Human resource management for nursing in Europe: A study on impact of nurse deployment on patient safety. Retrieved August 24, 2010 from RN4cast.eu/en/

Shapiro, J. (2008). Health care lessons from France. Retrieved August 24, 2010 from npr.org/templates/php?story/storyId=92419273

Tanner, M. (2008). *The grass is not always greener: A look at national health care systems around the world.* Cato policy analysis no. 613. Retrieved from http://www.cato.org/pub_display.php?pub_id=9272

UNO. (2004). Un.org/esa/population/publications/WorldPop.pdf

WHO. (2000). http://www.euro.who.int/documents/e83126.pdf WHO Health care systems in transition: France (WHO).

WHO. (2004). Who.int/whosis/database/core/core_select_process.cfm

WHO. France country profile. Retrieved from who.intl/profiles_countries_c-f.pdf

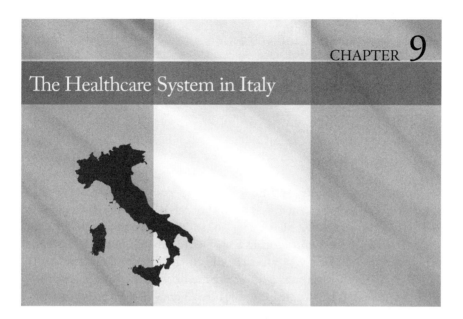

CHAPTER 9

The Healthcare System in Italy

One can never consent to creep when one feels an impulse to soar.

—Helen Keller

BEHAVIORAL OBJECTIVES

At the end of this chapter the learner will be able to:

1. Describe how health care in Italy is structured and financed.
2. Discuss the relationship of regional differences and access to health care.
3. Discuss the incidence and prevalence of disease.
4. Discuss Italy's preventive measures and health promotion activities.
5. Describe the country's health care in terms of positive impact on public health and future challenges.

KEY CONCEPTS

Capitation

Co-payments

DRGs

Essential levels of care

Hospital trusts
National Health Service (NHS)
Positive and negative lists
The north-south divide

INTRODUCTION

Italy, officially known as the Italian Republic, covers an area of 301,225 square km. (116,303 square miles) and is bordered by France, Switzerland, Austria, and Slovenia. Known by its boot-like shape, Italy is equivalent to the size of Georgia and Florida combined. Italy became a democratic republic in 1946 a few years after the fall of the fascist regime in WWII. Italy has OECD status and is a founding member of the European Union (EU). According to the Central Intelligence Agency (CIA), the literacy rate in Italy is high, at 99% (CIA, 2011). In 2011, the population of Italy was estimated at 60.6 million. Italy is an industrialized country and is ranked as the world's seventh largest market economy (U.S. Department of State Background Note, 2011). However, Italy is struggling with an exceedingly high public debt and fiscal deficit. The proportion of the population under 15 is 14% and the proportion of the population above the age of 60 years is 24% (WHO 2004). The main language used in the country is Italian. The largest ethnic group is Italian. The largest religious group is Roman Catholic.

Indicators for infant mortality and life expectancy suggest that, "Italy has a very healthy population" (Maio & Manzoli, 2002, p. 301). The total estimated infant mortality rate per 1,000 live births is 3:38 deaths; (male: 3.59 deaths/1,000 live births; female: 3.16 deaths/1,000 live births) (CIA, 2011). The estimated life expectancy for men is 79.16 and it is 84.53 for women (CIA, 2011). Adult mortality for men is 91:1,000 and for women, 47:1000 (World Health Organization, 2006). Demographic concerns over the past two decades involve Italy's persistent low fertility rates. Current estimates indicate Italy's total fertility rate as 1.39, resulting in birth rates falling below replacement levels of 2.1 children per woman (CIA, 2011; Maio & Manzoli, 2002). Italy's population challenges include a decline in the younger age groups and a rapidly aging population.

HISTORICAL

Since its inception in 1978, Italy's National Health Service (NHS) has undergone a series of reforms aimed at ensuring the equitable distribution

Table 9-1 The Italian national health service principles.

Human dignity

Every individual has to be treated with equal dignity and have equal rights irrespective of his or her personal or social characteristics.

Protection

The individual health has to be protected with appropriate preventive measures and interventions.

Need

Everyone has access to health care and available resources to meet the primary health-care needs.

Solidarity with the most vulnerable people

Available resources have to be primarily allocated to support groups of people, individuals, groups of people, individuals and certain diseases that are socially, clinically, and epidemiologically important.

Effectiveness and appropriateness of health interventions

Resources must be channeled to services with scientifically demonstrated effectiveness and to individuals who can benefit the most from them.

Equity

Any individual must have access to the healthcare system with no differentiation or discrimination among citizens and no barrier at the point of use.

Source: Health in Italy in the 21st century. Copenhagen, WHO Regional Office for Europe, 1999:169.

of public health services throughout the Italian state. "NHS was created to achieve the objective of the Italian Constitution which declares that the Italian state has the responsibility of safeguarding the health of each citizen as an individual asset and a community interest" (Maio & Manzoli, 2002, p. 302). **Table 9-1** identifies seven fundamental principles that establish the framework of Italy's health service including human dignity and equity (Ministerio delia Sanita, 2009).

While the Ministry of Health retains ultimate responsibility for NHS, several legislative measures since 1992 have culminated in administrative power progressively transferring to Italy's 20 regions. Some of the challenges facing Italy's health care today are embedded in failed compulsory insurance schemes dating back to 1943 that set into motion the questionable allocation of funds, overspending, and political harangues between the state and the regions. Alternatively, Italy's strengths in providing health care derive from building on lessons learned. During the 1990s Italy implemented several cost containment strategies (e.g., price controls on drugs, keeping NHS salaries in line with inflation) to develop a more efficient system of health care. "What appears to have been crucial to the success of Italy's cost-containment was the shared recognition that, in contrast with past experience, the central government would not bail out regional health systems burdened with large deficits" (Clements, Coady, & Gupta, 2012, p.14).

At the beginning of the 21st century, significant Constitutional reform passed on more decisional authority down to Italy's 20 regions, presenting Italy with new challenges for developing a coordinated, quality system of health care.

STRUCTURE

Italy's healthcare system is region-based and highly decentralized. The health service structure encompasses three levels: national (state), regional, and local. The Ministry of Health operates as the central organization of NHS and is responsible for healthcare planning, healthcare financing, and ensuring the uniform delivery of the benefits package. The regions are responsible for ensuring access to the benefits package through their regional health departments, local healthcare agencies (LHAs), and public and private health services providers. Regional governments are aimed at identifying the unique needs of their populations. Due to decentralization, the regions have considerable autonomy in managing their own budgets. This means they are also "required to fund any deficit that might occur from their own resources" (Maio & Manzoli, 2002, p. 302).

At the local level, LHAs are geographically situated throughout the regions and provide service to specific populations. LHAs are in charge of providing a coordinated, comprehensive level of care through their own facilities or through other accredited private providers. Units of care called hospital trusts, as well as university-centered research hospitals provide secondary and tertiary care (Maio & Manzoli, 2002).

Italy has one of the highest numbers of physicians on record worldwide. According to Action for Global Health (2011), Italy has 215,000 doctors or 37 doctors per 10,000 people. Ironically, having so many doctors has created a human resource health crisis. Italy is facing a growing shortage of nurses. The high rate of doctors outstrips the available supply of nurses. "There are different estimates of the size of the national shortage but all estimates place it above 50,000 nurses" (Action for Global Health, 2012, p. 30). There were 364,663 nurses or approximately 60 nurses for every 10,000 people in 2009 (Action for Global Health, 2011). Budget constraints, high retirement rates, and the trend toward specialization over primary care are some of the factors that have contributed to the nursing shortage. The nursing profession is subject to the bias toward professions dominated by women in terms of being undervalued and underpaid. Italy has recruited nurses from foreign countries to manage the shortage. However, this strategy has created a resource crisis for other countries. Most of the foreign nurses come from countries such as India and Peru where their services are *"desperately"* (Action for Global Health, 2011, p. 30) needed, particularly in healthcare coverage for maternal and child immunization (Action for Global Health, 2011).

In 2005, the average monthly salary for doctors was $3,294 and the average monthly salary for nurses was $1,304 to 1,359 (worldsalaries.org). Medical education is regulated by the Ministry of Health. Becoming a physician in Italy requires six years of medical school, a minimum of six months working in a hospital ward, and passing a state examination. Qualifying as a specialist involves successful completion of an exam for admittance to the specialist school, and four to six more years of training, depending on the choice of specialization. Nursing education includes completing a three year university degree and a state examination.

FINANCING

Italy's health care is financed through national and regional taxation, i.e., payroll and value added taxes. The NHS provides universal coverage throughout the Italian state as a single payer (Maio & Manzoli, 2002). Physicians are paid on a capitation basis, i.e., a fixed payment at regular intervals for enrolled patients, and hospitals are paid through Diagnosis Related Groups (DRGs).

Under the NHS structure, the 20 regions are responsible for ensuring the equitable delivery of the *essential levels of care* (the basic benefits package). "The Ministry of Health funds these regions according to a formula based on weighted capitation and past spending. Then the regions allocate these funds to the Local Health Authorities (LHA)" (Healthcare Economist, 2008).

Italy's attempts to distribute financial resources equitably are attenuated by a number of long standing issues:

- *Decentralization*: In theory, the state and the regions share the responsibility for enacting the essential levels of care; in practice, however, the regions have full administrative control of funding and regulating health care
- *Regional Differences*: Tax revenues favor regions with a stronger industrial economy resulting in huge regional differences in the organization and quality of healthcare services

The Benefits Package: Essential Levels of Care

Although voluntary health insurance is available, NHS is the dominant source of health care. Typically, middle to high income groups purchase private insurance. The core package of benefits (*the essential levels of care*) is described in a catalogue or "health benefit basket" that provides positive and negative lists of healthcare coverage including lists for pharmaceuticals. The positive lists describe the core services NHS is required to provide *uniformly to all regions;* the negative list identifies services that are excluded based on a variety of criteria including proven clinical ineffectiveness. Regions have the discretion to provide payment for services not covered by the core package but they must use their own funding resources.

Important general observations of the package include the following:

- Inpatient and primary care are free at the point of use. Patients pay *co-payments*, i.e., out-of-pocket payments for a fraction of the actual cost of care, for tests, diagnostic procedures, and prescription drugs. Co-payments can run as high as 30%. The elderly, pregnant women, and children (about 40% of the population) are exempt from cost sharing (Healthcare Economist, 2008).
- Dental care is not covered by the basic package except for children 0–16, vulnerable populations (people with rare diseases, people with HIV and people in need of urgent or emergency care). "Public coverage of dental services has always been a debated issue in the Italian NHS. Public coverage excludes almost all types of dental services from the nationally defined benefit package" (Torbica & Fattore, 2005, p. 550).
- Hospital coverage is not clearly defined in the package; however, Italian hospitals are paid on nationally predetermined rates based on Diagnostic Related Group classifications (DRGs). DRGs are criticized as roadblocks to innovative practice: "Fixed and outdated tariffs may discourage the adoption of new expensive technologies and may force hospitals to look for alternative sources of funding, often resulting in wide disparities of their availability to citizens" (Torbica & Fattore, 2005, p. 548).

Examples of health services not considered appropriate for coverage include the following:

- Plastic surgery not following accidents, diseases, or genetic malformations
- Ritual circumcision
- Non-conventional medicine (e.g., acupuncture, phyto-therapy, homeopathy, chiropractic)
- Medical certifications, except for scholars
- Non-obligatory vaccinations for traveling purposes

- Some outpatient and physiotherapy and rehabilitation services (e.g., assisted exercises in water; short-wave diathermy, ultra-sound therapy)

Certain Ambulatory and Diagnostic Services are included in the entitlement on a case by case basis:

- Bone density testing (available where there is proven clinical effectiveness)
- Refractory laser surgery
- Orthodontic service

Hospital procedures that should be recommended for substitute treatments and/or other levels of care

- Carpal tunnel release
- Cataract surgery
- Hypertension care

Source: Torbica & Fattore (2005); Fattore, (2004)

Italy's total health spending accounted for 8 to 10% of GDP between 2007 and 2010, slightly above the average of 9.0% in OCED countries (WHO, 2012; World Bank, 2012; OCED Health Data, 2011).

INTERVENTIONAL

General Practitioners (GPs) provide most of the primary care in the Italian system and also serve as gatekeepers in charge of referrals to a hospital or specialist. GPs write prescriptions for diagnostic interventions or drugs (Torbica & Fattore, 2005). "Once the general practitioner has authorized the visit or the procedure, the patient is free to choose any provider among those credited by the NHS anywhere in Italy" (Torbica & Fattore, 2005, p.550). In case of an urgent need for care or an emergency, a person can go directly to a Guardia Medica station where on-call physicians are available to provide medical care; ambulance service is free (Maio & Manzoli, 2002).

Despite an apparently generous system, Italian citizens typically indicate low satisfaction with the efficiency and quality of their health care (Maiod & Manzol, (2002); Blendon, Kim, & Benson, 2001). Following the GP's referral, patients move from one long wait list to the next for each level of care they may require. Available data suggests that the average wait time for a mammogram is 70 days and for an endoscopy is 74 days (Healthcare Economist, 2005).

Long-Term Care (LTC)

Italy's long-term care system provides services to the elderly, the disabled, persons with drug and/or alcohol dependency, and individuals who require psychiatric services. Long-term care is delivered by public and private providers of health and personal social care. "Health services provided by the National Health Service are free-of-charge, whereas social care is means-tested, and users can pay up to the full cost of it" (Tediosi & Gabriele, 2010, p. 1).

Among OECD countries, Italy has one of the lowest rates of long term bed availability. In their study of patterns of long term care in several European countries, Damiani et al. observe the following: "The provision of long term care beds in institutions (other than hospitals) ranges from less than 2% of the population aged 65 and over in Italy to 8% in Sweden, while the percentage of the elderly who are cared for either in institutions or at home ranges from less than 5% in Italy to more than 20% in Norway" (2011, p. 2).

Italy provides long-term care for the elderly in three modalities: community home care, residential care, and cash allowances (Tediosi & Gabriele, 2010). Community home care is for people who do not have serious debilitating illnesses. Home-based care is financed by the government and includes services such as primary care, rehabilitation, medical equipment, and drug deliveries (Tediosi & Gabriele, 2010) Access to home care requires an application to the local health authorities (LHAs) who then determine the person's eligibility for this level of service (Tediosi & Gabriele, 2010).

Italy provides three different types of residential services: nursing homes for dependent patients; residents aimed at a specific time period for release and designed for people who need assistance with recovering as much psych-motor and mental capacity as possible; and assisted living situations for people who are mainly self-sufficient (Tediosid & Gabriele, 2010). "The number of elderly persons in institutional care is still relatively low by international standards, being 19.8 per 1,000 inhabitants aged 65 or older (Tediosi & Gabriele, 2010, p. 1).

Gaining access to residential care requires a few more steps. The patient must have a doctor's referral to request institutional care; the doctor completes the application and then a residential assessment team evaluates whether the person should be admitted.

Cash benefits are paid to disabled people (irrespective of age or income) and are provided by the National Institute of Social Security (INPS). A person's eligibility for cash benefits is first assessed by the LHA and then passed on to an INPS commission for a final decision. "Persons eligible for this cash benefit must be assessed as 100% disabled and dependent, i.e., unable to walk without the permanent help of a companion or unable to carry out the activities of daily living and in need of continuous assistance; and not in a residential institution whereby the costs are charged to the public administration. This cash benefit is provided every month; beneficiaries are free to use it to purchase LTC services or not, and in 2009, the monthly benefit was set at $472" (Tediosi & Gabriele, 2010, p. 4).

The quality and effectiveness of Italy's long-term care system is called into question by the following issues:

- The lack of an integrated network of delivery between health and social care service.
- Wide regional differences in public expenditures for long-term care services
- Inadequate funding of personal social services
- The lack of a national policy to provide monetary support to informal caregivers (e.g., family members). Despite universal coverage, families not only share a large part of the financial care for their elderly relatives; they often become the principal caregivers.

PREVENTIVE

Under Italy's healthcare system, each LHA has a division of health care responsible for prevention and health promotion. Within the past decade, Italy has initiated several preventive measures that emphasize an integrated approach to healthcare delivery. The National Health Plans 2006–2008 has targeted syndromic surveillance systems as an important innovation for improving public health. Recognizing the serious role the General Practitioner (GP) plays in prevention, Italy has planned training programs on cardiovascular prevention for GPs in monitoring cardiovascular risk and risk factor trends in patients, including patient records of prescribed therapies and life style recommendations (Donfrancesco et al., 2008).

The European heat wave of 2003 took at least 35,000 lives; nearly 4,200 lives were lost in Italy (Bhattacharya, 2005). In 2004, the Italian Department for Civil Protection and the Ministry of Health implemented a national program for the prevention of heat-health effects during summer. Within five years of operation, the program reached national coverage of 93% of the population aged 65 and over living in urban areas. The Italian program is recognized as " an important example of a collaborative network with a central coordination based on city-specific Heat Health Watch Warning Systems (HHWWS), mortality surveillance systems, and a wide range of local prevention activities" (Michelozzi et al., 2010, p. 2270).

In Italy, around 270,000 road traffic accidents occur annually, causing almost 330,000 injuries and 7,000 deaths (LaTorre, Van Beeck, Quaranta, Mannocci & Ricciardl, 2007). In regard to domestic accidents, Sanson et al. assert that, "despite the dimension of the problem, rare structured initiatives have been realized. A turning point was represented by the National Prevention Plan and the National Health Plan 2006–2008 which promoted a national working group and stimulated regional studies and initiatives on the prevention of domestic accidents." (2010, p.1).

Italy has also initiated several quality information systems to make information more useful to patients (e.g., avoiding jargon).

RESOURCES

A number of cultural beliefs concerning health, such as the evil eye, are practiced by older Italians. Traditional treatment is supplemented with home remedies such as the use of healers, potion makers, and the concept of healing hands designed to relieve soreness and repair broken bones. New Age approaches to health are steadily being adopted by Italian citizens and gaining approval from once reluctant physicians. Complementary/alternative medicine (CAM) is not financed under the healthcare package except where treatment may benefit pathologies such as rheumatism or osteoarthritis (Torbica & Fattore, 2005). Available survey data suggest women are the main consumers of CAM and that people aged 35–44 are the most frequent group to utilize alternative approaches to health care. In their look at the use of CAM, among women experiencing menopausal symptoms, Cardini and colleagues found that patients were more likely than their physician, to ask for alternative treatments, and that the three most popular practitioners consulted were herbalists, nutritionists, and homeopaths (Cardini, Grazia, Lombardo, & van der Sluijs, 2010).

MAJOR HEALTH ISSUES

Table 9-2 lists the top 10 health issues in Italy by number and percent, and years of life lost. Cardiovascular disease is the leading cause of death in Italy, followed by cancer and respiratory diseases. Considerable attention is being given to addressing, in particular, obesity and smoking, both of which are precursors to the development of these leading causes of death

Table 9-2 Top 10 causes of death (all ages) in Italy, 2002, with the number and percent of years of life lost by disease.

Disease	Deaths	Number (%)	Years of Life Lost (%)
All Causes	570	100	100
1. Ischemic heart disease	92	16	13
2. Cerebrovascular disease	69	12	8
3. Trachea, bronchus, lung cancers	32	6	7
4. Hypertensive heart disease	20	4	2
5. Chronic obstructive pulmonary disease	20	4	2
6. Diabetes mellitus	19	3	3
7. Colon and rectal cancers	17	3	4
8. Lower respiratory infections	14	3	2
9. Alzheimer and other dementias	13	2	1
10. Breast cancer	11	2	3

Data From: Death and DALY estimates by cause, 2002.

http://www.who.int/entity/healthinfo/statistics/bodgbddeathdalyestimates.xls

DISPARITIES

Italy's efforts to decrease disparities are continuously challenged by regional variations in healthcare delivery. "Out of 13 European countries, Italy's regional income disparities are the most pronounced resulting in high regional health disparities" (Franzini & Giannoni, 2010, p. 1). Marked socio economic differences are evident between the developed industrial north, and the less developed, welfare-dependent agricultural south with high unemployment (CIA, 2011). In what the literature frequently refers to as the north-south divide, residents in the southern regions are more likely than their northern counterparts, to report poor self-assessed health, and less satisfaction with health services. The southern region is associated with higher rates of chronic disease, higher cancer rates, and higher mortality rates (Franzini & Giannoni, 2010). Due to inadequate medical services in the southern areas, patients migrate to the northern areas for treatment out of a belief that the services are better, and for the diagnostic services they may require.

SUMMARY

With France in the lead, Italy is favorably regarded as the second best healthcare system in the world, particularly with respect to health status, fairness in financial contribution, and responsiveness to people's expectations of the health system (Maio & Manzoli, 2002). However, as several experts and researchers observe, this ranking is controversial because it does not consider public perceptions of the system. Since its inception in 1978, the Italian National Health Service has demonstrated considerable success in protecting public health through effective therapeutic measures and prevention campaigns resulting in reduced rates of cervical cancer, infectious diseases, and increased life expectancy. However, Italy's high standing and accomplishments are overshadowed by sharp regional differences in healthcare delivery. The marked regional differences in socio-economic status create the north-south divide that continues to challenge Italy's efforts to provide a uniform, equitable system of health care.

Discussion Questions

1. In Italy, inpatient care and primary care are free. In your opinion, how does free coverage affect quality of care?

2. Explain the north-south divide. Have you observed a similar "divide" in your work experience? For example, are there certain areas of a town or city that provide better health care? Over time, patients may have a variety of experiences with healthcare services. What attitudes and opinions do patients express about their experiences? Do their opinions reflect a divide?

3. Review the examples from the Italian benefits package and describe the list of excluded items; compare the list with your own coverage. What does Italy exclude that you think should be covered by the government?

4. Torbica and Fattore (2005) suggest that DRGs impede medical progress. What are your views on this issue?

Case Scenario

Marietta: No disrespect!

Marietta is an 18-year-old who waited several months for an appointment for a required physical examination needed before she can begin her college-based nursing program. Just as she was resolved to the fact that she was not going to make the deadline for submission of a satisfactory physical she got the appointment. Her parents have, for over a year, discouraged her from pursuing a career in nursing, arguing that it pays poorly, is not highly regarded, and she would be bothered every day with patient complaints about the poor care and long waits to be seen by a doctor. She stood firm, told them that she planned to make a difference as a nurse, and continued focusing on fulfilling her dream. Excited, she arrived at the clinic 20 minutes early. As she sat in the overcrowded waiting room, she became slightly nervous about the impatience of the people waiting to be seen. She waited over an hour in the waiting room before being called into an examining room and waited an additional 20 minutes for the doctor. Just a few minutes into the first part of the physical exam Marietta was asked about her choice of nursing as a career. The physician asked, "Why nursing, and not medicine?" and mumbled in an almost inaudible tone, "You'll probably die a pauper if you choose nursing." Marietta was speechless, hung her head, and did not respond.

DISCUSSION POINTS

1. Considering that the healthcare system in Italy is considered the second best in the world, explain Marietta's long wait for a physical examination. Is this typical of the Italian system?
2. Knowing what you do about the shortage of nurses in Italy and the impact it likely has on healthcare delivery, why do you think the physician responded as he did?
3. Have you ever witnessed similar behavior in your work area? If so, what were the circumstances and how was it handled?
4. What do you think about Marietta's reaction? Put yourself in her place; how would you have responded?

References

Action for Global Health. (January 2011). Retrieved from www.actionforglobal health.eu

Bhattacharya, S. (October 10, 2005). European heat wave caused 3500 deaths. *New Scientist.* Retrieved from www.newscientist.com/.../dn4259-european-heatwave -caused-3500deaths.html

Blendon, R. J., Kim, M., & Benson, J.M. (2001). *The public versus the World Health Organization on health system performance.* Health Affairs, 20 (3), 10–20.

Cardini, F., Grazia, L., Lombardo, F., & van der Sluijs, C. (2010). The use of complementary and alternative medicine by women experiencing menopausal symptoms in Bolgona. *BMC Women's Health, 10*(7). Retreived from http://www .biomedcentral.com/1472-6874-10/7

Clements, B., Coady, D., & Gupta, S. (Eds.). (2012). *The economics of public health care reform in advanced and emerging Economics.* Washington, D.C .: International Monetary Fund.

Central Intelligence Agency. (2011). *CIA World Factbook.* Retrieved from https://www.cia.gov/library/publications/the-world-factbook/geos/it.html

Damiani et al. (2011). Patterns of long term care in 29 European countries: evidence from an exploratory study. *BMC Health Services Research,* 11:316 doi: 10.1186/1472-6963-11-316. Retrieved from http:// www.biomedcentral.com/1472-6963/11/316

Donfrancesco, C., LoNoce, C., Brignoli, O., Riccardi, G., Ciccarelli, Dima, F., Palmieri, L., & Giampaoli, S. (2008). Italian network for obesity and cardiovascular disease surveillance: a pilot project. *BMC Family Practice, 9*(53). doi: 10.1186/147-2296-9-53

Fattore, G. (2004). Health service benefit catalogues in Europe: Country report: Italy. Health Basket Project. SP21-ct-2004-501588. Retrieved from www.ehma.org/files/Benefit_Report_Italy.pdf

Franzini, L. & Giannoni, M. (2010). Determinants of health disparities between Italian regions. *BMC Public Health,* 10, 1471–2458. doi: 10.1186/1471-2458-10296

Healthcare Economist. (2008). Health care around the world: Italy. Retrieved from http://healthcare- economist.com/2008/04/15

LaTorre, G., Van Beeck, E., Quaranta, G., Mannocci, A., & Ricciardi, W. (2007). Determinants of within-country variation in traffic accident mortality in Italy: a geographical analysis. *International Journal of Health Geographics, 6*(49). doi:10.1186/1476-72X-6-49

Maio, V. & Manzoli, L. (2002). The Italian health care system: W.H O. ranking versus public perception. *P&T, 27*(6), 301–308. News Scientist. Retrieved from www.newscientist.com/.../dn4259-european-heatwave-caused-35000-deaths.html

Michelozzi, P., et al. (2010). Surveillance of summer mortality and preparedness to reduce the health impact of heat waves in Italy. *International Journal of Environmental Research Public Health, 7*(5), 2256–2273. doi: 10.3390/jerph7052256

OECD. (2011). Help wanted? Providing and paying for long-term care. Retrieved from www.oecd.org/dataoecd/54/11/47890836.pdf

OECD Health Data. (2011). Retrieved from www.oecd.org/health/healthdata.

Sanson, S., et al. (April 14–15 2010). Are inequalities playing a major role in the domestic accident context: What can we do? Experimental studies in North Eastern Italy. The Eighteenth International Conference on Health Promoting Hospitals and Health Services: Tackling Causes and Consequences of Inequalities in Health. Manchester, United Kingdom.

Tediosi, F. & Gabriele, S. (2010). The long-term care system for the elderly in Italy. *ENEPERI Research Report No. 80.* Retrieved from www.ceps.eu

Torbica, A. & Fattore, G. (2005). The "essential levels of care" in Italy: when being explicit serves the devolution of powers. *European Journal of Health Economics, 6,* 46–52. doi: 10.1007/s10198-005-0318-x

U.S. Department of State Background Note. (2011). Italy. http://www.state.gov/r/pa/ei/bgn/4033.htm

WHO. (2004). Who.int/whosis/database/core/core_select_process.cfm

World Bank. (2012). data.worldbank.org/indicator/SH.XPD.TOTL.ZS

World Health Organization. (2006). Mortality Country Fact Sheet 2006. Retrieved from www. euro.who.int./en

World Health Organization. (2012). Selected basic statistics. Retrieved from www.euro.who.int/en/where-we-work/member-states/italy/selected-basic-statistics

Worldsalaries.org. Retrieved from http://www.worldsalaries.org/italy.shtml

Part III

Health Care in Developing Countries

CHAPTER 10

The Healthcare System in Brazil

We must become the change we want to see.

—Mahatma Gandhi

BEHAVIORAL OBJECTIVES

At the end of this chapter the learner will be able to:

1. Discuss the incidence and prevalence of disease.
2. Identify key factors that affect Brazil's health status.
3. Describe Brazil's healthcare structure and financing.
4. Discuss the relationship of regional differences and access to health care.
5. Describe Brazil's healthcare initiatives and challenges.

KEY CONCEPTS

The Bolsa Familia Program
Chronic underfunding
Epidemiological transition
Family Health Program
Simpatias
Unified Health System

INTRODUCTION

Brazil, officially known as the Federated Republic of Brazil, is the largest country in Latin America and covers 8,511,965 sq. km. (3,290,000 square miles) a land area slightly smaller than the United States (U.S. Department of State Background Note Brazil 2010). The country comprises five geographical regions, 26 states, The Federal District, and 5,560 municipalities (CIA, 2011). As the fifth most populated country in the world, Brazil's population is generally estimated between 190–193 million. However, projections in 2011 estimated Brazil's population at 203,429,773 million people (CIA, 2011).

The proportion of the population under the age of 15 years is 28% (UNO, 2004) and the proportion of the population above the age of 60 years is 8% (WHO 2004). The main language used in the country is Portuguese. The largest ethnic group is Portuguese and other ethnic groups are mixed European American and African. The majority (74%) of Brazil's population is Roman Catholic (CIA, 2011) and the other religious group is Protestant.

The wide diversity of the population is reflected in several ethnic groups including the Portuguese who colonized Brazil in the 16th century, Africans who were brought as slaves, Europeans, Arabs, and Japanese (US Department of State Background Note Brazil 2010). The literacy rate is approximately 90.3%. The estimated life expectancy at birth is 72.53 years: 68.97 for men and 76.27 for women (CIA, 2011). According to United Nations forecasts, 32 countries will have ten million people over the age of 60 by 2050. Brazil is expected to have 60 million. The total estimated infant mortality rate per 1,000 live births is 21.17 deaths: 24.63 male deaths/1,000 live births and 17.53 female deaths /1,000 live births. The total fertility rate is 2.18 (CIA, 2011).

Although ranked as the eighth wealthiest economy (The World Bank, n.d), Brazil is marked by widespread regional and social inequalities. There is a desperate regional divide in Brazil that pits one socioeconomic group against the other. This has a tendency to impact the distribution of resources. For example, the Northeastern region of Brazil is the poorest region. Ironically, it is home to the African and indigenous populations. In contrast, the Southeastern region, where the majority of Brazilians live, is largely inhabited and influenced by Europeans.

HISTORICAL

Brazil's Unified Health System, *Sistemia Unico de Saude* (SUS), also known as the National Health System (NHS), was established by the Constitution of

1988 after more than two decades of military dictatorship. The Constitution universalized access to medical care declaring that all citizens have a right to health and that the government has a responsibility to protect that right. Until then Brazil's health system favored those who were financially well off, and the working class. Drawing on the SUS database (datasus) and the work of Braga & Paula (1981), Paim et al. provide a look at a system that was predominately private and elitist: "The health system consisted of an under-funded Ministry of Health and the social security system, which provided medical care through the retirement and pension institutes, delivered on the basis of occupational categories (i.e., bankers, railroad workers, etc.), each with different services and levels of coverage. Individuals with causal employment had an inadequate supply of public services, philanthropic care, and out- of-pocket private healthcare services (2011, p.1783). Healthcare reform in Brazil took place at the same time the country transitioned to democracy. Civilians returned to power in 1985, setting into motion the development of a system of health care aimed at equal access, comprehensive care, prevention, and community participation at all levels of government (Paim, Travassos, Almeida Bahia, & Macinko, 2011; Hudson, 1997).

STRUCTURE

Brazil's health care is a decentralized, integrated system utilizing a network of public and private organizations to deliver healthcare service to the population. Administratively, the Ministry of Health provides federal governance of the system. Described as a highly innovative approach to ensure the voice of the stakeholder, Brazil's healthcare structure consists of health councils, and intermanagerial committees representing each level of government; health sector providers and the citizenry participate in bipartite and tripartite negotiations on health policies and programs (Paim et al., 2011).

Approximately 78.8% of Brazil's population depends exclusively on SUS for their healthcare needs. The remaining 21.2% of the population is covered by the Supplementary System and has the right to access the health services of the SUS. The National Supplementary Health Agency, a regulatory body created in 2000, monitors compliance with statutory law that makes it "illegal for insurance companies to deny coverage to patients with pre-existing conditions or to set limits on the use of specific healthcare services or procedures" (Paim et al., 2011, p. 1787).

The *Family Health Program* is the main portal of basic health care to the population. In 2005 the Family Health Program provided service to over 73 million people (40% of the population) through 22,683 multidisciplinary teams in 4,837 cities (WHO Country Cooperation Strategy, n.d.).

According to WHO Health Report (2008), in 2005, there were 12 physicians per 10,000 inhabitants. SUS has 5.9 thousand registered hospitals, 64,000 primary healthcare units, and 28,000 Family Health Care Teams active in over 5,560 municipalities. Each Health Care Team serves up to 2,000 families or 10,000 people. The public hospital network includes 69 federal, 618 state, and 2,278 municipal hospitals, across all States. All university hospitals serve the public health system. The system performs 2.3 billion clinical procedures every year including 15.8 thousand transplants, 213 thousand cardiac surgeries, 9 million chemotherapy and radiotherapy procedures, and 11.3 million interments; 13 million hospitalizations are on record for 2005 with an average stay of 5.9 days (www.brasil.gov.br/sobre/health/service/what-does-sus-stand-for-1).

FINANCING

Healthcare financing in Brazil includes public funding (tax revenues) and private sources of funding (e.g., employer health plans, private health insurance, and out-of-pocket payments). Paradoxically, Brazil, as one of the largest universal healthcare systems in the world, is making more private expenditures on health care than public expenditures. In 2007, Brazil's health expenditures were 8.4% of GDP (Paim et al., 2011; Hennigan, 2010) rising to a total expenditure on health of 9.0% in 2009 (OECD, 2010). These expenditures are considered low when compared with the UK (82%), Italy (77%); Spain (71.8%), and are lower than the United States (45.5%) and Mexico (46.9%) (Paim et al., 2011).

"Funding for the SUS has not been sufficient to ensure adequate or stable financial resources for the public system. Because social contributions have been larger than contributions from taxes, which are divided between federal, state, and municipal governments, the SUS has remained underfinanced" (Paim et al., 2011, p. 1778).

The persistent gap between what the government guarantees for health care and what it can actually deliver, known as *chronic underfunding* (Hennigan, 2010) has led to service issues (e.g., long wait lists for appointments, staff shortages) that compromise good primary care, and there is the possibility that increasing numbers of citizens, particularly Brazil's growing middle class, may opt for private health plans—a trend that one medical expert observes could create an apartheid in the provision of health care (Hennigan, 2010).

INTERVENTIONAL

Brazil's healthcare system is based on a model of primary care. Through the Family Health Program, Basic Health Units (UBS) serve as entry points for people seeking medical help (Diabetes Foundation). The Family Health Program uses multi-professional teams that are typically composed of a physician, a nurse, a medical assistant, and community health workers (Hennigan, 2010). The family health teams are located at UBSs and are assigned to specific geographical areas of defined populations of 600–1,000 families (Paim et al., 2011). Over 30,000 teams of healthcare workers cover up to 95% of Brazil's municipalities. The family health strategy emphasizes continuity of care, including diagnosis, medication, lifestyle advice, and referral to secondary and tertiary care. Health care is free at the point of use from all public and private health services funded by the government (WHO Bulletin, 2010).

"In 2009, 95.4 million people (52% of the population) were served by the family health program. Out of this total 73.9 million lived in urban areas and 21.7 million lived in rural areas, which represents a coverage of 47% for urban areas and 73% for rural areas. Coverage is highest in the poorer northeastern region, reaching 72% and lowest in the wealthier southeastern region with only 36% coverage suggesting that the program has worked best where it is most needed" (Wehrmeister & Peres, 2003).

PREVENTIVE

An ongoing challenge of Brazil's health care is addressing significant disparities in health coverage. However, two initiatives that successfully demonstrate principles of equitable access to health care are Brazil's HIV/AIDS preventive campaigns and the National Immunization Program (Greco & Simao, 2007). There have been no cases of poliomyelitis in Brazil since 1947 or measles since 2000 (Paim et al., 2011). Available data indicate that deaths from AIDS and HIV-related hospitalizations in Brazil have fallen by 50% and 70–80% respectively, since 1997 (AVERT.org). "Since most private insurance providers would not cover the high cost of the antiretroviral drugs, even the middle and upper classes resorted to the public system which responded effectively" (Guanais, 2010, p. 19).

In an effort to improve medical coverage, Brazil has enacted reforms to address the unique needs of indigenous populations and black communities through the National Indigenous Health Policy (Paim et al., 2011) which provides health care, environmental surveillance, and sanitation measures. Considerable attention has been given to individuals suffering from mental illness. Psychiatric reform has led to the development of community-based care centers that provide psychosocial support and rehabilitation (Paim et al., 2011).

The SUS is credited with a remarkable decline in mortality for children under 5 (from 33.7/1,000 in 1996 to 22.6/1,000 in 2004), improved access to dental care in 86 municipalities in 21 states, and 90% subsidization of many essential drugs (Paim et al., 2011; WHO Bulletin, 2008). In 2008, efforts to improve emergency services were initiated with the installation of 391 twenty-four-hour emergency care clinics working in conjunction with the emergency mobile care service (Paim et al., 2011).

Under the *Bolsa Familia Program*, poor families receive a monthly cash benefit based on their compliance with conditions such as ensuring their children attend school and that they are immunized. Pregnant women are required to participate in all prenatal and postnatal appointments (Guanais, 2010). *Bolsa Familia* is regarded as playing a key role in declining illiteracy rates. Between 2003 and 2009, poverty (PPP $2 per day) has fallen from 22 percent of the population to 7 percent (Azeredo & Aguilar, 2010). In cooperative arrangements with the World Bank, Brazil has launched a second *Bolsa Familia Program*, aimed at strengthening program goals and developing strategies to help beneficiaries of the program exit poverty.

RESOURCES

Alternative medicine is not a fad or a trend in Brazil; rather, traditional remedies and rituals are deeply embedded in the culture. Self-care often reflects practices passed down through the generations. Traditional medicine is so highly valued in Brazil that the fear of losing centuries-old knowledge, most of it transmitted orally, prompted the Ministry of Health to finance a research program in 2009 aimed at recovering folk practices, and expanding the number of herbal medicines that could be available to the public. The move is not only viewed as a cost effective measure but in terms of health promotion, supports the appropriate use of herbal remedies (Frayssinet, 2011).

For many Brazilians, irrespective of their socioeconomic status, folk remedies are articles of faith, holding the potential for spiritual comfort, healing, and miracles. Public health markets selling plant and animal remedies are common throughout Brazil. In a study on the use of herbal remedies, the urban participants identified over 300 different plants used for medicinal purposes (Brandão, Acúrcio, Montemor, Melo, & Marlière, 2006). Animal parts are used for amulets and charms in magic-religious diagnosis. "The use of some medicinal animals is associated with popular beliefs locally known as *simpatias*. These *simpatias* are often secretive in nature, so that the people receiving the treatment cannot know what they are taking, otherwise the remedy will not be effective" (Ferreira, Brito, Riberiro, Saraiva, Almeida & Alves, 2009, p. 24)

MAJOR HEALTH ISSUES

Table 10-1 lists the top 10 health issues by number and percent, and years of life lost. A concerning trend in Brazil's mortality rates is the *epidemiological transition* of a rise in non-communicable diseases and premature death due to violence and road accidents. "Diseases of the circulatory system are the leading cause of death, followed by cancer and external causes (largely, homicide and traffic accidents)" (Paim et al., 2011, p. 1779, Reichenheim et al., 2011). In 2007, chronic diseases accounted for 72% of all deaths in Brazil compared to 46% of all deaths attributed to infectious diseases in 1930. Urbanization, greater income, and improved access to food accompanied by poor nutrition habits, are identified as some of the critical factors affecting the higher incidence of chronic diseases (Schmidt et al., 2011). Schramm, Oliviera, and Leite, (2004) identify cardiovascular diseases, diabetes, cancer, chronic respiratory disease, and neuropsychiatric disorders as the major causes of Brazil's disease burden. The related risk factors of obesity, hypertension, and diabetes are critical problems in Brazil as are smoking, inactivity, and alcohol abuse (Gaziano, Galea, & Reddy, 2007).

In 2008, 1 out of 10 Brazilians reported being assaulted or mugged, and 17% of the population reported being robbed; survey results indicated only 2 out of 5 Brazilians felt safe walking home alone at night (The Legatum Prosperity Index 2010). According to the last updated results in 2009 of the Global Burden of Disease Project (GBD 2005) in 2005, road crashes resulted

Table 10-1 Top 10 causes of death (all ages) in Brazil, 2002, with the number and percent of years of life lost by disease.

Deaths Disease	Number	Percent	Years of Life Lost %
1. Ischemic heart disease	139	11	7
2. Cerebrovascular disease	129	11	6
3. Perinatal conditions	70	6	14
4. Violence	57	5	9
5. Diabetes mellitus	53	4	3
6. Lower respiratory infections	51	4	4
7. Chronic obstructive pulmonary disease	46	4	2
8. Hypertensive heart disease	36	3	2
9. Road traffic accidents	34	2	2
10. Inflammatory heart diseases	22	2	1

Data From: Death and DALY estimates by cause, 2002.

http://www.who.int/entity/healthinfo/statistics/bodgbddeathdalyestimates.xls

in 38,982 deaths in Brazil representing an annual rate of 21.3 deaths per 100,000 people. Of the six countries in the Latin American region that were analyzed in this project, Brazil had the second highest road death rate; Ecuador placed first. The road death rate of Brazil was 3.7 times the death rate in countries with the best road safety performance (Sweden, UK, and Netherlands). Most road deaths in Brazil occur among adult males over the age of 20 (www.roadinjuries.globalburdenofinjuries.org/brazil).

DISPARITIES

Regional differences in health care are evidenced in the prosperous south and southeast regions and the poorer north and northeast regions. In 2006 for example, the infant mortality rate in the northeast was 2–24 times higher than the south region (Paim et al., 2011). Access to hospital care is difficult for those living in poor municipalities where hospital capacity is low: "This situation is cause for concern because one in five hospital admissions in the SUS are to hospitals outside of the patient's home municipality" (Paim et al., 2011, p. 1791). Compared to lower-income groups, some of whom report never having visited a dentist, higher income groups are likely to have greater physician contact, report better health, and experience fewer problems with wait times. Some researchers suggest that the perception of social inequalities in health should consider the different attitudes and behaviors of low-income groups who may have negative perceptions of health care and delay attention to the medical treatment they may require (Mendes, Martins, Rozenfeld, & Travassos, 2009).

SUMMARY

Primary care is the cornerstone of Brazil's healthcare system. Under SUS, public health has thrived due to a substantial increase in primary care clinics and aggressive immunization and child health initiatives. However, Brazil faces continuing challenges in financing public health, monitoring the allocation of resources, coordinating public health services, and reducing regional disparities in medical coverage.

Discussion Questions

1. *The Family Health Program* is regarded as the cornerstone of primary care. Describe your views of this healthcare strategy. What features of this model do you think would work well in your health setting?

2. Discuss the *Bolsa Familia Program*. Are cash transfers a good idea? Why or why not? Would this model work in the community you serve? Discuss the possible advantages and drawbacks of implementing this strategy in your community.

3. Brazil's healthcare structure emphasizes citizen participation at every level of government. Describe your views on this approach. To what extent are citizens involved with healthcare planning in your work setting? Discuss your views on how the public should be involved in health care. Describe what you believe are good examples of public involvement in healthcare initiatives and/or planning.

4. Discuss Brazil's *epidemiological transition*. Compare Brazil's transition to trends in health you have observed. What is similar? What is different? What challenges face healthcare providers in addressing transition issues?

5. Brazil's health care has launched research studies to expand the development of herb-based medicinal compounds. Discuss the advantages and possible drawbacks of this strategy.

Case Scenario

Raphael: Refusal of Treatment

Raphael, a 24-year-old Brazilian male was in a minor traffic accident where he collided with another car. Raphael recalls twisting his right arm as he swerved to avoid the collision. He recalls his chest hitting the steering wheel but denies loss of consciousness. He was treated at the scene by a doctor on the mobile emergency medical unit. Despite no obvious major injuries Raphael was taken to a nearby hospital to be further assessed. After waiting two hours, feeling a little sore on his left side but fine otherwise, Raphael left the packed hospital emergency room without being seen. He suspected his soreness would disappear after a few days. However, the next day, the previously vague, tolerable left sided pain he had been treating with "herbal rubs," became slightly worse. Raphael described his pain as a constant aching, much worse when breathing in than out. When Raphael became lightheaded on the third day and the pain was now more severe, his grandfather told him he needed much stronger medicine than he had been taking. Later the same day his grandfather summoned family members and presided over a family vigil where Raphael was given an unidentified herbal concoction to drink as his father and grandfather chanted harmonious, prayer-like lyrics. He was told only that the concoction would surely make him better. When Raphael began vomiting during the ceremony, he was taken to the hospital where they discovered he had been slowly bleeding from a small tear in his spleen that probably occurred when his chest hit the steering wheel during the accident. The doctor told Raphael and his family that had the tear in his spleen been larger he would not have survived without surgery.

Discussion Points

1. What, in your opinion, prompted Raphael to leave the hospital without being seen? Explain the rationale for Raphael's behavior.
2. What lessons do you believe Raphael and his family learned from this experience?
3. Have you ever heard of someone leaving a hospital without being seen? If so, what were the circumstances involved? Describe the consequences of the person's actions?
4. Had Raphael not vomited during the ceremony what do you believe the outcome would have been as the tear was a small one?

REFERENCES

AVERT.org. (n.d.). International HIV and AIDS Charity. Retrieved from http://www .avert.org/

Azeredo, M. & Aguilar, G. (September 17, 2010). The World Bank. Brazil's Landmark Bolsa Familia Program Receives US$200 Million Loan. Press Release No: 2011/093/LAC. Retrieved from http://go.worldbank.org/2X91DMDOJ0

Braga, J. C. & Paula, S. G. (1981). Health and Welfare. New York: Cebes-Hucitec.

Brandão, M. G., Acúrcio, F. A., Montemor, R. L., Melo, R. L., & Marlière, L. (2006). Complementary/Alternative medicine in Latin America: Use of herbal remedies among a Brazilian metropolitan area population. *Journal of Complementary and Integrative Medicine, 3*(1) Article 5, doi: 10.2202/1553-3840.1025

CIA World Factbook. (2011). Retrieved from: https://www.cia.gov

DATASUS. Retrieved from http://www2.datasus.gov.br/DATASUS/index.php

Diabetes Foundation. Brazil: Bridging the gap between health care worker and patient. Retrived from http://world diabetes foundation.org/composite-3326.htm

Ferreira, F. S., Brito, S.V., Riberiro, S.C.C., Saraiva, A. F., Almeida, W. O., & Alves, R. N. (2009). Animal-based folk remedies sold in public markets in Crato and Juazeiro do Norte, Ceará, Brazil. *BMC complementary and alternative medicine,* 9. Retrieved from http://www.biomedsearch.com/nih/Animal-based -folk-remedies-sold/19493345.html

Frayssinet, F. (June 6, 2011). Public health embraces herbal medicine. Retrieved from http://ipsnews.net/print.asp?idnews=47057

Gaziano, T. A., Galea, C., & Reddy, K. S. (2007). Scaling up interventions for chronic disease prevention: The evidence. *Lancet, 376,* 1619–1623. In: Schmidt, M. I., Duncan, B. B., Azevedo e Silva, G., Menezes, A. M., Monteiro, C., A., Barreto, S. M.,

Chor, D., & Menezes, P. (2011). Chronic non-communicable diseases in Brazil: burden and current challenges. Retrieved from www.thelancet.com

Global Burden of Disease Project (GBD). (2005). Retrieved from www.roadinjuries.globalburdenofinjuries.org/brazil

Greco, D. B. & Simao, M. (2007). Brazilian policy of universal access to AIDS treatment: Sustainability challenges and perspectives. *AIDS, 21,* (Supplement 4) S37-45. In: Guanais, F. C. (2010). Health equity in Brazil. *BMJ, 341,* c6542.doi: 10.1136/bmj.c6542

Guanais, F. C. (2010). Health equity in Brazil. *BMJ, 341,* c6542.doi:10.1136/bmj.c6542

Hennigan, T. (2010). Economic success threatens aspirations of Brazil's public health system. *BMJ, 341,* c5453. doi: 10.1136/BMJ. c5453

Hudson, R. A. (Ed.). (1997). Brazil: A country study. Washington: GPO for the Library of Congress, 1997. Retrieved from countrystudies.us/brazil

The Legatum Prosperity Index. (2010). Retrieved from prosperity.com/country/aspx?id=BR

Mendes, W., Martins, M., Rozenfeld, S., & Travassos, C. (2009). The assessment of adverse events in hospitals in Brazil. *International Journal of Quality Health Care,* 21, 279-284. In: Paim, J., Travassos, C., Almeida, C., Bahia, L., & Macinko, J. (2011). *Lancet,* 1778-1797, doi: 10.1016/50140-6736(11)60054-8

OECD. (2010). Health Data 2010. Retrieved from www.oecd.orgdataoecd/20/41.45.45703986.pdf

Paim, J., Travassos, C., Almeida, C., Bahia, L., & Macinko, J. (2011). *Lancet,* 1778-1797, doi: 10.1016/50140-6736(11)60054-8

Reichenheim, M. E., de Souza, E. R., Moraes, C. L., Prado de Mello Jorge, M. H., Passos da Silva, C. M. F., & de Souza Minayo, M. C. (2011). Violence and injuries in Brazil: The effect, progress made, and challenges ahead. *Lancet,* 1962-1975, doi: 10.1006/S0140-6736(11)60053-6. In: Paim, J., Travassos, C., Almeida, C., Bahia, L., & Macinko, J. (2011). *Lancet,* 1778-1797, doi: 10.1016/50140-6736(11)60054-8

Schmidt, M. I., Duncan, B. B., Azevedo eSilva, G., Menezes, A. M., Monteiro, C. A., Barreto, S. M., Chor, D., & Menezes, P. (2011). Chronic non-communicable diseases in Brazil: burden and current challenges. *Lancet,* 377, 1949-1961. Retrieved from www.thelancet.com

Schramm, J. M., Oliviera, A. F., & Leite, J. C. (2004). Transicao epidemiologicae estudo de carga de doencias no Brasil. *Cien Saude Coletiva,* 9, 897-908. In: Schmidt, M. I., Duncan, B. B., e Silva, G., Menezes, A. M., Monteiro, C. A., Barreto, S. M., Chor, D., & Menezes, P. (2011). *Lancet,* 377, 1949-1961. Retrieved from www.thelancet.com

UNO. (2004). Un.org/esa/population/publications/WorldPop.pdf

US Department of State Background Note Brazil. (2010). Retrieved from http://www.state.gov/r/pa/ei/bgn/

www.brasil.gov.br/sobre/health/service/what-does-sus-stand-for-1

www.roadinjuries.globalburdenofinjuries.org/brazil

Wehrmeister, F. C. & Peres, K. G. (2003). Regional inequalities in the prevalence of asthma diagnosis in children: an analysis of the Brazilian National Household

Sample Survey (in Portuguese). *Cad Saude Publica 2010:26*: 1839–1852 (Medicine) (Web of Science). In: Guanais, F. C. (2010). Progress in a land of extremes. *BMJ*; 341, c6542. Doi: 10.1136/bmj.c6542.

WHO. (2004). Who.int/whosis/database/core/core_select_process.cfm

World Health Organization. Bulletin of the World Health Organization. (September 2008). Flawed but fair: Brazil's health system reaches out to the poor. *86*(4) Retrieved from http://www/who.int/bulletin/volumes /88/4/08-030408/en/

World Health Organization. Bulletin of the World Health Organization. (September 2010). Brazil's march towards universal coverage. *88*(9) Retrieved from http://www /who.int/bulletin/volumes /88/9/10-020910en

World Health Organization. (n.d.). Country Cooperation Strategy at a glance.

World Health Organization. The World Health Report. (2008). Primary care in action, now more than ever. Retrieved from http://www/who.int/whr/2008 /media _centre/country_profiles/en/index

CHAPTER **11**

The Healthcare System in Cuba

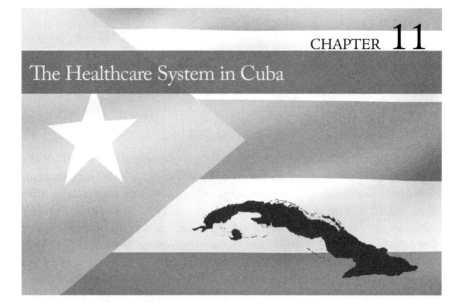

Knowing is not enough; we must apply. Willing is not enough; we must do.

— Goethe

BEHAVIORAL OBJECTIVES

At the end of this chapter the learner will be able to:

1. Discuss how Cuba's healthcare system emerged.
2. Discuss the incidence and prevalence of disease.
3. Discuss the top three diseases and related challenges.
4. Determine how health care is structured, financed, and accessed.
5. Identify funding priorities, initiatives, and challenges.
6. Describe health practices that are commonly used to maintain and restore health.
7. Explain how social determinants affect health-seeking beliefs and practices.

KEY CONCEPTS

Centers of excellence

Cholera

Dengue

Leptospirosis

Polyclinic

INTRODUCTION

The population of Cuba is 11,257,105. It is the largest of the islands in the West Indies and lies 90 miles south of Florida, just below the Bahamas. Although it is considered a developing country, it has many characteristics of an industrialized country. The land area is 110,860 sq. km (Nation's encyclopedia, 2009). Cuba has a low birth rate, an associated low infant mortality rate of 5.3, a combined infant and neonatal mortality rate of 7.2, a life expectancy rate of 79.5 for women and 75.8 for men, and a high literacy rate (CIA, 2001). The proportion of Cuba's population that is under 15 years old is 19% (UNO, 2004), and the over 60 population is 14% (WHO, 2004). Spanish is the predominant language spoken; the largest ethnic groups are European (Spanish descent) and African (descent), and other ethnic groups are racially mixed Asians. The major religious groups are Roman Catholic (about 83%), Protestant, other Christians, and traditional African (e.g., Yoruba) (WHO, 2005).

Table 11-1 highlights health indicators and outcome data (Cuba Health Data, MINSAP, 2005). Cuba is a male-dominated society with a higher divorce rate than the United States. According to the World Bank, per capita income in Cuba is less than $1,000 per year. Cuban estimates are slightly higher, ranging from $2,000–5,000 per year (Cooper, 2006).

HISTORICAL

Health and education is, and has always been, defined by Cubans as a social responsibility of government and a birthright of every Cuban citizen. They have a strong national health system that provides universal, accessible, free health services to the entire Cuban population irrespective of their economic status. In 1960, strong initiatives were implemented to address healthcare needs of the country that included such things as establishing 50 new rural hospitals, 160 urban, community clinics (also referred to as polyclinics), and a national immunization program that resulted in the widespread vaccination of children across the country.

Cuba also trained a record number of healthcare professionals. By mid-1980 there were over 55 healthcare fields, a serious focus on tertiary care, specializations, and research into the causes and treatment of diseases.

Table 11-1 Health indicators and outcomes per total population in Cuba.

Indicator	Population
Total Population	11,257,105
Infant and Maternal Health	
Total live births	120,716
Percent of in-hospital live births	99.5
Crude birth rate per 1,000 population	10.7
Fertility rate per 1,000 females ages 15–49	39.9
Global fertility rate (children/women)	1.46
Infant mortality	5.3
Under five mortality	8.0
Perinatal mortality per 1,000 live births	15.5
Maternal mortality per 100,000 live births	52.2
Percent of children fully immunized against tuberculosis and measles	99.0
Life expectancy men	75.8
Life expectancy women	79.5

Source: Cuba Health Data. MINSAP, Health Statistic's Yearbook, 2005. Retrieved from Medical Education Cooperation with Cuba (MEDICC) http://www.medicc.org /publications/cuba_health_reports/cuba-health-data.php. Updated statistics are available at http://www.medicc.org

There was a major downturn in the economy in the early 1990s during which Cuba lost some of its healthcare gains but by the mid-1990s they were already expanding their national healthcare efforts and were entrenched in building very strong entities that they referred to as national institutes (*centers of excellence*) where physicians and nurses were partnered in teams in practices set up in neighborhoods where they focused intensively on health promotion, disease prevention, and early intervention that resulted in remarkable outcomes. Cuba's healthcare system is notably one of the best in the world.

STRUCTURE

Cuba has a National Health Care System with many well-prepared health professions, including physicians. The system claims to provide universal, accessible, free health services for all Cubans. Health care is structured in strategically placed, physician and nurse run neighborhood polyclinics (centers of excellence) within walking distance of most residents.

There are 470 such polyclinics, and an additional 289 maternity homes. There are also a total of 248 hospitals with a combined capacity of 54,857 hospital beds.

In 2004, the total number of physicians in Cuba was 70,594 (62.7 physicians per 10,000 persons in the population, and 1 physician for every 170 persons). This is the second highest doctor-patient ratio in the world, second only to Italy (United Nations Report, nd; PAHO, 2008). The majority (33,769) were family physicians who serve 99.4 percent of the population. The government pays for the six years of medical school which includes room and board and a stipend. There is no debt after graduation but physician salaries are relatively low. Upon finishing medical school students are encouraged to complete two years of national service in rural areas before returning to complete three years of residency where family is emphasized (Drain & Barry, 2010). Cuba has also trained more than 10,000 Latin American physicians from approximately 33 countries. Once trained, these physicians return to their countries to practice in poor communities (Drain & Barry, 2010).

Cuban physicians are highly trained and highly respected. Despite limited economic resources Cuba has used its human resources effectively. Since 1990, Cuba has placed physicians, nurses, dentists, and other healthcare professionals in over 52 developing countries to share their experiences and practice expertise (Waki, 2002; Republic of Cuba, 2001). Cuban physicians are credited with assisting physicians and other healthcare professionals in the developing world to advance their skills in the treatment and management of diseases and in the use of diagnostic technology.

There are 79.5 nurses and 9.4 dentists per every 10,000 persons in the population. In the Cuban system, nurses make home visits, and partner with physicians in addressing health promotion, disease prevention, and addressing health problems early to prevent complications.

FINANCING

Cuba spends slightly more than $300.00 per person annually on health care, considerably less than the $7,000 per person the United States spends annually (Drain & Barry, 2010). The fiscal management and provision of Cuba's NHS is not easy. The Kaiser Family Foundation, a non-governmental organization that evaluated Cuba's healthcare system in 2000–2001 described Cuba as "a shining example of the power of public health to transform the health of an entire country by a commitment to prevention and by careful management of its medical resources" (Essif, 2001).

Cuba has been financially challenged for decades. During the early 1990s the loss of financial support from the Soviet Union (Graham, 1998), and the U.S. embargo resulted in Cuba experiencing trade restrictions on food and medicines, increased shipping costs, and in 1986 defaulting on its debts to Western banks (American Association for World Health, 1997).

Diagnostic tests and medications for patients in the hospital are free. Health care is generally free for everyone. However, there are limited items, such as some medications prescribed for outpatients; some dental, hearing, and orthopedic procedures; wheelchairs; and crutches. Again, patients who cannot afford these things are not charged (Garfield & Santana, n.d).

For more than 20 years, Cuba has served health tourists from around the world. Cuba attracts approximately 20,000 paying health tourists, who come for eye surgery, neurological disorders such as multiple sclerosis and Parkinson's disease, cosmetic surgery, treatment for addictions, and ortho-pedics. The majority of these tourists come from all over Latin America, Europe, Canada, and most recently the United States. Cuba is also a great exporter of vaccines. Cuba's medical tourism industry generates revenues of around $40 million annually. This money gives a tremendous boost to the Cuban economy. Some of this income is used to fund healthcare initiatives (Lasa, 2001). Throughout many years of fiscal challenges, Cuba's budgetary support for medical professionals, and operational costs of hospitals and clinics remained strong (Lasa, 2001).

INTERVENTIONAL

Physicians and nurses live in communities where they practice. As a consequence, they become an integral part of the community where they assist with emergencies, and encourage consistency of preventive measures (van Gelder, 2006). In addition to this, doctor-nurse teams working and living in the same communities as their patients are in a position to better understand the problems experienced by those patients. It also affords them a better opportunity to address health problems within the context of their patient's homes, families, and neighborhoods. If a patient misses too many appointments, they will probably receive a visit from their neighborhood physician or nurse (van Gelder, 2006).

Healthcare interventions include health promotion actions that encourage healthy lifestyles and early treatment for problems so that better outcomes can be achieved. The healthcare focus is on primary care and prevention that is designed to keep people healthy and active. When people do become ill, early intervention is central in preventing the problem from getting worse. The majority of the interventions are directed at encouraging healthy lifestyles and preventing illness. Health services are free; however, under-the-table payments are sometimes made to particular health professionals for which the patient receives speedier and better-quality services (de Gordon, n.d.). In Cuba, biomedical and traditional health practices are valued.

Interventions are hampered by the lack of basic medical supplies such as latex and surgical gloves, bone marrow aspiration needles, cancer drugs, antibiotics, anesthetics, and radiology machines.

PREVENTIVE

Prevention of diseases is key to Cuba achieving successful health outcomes. This is perhaps best seen by Cuba being among the first countries to early immunize its population, and eradicate polio, malaria, and diphtheria. Being a tropical country, the eradication of malaria was not an easy accomplishment. By the 1990s, Cuban children were being immunized against 13 childhood diseases, more than any other country, including the United States. In 2006, 99% of the children in Cuba were fully immunized against tuberculosis and measles. There is a low infant mortality rate and 99.9 percent of Cuban babies are born in hospitals.

Community-oriented primary care networks accessible to virtually every family tremendously strengthened Cuba's focus on assisting families to stay healthy, preventing illness, and especially making strides in cleaning up the environment, as well as providing special prenatal care, care to children, and the elderly.

Cuba has committed considerable effort and resources in the area of research into the epidemiology and treatment of diseases, such as sickle cell disease; *cholera*, an acute bacterial infection that presents with excessive diarrhea; *dengue*, mosquito carrying viruses causing severe fever and muscle and skeletal pain; TB; and *leptospirosis*, another severe bacterial infection causing high fever, headache, muscle aches, vomiting, diarrhea and jaundice. Cubans also conduct clinical trials.

RESOURCES

Cubans share a rich cultural heritage and they use both modern medical practitioners as well as traditional methods of treating health problems and preventing illness. The use of alternative therapies and herbal medicines is widespread. There is also a strong sense of community and resourcefulness among Cubans. Literally all AIDS patients are cared for in clinic-like, sanatorium-based facilities. Years ago, from the moment of diagnosis, HIV positive patients were relegated to these small clinic-based communities. Although today they have the option to be treated on an outpatient basis many choose to remain in the sanatorium where they are ensured better care (Merz, 2005).

One of Cuba's greatest resources is the abundance of physicians in their healthcare system. Medical students are socialized early to serve the public, and to enter family medicine practices. Placing nurse/physician clinics strategically where they are most needed serves to strengthen families and communities.

MAJOR HEALTH ISSUES

One of the most challenging healthcare problems in Cuba is unsafe drinking water and the treatment of associated waterborne diseases. An aged water treatment system is partly to blame. This is especially troublesome because parts needed to repair the system, and the much needed water purification chemicals, are too costly to be purchased. Visitors to Cuba are able to purchase bottled water that the average Cuban cannot afford (Randal, 2000). Cuba has also made very little progress in the treatment of cancer.

Some of the health challenges seen in Cuba stem from cultural values. There is a high incidence of obesity. Plump women, babies, and children are considered healthy, a sign of affluency and that they are being well provided for by loved ones. A spicy diet that is high in fat, cholesterol, sugar, and is often fried is part of the problem and accounts for the similarity of health problems to the Western world. In fact, the top three causes of death in Cuba are identical to the United States. The top ten diseases causing death in Cuba are outlined in **Table 11-2**.

DISPARITIES

Although under the Cuban Constitution everyone receives free care, wealthy Cubans are sometimes able to get faster access to care. Cuba's attention to health promotion and the establishment of physician/nurse primary care clinics in neighborhoods has done very well in narrowing the disparity gap between the haves and have nots. The only health indicator that hints of a disparity in Cuba is the relatively high maternal mortality rate of 52.2 per 100,000 live births while at the same time enjoying a relatively low infant mortality rate. The connection between infant and maternal mortality that is often seen is not observed in Cuba.

Table 11-2 Top 10 causes of death (all ages) in Cuba, 2002, with the number and percent of years of life lost by disease.

Disease Deaths	Number	Percent	Years of Life Lost %
All causes	76	100	100
Ischemic heart disease	16	21	15
Cerebrovascular disease	7	10	8
Lower respiratory infections	6	9	5
Trachea, bronchus, lung cancers	3	5	5
Chronic obstructive pulmonary disease	2	3	2
Prostate cancer	1	3	1
Colon and rectal cancers	1	2	2
Self-inflicted injuries	1	2	5
Falls	1	2	1
Alzheimer and other dementias	1	2	1

Data From: Death and DALY estimates by cause, 2002.

http://www.who.int/entity/healthinfo/statistics/bodgbddeathdalyestimates.xls

SUMMARY

The Cuban healthcare system has many positive qualities. If studied carefully much can be learned from the Cuban system. If the accomplishments of Cuba could be reproduced across a broad range of poor and middle income countries, health globally could potentially be transformed (Cooper et al., 2006). Despite the many health challenges in Cuba, in many areas it is doing better than some high income industrialized countries. For example, it outpaces other Latin American countries and the United States in its supply of physicians and dentists per 100,000 in the population.

Discussion Questions

1. In Cuba, doctors and nurses live where they practice. Discuss the advantages of this situation in terms of health outcomes. Are there any drawbacks?

2. Discuss the Cuban diet and its effect on health. To what extent, if any, do you see similar nutrition problems in your work setting? What types of health promotion activities would be effective in addressing Cuba's nutrition challenges. Discuss the pros and cons of these interventions in your work setting.

3. Discuss Cuba's community resources in relation to treating HIV/AIDS. How does your community respond to the needs of those with HIV/AIDS?

4. Cuba's intervention and health promotion activities are family- and community-centered. Discuss the advantages of this strategy.

5. Cuba has placed a high priority on education in general. Explain how education as a priority has impacted Cuba's health status.

Case Scenario

Michael Moore and Cuba

In the United States, the cost of medications to treat common chronic illnesses has escalated so tremendously that many patients stop taking essential medications because they can no longer afford them, whereas in other countries, the cost of the same medication is often less than $1.00. Michael Moore makes this point in *"Sicko,"* his widely debated documentary which spotlights the advanced system of health care in Cuba. In the aftermath of 9/11, many Ground Zero firefighters developed chronic lung problems. They could not afford the respiratory medications and inhalers needed to simply breathe, but in Cuba, and as *"Sicko"* dramatically reveals, firefighters were given the same medications for a fraction of the cost they would have paid in the United States.

DISCUSSION POINTS

1. How does obtaining medication at a low cost in Cuba strike you? Is it a feasible (*sensible*) idea? Why or why not?
2. Would you ever consider Cuba as an alternative to health care? Why or why not? How does being a health practitioner influence your point of view?
3. Do you know people who go to Cuba for medications? What observations have you made?
4. What aspects of Cuba's health system do you think would work out well in the United States?

References

American Association for World Health. (1997). http://www.ncbi.nlm.nih.gov/entrez
Cooper, R. S., Kennelly, J. F., & Ordunez-Garcia, P. (2006). Health in Cuba. *International Journal of Epidemiology.* 35:4 health in Cuba in PubMed.817-824.
Cuba Health Data. MINSAP, Health Statistic's Yearbook (2005). Retrieved from Medical Education Cooperation with Cuba (MEDICC) www.Medicc.org /publication/cuba_ health.../cuba-health-data.php

Drain, P. K. & Barry, M. (2010). Fifty years of US Embargo: Cuba's health outcomes and lessons, *Science, 3218*(5977). www.wired.com/wiredscience/2010/04/cuban-lesson-lessons/

Garfield, R. & Santana, S. (n.d.). *The impact of the economic crisis and the US embargo on health in Cuba.* New York: Columbia University. http://www.pubmedcentral.nih.gov

Graham, J. (1998). The devastating medical results of the U.S. embargo against Cuba. *Journal of International Association of Physicians.* National Institute of Health: AIDS Care. 4:4, 34-5

de Gordon, A. M. (n.d.). Cuba's health in transition and the Central and Eastern European countries experience. http://www.finlay-online.com/finlayinstitute/healthintransiton.htm.

Lasa International. (2001). Structural reform and medical commerce: The political economy of Cuban health care in the special period. http://lasa.international.pitt.edu/Lasa2001/DunningThad.pdf

Merz, C. (2005). The Cuban paradox. *Harvard Public Health Review.* Harvard School of Public Health.

Nation's Encyclopedia. (2009, October). Nationsencyclopedia.com/Americas/Cuba-location-size and extent.html

Pan American Health Organization (PAHO). (2008). Health agenda for the Americas: Cuba. Health_agenda_for_the_Americas_2008-2017.pdf.new.paho.org/h

Randal, J. (2000). Does the U.S. embargo affect Cuban health care? *Journal of the National Cancer Institute.* 92:12. Doi: 10.1093/jnci/92:12,963

Republic of Cuba. (2001). Comprehensive health program for Central America, The Caribbean and Africa. Republic of Cuba: Ministry of Health.

United Nations Human Development Reports. (n.d.). Commitment to health: Resources, access and services. Retrieved, 11/10/10 from http://hdr.undp.org/statistics/data/indicators. cfm?x=58&y=2&z=1

UNO. (2004). Un.org/esa/population/publications/WorldPop.pdf

van Gelder, S. (2006). Cuba's cure: Why is Cuba exporting its health care miracle to the world's poor? http:www.yesmagazine.org/issues/latin-america-rising/cuba-cure

Waki, S. (2002). Mobilisation of Cuban doctors in developing countries. *Lancet,* 360–392.

WHO. (2004). Who.int/whosis/database/core/core_select_process.cfm

WHO. (2005). who.int/health/evidence/atlas/profiles _ countries_c_d.pdf

CHAPTER 12

The Healthcare System in India

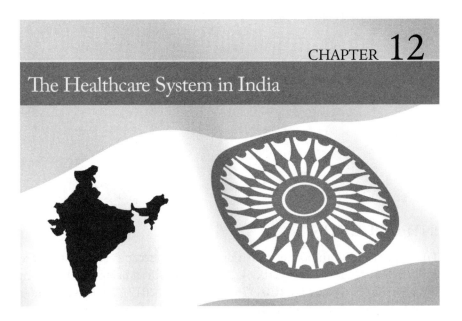

The roof of the house fights the rain, but he who is sheltered ignores it.

—Nigerian Proverb

BEHAVIORAL OBJECTIVES

At the end of this chapter the learner will be able to:

1. Discuss the how India's healthcare system emerged.
2. Discuss the incidence and prevalence of disease.
3. Discuss the top three diseases and related challenges.
4. Determine how health care is structured, financed, and accessed.
5. Identify funding priorities, initiatives, and challenges.
6. Describe health practices that are commonly used to maintain and restore health.
7. Explain how social determinants affect health-seeking beliefs and practices.

KEY CONCEPTS

Activities of daily living

Ayurvedic medicine

Caste

Dalits

Fatalistic

Harijans

Shundras

Telemedicine

Unani

Vaisyas

INTRODUCTION

The population in India has grown over the past decade. Today, there are 1,205,073,612 (CIA World Factbook, 2012) people in India. India's land area is 2,973,192,059 square km (CIA World Factbook, 2012). There is an under 5-year-old mortality rate of 85:1,000 and life expectancy of 62 years. India's largest ethnic groups are Indo-Aryan, and Dravidian. Its major religions are Hindu, Muslim, Sikh, and Christian (WHO, 2005). India has a low literacy rate, and, as is true of most developing countries, it has a high infant mortality rate. Similar to Ghana, India is devastatingly poor but the economy is improving as a consequence of the United States' overseas cheap labor employment opportunities. India is a male-dominated society. Women are subservient to males. Many women do not aspire to work outside the home, (or are content with remaining home, or not working outside the home). Men have traditionally had first priority for attending school.

India's Ministry of Health has a poorly managed and funded National Health Care System. Residents receive acute care only. True of much of the developing world, many chronic, infectious diseases due to major public health problems like contaminated water and poor sanitation plague India. India's endemic problems include cholera, and CR-Malaria. There are incentives (money and prizes) given for voluntary male sterilization. The predominant religion is Hindu, which accounts for approximately 83% of those native to India. Approximately 11% are Islamic Muslim. It is not uncommon for Indians to take the *fatalistic* view of health and view sickness as God's will. Death is welcomed as natural, cremation is preferred, and there is an anticipation of reincarnation.

HISTORICAL

Indians practice what is called Ayurvedic medicine (also called *ayurveda*) a traditional medicine utilizing the healing arts that balances the use of herbal remedies and medical practices. Many rural and urban poor rely on alternative treatments such as acupuncture, Ayurvedic, and Unani medicine. According to Spector (2009), Ayurvedic medicine, a 4,000 year old method of healing the body, is one of the oldest systems of medicine in the world. It is accredited with laying the foundation for Chinese medicine. It is similar to CAM in that herbs, specialized diets, and natural therapies are used to integrate and balance the body, mind, and spirit. Similarly, *Unani* medicine is based on the humoral theory that presupposes the presence of four humors; Dum (blood), Balgham (phlegm), Safra (yellow bile), and Sauda (black bile). The body, when in balance, has the power to maintain balance of these humors (unanidoctors.com, n.d.).

Universal health enjoys a long history in India. In similarity to other developing countries, during the mid-80s with healthcare expenditures varying greatly among states and union territories, Indian leaders committed to health for all by 2000. There has been a growth in the health industry of about 12% per year in the last four years (moneycontrol.com, 2007).

STRUCTURE

There is a serious health provider shortage in India. Forty percent of the primary health centers are understaffed. According to the WHO (sero.who.int, n.d.) India produces over 25,000 physicians annually in the modern system of medicine and more than 400 a year in the Indian system of medicine and homeopathy (IM&H). Yet, there remains a tremendous shortage of not only physicians but nurses and paramedics. India licenses approximately 18,000 new physicians every year, as many migrate to more prosperous, developing countries to practice. According to the Planning Commission Government of India (2002–2007), in 2000, there were approximately 1.25 million doctors and 0.8 million nurses in India; one doctor for every 1,800 people. When counting the indigenous doctors and homeopaths this ratio is one doctor for 800 people. The overall ratio of doctors to population in rural area is almost six times lower than that in the urban population (Central Bureau of Health Intelligence, 2001). It is difficult to determine the accuracy in physician numbers because, although doctors are registered to practice in India, many have emigrated to other countries to practice and some are left in the system even after they have died (Medical & Tourism).

Despite the existence of well-funded healthcare centers of excellence, India has poor health outcomes. These state of the art centers are too few and inadequate to meet the healthcare needs of the masses. The number of hospital beds in India grew from 11,174 (57% private) in 1991 to 18,218 (75% private) in 2007 (Central Bureau of Health Intelligence, 2001). India also has a large gap in the availability of hospital beds to serve the people in rural areas. Its infrastructure has failed to keep pace with the growing economy. India also does over a 260 billion (INR) pharmaceutical business, exporting a significant amount of the drugs manufactured (Ministry of Chemicals and Fertilizers, 2001–2002).

FINANCING

India spends a total of $14.8 billion annually on health care. This equates to approximately 5.2% of its GDP. It is predicted that India will spend $33.6 billion by 2012, which accounts for 8.5% of the GDP (WHO, 2007). India's healthcare system is a system that is grossly inadequate and underfunded. According to WHO (2003) "only five other countries in the world are worse off than India regarding public health spending" (Burundi, Myanmar, Pakistan, Sudan, and Cambodia). Despite relatively low overall spending on health care, state expenditures are even lower, only (0.9%) of the GDP (Deogaonkar, 2004).

The state government contributes approximately 15.2% to the financing of health care, the central government contributes 5.2%, third party insurance companies and employers contribute 3.3%, and municipal and foreign donors contribute an additional 1.3%. The World Bank suggests that nearly 59% of this money goes to fund primary health care (curative, preventive, and health promotion). Another 39% is spent on secondary and tertiary inpatient care. The government run General Insurance Company (GIC) along with four subsidiaries are the major providers of insurance. Out-of-pocket expenditures are high and account for 98.4% of the total health expenditures by household.

The private sector accounts for more than 80% of total healthcare expenditures in India. "Eighty-two percent of health expenditure in India is made as out of pocket payments by the user of the service," (Deogaonkar, 2004, p. 4). The per capita expenditure on public health is seven times lower in rural areas than urban areas (Central Bureau of Health Intelligence, 2001).

INTERVENTIONAL

According to the Indian Institute of Medicine (2005), private firms provide approximately 60% of all outpatient care in India, and approximately 40% of all inpatient care. Approximately 70% of the hospitals in India are private sector owned and operated. One of the most significant attempts at providing quality care interventions in India is the promotion of the use of primary health centers in delivery of care. However, these centers are understaffed, personnel are underpaid, and equipment and supplies are lacking (Deogaonkar, 2004).

Approximately one million Indians die each year because of the insufficient treatment facilities and lack of personnel to meet the care demands of the country. Another major interventional consideration is that the northern areas of India have the greatest healthcare needs yet this area tends to have the most difficult access challenges. There is also an urban/rural divide reflected by the significantly fewer hospitals and services in the rural Indian communities as compared to the urban areas. For example, in 2005 there were 178 hospitals and 3.6 clinics in urban areas compared to 9.85 and 0.36 in rural areas. The federal government funded program called the National Rural Health Mission 2005–2012 works to improve rural health.

In India, long-term care and care of older adults are regarded as better than in many other countries. In fact, individuals are beginning to retire to India in search of better long-term care options. India is not only a top destination for medical tourism for persons searching for low cost surgery and other treatments but it is becoming a popular destination for retirement. According to Chicago Tribune reporter Kidd Stewart (2007, p.3) outsourcing ill parents to India costs considerably less than caring for them in the United States. In India, $2,000 a month covers a nursing home stay in a resort-like plush facility on the coast of India for two persons. This cost also covers food, utilities, medications, telephone, 24-hour staffing by very low paid, but good staff. Medications are about 20% less than the same drugs in the United States. Although there appears to be substantial accommodations for older adults in the Indian system of health, these facilities are not available to older people who have mental and/or physical disabilities. It is suspected these individuals would require assistance in carrying out activities of daily living (Dey, 2006), which includes such things as bathing, dressing, meal preparations, and light housekeeping.

In regard to medical tourism, it has become a big business in India. It is estimated that medical tourism made an estimated $350 million in 2006. It is predicted to grow into a $2 billion industry by 2012 (Confederation of India Industry, 2006). India proposes that it delivers the best treatment, often at less than one-tenth the cost of the same treatment in the United States and other industrialized countries. Its private hospitals excel in cardiology, joint replacements, orthopedics, gastroenterology, ophthalmology, transplants, and urology (India Brand Foundation Report, 2007). For example, according to the Brand Foundation Report, cardiac surgery in the United States costs $50,000; it costs $14,200 in Thailand and $4,000 in India. A liver transplant costs approximately $500,000 in the United States, $75,000 in Thailand, and $45,000 in India. It is believed that medical tourism leverages India's well educated, English speaking medical staff, and its state of the art private hospitals and diagnostic facilities.

Many western tourists travel to India also seeking alternative medicine treatment such as ayurveda. For example, the number of medical tourists visiting Kerala in southwestern India was approximately 15,000 in 2006, but it was predicted that this number would reach 100,000 by 2010 (Blonnet, 2007). There is a new initiative underway to establish a public/private partnership for the purpose of building a 900 bed, "Medi City" on 43 acres of land near the outskirts of Delhi. It is suspected that this facility will have the capacity to offer 17 super specialties, and a medical college and para-medical college, with an integration of allopathic and alternative medicine and care including unani, ayurvedic, homeopathic, and telemedicine. *Telemedicine* is an approach to practicing medicine that allows for the diagnosis and treatment of diseases remotely over long distances by use of videoconferencing, cabled networks, and the internet. There are already approximately 100 telemedicine centers in India. Telemedicine is popular in many industrialized countries (Blonnet, 2007).

In general, Indians lack dental coverage (Parkash et al., 2006). Dental care is almost unheard of in India. As people age in any system the quality of their lives is often determined by their health status, this includes dental health. If they are healthy and active they are likely to enjoy quality during their advancing age. Dey (2006) suggests that, "of the many determinants of the quality of life: financial security, emotional security and health and well being, the last one occupies the prime position, as all other issues become irrelevant in poor health" (p.134). Further, India lacks a clear policy or strategy for the development of health care for older people. A comprehensive care package that includes, "promotive, preventive, curative and rehabilitative services is essential for this population group" (Dey, 2006, p. 134).

PREVENTIVE

Prevention is perhaps the most serious challenge in Indian health care partly because of inadequate funding and a disparity in regard to access especially for the poor. Because health insurance is inaccessible to large numbers of Indians, prevention is a major problem.

All over India a vast number of its poorest residents are packed together in what is being referred to as the new slums. These make-shift, cardboard-constructed, shanty town appearing shelters that can be seen for miles in many areas of India. These communities lack clean water, electricity, sanitation (UN-HABITAT, 2007; Joshi, n.d.). These conditions are perfect breeding grounds for diseases, especially infections. To further complicate the situation, people living in the more permanent building structures exhibit similar health problems. Prevention under these circumstances is difficult.

As one visitor to India puts it, "from the comfort of my four star hotel room, I looked across the roadway and sprawled out for miles and miles, all I could see were flickers of light breaking through the otherwise total darkness, that I knew emanated from small make shift fires surrounding the cardboard shanties that seemed to consume the entire city. My heart was heavy with pain and a sense of shame for the conditions under which these people were striving to just survive. How blessed I felt to have more than just what I needed to not just survive but to thrive."

As lifestyles began changing in India due to improved economic growth, much of which is related to jobs being outsourced to India from the industrialized world, there has been a growth in India's middle class. There has also been an increase in some of the same top diseases such as cardiovascular diseases and diabetes that are seen in the developed world.

RESOURCES

Family is a major human resource in India. Although every region has its own unique characteristics and traditions, especially in relation to housing preferences and lifestyles, there are many similarities. Despite the customs, language, religion, or caste affiliations, Indians live together, relatively harmoniously. Family, defined as extended, is a source of support throughout life in India. Roles and responsibilities are influenced by age and gender. Children are cherished and considered as gifts from God and they have full support from their families for their entire lives because family progress, unity, and support is held in the highest regard for life.

There are genuine displays of respect for family, especially parental and elder respect. Parents and grandparents are looked to for guidance and support through many of life's challenges. For example, arranged marriages are still the norm although younger Indians however, through their intrigue by the western world's love-based marriages, are beginning to pressure their parents to respect their individual choices of a spouse. They are also beginning to reject the tradition of marriage signifying the joining of two families as one. Public display of affection, even between married couples is taboo and often misinterpreted by outsiders. This is especially misunderstood by health professionals in the western world.

In regard to roles, responsibilities, and financial support, although men have traditionally assumed primary responsibility for financially supporting their families, women are beginning to work more. But, especially in the urban areas, women have for many years often worked and contributed to the family's income. Despite working, women remain primarily responsible for maintaining the household and caring for the children and aged relatives (Rampur, 2009). This is especially difficult if the parent or grandparent happens to be chronically ill. However, even though the woman has a career, she must still care for sick family members.

There are a variety of living conditions in India. Rich urban families enjoy modern homes, servants, and cars; the middle classes usually live in apartments or smaller homes. Poor families live in simple huts or scantly roofed houses. Many of India's poorest residents live in what is referred to as the 21st century slums which presents some of India's greatest challenges.

Religion is also a strong support for families who are ill and particularly those at or near the end of their lives. Approximately 82% of Indians practice Hinduism. Reincarnation is central to the Hindu religion. Other religions include Buddhism, Christianity, Sikhism, Islam, and most recently, Methodist. Although only 3% of the Indian population is Christian, 50% of Dalits (the untouchables, oppressed) are Christians (www.hrw.org 2000). The cultural and religious backgrounds of patients and their families should be included in the assessment made by health professionals attempting to identify the best treatment options for the patient.

MAJOR HEALTH ISSUES

India is a disease-ridden country. Its people suffer from such diseases as malaria and tuberculosis. In fact, one-third of the world's tuberculosis cases are in India. Also, polio, although eradicated in most of the world is still prevalent in India. Although there has been a decrease in the incidence of diseases such as polio, leprosy, and neonatal tetanus in India, there has been a rise in drug resistant dengue fever, viral hepatitis, tuberculosis, malaria, and pneumonia (Gubler, 1999). There is also an unusually high incidence of Type 2 diabetes (Abate & Chandalia, 2001) known also as non-insulin dependent diabetes.

The lack of clean water, poor sanitation, growth of new 21st century slums, and malnutrition are but a few of the challenges overshadowing efforts by the country to promote health and prevent illness. India's malnutrition rates are among the highest in the world, contributing to almost 6 million deaths of children every year, more than half the world's total (Pandey, 2006).

According to the WHO, 900,000 Indians die each year because they consume contaminated drinking water and are breathing polluted air (Robinson, 2008). The majority of these deaths, approximately 700,000, result from diarrheal illnesses contracted from contaminants in the water supply. The number of persons living with AIDS in India is estimated to between 2 and 3 million. The top ten diseases causing death and years of life lost due to these diseases in India are listed on **Table 12-1**.

Disparities

One-fifth of maternal deaths and one quarter of child deaths in the world occur in India (UNICEF, 2009). Also India has one of the lowest life expectancies and highest infant and child mortality rates in the world (WHO, 2010). There is also a rural/urban divide in India reflected by major access problems especially in the rural areas of India. This is reflected by substantial rural/urban differentials in the allocation of resources, and the lack of available doctors and hospitals. However, there is a noticeable access problem in the urban cities of India partly as a result of urban slums that become the foundation of communicable diseases that widely spread under these conditions. Also data from urban slums show infant and under-five mortality rates for the poorest 40% of the urban population are as high as the rural areas (Deogaonkar, 2004).

Table 12-1 Top 10 causes of death (all ages) in India, 2002, with the number and percent of years of life lost by disease.

Disease Deaths	Number	Percent	Years of life lost %
All causes	105	100	100
1. Ischemic heart disease	153	15	7
2. Lower respiratory infections	110	11	13
3. Cerebrovascular disease	771	7	3
4. Perinatal conditions	762	7	13
5. Chronic obstructive pulmonary disease	485	5	2
6. Diarrheal diseases	456	4	8
7. Tuberculosis	364	4	4
8. HIV/AIDS	361	3	4
9. Road traffic accidents	189	2	2
10. Self-inflicted injuries	182	2	3

Data From: Death and DALY estimates by cause, 2002.

http://www.who.int/entity/healthinfo/statistics/bodgbddeathdalyestimates.xls

Health outcomes, though improved over the years, are still strongly determined by factors such as gender, caste, wealth, education, and geography (Subramanian, Ackerson, Subramanyam, & Sivaramakrishnan, 2008; Subramanian, Nandy, Irving, Gordon, Lambert, & Davey Smith, 2006; Subramanian, Davey Smith, & Subramanyam, 2006). India's 3500 year old caste system, although illegal today, is still practiced. It is the longest surviving social hierarchy existing in the world. The system is typically characterized by four distinct levels, and once you are born into a caste you remain in that caste for life. The highest caste is Brahmins, the thinkers, philosophers, priests, and teachers. The next highest caste is Ksyatriyas, the rulers and warriors who are concerned with defending and governing the state. The third level, the Vaisyas, are merchants and traders, and the fourth level, the *Shundras,* are laborers, artisans, and menial workers. The Shundras became known as the *Harijans* (God's children), previously referred to as the untouchables, and most recently this group has been called *Dalit,* or oppressed (Murthy & Daniels, 2005). A major concern when a patient enters the healthcare system is that they receive quality care irrespective of who they are or their financial status.

SUMMARY

Similar to other countries, the hallmark difference in India's healthcare system is primary care. Despite a lack of resources, there has been substantial improvement in the addressing of many health problems plaguing this society. Initiatives such as primary care centers of excellence, major pharmaceutical business, and medical health tourism have been successful. However, there is a need to expand insurance coverage and services to rural areas. Overcrowding, regional funding differences, disparities in access to healthcare services, and the lack of dental care are among some of India's greatest challenges.

Discussion Questions

1. Among the many challenges India faces in its healthcare system are the 21st century slums. Why has this become such an uncontrolled problem in India? What specific strategies can you identify to minimize the effect on the overall health of Indian people?

2. Describe India's greatest public health challenge. Can you identify similar challenges in your setting? What, if anything, can be done to address this problem?

3. The caste system is one of the oldest hierarchical systems in the world. How does the caste system influence health decisions, beliefs, and practices in India? Identify beliefs and practices in your healthcare setting that compare to the caste system?

4. India is beginning to experience a shift in its economy. If you headed the Ministry of Health of India, as financial resources were available what would you identify as your greatest health priority, and why?

Case Scenario

Misunderstood

Mrs. Madan, a 28-year-old East Indian came to the United States three months ago to join her husband who has been in the United States for one year. She is approximately 5 months pregnant with her first child but has not yet been examined by a doctor. She arrives in a local emergency department, accompanied by her husband with whom she has no physical contact throughout the encounter. When the couple entered the emergency department Mrs. Madan walked several feet behind her husband, her eyes were red and slightly swollen. The admitting nurse said she assumed she had been crying. When asked direct questions she repeatedly deferred to her husband who insisted on being present for the entire assessment, but otherwise sat silently across the room. Mr. Madan reports his wife was complaining of a headache, toothache, vomiting, diarrhea, and very little sleep for three days. They are concerned about the effect of Mrs. Madan's condition on the baby.

Throughout the emergency department stay, Mrs. Madan spoke very little, allowing her husband to be her spokesperson. During her exam the women's health nurse practitioner closely examined her for bruises, but found none. After the exam, the nurse practitioner told Mr. Madan his wife was dehydrated, and the plan was to draw blood to send to the lab, hydrate her intravenously, watch her overnight, and reevaluate her the next morning. He agreed, told his wife he would see her in the morning and left the hospital. The nurse practitioner questioned Mrs. Madan about her husband's seeming lack of concern, and asked about her red eyes and the possibility of spousal abuse? She was offended, and insisted her husband was a good man, supportive and affectionate when in private. Mr. Madan returned early the next morning to find his wife and unborn baby were both fine and that his wife could go home. She was encouraged to rest and drink plenty of fluids, and was given multivitamin samples and a referral to be seen the next day by an obstetrician. He thanked the staff and took his wife home.

DISCUSSION POINTS

1. What do you believe accounted for Mrs. Madan's dehydration?
2. Explain the nurse practitioner's actions regarding the assumption that Mrs. Madan was a victim of spousal abuse? Why did she not confront the husband?
3. Why did Mrs. Madan refuse to speak for herself? What do you think about Mrs. Madan allowing her husband to speak for her?
4. What do you think accounts for Mrs. Madan's three day toothache? Why didn't the nurse practitioner make a dental referral for Mrs. Madan?

REFERENCES

Abate, N. & Chandalia, M. (2001). Ethnicity and type 2 diabetes: Focus on Asian Indians. *Journal of Diabetes and its Complications, 15,* 320–327.

Blonnet. (2007). http://www.blonnet.com/2007/04/02/stories/2007040205221500.htm

Centers for Disease Control. http://www.cdc.gov/nicdod/dvbid/dengue/

Central Bureau of Health Intelligence. (2001). Directorate general of health services, Ministry of health and family welfare. Health information of India.

CIA World Factbook. (2012). Retrieved on 7/12/12 from, http://www.files.explore.org/files/The_World_Factbook_-India.pdf

Confederation of India Industry, McKinsey, Finance wire July, 2006.

Daniels, A. (2005). Restorative justice and India's caste system.

Daniels, A. (2005). The caste system in India. Retrieved from: http//:www.adaniel.tripod.com/castes.htm

Deogaonkar, M. (2004). Socioeconomic inequality and its effect on healthcare delivery in India: Inequality and health care. *Electronic Journal of Sociology.* p. 7.

Dey, A. B. (2006, December). Emerging challenges of old age care in India. *Journal of the Indian Academy of Geriatrics, 2*(4).

Gates, B. (n.d.). Senate Foreign Relations. Lack of dental health professionals.com http://cii.in/menu_content.php?menu_id=238

Gubler, D. J. (1999). Prevention and control of dengue and dengue haemorrhagic fever. WHO Regional publication. SEARO No. 29: New Delhi, India. Retrieved, December 18, 2010 from http://www.cdc.gov/nicidod/dvbid/pubs/dengue-pubs.htm

Hrw. world atlas-India. Go.hrw.com/atlas/norm_ htm/india.htm. Religions based on 2000 data.

India Brand Foundation Report. (n.d.), IBEF Research. ibef.org/aboutus.aspx.

Infoplease. (2010). A profile of the world factbook.geography_India. http://infoplease.com/ipa0762380.html

Joshi, R., Jaw, S., & Wu, Y. (n.d.). 21st century slums in India presents the greatest health challenges in India.

Kidd-Stewart, J. (2007, October 7). Outsourcing ill parents to India: Outsourcing for retirement. *Chicago Tribune*, p. 3.

Medical+Tourism. (n.d.). http://202.131.96.59:8080/dspace/bitstream123456789 /113/1/Medical+Tourism-Pheba+Chacko.pdf.

Ministry of Chemicals and Fertilizers, Government of India. Annual report, 2001–2002.

Moneycontrol.com. (2007, June 27). India's healthcare industry to see mammoth growth: McKinsey. Retrieved December 10, 2010 from http://www.moneycontrol .com/news/business/india's-healthcare-industry-to-see-mammoth-growth –mckinsey-289024.html

Pandey, G. (2006). Hunger critical in South Asia. http://news.bbc.co.uk/2/hi /south_asia/6046718.stm.BBC

Parkash, H., Mathur, VP., Duggal, R., & Jhuraney, B. (2006). Dental workforce issues: A global concern. *Journal of Dental Education, 70*(11), 22–26.

Planning Commission Government of India. (2002–2007). Tenth five year plan, volume II. In: Deogaonkar, M. Socioeconomic inequality and its effect on healthcare delivery in India: Inequality and health care, 2004.

Rampur, S. (2009, April 22). Family life in India. Buzzle/articles/family-life—in -India.html Searo.who.int. http://searo. Nationalhealthprofile/ linkfiles/India.

Robinson, S. (2008). India's medical emergency. Time Magazine, May 1, 2008. Retrieved 10 November, 2010 from www.time.com/time/magazine/article /0,9171,1736516-1,00.html

Spector, R. (2009). *Cultural Diversity in Health and Illness.* New Jersey: Pearson-Prentice Hall.

Searo.who.int.http://searo.who.int. *The Times of India.* Retrieved November 12, 2010 from http://economictimes.indiatimes.com/healthcare/lacking_healthcare _ a_million_Indians_die_every_year_Oxford_University/articleshow/4066183

Subramanin, S., Ackerson, V. K., Subramyam, M. A., & Sivaramakrishnan, K. (2008). Health inequalities in India: The axes of stratification. *Brown Journal of World Affairs.*14, 127–139.

Subramanin, S., Nandy, S., Irving, M., Gordon, D., Lambert, H., & Davey Smith, G. (2006). The mortality divide in India: The differential contributions of gender, caste, and standard of living across the life course. *American Journal of Public Health.* 96, 818–25.

Subramanian, K., Davey Smith, G., & Subramanyam, M. (2008). Indigenous health and socioeconomic status in India. *PLoS Medicine.* 3:e421

Unanidoctors.com (n.d). Unani Medicine. www.unanidoctors.com/unanimedicine .htm

UN-HABITAT. (2007). Slums of the world: The face of urban poverty in the new millennium? http://www.unhabitat.org/publication/slumreport.pdf

UNICEF. (2009). *The state of the world's children: Maternal and newborn health.* New York: United Nations Children's Fund. New York: United Nations.

WHO. (2003). *The world health report 2003*. India country profile health resources. Sero.who.int/en/section313/section1519_10852.htm

WHO. (2005). www.who.int/profiles_countries, 2005

WHO. (2007). Status report on macroeconomics and health, India. Retrieved December 10, 2010 from http://www.who.int/macrohealth/action/en/rep04 _india.pdf

WHO. (2010). Global health Indicators: Part II. Retrieved December 10, 2011 from http://www.who.int/whosis/whostat/EN_WHS10_part2.pdf

CHAPTER 13

The Healthcare System in the Russian Federation

Understanding human needs is half the job of meeting them.

—Adlai Stevenson

BEHAVIORAL OBJECTIVES

At the end of this chapter the learner will be able to:

1. Explain the impact of transition on Russia's health status.
2. Explain the influence of Soviet health care on the new Russia.
3. Identify key factors that affect health promotion in Russia.
4. Describe challenges to providing efficiently run health care in the Russian Federation.
5. Identify the strengths and weaknesses of Russia's health care.

KEY CONCEPTS

Overcapacity

San–epid network

Semashko Model

The Guaranteed Package Program

INTRODUCTION

Russia, officially known as the Russian Federation, is the largest country in the world, covering an area of 17 million square km (6.5 million square miles) estimated at 1.8 times the size of the United States (U.S. Department of State Background Note Russia, 2011). This vast country is located in Northern Asia between Europe and the Pacific Ocean. Russia's enormous geography is matched by its wide diversity. The Russian population descends from over 100 ethnic groups; 79.8% are ethnic Russians; 3.8% Tatar, 2% Ukrainian, and 14.4%, other (U.S. Department of State, Background Note Russia, 2011). With a population density of 9 people per square km (22 persons per square mile) Russia is sparsely populated; most people live in the urban areas such as Moscow, the capital of Russia, and St. Petersburg, Russia's second largest city. The proportion of the population under 15 is 15% (UNO 2004) and the population above the age of 60 years is 18%. The main language used in the country is Russian. The largest ethnic group is Russian. The largest religious group is Russian Orthodox (75%) and the other religious group is Muslim.

Russia has one of the highest literacy rates in the world at 99.4 % (CIA, 2011). The Russians are noted for their pioneer work in laser eye surgery and heart surgery. With the dissolution of the Soviet Union, Russia moved from a centrally planned economy to a market economy (World Bank, 2011).

Russia's health status has been described as grim, dire, substandard, and below Western standards. Another observation emphasizes the magnitude of Russia's problems: "On virtually every health indicator, Russia lags considerably behind her European neighbors and is among the most vulnerable of the European and Eurasian countries" (Gerry, 2011).

The breakup of the Soviet Union stands as the extraordinary experience that profoundly affected Russia's health outcomes. "Russia continues to struggle with a health and mortality crisis. The deterioration in basic indicators of health and human welfare that began in the Soviet period and accelerated after the Soviet collapse has yet to be overcome" (Tompson, 2007, p.6). The transition from communism found the new Russia facing economic uncertainty, political turmoil, and psychological trauma. People were not prepared for the "drastic reversal" (Nuti, 2009, p. 33) of their everyday lives. Transition brought unemployment, poverty, the loss of free or subsidized services, and feelings of vulnerability and powerlessness (Nuti, 2009). Public funding for health took a heavy blow, seriously impacting "all aspects of medical care from prevention to emergency treatment" (Curtis, 1996).

For several decades, and most prominently, since the fall of the Soviet Union in 1991, the Russian population has been shrinking. By the turn of the 21st century, the Russian population declined by six million (Gerry, 2011). Russia's severe demographic decline can be attributed to abnormally high mortality rates, particularly for adult males, and exceptionally low birth rates (Kumo, 2010). The replacement rate to maintain a population is considered to be 2.1 births per woman (CIA, 2010). Russia's total fertility rate falls short of this standard. In 1989, a few years before the breakup of the Soviet Union, Russia's fertility rate was 2.01, then plummeted to 1.20 in both 1999 and 2000, and rose to 1.5 in 2007 (Kumo, 2010). "Countries elsewhere in Europe have fertility levels that are equally low or even lower, but the Russian demographic predicament is aggravated by mortality that is exceptionally high by modern standards" (Vladimir Putin on Raising Russia's Birth Rate., June 2006, p.385).

Mortality rates for working-age males (15–64) and middle-aged males (40–64) have become part of Russia's disturbing mortality profile (Shishkin & Vlassov, 2009; Marquez, Suhrcke, McKee, & Rocco, 2007) "Russian male mortality rates are higher than those of other countries with similar per capita incomes. The only countries that are farther above the trend line are countries in Africa that have suffered from HIV AIDS" (Marquez et al., 2007, p. 1040). Russian life expectancy at birth is 66.46 years: 72.18 years for women, and 60.11 years for men (CIA, 2012). "At present levels of mortality, fewer than six out of ten fifteen-year-old Russian males can expect to survive to age sixty while almost eight out of ten Brazilian or Turkish males and nine out of ten British males that same age can expect to do so" (Marquez et al., 2007, p. 1041). Current data based on WHO estimates indicate 40 million smokers in Russia; the prevalence of smoking any tobacco products in adults is 70% in males and 28% in females; and there are an officially registered 2.5 million alcoholics: 80% male and 20% female (USAID, 2010).

The infant mortality rate in 2010 was 9 deaths per 1,000, down from 10 in 2009 and 11 in 2008 (World Bank, 2012). Abortion has figured significantly in Russia's declining population and appears to be used as the primary method of birth control. In their look at contraceptive use in several countries, Deschner and Cohen (2003) observed, "Russia legalized abortion in 1955 in response to the public health problem of illegal procedures. At that time, it was not uncommon for a woman wanting only two children to have 10 or more abortions in her lifetime, and as late as 1990, Russia's abortion rate was well over 100 per 1,000 women of reproductive age" (p.8).

According to USAID 2010 and United Nations Millennium Goal documents, despite the decline in abortion rates over the past decade as well as reform efforts to improve the maternal health of women, Russia's abortion rate (53.7/1,000, UNdata, 2012) remains among the world's highest, profoundly affecting maternal mortality, morbidity, and overall fertility rates

(Westoff, 2005). An uncertain economy and the loss of free or low cost child care since the transition may be contributing factors to Russia's low birth rates (Kumo, 2010). Russian mortality is further affected by growing incidences of TB and HIV. According to the National Foundation of Infectious Diseases (NFID) nearly 2 billion people, one third of the world's population, have TB. In 2008, an estimated 440,000 people worldwide had multi drug resistant Tuberculosis (MDR-TB) one-third of whom died. Based on WHO data in 2007, Russia has an estimated 115 TB cases per 100,000 population (UNdata, 2012).

Global statistics estimate 33.3 million people around the world living with HIV/AIDS in 2009 (UNAIDS Global Report, 2010). Russia has the second-highest HIV prevalence in Eastern Europe and Eurasia: 1.1% of the adult population, compared in 2007 with 0.2% in the United Kingdom, and 0.4% in France (UNAIDS Global Report, 2010). An estimated 940,000 people in Russia were living with HIV in 2007. In 2009, approximately 1.4 million people in Russia, Eastern Europe, and Central Asia were living with HIV; around 130,000 became infected in 2009 and 76,000 died (AVERT.org).

HISTORICAL

Russia's current system of health care is rooted in its communist past. The Soviet approach to health care was based on a belief in preserving a healthy workforce, and supporting the health of mothers and children for the future security of the nation (Curtis, 1996).The Soviet system of health care followed the *Semashko Model*, a highly centralized, tax funded system (Grielen, Boerma, & Groenewegen, 2000) developed by Nikolai Semashko, People's Commissar of Public Health from 1918 to 1930. Semashko was involved in restructuring a health system devastated by the impact of World War I and the famine and disease following the Russian Revolution. Under this model, medical personnel were hired by the state, and medical facilities were government owned and regulated. The tight control of this health system extended to the Ministry of Health, charged with the responsibility of ensuring compliance with state norms.

The Semashko system is noted for its strong emphasis on the control of epidemics and infectious diseases which resulted in the development of the Public Health Sanitation Epidemiological system or *san-epid network*. Additional positive contributions associated with the Semashko model include an advanced curative service infrastructure, and the establishment of primary health care in rural and urban settings through health posts or polyclinics (Vienonen & Vohlonen, 2001). In 1978, Russia hosted the first Alma Ata Conference on Primary Health Care which urged the world community to recognize that helping people attain good health required action on social and economic levels, not just health, and that primary care was the first critical step in bringing people through a quality healthcare process (Vienonen & Vohlonen, 2001).

In spite of these accomplishments, the Semashko Model had many weaknesses that the new Russia is now struggling to overcome. For example, the system's intense resolve to control infectious diseases led to the over-provision of beds. Because Soviet Russia placed so much emphasis on hospital and specialist care, primary care was marginalized (Vienonen & Vohlonen, 2001). Tompson (2007) adds that attention to noncommunicable diseases also suffered under this model. Although the Semashko Model idealized quality professional care, physicians were undervalued, poorly trained, and paid low wages—a situation which created a long standing tradition of de facto privatization or under-the-table payments (Curtis, 1996). While staff numbers were high, Rechel and Mckee (2009) point out that "access to labor saving technology was poor" (p.1186). Another weakness of the Semashko Model was the lack of evidence-based practice (Vienonen & Vohlonen, 2001).

STRUCTURE

With the collapse of the Soviet Union, the Russian Federation moved to a decentralized organization of health care. The Russian Federation consists of 83 federal subjects. Under the current structure, administrative responsibilities are divided at the federal (state), regional (oblast), and municipal levels. The Ministry of Health operates as the highest administrative level formulating healthcare policy, and providing oversight of the healthcare system. Russia's healthcare delivery is hierarchically organized. Basic services are available in rural areas and more complex medical and diagnostic services are available in urban settings. The cities include several specialized hospitals (e.g., emergency care, cardiology) and separate facilities for specific diseases (e.g., tuberculosis, sexually transmitted diseases) known as dispensaries (Borowitz et al., 1999). In the urban setting, "First contact primary care is delivered through a wide array of healthcare institutions including adult and children polyclinics, women's consultation centers, and for specific diseases, the outpatient component of dispensaries" (Borowitz et al., 1999, p.8). Primary care in rural settings is geographically situated covering specific populations (1,500–2,000 people). The first contact for most people seeking help in rural settings is a health center that may be staffed by a physician, a midwife, and a dentist. Smaller rural clinics, known as health posts, or Feldsher stations, provide simple treatments, referral, and health promotion (Borowitz et al., 1999). Feldshers, referred to as physician assistants, have three and one-half years of medical education beyond high school. Feldsher training includes three to eight weeks rotating through clinical specialities such as internal medicine, pediatrics, surgery, gynecology and orthopedics (Multak, 2010). Feldshers play a critical role in primary care in the rural setting, often acting independently and serving large populations. In her detailed account of feldsher training and practice in the Ukraine, Multak (2010) adds, "Feldshers in rural clinics perform history and physical exam, prescribe medications, perform follow-up-evaluations, and refer patients to physicians in the hospitals when needed" (p.45). In Russia's decentralized system of health care, the regions and the municipalities are the major actors in the provision of health care to the population (System Overview, 2010; Tompson, 2007). Russia's move to a decentralized system was founded on the expectation that the unique needs of the people would be identified more accurately and addressed more efficiently; decentralization would facilitate equitable access to health care. However, what would appear as a positive approach to healthcare organization has generated several problems.

Significant weaknesses in Russia's healthcare delivery system are attributed to a lack of communication between healthcare givers, creating problems in duplication of services, patients frequently using emergency services, and huge gaps in continuity of care. Vienonen & Vohlonen (2001) observe that "the primary healthcare system, although it exists as a collection of physical settings and staff, is poorly thought through, and underutilized" (p. 2). Further, the authors assert that improving primary care will require strong legislation and appropriate economic incentives: "So far, no one in Russian health policy has really wanted to challenge the establishment of specialist clinics which are bound to experience a major decline in their clientele and revenues if the first contact level (general practice) is really allowed to function" (p. 7).

FINANCING

Healthcare financing in the Russian Federation includes public and private funding; however, the predominant financing scheme is the public sector (Tompson, 2007). Analysts of Russia's healthcare systems suggest that the lack of regulation of private healthcare and voluntary insurance programs significantly reduces the availability and quality of medical services for people under universal coverage by the state (Davydov & Shepin, 2010). One Russian physician offers her perspective on why private healthcare and voluntary health insurance programs are not popular options:

"The state fund covers a basic healthcare package; however citizens who can afford private insurance can ensure that they receive the best medical care available. Private medical services include treatment by specialists, hospitalization, prescriptions, pregnancy and childbirth, and rehabilitation. Few can afford this option; but those in dire need of good medical care may be forced to take out private insurance; for example a retired pensioner is entitled to free health care in at least one institution. If the treatment given in that institution is not satisfactory, he must decide whether to spend five years of pension allowance on a single year of health care" (Personal narrative, March, 2011).

Russia uses a budget/insurance model (Davydov & Shepin, 2010) to finance public health. Article 41 of the Russian Constitution guarantees every citizen the right to free health care. This is achieved through federal, regional, and municipality budgets in addition to the Mandatory Medical Insurance program passed into law in 1993. The Russian Federation introduced the insurance program to increase government funding for health care, expand patient options for medical care, and stimulate competition between providers and insurers, hoping thereby to lead to increased quality and delivery of medical services and increase the overall effectiveness of the healthcare system (System Overview, 2010; Tompson, 2007). "The introduction of this purchaser–provider split was also expected to help facilitate the restructuring of care, as resources would migrate to where there was greatest demand, allowing for a reduction in excess capacity in the hospital sector and stimulating the development of primary care" (Tompson, 2007).

At the federal level, the compulsory insurance scheme covers the basic medical services provided by the Guaranteed Package Program legislated in 1998. The Package does not cover pharmaceuticals for outpatients, and coverage for dental work is restricted to basic work for children, veterans, and other groups not specifically identified. Following is one Russian doctor's explanation of how health care is financed:

> For the state healthcare fund, employees and employers pay around 2 to 3% of wages to a social tax and then a small percentage of that money goes into the healthcare fund. Dependent family members are covered by the contributions paid by employed family members. The unemployed, old age pensioners, and people on long-term sickness benefit are also entitled to free health, with the state covering their contribution. Vulnerable groups are not exempt from fees payable directly to doctors, which again makes health care virtually impossible for them. The self-employed must pay for their own contributions in full. Foreigners immigrating to Russia without jobs must produce proof

of private health insurance in order to obtain their residence permit. Dental care in Russia is expensive, and most citizens cannot afford the treatment. Dentists are known as *zubnoiyvratch* which means, tooth doctor. Citizens must pay for dental treatments themselves including check-ups (Personal Narrative, March 2011).

Criticized as creating more problems than it was intended to resolve, the compulsory insurance plan is regarded as a nominal attempt to provide universal health care. In practice, there are low incentives for competition among service providers, and the guarantees of the free health package require more clarity. A core issue is the lack of adequate funding to support the ideal of free health care.

Russia's health expenditures are low (about 3.6% of GDP in 2008) compared with European Union countries, which spend from 6 to 8% of GDP on average "In 1995, less than 1% of Russia's budget was earmarked for public health, compared with 6% in Britain and more than 12% in the United States" (Curtis, 1996). Since 2001, per capita health spending has fluctuated between 2.7 and 3.6 % (Marquez et al., 2007). Slightly improved, although still below the level of countries with similar per capita, (Tompson, 2007), Russia's total expenditure on health in 2009 was 5.4% of GDP (Marquez, 2009).

According to WHO 2011, on average, in 2006 Russia's healthcare workforce comprised 431 physicians per 100,000 people. On average, there were 966 hospital beds per 100,000 and 23.67 inpatient care admissions per 100 people. Only 12% of all physicians in the Russian Federation are working in primary care as general practitioners (GPs). In his study of healthcare reform, Tompson (2007) observes that "an estimated 35% of primary care consultations result in specialist referrals, around 5–10 times the rate typical of OECD countries" (p.17).

Drawing on data verified by the Russian National Research Institute of Public Health, Davydov and Shepin (2010, p. 76) report the following statistics:

- The current number of medical facilities is 5,993 hospitals, 7,951 health centers, 2,330 outpatient/polyclinics, and 827 dental clinics.
- In 2008, 621,000 doctors and 1.3 million nurses were employed in Russian health care.
- The number of doctors per 10,000 people was 43.8 but only 12.1 in rural areas.
- The number of nurses per 10,000 people was 73.1.
- In 2007, the hospitalization rate for 24-hour inpatient facilities was 22.5 per 100,000 people; the average inpatient stay was 13.2 days, and annual bed occupancy was 318 days. In rural areas, the

hospitalization rate was 24.5 per 100,000 people; the average inpatient stay was 13.7 days, and annual bed occupancy was 306 days.

The total number of doctor visits in 2007 was 1.3 billion of which 6.9% were home visits. Recent reforms over the last decade demonstrate Russia's commitment to improving its healthcare services. However, there are a number of persistent issues that raise barriers to effective delivery. Davydov and Shepin (2010) identify the poor organization of outpatient and inpatient services as a key concern. Similar to the observations of several researchers, these authors identify the following problems:

- Inefficient distribution of medical personnel between regions, cities, and rural areas
- Overspecialization resulting in marginalization of primary care and prevention
- Inadequate continuity of treatment between inpatient and outpatient facilities and polyclinics
- Overuse of emergency medical care: "The lack of a social care system combined with ineffective monitoring of patients with chronic problems has created a situation where emergency medical care is a widespread method of providing outpatient medical care to the population" (p. 74).

Russia's quality of health care is further compromised by a shortage of nurses. This shortfall in nurses runs "counter to the objective of developing primary medical care as a priority, the need to reduce the scale of the provision of high cost medical care, and the need to orientate health care towards prevention" (Davydov & Shepin, 2010, p. 78).

Unsatisfactory working conditions and low salaries (Davydov & Shepin, 2010) are major disincentives and increasing numbers of medical personnel (including physicians) either look for alternative ways to amplify their income or leave the healthcare field. In 1996 the average salary for a specialist in Moscow was $75 per month; senior doctors earned about $150 per month (Curtis, 1996). In 2007, the average monthly salary for doctors and nurses was $392 per month compared to $596 for industrial workers (Shishkin & Vlassov, 2009, p. 14).

Medical education is mainly state funded and regulated by The Ministry of Health. The typical route to obtaining a physician's degree involves six years of medical training including a one year internship under a specialist. "Training programs at medical institutes are adjusted to the needs of population in accordance with health priorities. Thus, when in the 1950s the non-communicable diseases became a real health problem; these subjects were strengthened and introduced more widely into curricula. When the role of primary health care became more evident in the 1970s, the training programs were adapted to this target-problem" (Vartanian, 2008, p. 3). Nursing education includes three years of schooling after the 11th grade, the mandatory level of completion for Russian students (Leak, Ivanov, & Brown, 2006).

INTERVENTIONAL

Russia's attempts to develop an accessible, well-coordinated system of primary care are linked to several challenges. One entrenched problem is historical—the Soviet emphasis on hospital care has translated to over-capacity in the new Russia. "Although the number of bed days per 1,000 population is falling, it is still 2–3 times higher than the figure reported in Western countries. The average length of stay in Russian hospitals is 1.5 times higher than in European Union (EU) countries. One third of patients who are admitted to hospital could be treated as outpatients" (Shishkin & Vlassov, 2009, p. 141). Overspecialization and patient beliefs that only the best qualified doctors go into hospital medicine are parts of a complex web of issues surrounding primary care.

Two key interventions are aimed at helping Russia turn the corner on obstacles to primary care. In 2006, government spending on health care took an impressive leap with the launching of the National Priority Project (NPP), one of four multibillion dollar projects aimed at addressing issues related to health, education, housing, and agriculture. The federal budget for *National Priority Project Health*, including *The Mother's Fund,* a childrearing program to assist parents of two or more children, was more than 400 billion rubles (approximately 7 billion dollars) over 2006–2009 (Kumo, 2010). "This substantial injection of finance to the Russian health system has funded the main activities of the NPP: increasing the salaries of primary and emergency care physicians; facilitating the purchase of primary care equipment, buttressing vaccination programs; providing free medical examinations; promoting fertility and constructing new high tech centers for tertiary care" (Gerry, 2011).

The NPP is credited with an improved birth rate by 23%, a drop in the death rate by 11%, and an increase in the average life expectancy from 61 to 68.98 years. The Project's favorable reviews include the opening of 502 adult health centers, and the construction of new perinatal centers in 22 regions of Russia (Kavkaza, 2011). In spite of a number of positive gains, researchers question the long-term impact of the NPP. As one representative comment suggests: "The overall population decline may have slowed but it has not altogether halted" (Kumo, 2010).

Healthcare Development Concept to 2020 extends the goals of the NPP and is Russia's most recent reform. With a start date of 2011, the government pledged over 10 billion dollars to reconstruct and update medical institutions, raise salaries of medical personnel, and purchase high technology equipment (Parfitt, 2009). The reform targets some of Russia's most pressing health issues, in particular, reducing mortality from cardiovascular diseases. The plan calls for new equipment to detect early stages of cancer, improved paramedic care for victims of traffic accidents, and greater quality and availability of Russian produced medicines (Parfitt, 2009).

Healthcare Development Concept to 2020 emphasizes a transition to insurance-based health care or as Shishkin and Vlassov (2009) explain, modernizing the government's mandatory insurance (introduced in 1993) to "a real insurance system with free selection of the insurance company and the healthcare facility" (p.141). This approach not only enhances patients' choices but induces competition for customers among providers (Gerry, 2011).

Described as a reform with ambitious goals, the efforts of *Healthcare Development Concept to 2020* to improve health care include better financial management, and strengthening the system of primary care. Although highly praised as a courageous initiative, detractors of *Healthcare Development Concept to 2020* are concerned about funding—where is the money for reform coming from as Russia struggles to overcome the economic crisis of 2008?

Critics also assert that new buildings and the latest medical technology are only partial solutions to Russia's health crisis; healthcare reform must direct more attention to the social issues that undermine good health. Andrei Dyomin, President of the Russian Public Health Society, provides a perspective on where health reform should focus:

> As for reducing mortality, there's a risk that health care will become the responsible party; and it cannot take responsibility because most of the health issues originate not in risk factors but in social conditions— education, work places, flats, environmental issues. It's a multisectoral problem which necessitates sophisticated public policies. What is important is that we don't go down the road of building high-tech centers to resuscitate babies instead of improving conditions for parents, or forming new police regiments instead of improving social security" (Parfitt quoting Dyomin, 2009, *Lancet*, p. 110).

Social services for the elderly in Russia, as well as the mentally ill, the disabled and other special needs groups, has been plagued by inadequate funding, poorly equipped facilities and very few care centers or nursing homes to meet the demand for long-term care (Tompson, 2007). These problems exacerbate Russia's longstanding issue of *overcapacity*. "Many patients, particularly elderly patients, are hospitalized for long periods simply because they cannot manage alone and there are no alternative care arrangements available" (Tompson, 2007, p.17).

Recognizing these issues, Russia has vowed to make improving the quality of life for the elderly a major goal of its restructuring agenda. In 2010, President Dimitry Medvedev directed Health and Social Development Ministry to draft plans to improve the state pension system, examine the unique access issues of the elderly across regions, provide affordable medical assistance and medications, renovate or construct new buildings of social institutions, and develop a reward system for social workers (Borisov, October 25, 2010).

PREVENTIVE

Russia is aware of the costly burden, economically and socially, of having emphasized acute curative care over preventive care. Over the past decade, the government has engaged more pronounced efforts to incorporate preventive programs in the healthcare system. Important linkages have been established with UNAIDS, a non-governmental organization (NGO) for the prevention and treatment of HIV AIDS (*see* Shishkin & Vlassov, 2009, p.143). Alcohol consumption and smoking are major contributors to Russia's high rate of mortality, particularly in relation to non-communicable diseases and injuries (NCDIs). To move more aggressively on these issues, Russia joined the World Health Organization's Framework Convention on Tobacco in 2008. Picking up from Gorbachev's largely unsuccessful anti-alcohol campaign in the 1980s, Russia announced vigorous plans to reduce alcohol abuse including the construction of 500 health centers, and the creation of criminal sanctions for retailers who do not follow alcohol sales laws (RIA Novosti, 2010).

According to WHO data, non-communicable diseases and injuries (self-inflicted and accidental) are Russia's highest cost conditions, and account for over 50% of Russia's total health expenditures in 2003 (Marquez et al., 2007). A number of challenges are associated with attempts to improve the prevention and control of NCDIs, starting with a lack of sufficient medical personnel that are adequately trained for NCDIs. Just as importantly, physicians and other medical staff may not subscribe to health promotion as a best practice (Marquez et al., 2007). Along these same lines, prevention and treatment of chronic diseases requires a close doctor-patient relationship and places more responsibility on the patient (Borowitz et al., 1999). Patient empowerment and responsibility is a significant departure from Russia's historically passive model of simply dispensing treatment.

> During Soviet times, the population had no voice in the healthcare system. The system was driven by providers and patients were seen as compliant objects who should be grateful for the limited time that physicians might provide. Patients had no options since they could not choose another provider if they were dissatisfied with care and their complaints would fall on deaf ears. The provider had all of the power in terms of healthcare decisions and physicians were seen as instruments of the state. A telling example is that Soviet physicians did not take the Hippocratic Oath because the principal role of a physician was not as an agent of the patient but as agent of the state: the physician's role was to ensure a productive workforce. Physicians did not give to their patients even elementary information about their clinical conditions, thus attenuating the already weak doctor-patient relationship" (Borowitz et al., 1999, p. 38).

RESOURCES

For many Russians, including Russian physicians themselves, health care takes the form of herbal medicine, mysticism, acupuncture, and faith healing. Due to the high cost of medication, people take care of themselves using long-practiced folk remedies such as cupping, wrapping up in vinegar soaked blankets, using garlic to ward off the spread of disease, and drinking green tea laced with mint to cure headaches. Russian herbal treatments are viewed with respect and researched in medical universities for modern applications. By 1995, 80% of the Russian population sought out medical assistance from practitioners of alternative medicine (Curtis, 1996).

MAJOR HEALTH ISSUES

Table 13-1 lists the top ten health issues which account for Russia's poor health outcomes by number, percent, and years of life lost. Cardiovascular disease is the leading cause of death in Russia and accounts for the high mortality among working-age men. Recent estimates through 2008 show cardiovascular disease as causing over half of all deaths in Russia (Gerry, 2011). According to World Health estimates, 75% of all deaths in the Russian Federation are attributable to non-communicable diseases (e.g., heart attacks, strokes, cancers) and external causes (e.g., injuries,

Table 13-1 Top 10 causes of death (all ages) in the Russian Federation, 2002, with the number and percent of years of life lost by disease.

Deaths	Number	Percent	Years of Life Lost (%)
All Causes	240	100	100
1. Ischemic heart disease	711	30	21
2. Cerebrovascular disease	533	22	13
3. Poisonings	66	3	5
4. Self-inflicted injuries	59	3	5
5. Trachea, bronchus, lung cancers	58	2	2
6. Violence	47	2	4
7. Road traffic accidents	44	2	4
8. Stomach cancer	44	2	2
9. Colon and rectal cancers	38	2	1
10. Cirrhosis of the liver	37	2	2

Data From: Death and DALY estimates by cause, 2002.

http://www.who.int/entity/healthinfo/statistics/bodgbddeathdalyestimates.xls

homicides, suicides, alcohol poisonings) primarily injuries caused by traffic accidents. Noting that Russia has one of the worse traffic fatality records in the European Union (e.g., five times higher than countries such as Hungary and Poland) and twice that of the United States, Marquez and Bliss (2010) point out the heavy costs of Russia's phenomenal traffic issues: "Estimates by the Russian Ministry of Internal Affairs in 2005 indicate that the cost of road crashes in Russia absorbs about 2.5 percent of gross domestic product (GDP) or about USD 26 billion annually" (2010, p.4). Alcoholism and smoking are regarded as the root causes of Russia's demographic crisis and poor health status. "Every year around 1 million people perish as a result of these twin evils: 400,000 from smoking and 600,000 from drinking, including murders and accidents caused by intoxicated people" (Parfitt, 2009, p. 3).

DISPARITIES

Mortality rates for Russia's three leading causes of death demonstrate an outstanding gender disparity. More Russian men than women die from cardiovascular disease, cancer, and road accidents. Alcohol consumption is blamed as a major contributor to the higher incidence of adult male mortality in noncommunicable diseases and injuries (Marquez et al., 2007).

Several explanations for women's lower mortality rates suggest that when faced with stress, women engage in coping behaviors that are "cardio protective", i.e., women are more inclined than men to ask for help (Weidner & Cain, 2003).

Although health care is free, decades of inadequate public funding and low salaries for medical workers have led to a steady rise in out-of-pocket payments. Access to health care is often dependent on one's ability to pay. Out-of-pocket payments are particularly onerous for the poor who spend 1.5 times more of their income for drugs and medical services than do the rich (Shishkin & Vlassov, 2009).

Inequalities in rural and urban settings are evident in the varying levels of socioeconomic status. The weaker infrastructure of medical services in rural areas leads to increased utilization of inpatient care. "Rural inhabitants are referred for outpatient care less often than people in urban areas and stay in hospital longer. This seems to be because of both lower use of primary healthcare services and low quality of diagnostics and limited accessibility of outpatient care in the rural areas" (Shishkin & Vlassov, 2009, p. 142). Disproportionate public spending at the regional level has compromised Russia's efforts to equalize access to health care. Marquez (2007) stresses that, "Analysis of spending at the regional level is of special importance because the overwhelming majority of the population receives medical care at regional or municipal levels" (p. 15).

Shishkin and Vlassov (2009) add that "The per capita public health funding is four to five times higher in rich regions compared to poor regions and the difference has been growing over the past decade" (p.141). Experts suggest that the uneven distribution of public funds can be attributed to Russia's complex decentralized system. The hope for a more equitable distribution of public funds rests in the development of a more coordinated, integrated approach to public financing and reform strategies that will close the persistent gap between the government's guarantees of free health care and insufficient funds.

SUMMARY

As a country in transition, the new Russia is facing a number of healthcare challenges. A major concern is a shrinking population; in addition to Russia's low birth rates and high death rates, Russia has the added challenge of a rapidly growing aging population. The high rate of mortality among middle-aged adult males, as well as the high incidence of preventable deaths, heads the list of Russia's poor health outcomes.

Russia's outstanding strength is a steadfast commitment to providing free health care to all of its citizens. However, Russia's health care is fraught with issues. One major weakness is a poorly organized system. Decentralization has created a highly fragmented, inefficient system lacking in transparency and oversight. The mandatory insurance system has not lived up to expectations for equalizing access to health care and public distribution of healthcare funds is largely uneven. Russian citizens often pay for medical care that should be free under the Guaranteed Package Program.

Low salaries of medical personnel have led to significant problems in out-of-pocket payments as well as a lack of motivation to practice. "Doctors and nurses are in short supply due to low wages which is resulting in doctors and nurses going abroad and offering their services" (Personal narrative, March 2011). Russia's long-time emphasis on secondary and tertiary care over primary care accounts for myriad problems with over-hospitalization, and scant attention to health promotion—a critical component of primary care and true access.

Discussion Questions

1. Compare Russia's *Guaranteed Package Program* with health insurance coverage at your work setting. Are there any similarities? What differences do you notice? What surprises you about the coverage offered in the Guaranteed Package? Are there features of the Guaranteed Package that you feel should be included in your insurance plan?

2. Describe Russia's long-term care issues. Have you observed similar challenges as a healthcare professional? Russia is attempting reforms to improve the quality of life for the elderly. Do you agree with the direction Russia is taking? Why or why not? What recommendations do you have to ensure quality care for the elderly?

3. Describe issues which raise barriers to health promotion in the Russian Federation. How do these issues compare to your own observations as a healthcare professional?

4. According to a physician in the Ukraine, there are many private clinics that provide adequate health care, with very little waiting. These clinics are generally oriented towards the middle class. In recounting her healthcare experiences, the physician provided a representative price list of medical services as listed in **Table 13-2**. How does this listing compare with your knowledge of healthcare costs or the costs of services provided in your healthcare setting?

Table 13-2 Price list.

Private Clinic	Price Structure (US Dollars) Kiev as of Summer 2010
House visit of general doctor with an initial examination	$36.00
Follow-up visit in office	$13.00
Visit to a gynecologist with an examination	$19.00
Applying stitches to a wound (price per stitch)	$9.00
Local anesthesia	$11.00
Thyroid ultrasound	$13.00
TB fluorography	$5.00
Back x-ray	$11.00
Certificate of health allowing you to visit swimming pools	$9.00
General blood test	$6.00
General urine test	$4.00

Data from: DeLong, Rick. Health care in Ukraine: Where to Get Medical Services. Accessed April 11, 2012. http://www.tryukraine.com/info/healthcare.shtml

Case Scenario

Mr. Vladismar: Why Not CAM?

Mr. Vladismar is a 78-year-old who lives in a small rural community in the Russian Federation. He enjoyed reasonably good health for many years, which he attributed to hard work and healthy eating habits. He has been followed for four years by a doctor in a nearby private clinic for chronic breathing problems. He has been seen in the clinic by the same doctor five times in the past two month for worsening of his breathing problems and each time he has had his medications adjusted or changed. He is considered by his physician to be non-compliant, demanding and difficult to treat. During his last visit he became increasingly anxious and depressed about his chronic breathing problems and lack of energy. His doctor wants to draw blood to send for lab analysis but Mr. Vladismar refuses, saying it is too costly. He repeatedly questions the doctor about why he is not improving as he has been on so many different medicines and done everything he was told to do? After his last visit to the clinic, he told his wife he would not go back. Soon after, Mr. Vladismar began seeing a doctor who specializes in CAM;

although not yet improved he believes he will get better if he continues to see the CAM specialist.

DISCUSSION POINTS

1. To what extent have you witnessed similar patient behavior in your health setting? What strategies have worked for you and your colleagues?
2. What do you believe contributed to Mr. Vladismar's decline in health, and repeated visits to the clinic?
3. What explanation can you provide for Mr. Vladismar's refusal to pay the fee to have labs drawn and to his refusal to return to the clinic, especially as, according to the price list, these costs are relatively low?
4. Explain what could possibly have been done, if anything, to address Mr. Vladismar's concerns.

References

AVERT.org. (n.d.). International HIV and AIDS Charity. Retrieved from http://www.avert.org/

Borowitz, M., O'Dougherty, S., Wickham, C., Hafner, G., Simidjiyski, J., Van Develde, C.C., & McEeun, M. (September 1999). Conceptual Foundations for Central Asian Republics Health Reform Model. Submitted to the Zdrav Reform Program.

Borisov, S. (October 25, 2010). Russian authorities pledge to improve living standards for the elderly. Retrieved from rt.com/politics/medvedev-council-meeting-pensioners/2010

Central Intelligence Agency (CIA). (2011). World Factbook. Retrieved from https://www.cia.gov/library/publications/the-world-factbook/geos/it.html

Central Intelligence Agency (CIA). (2012). Word Factbook. Retrieved June 10, 2012 from https://www.cia.gov/library/publications/the-world-factbook/fields/2012.html

Chesnokova, Y. (January 13, 2010). Russia plans to cut alcohol consumption in half by 2020. RIA Novosti. Retrieved from http://en.rian.ru/russia/20100113/157537462.html

Curtis, G. E. (Ed.). (1996). Russia: A Country Study. Washington: GPO for the Library of Congress. Retrieved from http://countrystudies.us/russia

Davydov, M. I. & Shepin, O. P. (2010). The Russian healthcare system. *Medical Solutions,* 74–78. Retrieved from www.siemens.com/healthcare.magazine

DeLong, R. (2003-2011). Health care in the Ukraine: Where to get medical services. Retrieved from www.tryukraine.com/info/healthcare.shtml

Deschner, A. & Cohen, S. (2003). Contraceptive use is key to reducing abortion worldwide. *The Guttmacher Report on Public Policy,* 6(4). Retrieved from http://www.guttmacher.org/pubs/tgr/06/4/gr060407.html

Gerry, C. (February 14, 2011). *Russian health care: A healthy future?* Retrieved from: http://.modernrussia.com/content/russian-health-care-healthy-future

Grielen, S. J., Boerma, W.G.W., & Groenewegen, P. P. (2000). Unity or diversity? Task profiles of general practitioners in Central and Eastern Europe. *European Journal of Public Health, 10*(4), 249–254.

Kavkaza, V. (February 26, 2011). Russian population stops downward trajectory. RIA Novosti. Retrieved from vestnikkavkaza.net/news/society/1143.html.

Kumo, K. (June 2, 2010). *Explaining fertility trends in Russia.* Retrieved from www .VoxEU.org

Leak, A., Ivanov, L., & Brown, H. (2006). Nursing Administration in Russia. *The Journal of Nursing Administration, 36*(4), 177–180.

Marquez, P. (June 22–24, 2009). Addressing health challenges in the Russian Federation: From theory to action. WHO Consultation on Intersectoral Action (ISA) for the Prevention of Noncommunicable conditions (NCC). Kobe, Japan. Retrieved from http://siteresources.worldbank.org/INTECAREGTOPHEANUT /Resources/russiahealthchallengesjune2009.pdf

Marquez, P. & Bliss, T. (2010). The goal is zero: Making roads safe in Russia to reduce injuries and premature deaths. Retrieved June 11, 2012 from siteresources. worldbank.org.

Marquez, P., Suhrcke, M., McKee, M., & Rocco, L. (2007). Adult health in the Russian Federation: More than just a health problem. *Health Affairs, 26*(4), 1040–1051. doi: 10.1377hlrhalf26.41040

Multak, N. (2010). An update on feldsher training and practice in the Ukraine. The Journal of Physician Assistant Education, 21(3), 44–45.

Nuti, D. M. (September 18–19, 2009). Reflections on transition: Twenty years after the fall of the Berlin Wall. An International Conference at the United Nations University–Wider Institute, Helsinki, Finland.

OECD. (2010). Country Statistical profile Russian Federation. Retrieved from www .oecd-Ilibrary.org/economics

Parfitt, T. (2009). Russia releases draft health-care plan. *Lancet, 373*(9658), 109–110 doi: 10.1016/501406736 (09) 60021-0.

Rechel, B. & McKee, M. (2009). Health reform in central and eastern Europe and the former Soviet Union. *Lancet, 3*(4), 1186–1195. Retrieved from www.theLancet .com

Shishkin, S. & Vlassov, V. (2009). Russia's healthcare system: in need of modernization. *BMJ, 339*, 141–143. doi:10.1136bmjb2132

System Overview: Russian Healthcare System Overview. (2010). Prepared by the Stockholm region office in St. Petersburg. Retrieved from www.swecare.se /virtupload/content/205/Rus_HC_System_Overview.pdf

Tompson, W. (2007). Healthcare reform in Russia: Problems and prospects. *Economics Department Working Paper No. 538. ECO/WKP (2006)66. Economics Department, Organisation for Economic Co-operation and Development.*

UNAIDS Global Report. (2010). Retrieved June 8, 2012 from www.unaids.org /documents/20101123_globalreport_em.pdf

UNdata- the United Nations. Retrieved from http://data.un.org/DataMartInfo .aspx

UNO. (2004). Retrieved January 24, 2010 from Un.org/esa/population/publications /WorldPopulation.pdf

USAID. (2010). Health in Russia. Retreived, January 25, 2010 from http://russia .usaid.gov/programs/health /overview

U.S. Department of State. (2011). Background Note Russia. Retrieved January 11, 2011 from http://www.state.gov/r/pa/ei/bgn/3183.htm

Vartanian, F. (December, 2008). *Medical Education in Russia.* Retrieved from www .globecpd.org/pdfs/educationinrussia.pdf

Vienonen, M. A. & Vohlonen, I. J. (2001). Integrated health care in Russia: To be or not to be? *International Journal of Integrated Care.* Retrieved from http://www .ncbi.nlm.niih.gov/pmc/articles/PMC1525341

Vladimir Putin on Raising Russia's Birth Rate. (June 2006). *Population and Development Review*, Population Council, *32*(2), 385–389.

Weidner, G. & Cain, V. S. (2003). The gender gap in heart disease: Lessons from Eastern Europe. *American Journal of Public Health. 93*(5), 768–770.

Westoff, C. F. (2005). Recent trends in abortion and contraception in 12 countries. *DHS Analytical Studies No. 8.* Calverton, Maryland: ORC Macro. Retrieved from http://pdf.usaid.gov/pdf_docs/pnadb984.pdf

World Health Organization (WHO). (2011.) Russian Federation Selected Basic Statistics. Retrieved from http://www.euro.who.int

World Bank. (2011). Retrieved January 22, 2011 from www.worldbank.or/en/country /russia/overview

World Bank. (2012). Retrieved June 11, 2012 from data.worldbank.org/indicator /SP.DYN.IMRT.IN

CHAPTER 14

The Healthcare System in Ghana

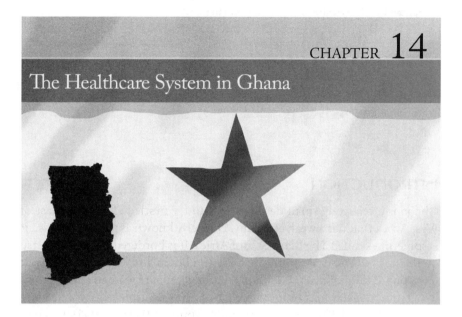

When you follow the path of your father, you learn to walk like him.

—Ashanti proverb

BEHAVIORAL OBJECTIVES

At the end of this chapter the learner will be able to:

1. Discuss how Ghana's healthcare system emerged.
2. Discuss the incidence and prevalence of disease.
3. Discuss the top three diseases and related challenges.
4. Determine how health care is structured, financed, and accessed.
5. Identify funding priorities, initiatives, and challenges.
6. Describe health practices that are commonly used to maintain and restore health.
7. Explain how social determinants affect health-seeking beliefs and practices.

KEY CONCEPTS

Allopathic

Cash 'n carry

Primary care initiative

Physician's bill of Rights

Traditional birth attendant

Traditional healers

WE-ISM

INTRODUCTION

Ghana is a relatively small developing country nestled along the coast of West Africa that has a weak economy. Formerly known as the Gold Coast, it is sometimes called The Black Star of Africa. It is bordered by Burkina Faso on the north, Cote d' Voire on the west, and Benin and Togo on the east. It has a population of over 18 million, 70% of whom are women and children living in rural areas. Fifty-nine percent of the population is between 15 and 64 years old, and 39% are 15 years old or younger (WHO, 2005). Ghana's land area is 238,000 sq. km. Ninety percent of Ghana's residents are native African, but there is a strong Dutch and Chinese presence in Ghana. The largest religious groups in Ghana are Christian, Indigenous religions, Catholic, and Muslim (WHO, 2005).

Life expectancy in 1997 was 58 for women and 47 for men. In 2000, life expectancy was 60 for women and 58 for men, an improvement of two years for women and an approximate ten year jump for men, and today it is 61.31 for women and 58.92 for men (CIA, 2010). There is a low divorce rate, and a high, but improving infant and neonatal mortality rate which has steadily decreased over the past 50 years. For example, the infant mortality rate based on 1,000 live births was: in 1965 (120:1,000), in 1989 (86:1,000) in 2005 (57:1,000) and in 2010 (52:1,000) (CIA, 2010). Ghana's literacy rate is 70% for men and 30% for women. Uneducated women in the Ghanaian system are relegated to a life of petty selling in the market working from sunup to sundown.

HISTORICAL

Since its independence in 1957, Ghana has been a two tier healthcare system, a system administered by the Ministry of Health and one entrenched in a highly respected system of traditional medicine. The Ministry of Health has traditionally funded maternal and child health with little funding for teen, adolescent, older adult, and trauma care.

Many challenges, not the least of which is a failing economy, include the inability to mass immunize, environmental hazards, unclean water, cross contamination of crops, and diarrheal diseases which result in a large number of infants dying before their first birthday. Complications of pregnancy are common.

STRUCTURE

Ghana has a dual system of health care that includes a Ministry of Health (government) controlled, funded, and operated hospital and clinic system, and an equally respected traditional (folk) system. Many Ghanaians use both systems, sometimes simultaneously. Under the Ministry of Health's primary care initiative, promising "Health for all by 2000," the government established polyclinics in the nine major regions of Ghana. The expectation was that when people became ill they would visit the polyclinic is their region first, and would be referred to hospitals only when necessary, thereby making health care accessible to all Ghanaians, even those in rural Ghana. However, soon after Ghanaians began using these clinics, they quickly learned that the clinics were poorly staffed, and equipment was substandard. Many stopped coming, and today the well-conceived polyclinics remain underutilized. Instead Ghanaians continued to travel longer distances to hospitals.

Korle Bu Hospital is the only major medical center in the entire country of Ghana. It has a state-of-the-art intensive care unit (again, the only one in the country), theatres known to the western world as operating rooms, and it has a rather distinguished reputation. Korle Bu, like all facilities in Ghana, must contend with unstable water and electricity supplies.

Of the approximately 22 million people making up the Ghanaian population, 12.6 million live in rural areas where only 30% of the *allopathic* (scientific, mostly hospital-based) physicians practice. The majority (70%) of health practitioners in rural Ghana are traditional healers who practice folk medicine combining the use of herbs, rituals, and sacrificial offerings in their practice. The remainder of those practicing in abundance in rural Ghana are community health nurses and *traditional birth attendants* (TBAs) who are trained to serve in roles similar to midwives, although they are unprepared to handle complicated deliveries. The majority of Ghana's physicians (70%) practice in urban areas, where only 30% of traditional healers practice.

Poorly staffed and equipped polyclinics in the nine regions of Ghana have well-educated physicians; however, most physicians choose to practice in the larger cities. Physicians rule in Ghana and the health system honors a *Physician's Bill of Rights*. Nurses in Ghana enter the profession by either completing a diploma or baccalaureate degree. They work in hospitals, clinics, and in the community. Their role is subservient to physicians rather than collegial. Nurses prepared at the master's degree level teach other nurses or are directors of nurses in hospitals and various community-based programs. There are no nurse practitioners in Ghana other than those working at the United States Embassy.

The well-trained medical and nursing professionals are experts at doing the best they can despite the lack of resources and infrastructure to support technology needs and maximization of outcomes. The government's "health for all" policy, although philosophically a good one, lacks the financial resources to fund it. It is doubtful that the polyclinics will ever be sustained and their benefits fully realized.

Columnist Quainoo (2003, February 22) calls physician salaries in Ghana "slave wages." In 2002, junior doctors at government hospitals in Ghana are paid 1.6 million cedis ($178.00) a month, while senior doctors receive a little over 2 million cedis ($230). Quainoo goes on to say that doctors with cars are given a mere 150,000 cedis ($17.00) maintenance allowance and 30 gallons of petrol worth 600,000 cedis ($66.00). Doctors without cars are not entitled to these extra allowances. Dissatisfied physicians leave Ghana in high numbers.

High attrition of skilled employees, such as physicians and nurses, can result in an understaffed public healthcare system that is often seen in developing countries. In addition, according to a Ghanaian Conference Report, of the approximate 2,800 nurse midwives practicing throughout Ghana, approximately 90% will be retiring in the next four years. This is expected to create a gap of 3,500 midwives needed to assist in addressing the critical issues of infant and child mortality and morbidity (Daily Graphic, November, 2007).

Wage differentials often account for physicians, nurses, and other skilled healthcare workers migrating to other countries to practice. Migration of Ghanaian physicians and nurses to countries where they could be better compensated has become a workforce supply and demand problem (Chen and Boufford, 2005). Frimpong (2002) reveals that in 2002 there were 600 Ghanaian medical practitioners practicing in New York alone. Another 62% of those still practicing in Ghana intended to emigrate (p. 47), despite the fact that Ghana was, and still is, in dire need of their services. Seventy percent of the physicians trained between 1993 and 2002 left the country after graduating (Antwi & Phillips, 2011; Okeke, 2009; Safo, 2003; Loewenson & Thomson, 2002; Dovlo et al., 1999). The exodus of medical professionals is mirrored in other health sector professions. Out of 944 pharmacists trained between 1995 and 2002, a total of 410 were presumed to have left the country by the end of 2002. The number of nurses and midwives immigrating to foreign countries exceeded that of other health professional categories. Of the 10,145 nurses trained during that same period, 1,996 were deemed to have left Ghana by the end of 2002 (Safo, 2003). Similarly, the Ghana Nurses Association reported in 1999 that, "over a four year span from 1999 to 2002, Ghana lost approximately 2,500 nurses to Europe" (Awases, Gbary, & Chatora, 2003, p. 35). With an annual 328 yield of nurses in 1999, Loewenson and Thomson (2002) reported Ghana's net loss of its nursing workforce in 1999 as equivalent to its yield. This is an incredible blow to service demand.

In most regions, the ratio of physicians to Ghanaians is 1:12,000, but 1:36,000 in the Volta River Region, as compared to traditional healers who number 1:400 in most regions, and 1:185 in the Volta River Region (Republic of Ghana, 1995). The higher ratio of traditional healers to physicians throughout Ghana makes them far more accessible to the people, especially those in rural areas. Traditional healers are popular in Ghana because they are located in both cities and in rural communities. They are also more available, acceptable by many, and affordable. Traditional healers are typically well-known, accepted members of the community and generally will provide services in exchange for a commodity or foodstuffs such as cloth, chickens, goats, and auto repair services.

Reproductive health remains a challenge for Ghana's health sector particularly as very few (35%) of all deliveries are attended by a qualified medical practitioner; rather the overwhelming majority of women either deliver at home or seek assistance from a traditional helper such as traditional birth attendants (TBAs) (IRIN, August 5, 2008). The WHO estimates that "560 pregnant women will die out of every 100,000 that go into labor" (IRIN, August 5, 2008). Also, over 214 Ghanaian women will die in the process of delivery (Modern Ghana, August 7, 2008). The use of traditional birth attendants and birthing centers, although helpful in providing some of the care of women mostly during the delivery period, is not always the right care solution as illustrated in the case scenario discussed later.

FINANCING

Ghana is a developing country that has a severely devalued Cedi (Ghanaian currency). Although rich in timber, gold, and diamonds, the country has no infrastructure to manufacture or export any of these. The Ministry of Health, financed by the government, funds the health system that includes the hospitals and salaries of health professionals, including physicians. Physicians receive housing and small transportation stipends. Seventy percent of the healthcare budget is for curative versus health promotion and disease prevention. Ghana's healthcare funding priority is maternal child health. Little funding is allocated for older adult and long-term care. Older adults are generally cared for at home by close family members until death.

There is a *cash 'n carry* system that requires that the person pays for medications and hospital services upfront. With the exception of a certain number of indigent patients cared for and written off under a special bad debt program, hospital admissions and the medications administered during hospitalization are based on a patient's ability to pay for services. Those who have the ability to pay will get the bed and the medications, those without the resources do not. Prior to implementation of the *Cash 'n Carry* system January 1992, the Ministry of Finance and Economic Planning provided initial seed capital for free drugs to patients with the expectation that the hospitals would sell the drugs to patients and use the resources to purchase additional drugs to replenish their supplies (Aseno-Okyere et al., 1998). For example, if family fails to purchase needed medications such as antibiotics and narcotic analgesics for their hospitalized family member the patient goes without. I can recall a burn patient having her burns debrided without analgesics because the family did not make it from the chemical store in time with her narcotic analgesic (pain medication).

Many have argued for developing countries such as Ghana to move toward universal health coverage by utilizing a prepayment financing mechanism especially as user fees and direct payments present a hardship for the poor. However, evidence shows that simply removing user fees, as some have advocated, is not a sustainable solution to healthcare financing (Akazili, Gyapong, & McIntyre, 2011). Hercot and colleagues (Hercot, Meessen, Riddle, & Gilson, 2011, p. ii5) propose that "more attention should be paid by researchers to the production of knowledge that meets the needs of people managing policy changes in low income countries." The authors state that, "good practice hypotheses derived from existing public policy and health financing policy later can assist in a review of removing user fees for health services reforms in low income countries" (Hercot et al., 2011, p. ii5).

There are systematic problems in financing of health care such as the untimely, and unpredictable, methods of processing payments to various districts. Asante et al. (2007) argue that, "first quarter government allocations to districts are often not received until second quarter... and fourth quarter payments may not be received at all." The results of a peer reviewed evaluation of the NHIS revealed that routine data treated as confidential information on the DMIS rarely filters up to the national level and there is untimely disclosure of annual and financial reports (Witter et al., 2007).

INTERVENTIONAL

There are few emergency vehicles. Usually, when an accident occurs someone puts the individual in their car or truck and races them to the nearest hospital where there is usually little or no major emergency or trauma care available and the person dies anyway. The is also no reliance on technology except radiology at hospitals other than at Korle Bu Hospital which even there is limited to the theatres and intensive care units. Providers in the Ghanaian system must respect the values of the people they serve. Physicians, however, often openly disrespect patients who vacillate between traditional healers and hospital doctors. Hospitals provide two meals a day for hospitalized patients and the family provides one meal a day. The family also provides linen.

The majority of healthcare funding is allocated to maternal and child health. Many interventions and campaigns focus on healthy childbearing practices, and child health and development. Ghanaians of all ages actively walk long distances. Their diet routinely includes vegetables (including yams), stews, soups, and rice. Obesity is rarely seen. Younger Ghanaians, influenced by foreigners who smoke, are beginning to experiment with smoking. Recent interventions by nurses and physicians are aimed at discussing the associated health risks of smoking and discouraging the practice.

Perhaps one of the greatest interventional assets among the Ghanaian healthcare workforce is that, despite low wages, Witter et al. (2007) report findings from a survey of health workers showed a strong commitment despite long work hours, and morale was not affected.

PREVENTIVE

Ghana has many environmental challenges due to it tropical climate, rainy season, dry season, malaria breeding mosquitoes, unclean drinking water (especially in rural areas), piped in water in some areas of larger cities, poor sewage, pit latrines everywhere, cross contamination of crops, burning of rubbish, unstable electricity in urban areas, often no electricity in rural areas, and no refrigeration.

Other challenges that interfere with preventive health measures include the market culture and women's work which is from sunup to sundown and includes heavy lifting; numerous older vehicles releasing exhaust into the atmosphere; and the burning of rubbish despite that the fumes are chronic irritants to the lungs when inhaled.

A major problem making prevention difficult is that Ghanaians tend to self-treat until the health problem gets out of hand before seeking professional care. Also, almost every meal begins with palm oil additives which probably contribute to blood pressure related deaths. However, autopsies are not routinely done in Ghana; therefore, causes of death are not well documented.

RESOURCES

Children are revered in Ghanaian culture. Ghana is a society that values women for the number of children they have. They are considered a major resource. Consequently, Ghanaian women are rarely childless by choice. African reproduction is considered a way of replenishing the family lineage and building the community. People strive to have large families to fulfill their role in society and to build up the strength of constituent groups (Addo & Goody, 1977). To complicate this value, the infant mortality rate is unusually high (CIA, 2010). Many children do not survive beyond their first birthday and they die from preventable problems such as diarrhea. Women, as a consequence, attempt to have many children hoping that some will survive, and attempt to conceive a boy as male babies are preferred. Girls, although not preferred, are later appreciated for the love and assistance they render around the home especially when the parents become older adults or ill. Among most ethnic groups of Ghana, prolific childbearing is honored. For example, a mother of ten children may be given a public congratulatory ceremony. In most regions of Ghana, a woman has no social status until she becomes a mother.

The role of family is very important in Ghana. *We-ism* demonstrates a valuing of family, nuclear and extended. This strong kinship tie makes the strong statement suggesting that, I am because we are, and we are because I am, translating to we are all responsible for one another. If you become successful it is your responsibility to help other family members. In a typical Ghanaian home you will find nieces, nephews, and cousins living with a family who is paying their school fees and living expenses. They are also assisted to attend high school and sometimes college. Chiefs, elders, and folk traditions are all resources for the ill and make significant contributions in assisting people to stay in their communities while maintaining their health. Male elders are particularly respected and are often among the first with whom people consult when they are ill.

When a patient is hospitalized, family members must purchase and deliver to the hospital many of the prescribed medications to be used during their care. They must also provide one meal a day but may choose which meal.

Organized religion is prominent. Religious symbols and messages are literally everywhere (on buildings, vehicles, bridges, billboards). The formal religions are primarily Christian, particularly Roman Catholic and Protestant, and there is a strong Muslim presence. The Anglican Church still has a notable presence in Ghana (Kirby, 1993).

The grieving experience in Ghana is traditionally somewhat lengthy, with weekly, monthly, and yearly tributes to the deceased, and it is characteristically reflected by massive community support. Wakes are typically held in the family residence. Women are critically important in the care and preparation of the repast feast that often spans more than one day.

MAJOR HEALTH ISSUES

Health problems endemic to Ghana are polio, cholera, yellow fever, guinea worm, and C-Resistant malaria. Although improved over the last 20 years, Ghana's piped water and electricity are still unstable and in some village communities non-existent. There are illnesses for which Ghanaians will not consult an *allopathic* (scientific, hospital) doctor because such problems are considered conditions that defy scientific understanding. These include boils, rashes, and headaches. There are also problems creating such urgency that Ghanaians are lead to only consult an allopathic doctor; these include respiratory and heart problems and malaria.

Typical of most developing countries, infections lead the way as the top killers annually. The top ten causes of death and the years of life lost in Ghana according to the WHO (2006) are outlined on **Table 14-1**. Each of

Table 14-1 Top 10 causes of death (all ages) in Ghana, 2002, with the number and percent of years of life lost by disease.

Disease Deaths	Number	Percent	Years of Life Lost %
All causes	207	100	100
1. HIV/AIDS	30	15	17
2. Malaria	23	11	16
3. Lower respiratory infection	16	8	10
4. Perinatal conditions	16	8	12
5. Cerebrovascular accidents	11	6	2
6. Ischemic heart disease	10	5	2
7. Diarrheal conditions	9	5	6
8. Tuberculosis	8	4	4
9. Road traffic accidents	5	3	3
10. COPD	3	2	1

Data From: Death and DALY estimates by cause, 2002.

http://www.who.int/entity/healthinfo/statistics/bodgbddeathdalyestimates.xls

the diseases listed are preventable, and many can be successfully treated when diagnosed early and the appropriate intervention applied.

DISPARITIES

Ghana's poorest residents are women and children. The majority of women and children live in rural areas where there are few scientific/allopathic physicians. Care in rural Ghana is primarily provided by community health nurses, traditional birth attendants, and traditional healers. The majority of physicians live and practice in urban areas. The cash 'n carry system of operation favors patients who can afford care. Kirby (1993) suggests that delivering better health care may be impeded by an individual's religious orientation, traditional beliefs, and practices.

SUMMARY

A major strength of the system of healthcare in Ghana is that the country has many well-qualified physicians and nurses dedicated to practice. Major weaknesses in the system are many. The majority of Ghanaians (70%) live in rural areas but the majority of well-educated physicians live in the cities. There is a serious need for physicians in rural areas. Although the poly-clinic concept is a good one, it just does not work because the clinics are not well staffed or equipped. The Ministry of Health's lack of necessary resources, a Physician's Bill of Rights and a cash 'n carry system are also major weaknesses.

Discussion Questions

1. Typical of most developing countries, Ghana lacks the resources to address many of the 21st century health challenges it faces. Discuss the basic "Health for all by year 2000" primary care initiative and why it failed.

2. Describe the health funding priority in Ghana and the rationale for directing the majority of its healthcare budget to this initiative.

3. Discuss the concept of We-ism in Ghana. What are the strengths and weaknesses of such a commitment as this? How does this concept compare to practices in your setting?

4. Imagine living in a remote Ghanaian village for six months without electricity, running water, bathrooms, or emergency medical care. What strategies might you employ to remain healthy?

Case Scenario

A Complicated Delivery

Adowa is a healthy 26-year-old professional female in the third trimester of her first pregnancy. She has received routine prenatal care since her first month of pregnancy, and mother and unborn child are progressing well. Her husband, Kwabena, is a prominent attorney, his father is also an attorney; Adowa's parents are both Ghanaian dignitaries. Being persons of substantial financial means, the parents on both sides are excited about the birth of their first grandchild and convince the couple that it would be best if Adowa spends her last two months in a prominent birthing center, generally reserved for only the most affluent. Adowa and Kwabena were initially reluctant because she was feeling well, had thus far had an uneventful pregnancy, and they lived only 20 minutes away from the Korle Bu Hospital, the only fully-equipped medical center in the country. However, after a few days of their parents' urging, and so as not to disappoint them, the couple finally agreed to the birthing center.

Promptly upon reaching 7 months of pregnancy, Adowa was admitted to the birthing center about 40 miles west of their home, the opposite direction of the Korle Bu Hospital. When she reached 8½ months pregnancy, Adowa's parents received a call that she was in labor and they should come right away. Filled with excitement, they left for the birthing center. Adowa had unexpectedly awakened with terrific pain in her abdomen and back, and was in obvious labor; but by the time her parents reached the center their daughter was dead, and the baby had already been rushed to the Korle Bu Medical Center by a private automobile, without oxygen. The only explanation offered the parents was that their daughter died in childbirth. The baby, once at Korle Bu, was stabilized and miraculously did well. Kwabena, having received the call late, was waiting for the parents at Korle Bu. The young husband, along with the entire family, was devastated to learn that his healthy, energetic wife, who had no complaints when he saw her a day ago, was now dead. Kwabena blamed the birthing center, the parents for convincing them to go in the first place, and mostly he blamed himself for not having the courage to go against the wishes of his parents and in-laws. Especially because, as he said, "She would have had a much better chance had she been at Korle Bu."

DISCUSSION POINTS

1. Ironically, money and privilege did not prevent a tragic ending in this situation. What factors do you think account for the wife's death?

2. Should Kwabena have been more assertive with the parents about staying close to home and using the services at Korle Bu? Had he been more assertive, would things have turned out differently?

3. Why would a prominent birthing center have to rush the baby to Korle Bu? Why wouldn't the center be able to take care of the baby's needs?

4. As you think about the issues in this case, what is your understanding of true access in relation to class differences? For example, does being wealthy guarantee the best medical service possible?

REFERENCES

Akazili, J., Gyapong, J., & McIntyre, D. (2011). Who pays for health care in Ghana? *International Journal for Equity in Health, 10*(26). Doi:10.186/1475-9276-10-26

Antwi, J. & Phillips, D. (2011, February). Wages and health worker retention: Evidence from public sector wage reforms in Ghana. HNP discussion paper. International Bank for Reconciliation and Development. Health Nutrition and Population. The World Bank. 1–40.

Asante, F. A., Chikwana, C., Daniels, A., & Amar-Klemesu, M. (2007). Evaluating the economic outcomes of the policy of fee exemption for maternal delivery care in Ghana. *Ghana Medical Journal* 41:110–17.

Aseno-Okyere, W.K., Osei-Akoto, I., Anum, A., & Adukonu, A. (1999). The behavior of health workers in an era of cost-sharing: Ghana's drug cash and carry system. *Tropical Medicine and International Health.* 4:8, 586–593.

Awases, M., Gbary, A., & Chatora, R. (2003). In: Antwi, J. & Phillips, D. (2010). *Home wages and migration: Evidence from health sector wage changes in Ghana.* 1850–1852

CIA. (2010). Ghana Infant mortality rate: Demographics. Retrieved August 14, 2010 from http://indexmundi.com/ghana/infant_mortalityrate.html

CIA. (2010). *World factbook.* Cia.gov/library/publications/the-world-factbook/geo/gh.html

Daily Graphic. (2007, 15 November). Modern Ghana. Retrieved November 11, 2010 from http://www.modernghana.com/news/14768/1/improve-our-conditions-to-attract-the-young-midwiv.html

Daily Graphic. (2008, 7 August). Modern Ghana. In: *Health care in Ghana.* (March 2009). Austrian Red Cross, ACCORD, UNHCR & Austrian Federal Minster of the Interior 9–10.

Dovlo, D. & Nyonator, F. (1999). Migration of graduates of the University of Ghana Medical School: A preliminary rapid appraisal. *Human Resources for Health Development Journal, 3*(1). 34–37.

Frimpong, D. (2002). In: Liese, B. & Dussault, G. (2004). The state of the health workforce in Sub-Saharan Africa: Evidence of crisis and analysis of contributing factors. p. 35, Table 8. "Brain loss in 9 SSA countries, by profession."

Washington, DC:, Human Development Sector, The World Bank, Africa Region. *Home wages and migration: Evidence from health sector wage changes in Ghana. p.* 47

Goody, J. & Addo, N. (1977). *Siblings in Ghana.* University of Ghana Population Study. Vol. 9, Legon, Accra, University of Ghana Press. Retrieved November 10, 2011 from annual reviews.org/pdf/10.1146/annurev.an.20.100191.000245 (application)

Hercot, D., Meessen, B., Riddle, V., & Gilson, L. (2011). Removing user fees for health services in low-income countries: A multi-country review framework for assessing the process of policy changes. Oxford University Press in association with the London School of Hygiene and Tropical Medicine. doi:10.1093heapol/czr063. In: *Evaluating knowledge, management, best practices and high quality lessons learned.* Retrieved from http://heapol.oxfordjournals/content/26/suppl_2 /ii5.full.pdf+html

IRIN. (August 2008). Health Care in Ghana. In: *Health care in Ghana.* (March 2009). Austrian Red Cross, ACCORD, UNHCR & Austrian Federal Minster of the Interior 9–10.

Kirby, J. P. (1993). The Islamic dialogue with African traditional religion: Divination and health care. *Social Science and Health Care, 36*(3) 237–247.

Loewenson, R. & Thomson, C. (2002). *Regional Network for equity in health in Southern Africa (EQUINET) Health System Trust.* In: Liese, B. & Dussault, G. (2004). The state of the health workforce in Sub-Saharan Africa: Evidence of crisis and analysis of contributing factors. p. 35, Table 8, table title, "Brain loss in 9 SSA countries, by profession." Washington, DC:, Human Development Sector, The World Bank, Africa Region.

Okeke, E. N. (2009). Empirical investigation of why doctors migrate and women fail to go for screening. Unpublished doctoral dissertation. Health Services Organization and Policy, University of Michigan. 1–127.

Quainoo, E. (2003, February 22). Ghanaian doctors deserve better: Feature article, p1. Daily Graphic, Modern Ghana. Retrieved, October 10, 2010 from http:// www. modernghana.com/news/111812/1/Ghanaian-doctors-deserve-better .html

Republic of Ghana. (1995). *Medium term health strategy: Towards vision 2020.* Accra: Ministry of Health.

Safo, A. (2003). 604 physicians abandon Ghana. In: Liese, B. (2004). *The state of the health workforce in Sub-Sharan Africa: Evidence of crisis and analysis of contributing factor.* Washington, DC: Human development sector Africa region, The World Bank. Evidence from health sector wage changes in Ghana.

Witter, S., Kusi, A., & Aikins, M. (2007). Working practices and incomes of health workers: Evidence from an evaluation of a delivery fee exemption scheme in Ghana. *Human Resources for Health. 3*(2).

World Health Organization (WHO). (2005). www.who.intl/profiles_countries

World Health Organization (WHO). (2006). Mortality country fact sheet.

World Health Organization (WHO). (2010). World Statistics 2010 WHO press. Geneva.

Part IV

Specific Challenges and Opportunities

CHAPTER 15

Prevalence and Management of Behavioral Health Care

BEHAVIORAL OBJECTIVES

At the end of this chapter the learner will be able to:

1. Describe how mental health care is structured and financed in selected countries.
2. Discuss the relationship of regional differences and access to behavioral/ mental health care.
3. Discuss the incidence and prevalence of mental illness.
4. Discuss the mental healthcare system in terms of impact and future challenges.

KEY CONCEPTS

Behavioral health

DALY

Global burden of disease

Incidence

Mental health

Normalization

Prevalence

Social care

YLL

INTRODUCTION

Although in some cases behavioral and psychiatric/mental are grouped under the same broad category, behavioral health problems are generally effectively treated on an outpatient basis with combination psychotherapy and pharmacotherapy (medications). Behavioral health professionals are licensed by the state in which they reside to practice, and they collaborate on the management of clients' behavioral problems. These professionals include psychiatrists, psychologists, psychiatric nurse practitioners, social workers, family counselors, and drug/alcohol and mental health counselors (Parker, 2002). Such chronic problems as dementia and mental retardation are considered psychiatric/mental problems rather than behavioral.

There is a distinct interconnectedness between mental health and health in general. The WHO defines health as, "a state of complete physical, mental, and social well-being, and not merely the absence of disease and infirmity" (WHO, 2001b, p. 1). Mental health on the other hand is defined as, "a state of well-being in which the individual realizes his or her own abilities, can cope with the normal stress of life, can work productively and fruitfully, and is able to make a contribution to his or her community ... it is determined by socioeconomic and environmental factors and it is linked to behavior" (WHO, 2001a , p. 1; WHO 2010, p. 1). For example, people are generally resilient enough to spring back when they are stressed, or depressed and are therefore able to maintain their baseline. However, when they lose their resiliency and remain stressed or depressed for long periods and are unable to cope, they become ill.

Globally, the prevalence of mental disorders is high (approximately 80 percent), yet few severely affected seek treatment (Demyttenaere, et al., 2004). Kleintjes, Lund, and Flisher (2010), in their analysis of mental health in children and adolescents across the four African countries studied, which included Ghana, found that stigma toward people with mental health problems was felt to contribute to active discrimination and the violation of the human rights of service users; whatever their age (p. 136). Respondents viewed this as significantly influencing their "willingness to disclose and seek help" (p. 136). The authors also found that "there is a low priority of mental health relative to other health programs; and there is a link between poverty and mental health" especially in regard to development of problems such as "stress, depression and anxiety" (p. 137).

To the extent that a persons' mental health is intact, they are more capable of maintaining their physical and social well-being. If their physical health is poor, or severely threatened by disease and the ills of poverty, it can negatively impact their mental and behavioral health. Herrman, Saxena, and Moodie (2005) suggest that physical illness is detrimental to mental health just as poor mental health is detrimental to physical health. Perhaps the more complex the physical health problem, the more likely a behavioral health problem will emerge. The same can be said for social problems and pressures that may result in risky behavior that consequently results in physical, mental, or behavioral health problems.

BEHAVIORAL HEALTH

When persons have diminished capacities—whether cognitive, emotional, attentional, interpersonal, motivational, or behavioral...that interferes with their enjoyment of life or adversely affects their interactions with society and the environment, they are considered to have a mental health disorder (Kirby, 2004, Report 1 p 68). Mental illnesses not only result in human suffering for the individuals experiencing the problem but it also affects their families, the healthcare system, the social system, the workplace, and society at large (IHE, p. 9). According to the WHO (2004) mental health problems present a global burden and in some countries it carries a stigma that impedes how communities address the problem. Further, not only are "mental health problems stigmatized in society globally, mental health is generally underfunded, and it presents a significant burden for countries throughout the world" (WHO, 2003, p. 18). The WHO also predicts that "by 2020 mental disorders will account for 15% of disability—adjusted life-years lost to illness" (p. 18).

Worthington and Rauch (2000) suggest that behavioral therapy consists of reconditioning patients' behaviors or the associations they have between a stimulus and response. Behavioral health, in much of the world, is an all-inclusive term that refers to the management of community-based, emotional instabilities, as well as psychiatric mental health problems that do not require hospitalization. It includes a variety of problems that can be managed on an out-patient basis, and emphasizes changing behavior. For example, according to Worthington and Rauch, (2000, p. 1147), "anxiousness is a normal human, or behavioral response to stress. However, distinguishing it from pathologic anxiety and anxiety disorders often requires a systematic evaluation and a thorough understanding of the individual patient's physical and psychological status. Unrecognized and untreated, anxiety disorders increase the cost of medical care and render patients vulnerable to further morbidity, including demoralization, hypochondriasis, depression, and varying degrees of disability. A comprehensive and empathic assessment of the anxious patient by the primary care physician permits a reasoned and often therapeutically effective approach to the difficult problems presented," by introducing behavioral interventions at the earliest point of contact (the community).

PREVALENCE AND MANAGEMENT OF BEHAVIORAL HEALTH CARE IN INDUSTRIALIZED (DEVELOPED) COUNTRIES

Behavioral and Mental Health in the United States

It has been well established, that access to delivery of high quality, afford-able health care in the United States health delivery system is generally a problem (USDHHS, 2006; Long, Chang, Ibrahim, & Asch, 2004; Burroughs et al., 2002; Smedley, Stith, & Nelson, 2002: Exner et al., 2001). However, access to behavioral health care and services in the United States (U.S.) is an even greater challenge. It has obvious shortcomings. According to the CDC (2007), 1 in 2 Americans in the United States has a diagnosable mental disorder each year, including 44 million adults and 13.7 million children. Although 80–90% of mental disorders are treatable, of those with a diagnosable mental disorder, fewer than half of the adults actually get help and only one-third of children get help. The CDC also reports that in 1999, suicide was the 8th leading cause of death in the United States. In 2009, suicide dropped to the 10th leading cause of death (CDC, 2010). However, since 1980 suicide has doubled among young African American males. Further, African Americans are more likely to experience a mental disorder than their European American counterparts, yet they are less likely to seek treatment. When they do seek treatment, they are more likely to receive inpatient care. Latino American women are more likely to suffer from depression than Latino men, and when Asian American/Pacific Islander females seek mental health care, they are more likely to be misdi-agnosed as "problem free" (CDC, 2007). Finally, American Indians/Alaskan Natives appear to suffer disproportionately from depression and substance abuse and they are overrepresented as hospitalized in-patients compared to European Americans (CDC, 2007).

The Public Health Act of 2000 defines the function of the National Institute of Mental Health (NIMH) and the Center for Mental Health Services (CMHS). The Children's Health Act of 2000 authorized the Substance Abuse and Mental Health Services Administration (SAMHSA). Patients who have documented addiction to controlled substances qualify for governmental disability payments. There are 7.7 psychiatric hospital beds per 10,000 of the population, and 3.1 beds in psychiatric hospitals in the United States. There are also, according to the WHO, 13.7 psychiatrists per 100,000 in the population (WHO, 2005). Feldman, Bachman, Cuffel, Friesen, and McCabe (2003) assert that there are 14.2 psychiatrists per 100,000 population. Both are substantial numbers. There are also 6.5 psychiatric nurses, 31.1 psychologists, and 35.3 social workers (WHO, 2005). (who.int/profiles_countries, 2005).

The National Health Reform Bill (the Obama Bill), although heavily pertaining to physical health, does encompass limited considerations for mental health. There are an array of social, psychological, and biological factors that determine a person's mental health and stability. Any one of these determinants can threaten a person's mental health. A good example of this is evidenced by the stressors of such things as poverty, violence, and poor working conditions (WHO, 2010, p 2). Laypersons often do not understand the distinction between behavioral health and mental health.

The essential levels of care covered by the United States' healthcare insurance policies are similar to general healthcare coverage. Despite a move decades ago toward deinstitutionalization of mental health services, resulting in the closure of many long-term mental healthcare facilities across the country, few changes have occurred in the funding of mental health. Also, due to the lack of community-based mental health providers, access to community-based mental health services are somewhat limited.

In the United States, behavioral health covers an array of disorders such as alcohol and other mood altering substances abuse and dependence, anxiety, depression, chronic fatigue, chronic and/or nonmalignant pain, insomnia, obesity, sexual dysfunction, and phobias (Worthington & Rauch, 2000). Phobias, according to Worthington & Rauch (2000) are "irrational fears related to specific stimuli that often result in an anxiety response that interferes with some aspect of people's ability to function" (p. 1148). Behavioral health also may include the management of people considered bipolar, relationship violence, and adolescent adjustment problems that could include bullying, which schools often fail to prevent and parents often feel helpless against.

The prevalence for many behavioral health problems are high, yet behavioral health provider availability in the United States is low. For example, anxiety disorders have an estimated lifetime prevalence of 25% in the general population, and account for frequent visits to the non-psychiatric provider (physicians and nurses in advanced practice roles such as NPs and CNs). "Evaluation and management of these patients are often challenging because they present with feelings of distress and concern about disease in the absence of objective evidence" (Worthington and Rauch, 2000, p. 1147). Goroll and Mulley (2000) suggest that, "patients with anxiety disorders are

50% more likely to be alcoholic; similarly, the prevalence of anxiety disorders is 50% higher in alcoholics" (p. 1149).

An important message from the AMA suggests that, "alcohol use and abuse is the major cause of preventable deaths associated with violence and motor vehicle accidents. Excessive alcohol intake strains personal relationships and may affect one's ability to keep a job, and it results in serious health problems including damage to the liver and brain" (Ringold, 2005 p. 1).

The most recent available national prevalence data on alcohol abuse and dependence is from 2000 and 2001. These data suggest that the United States has a very high prevalence of alcohol abuse and dependence, approaching 8% or nearly 14 million adults. The rates of abuse and dependence among persons 18–29 is twice those for the nation as a whole and alcohol use among 12- to 17-year-olds has drastically increased (NIH, 2009, p.1; Hanna, 2000, p. 1169). The CDC (2007) reported that overall, 6 in 10 (61.2%) of U.S. adults were current drinkers in 2005–2007 (CDC, p. 1).

During 2006–2009, the National Institute on Alcohol Abuse and Alcoholism (NIH, 2009) obtained data on alcohol use from surveying 44,000 children between ages 12 and 14 across geographical and socioeconomic areas. Reportedly 5.9% of 12- to 14-year-olds admitted to using alcohol during the month prior to the survey. Almost all of these kids got the alcohol for free, 45% reported getting their alcohol from a parent or other family member or taking it from their home without permission (NIH, 2009). Additionally 5,000 youths and teens under the age of 21 die annually as a result of underage drinking. These deaths include deaths from falls, burns, and drowning. Young people who use and abuse alcohol are also more likely to perform poorly in school, and engage in risky sexual and drug taking behavior (NIH, 2009).

In 2000, the overall estimated alcohol related cost to society associated with lost productivity, crime, accidental deaths, and fire exceeded $165 billion. The estimated direct cost of alcohol treatment and medical consequences of using and abusing alcohol approached $20 billion. More than $15 billion is paid for medical care alone (Hanna, 2000, p. 1169).

Primary care physicians are uniquely positioned to detect and treat harmful patterns of alcohol use. They are also best positioned to prevent alcohol related disorders and a host of related medical and social problems. Screening for alcohol problems long before they become disabling and more difficult to manage should be a routine part of every primary care practice. Timely recognition and intervention is critical. Alcoholism encompasses two distinct conditions; alcohol abuse and alcohol dependence (Hanna, 2000) commonly referred to as alcohol addiction. When persons become addicted to alcohol it greatly impacts not only their lives but the lives of their families, their co-workers, and their community. Once addicted, long-term family counseling, the use of support groups, detoxification, and substitution therapy is often necessary.

Depression is a complex problem that presents clinically as a variety of psychological and physical complaints. It is often not diagnosed early, and sometimes goes undiagnosed. Although many persons become occasionally depressed for short periods they are generally resilient and spring back before long. When depression is unresolved, it is called clinical depression. At this point it requires intervention and follow up that often includes the use of antidepressant medications and professional counseling.

Access to mental health services in the United States is based largely on insurance provisions which vary among subscribers. There is coverage under Medicare and Medicaid for individuals who are considered poor. In most cases, out-patient psychiatric mental health and behavioral health services have limited insurance coverage. Also, there are so few community-based behavioral health providers in some geographic localities that services are not available, and existing programs are limited; others are even threatening to close. As a consequence, primary care providers are among the first to evaluate and treat persons with behavioral health problems. However, referrals to behavioral health providers are difficult to obtain, and when they can be made wait lists are very long.

Behavior health managed care companies have reported that major segments of the U.S. population lack access to clinicians who are capable of properly evaluating the indication for prescribing and monitoring psychotropic medications (Christian, Dower, & O'Neil, 2007). With 14.2 psychiatrists per 100,000 people in the United States, a declining number of psychiatric mental health nurse practitioners, and persistent treatment barriers, Feldman et al. (2003) predict there will be continued lack of access to treatment and fewer incentives for behavioral health providers to enter into community practice.

Healthy People 2010 and 2020 call for more mental health providers to treat individuals in need of behavioral health. According to the United States Department of Health and Human Services (USDHHS) many employers of large workforces have established the goal to improve delivery of behavioral health care in general medical and mental health sectors (United States Department of Health and Human Services, 2007). The Substance Abuse and Mental Health Services Administration, the largest supporter of mental health grant opportunities for mental health innovation and demonstration programs recognizes the need for more community-based mental health research designed to assist providers in better responding to behavioral health needs at the community level. This organization actively advocates for increased numbers of mental health providers who are experienced in, and committed to, evidence-based practice to be community-based, rather than hospital-based (United States Department of Health and Human Services, 2007).

Although behavioral health is generally underfunded throughout the United States, some states are leading the way in behavioral health services to address the needs of children. One such state is New Mexico where access to behavioral health care and services for children and their families is a state priority. Bolson (2004) describes the New Mexico mental health system as one that utilizes state and federal funds to develop and maintain a statewide coordinated, comprehensive service delivery system that has three distinct characteristics. It is: flexible and designed to meet the needs of clients at the local level; inclusive of, and responsive to, the ethnic, cultural, racial, and socioeconomic diversity of the state; focused on results with clearly defined and measurable outcomes for the clients served (p. 4).

The Child Youth and Families Department (CYFD) of the Community Services Section of the Children's Behavioral Health and Community Services Bureau is a very successful program. It disseminates an extensive, service delivery manual that fully describes and defines the standards and guidelines to be followed for children receiving behavioral health services. The CYFD's goal is to improve and enhance the emotional, mental, and behavioral health of its children, youth, and families. Children are, without question, the clearly identified (service) population that includes youth up to age 21 (and their families) who have an open case file with one of three agencies that make formal referrals for services. These include, County Protective Services, the Juvenile Probation/Parole office, and the Tribal/Social Services. Children determined to be at risk for entry into CYFD's Protective Services, Juvenile Justice System, and/or Tribal Social Services can also be referred for behavioral health services. According to Bolson (2004), specific contributing factors defining the population meeting the specific service categories include:

- Severe behavioral, emotional, neurobiological problems/disorders or at risk of developing such problems
- Intention/plan to hurt self or others as evidenced by written, verbal, and/or behavioral indicators
- Child or parent suicide attempt during the past year
- Substance abusing behaviors by child or their parents
- Multiple delinquent acts or law enforcement contacts by child
- Multiple school problems, including suspension or expulsion from school during the last year

- Homeless/runaway
- Child or parent with mental illness
- Parents who are incarcerated, involved with the criminal justice system, or on parole or probation
- Physical, sexual, emotional abuse or neglect of the child (current or known history)
- Multi-generational history of familial maltreatment, neglect

Smith and Sederer's (2009) proposal of a "mental health home" is another interesting, yet feasible solution to addressing the needs of the homeless who have serious mental illness. As a consequence of their illness, the mentally ill homeless, failing to get access to care at the community level, are bounced from place to place. They often become incarcerated, and have repeated admissions to hospitals to address mental health crises that, with treatment, may have been prevented. The "mental health home" concept is based on an earlier "medical home" concept, primary care's solution to accessible and accountable services for persons with chronic medical problems. The authors justify the need for mental health homes suggesting that they will provide well-coordinated, integrated primary and preventive care, recovery orientation, evidence-based practices, and family and community outreach (Smith and Sederer, 2009).

Behavioral and Mental Health in Canada

Mental illnesses indirectly affect all Canadians through illness in a family member, friend, or colleague. The onset of most mental illnesses occurs during adolescence and young adulthood, and it affects people of all ages, educational and income levels, and cultures. Mental illnesses are costly to everyone (individuals, families, the healthcare system and the community). In 1993 the economic cost of mental illness was estimated to be $7.331 billion. Further, the stigma attached to mental illnesses presents a serious barrier perhaps best seen by how it impedes diagnosis and treatment and also lack of acceptance in the community (publichealth.gc.ca).

Canada's policy on mental health services dates back to 1988. The major policy components were, and still are, typical of the policies of most developed countries. These components are advocacy, promotion, prevention, treatment, and rehabilitation (WHO, 2005). Canada has 13 interlocking health insurance plans in 13 separate service delivery systems. Although the figures are somewhat dated (1991–1993) the total number of hospital beds per 10,000 in the population was 19.4. Of these, 9.1 were designated as beds in psychiatric hospitals. The number of psychiatrists per 100,000 population was 12, the number of psychiatric nurses was 44, and psychologists 35 (WHO, 2005). Eighty-six percent of hospitalizations for mental illness in Canada occur in general hospitals. The majority of these hospitalizations are due to anxiety disorders, bipolar disorders, schizophrenia, major depression, personality disorders, eating disorders, and suicidal behavior (publichealth.gc.ca).

Mood disorders, anxiety disorders, schizophrenia, personality disorders, and substance use disorders are among the problems that are responsible for the leading source of human mental disability in Canada (Kirby, Report 1, 2004, p. 68). The growing burden of mental illness in Canada in relation to utilization of healthcare resources, lost productivity, and human suffering has been well documented (Global Business and Economic Roundtable on Addiction and Mental Health, 2004; Health Canada, 2002; Romanow, 2002; Wilkerson, 2006).

One of the fundamental things a country must do before it can determine the amount needed to be spent on mental health is to have comprehensive estimates of the prevalence of mental health disorders in that country (IHE, 2008, p. 15). Prevalence data are used to estimate the proportion of a population that is suffering from an illness or disorder. Epidemiological studies have estimated that 21% of all Canadians will experience a mental illness or addiction in their lifetime (lifetime prevalence), while 3% will suffer a severe persistent disability (Health Canada, 2002). The highest prevalence of mental illness occurs among both men and women between ages 35 and 49. Canadian women have a 1.5-2 times higher prevalence rate than Canadian men for both diagnosed and undiagnosed populations (IHE, 2008, p. 12). The most common mental illnesses among Canadian adults are anxiety disorders which account for 12%, and mood disorders accounting for 9%. Another 6-9% of adult Canadians suffer from personality disorders (IHE, 2008, p. 10). Schizophrenia affects less than 1% of the Canadian population (Kirby, Report 1, 2004, 1, p. 85).

"It is estimated that 37% of Canadians experience some type of mental health problem. As a result of the migration process, many immigrant and refugee women suffer serious mental illnesses such as depression, schizophrenia, post-traumatic stress disorder, suicide and psychosis" (Donnelly et al., 2011, p. 2790). In 2003, approximately 1.9 million (7%) adult Canadians were diagnosed with mental disorders such as a mood or anxiety disorder or schizophrenia. It is estimated that another 1.6 million (6%) of adult Canadians with mental disorders went undiagnosed (Lim, Jacobs, Ohinmaa, Schopflocher, & Dewa, 2008). People with undiagnosed mental illness include those individuals who may have self-reported, those in poor mental health, those being seen by two or more mental health professionals, those who are seriously depressed, and those having had seriously considered suicide but none actually received a diagnosis of mental illness from a physician.

Approximately 50% of Canadians who suffer from severe mental illness develop alcohol or other drug abuse problems at some point (Alberta Mental Health Board, 2004, p. 4; Adlaf, Begin, & Sawka, 2004). Suicidal behavior is often a symptom of mental illness and addiction. Each year approximately 3,700 Canadians commit suicide and more than 90% of suicide victims have a diagnosable mental illness of substance use disorder (Kirby Report 3, 2004, p. 27; Langlois & Morrison, 2002). According to Clayton and Barcel (1999), there was an estimated mean economic cost per suicide death of almost $1 million (in 2006 dollars). Also, of the 3,700 Canadians committing suicide every year, Canada suffered an estimated premature mortality cost in 2006 of approximately $3.7 billion (IHE, 2008 p. 17).

Using the WHO's Global Burden of Disease measure, the *Disability-Adjusted Life Year* (DALY) expresses years of life lost (YLL) to premature mortality (due to suicide in cases of mental illness). It also expresses *years lived with a disability* (YLD) of specified severity and duration. One DALY is one lost year of healthy life. In order to calculate the total DALY for a given population, the YLLs and the YLDs for that condition is estimated and summed separately. The DALY as a health status indicator extends the concept of *potential years of life lost* (PYLL) due to premature death to include equivalent years of healthy life lost to disability (WHO, 2001).

The disease burden for behavioral health problems has progressively increased over several years. For example, measured in DALYs, neuropsychiatric conditions accounted for 10.5% of disease burden worldwide in 1990; 13% in 2002, and it is estimated to increase to 15% by 2020 (IHE Report, 2008, p. 13). Mathers & Loncar (2006) predict that unipolar depression, although the fourth leading cause of disease burden in 2002, is anticipated to become the second leading cause worldwide by 2030, outranked only by ischemic health disease. Further, in developed (industrialized) countries not only is unipolar depression projected to become the leading cause of disease burden by 2030, Alzheimer's disease, other dementias, and alcohol use disorders are also projected to be among the top four causes of disease burden (p. 13). Considering the disability component alone, Global Burden of Disease 2002 estimates that neuropsychiatric conditions accounted for 31.7% of all years lived with disability (YLDs), and unipolar depression was the leading cause of disability worldwide, accounting for 11.8% of the total TLDs (WHO, 2002):

> Factoring in the direct costs for social care, hospital services, physician services and pharmaceuticals, the cost of treating and caring for mental

health services in Canada exceeded $7.7 billion in 2006. This includes payments made by the Ministry of Health, Housing and Education, private insurance and out-of-pocket payments made directly by consumers (Jacobs et al., 2008). The indirect costs estimates are considerable (between $6.2 billion and $9.1 billion) during this same period, accounting for loss in work including short- and long-term disability. Because of the greater prevalence of mental illness during mid-career periods, this loss of productivity usually affects ages 36–55 (IHE, 2008, p. 15 & 16). Access to services is free including medications, hospitalization and treatments.

Many agree that investment in community-based services and support for such initiatives as safe and supportive housing can reduce other costs such as funds appropriated to combat crime, unemployment, poverty, and homelessness (Toronto-Peel Mental Health Implementation Task Force, 2002; Alberta Mental Health Board, 2004).

Loss of income and independence, and fear of being stigmatized may strongly influence whether a person with a behavioral problems seeks treatment. It may also affect whether the person adheres to the prescribed regimen, or, if treated, how effectively s/he reintegrates into the community after crises.

Behavioral and Mental Health in Japan

Japan is credited with having one of the lowest (4%) mental illness prevalence rates in the world, second only to Italy (0.5%) (Wilkinson & Pickett, 2007). However, the most common mental disorder in Japan is depression. The Ministry of Health is the core structure under which mental health services are provided in Japan. Prior to World War II, The Confinement and Protection for Lunatics Act of 1900, and The Mental Health of 1919 was all that existed. Japan has had a Mental Health Plan since 1950, and a Substance Abuse Policy since 1953 (WHO, 2005).

The 1950 Mental Hygiene Law allowed for compulsory institutionalizing of patients with mental problems. This law was revised in 1987 after two inpatient deaths occurred resulting in human rights initiatives for patients and a movement toward community care and rehabilitation (WHO, 2005). The revised law, which is reviewed every five years, emphasizes advocacy, promotion, prevention, treatment, and rehabilitation. In 1995 government plans were revealed for what was called "The Plan for People with Disabilities" which positioned Japan for normalization which focuses on community-based care for persons with mental illness. The most recent amendment to this legislation, in 2000, provided public funding support and exempted the family and patient of any responsibility for damages caused to self or others while the patient was being treated (WHO, 2005).

Since 1990, Japan has made significant attempts to address mental health in similar ways to other countries in the industrialized world. Mental health care is part of Japan's Primary Healthcare System. However, persons with severe mental disorders have no community options; rather, they are forced to use psychiatric emergency services (WHO, 2005). Japan places great emphasis on what is called *normalization*, which requires viewing mental illness as a disability and encouraging the integration of psychiatric inpatients into the community (Ito and Sederer, 1999; Nakatani, 2000).

Japan's expenditure on mental health is 0.5% of its GDP, a relatively small percentage of their total health expenditure (Ministry of Health, 2000), and it is 5% of its total healthcare budget. Primary funding sources, in descending order, are taxes, social insurance, out-of-pocket by family or patient, and private insurance (WHO, 2005). If a person is hospitalized for mental health treatment, Japan's payment structure favors shorter hospital stays and initiating community-based care as soon as possible. Individuals with mental disorders receive disability payments.

Japan has 28.4 psychiatric beds per 10,000 in the population. There are 20.6 specifically in mental hospitals. The number of psychiatric beds (with a 95% bed occupancy rate) is the highest number in the world, and is three times the number in the United Kingdom. The majority (89%) of psychiatric beds in Japan are in the private sector. There are approximately 1,250 facilities in Japan that offer day and night care for patients with behavioral and mental problems.

Mental health workers in Japan include psychiatrists, psychologists, general practitioners, therapists, social workers, and various levels of specialist nurses. Per 100,000 in Japan's population, there are 9.4 psychiatrists, 59 psychiatric nurses, 7 psychologists, and 15.7 social workers. The Japanese healthcare system has more than enough psychiatrists (13–23 times more than the number in Iraq and the Philippines) although many are not community-based. However, there are inadequate numbers of other mental health staff who are adequately trained to provide community care. This has slowed Japan's progress toward achieving its deinstitutionalization policy.

Although, Japan's focus is on community-based mental health services, mental health primary care workers are not rigorously evaluated so it is difficult to assess performance outcomes (Tsuchiya & Takei, 2004). There is also little published data on treatment efficacy and training of community-based providers of mental health services making it difficult to determine effectiveness of care and services. Although Japan's Ministry of Health allocates ample resources for research and monitoring of its mental health system including patient's rights and getting feedback from patients about quality of mental health care, (Hamid, Abanilla, Bauta, & Haung, 2008, p.469) this is an area in need of growth. The updated national database that has been useful in guiding their existing mental health policy and evaluating new policies (Hamid et al., p.469) is fully operational, although it is difficult to determine its full value.

There are specific programs in Japan to address disaster-affected populations, older adults, and children. For example, a ten year "Gold Plan" to promote health care and welfare for the Elderly has been in place since 1987. The Plan was revised and launched as, "Gold Plan 21" in 2003. There is also a Zero Physical Restraint Campaign (WHO, 2005).

Japan has been hit by devastating, life-changing natural disasters that have greatly impacted the general health and mental health of massive numbers of people. For example, the long-term health challenges resulting from the nuclear crisis in Fukushima in the aftermath of Japan's March 11, 2011 earthquake followed by the devastating tsunami, may never be fully understood. For tens of thousands of people who lost their loved ones, hundreds of thousands who lost their homes and their livelihood, compounded by the associated stress (Kennedy & Luthra, 2011) life as they knew it will never be the same. The full impact of this natural disaster on the mental health of all involved—survivors and responders—may never be known. It is suspected that prevalence of such problems as anxiety and depression will likely increase. Francesco Checchi, epidemiologist at London School of Hygiene and Tropical Medicine, stresses the importance of reinforcing public health surveillance of mortality and a number of other problems, including mental disorders as well as suicide (Kennedy and Luthra, 2011), expecting the incidence and prevalence to escalate. This is of particular importance as Japan already has a relatively high incidence of suicide.

According to the Organization for Economic Cooperation and Development (OCED), " in 2005, 140,000 people in OECD countries took their own lives, equating to 12 per 100,000 population...the rates were highest in Korea, Japan, and Hungary, at 19 or more deaths per 100,000" (OCED, 2008, p.3). Further, "although some countries have seen declines in their suicide rates of 40% or more in recent decades, Korea and Japan have seen significant increases" (OCED, 2008, p. 3).

Japan is one of the richest, healthiest countries on earth, with a vast capacity for disaster response (Kennedy & Luthra, 2011). It has an excellent record of tracking the effects of crises dating back to the 1945 atomic bomb crisis. Despite this, the enormity of the potential disaster-related mental health challenges of the 2011 earthquake and tsunami, may have far reaching implications.

Behavioral and Mental Health in the United Kingdom

Reference in the literature to the utilization of mental health services in the United Kingdom (UK), with the exception of England, is either inconsistent, or lacking. Although Scotland had a Mental Health Services Framework in 1997, referred to as "Our National Health: A Plan for Action, A Plan for Change," 2000; and Northern Ireland published its plan, "The Way Forward for Northern Ireland," in 1995, there were no overall UK mental health policies in place until 1998.

Delivering race equality (DRE) in mental health care prompted the change in mental health policies in the UK. The DRE was a five year action plan, that was an initiative launched for the purpose of improving services for minority ethnic communities. This emerged in a response to a report of the independent inquiry into the death of an African-Caribbean patient who died in 1998 in a medium-secure psychiatric unit after being restrained by staff (dh.gov.uk.en, 2007).

These policy frameworks, called National Service Frameworks (NSFs) were specifically designed to improve particular areas of care including mental health. The National Service Framework for Mental Health identifies key interventions representing nationally-arrived-at standards for the purpose of raising the overall quality of mental health care and services in the UK. By standardizing quality and decreasing variation in care (Boyle, 2008), actions such as utilizing standard treatment protocols and performance expectations should maximize the quality of mental and behavioral health care. Efforts are also made to increase efficiency of, especially, social care (Boyle, 2008). Social care includes a range of areas, such as living accommodations, employment, and training.

The typical UK mental health policy focuses on primary care, access to mental health services, and it especially addresses providing effective services for people with severe mental illness. It also provides services for caregivers and initiatives to reduce suicide. The UK's National Health Framework for Mental Health of 1999, and England's National Health Service (NHS) Plan for 2000, both addressed mental illness. England's NHS focuses on three major priorities geared more toward interventions and care that is more responsive to the needs of the mentally ill, rather than those in need of behavioral health. The priorities included firstly, that all in crisis will have access to crisis resolution/home treatment teams by 2005. Secondly, by 2006, all with a first episode psychosis will have access to intensive treatment from early intervention teams for the first three years. Finally, all with intensive needs will have access to assistive outreach teams by 2004 (WHO, 2005). One piece of the UK's mental health legislation covers England and Wales; a second piece covers Scotland, which is historically different from the English legislation; and a third covers Northern Ireland.

Although mental health policies were generally not enacted in the UK until 1998, disabled persons received partial coverage under several initiatives. The Disability Discrimination Act of 1995, seeking to end discrimination that many disabled persons were faced with, provided some coverage for the mentally disabled. This Act provided new rights for the disabled to access goods, facilities, services, and employment, as well as buying and renting property. The Disabled Living Allowance was also provided as an extra-cost, non-contributory benefit that was unrelated to income coverage. Department of Social Security welfare benefits also provided for persons with documented, longstanding disabilities (who.int/mental_ health). The most recent Disability Discrimination Act of 2005 amended the definition of 'mental illness' by removing the requirement that conditions be "clinically well-recognized." This enabled persons not already diagnosed by a doctor with well known conditions such as anxiety, depression, bipolar disorder, and schizophrenia to also be covered (opsi.gov.uk, 2005).

The overall prevalence of mental health disease in the UK is 23%. Depression and anxiety are among the most common mental health problems in the UK (17.5%), psychosis is 0.5%. There have been very few changes in the overall prevalence of mental health illness in England's healthcare system from 2002–2009 (Singleton, Bumpstead, O'Brien, Lee, & Meltzer, 2001, McManus, Meltzer, Brugha, Bebbington, & Jenkins, 2009).

Actual mental health services in the United Kingdom are covered under the National Health Service which provides free universal coverage for everyone at the point of use that often begins with the general practitioner. Although there are slight variations among countries, the free coverage generally includes medications, hospitalization, and other treatments. Access to mental health services is generally at the primary care level. Based on beds per 10,000 in the population, the total number considered psychiatric beds in the UK is 5.8. There is no differentiation between beds in psychiatric hospitals compared to those in general hospitals. Psychiatrists per 100,000 in the population number 11, psychiatric nurses number 104, psychologists number 9.0, and social workers number 58 (WHO, 2005).

The UK spends 10% of its health budget on mental health. Primary sources of funding come first from taxes, then private insurance, social insurance, and finally out of pocket expenditures are paid only if needed. Approximately 85% of expenses for health and social care of the mentally ill are paid by the NHS; whatever remains is covered by local authorities (www .dh.gov.uk). The Ministry of Health is the core structure under which mental health services are provided. Among the various departments falling under the administrative structure of the NHS' Ministry of Health, two are most immediately responsible for mental health. These are the Commission for Social Care Inspection and the Mental Health Act Commission. These two merged into one entity in 2008 (www.dh.gov.uk).

Early intervention is critically important in preventing severe mental illness. England has made some progress in addressing early intervention in psychosis (EIP) by linking with primary care providers to facilitate early diagnosis and referral, and linking with public service organizations, schools, universities, and the welfare and criminal justice system (Boyle, 2011). Although mental health problems present a significant burden of disease throughout the UK, it is best demonstrated by the economic and social burden in England (Sainsbury Centre of Mental Health, 2003a).

The economic and social costs of mental health problems in England were £77.4 billion in 2002–2003. Using the sample formula, the aggregated cost of mental health care in England was estimated to rise to £105.2 billion in 2009–2010 (Sainsbury Centre for Mental Health, 2003a). The sample formula is used to calculate the cost of EIP. This formula is based on the expectation that clients remain with services for 3 years, at an estimated cost of £5,000 per person, and it factors in a minimum cost at years 1, 2 and 3. The cost at year 3 represents recurrent annual cost costs of services Salisbury Centre for Mental Health, 2003a). The total cost of mental health care by category of costs for 2002–2003 includes £12.5 billion for health and social care, £23.1 billion for output losses generally occurring as adverse effects of mental illness resulting in the inability to work, and an additional £41.8 billion (54.0%) for human costs including things that negatively impact the quality of life. The predicted cost by category for 2009 –2010 is £21.3 for health and social care, £30.3 billion for economic output losses, and £53.6 (51.0%) billion for human suffering (Sainsbury Centre for Mental Health, 2003a).

The key findings in an Office for National Statistics (ONS) survey examining prevalence of mental health problems in populations 16 to 74 years old living in private households across Britain and England, were that

1 in 6 (16.5%) of the population exhibited symptoms in the week prior to interview sufficient to warrant a diagnosis of a common mental health problem, with women exhibiting higher rates than men overall; London had a slightly higher rate than England in general (18.2% compared to 16.5%); and England had the highest rate of depressive disorders (London Health Observatory, nd., p. 2).

In Wales, for example, there is a Mental Health Foundation that has worked with the Welsh Assembly to inform policy and improve mental health services there. Through their consultant efforts, they have witnessed improvement in user and caregiver service involvement across Wales (Mental Health Foundation, 2012).

Behavioral and Mental Health in France

France has had a National Mental Health Program in place since 1985. They also have a comprehensive national suicide prevention program and most recently, a program designed to prevent depression that is called, "Actions Against Depression." Among France's latest initiatives addressing mental health is a policy on the admission of patients to psychiatric hospitals under constraints (WHO, 2005). Sectorization, a concept dating back to World War II, where one team is responsible for both inpatient and outpatient care of persons within its parameters, is a concept that still exists. Of the approximately 1,000 sectors in France, there are different sectors for adult, adolescent, child, and forensic psychiatry that encompass community care and sheltered workshops (Jaeger, 1995).

The primary source of mental health funding in France is from social insurance. Funding of mental health in France is less dependent on taxes. France spends approximately 8% of its total health budget on mental health. With the exception of services by private sector psychologists and psychoanalysts, patients have free access to private or public mental health professionals of their choice. However, in the event that the patient is severely mentally ill or severely deprived financially, there is full coverage without cost. There is also special coverage and allowances for housing if the patient is disabled patient (WHO, 2005).

Mental health in France is part of the primary healthcare system with treatment of severe mental disorders provided at the primary care level. There is regular training of primary care professionals. The total number of psychiatric hospital beds per 10,000 in the population is 12. There are 22 psychiatrists per 100,000 in the population, 98 psychiatric nurses, and 5 psychologists (WHO, 2005). There is an urban rural service divide in France as the majority of psychiatrists and psychologists practice in the large cities, leaving somewhat of a void in the rural area where the few practicing mental health providers are backed up. Medical students pursuing clinical rotations in mental health are discouraged and even prevented from specializing in psychiatry. Psychiatric diagnoses of adults are made according to ICD-10 criteria, but patients younger than 20 years old are still categorized according to the French classification of child psychiatry (WHO, 2005).

France also has specific mental health programs for disaster affected populations, older adults, and children. In 2001, a program was launched to campaign against stigmatizing mental illness, and to reinforce patient rights, improve professional mental health practices, and improve prevention, rehabilitation, and community psychiatry (WHO, 2005).

Most high income countries have not conducted national or regional surveys that address mental health service use, access to care, and unmet needs (Alonso et al., 2004). The findings in one study that sought to determine use of mental health services in six European countries, including France and Italy, used odds ratio (OR) estimates, and their estimated (95%) confidence intervals (CI). Data were reported regarding how frequent individuals sought medical consultation. The most frequent consultations were reported to be among individuals with mental disorders. The rate of mood related consultations was reported as (36.5%, 95% CI 32.5 – 40). One third of the consultations were made with mental health professionals only (mostly psychiatrists rather than psychologists or counselors). These data suggest there is insufficient use of health services for mental disorders in Europe and a need for improvement. The most important factor associated with the use of health services was the presence of a mental disorder, particularly a mood disorder. There was a peak in use of services in females between the ages of 35 and 49 (Alonso et al., 2004).

Behavioral and Mental Health in Italy

For over thirty years, and with very few changes in policy, the National Mental Health Reform Act (1978) or Law 180, has served as the legislative framework for Italy's care of the mentally ill. Spearheaded by the pioneer efforts of psychiatrist Franco Basaglia, Law 180 (commonly referred to as the Basaglia Law) was aimed at ending the institutional abuses suffered by the mentally ill. In Basaglia's terms, "If mental illness is a loss of individuality and liberty, in the "looney bin" the mental patient can find nothing more than a place where he will be definitely lost, where he will be made the object of his illness and by those who treat him" (Basaglia, 1964, p. 2).

Law 180 called for the closing of psychiatric institutions, and prohibited the referral of new patients to mental hospitals; compulsory admissions (involuntary treatment of patients determined to be dangerous to themselves or others) were permitted only in situations where outpatient interventions were ineffective. The Basaglia Law stimulated the development of community-based comprehensive mental health services. As a result, Italy became the first developed country to care for the mentally ill relying solely on community resources (Lora, 2009).

Under Law 180, deinstitutionalization was more than simply a matter of closing doors; the radical move to dismantle psychiatric institutions symbolized a new way of thinking about addressing mental health problems. Reform was intended to remove the stigma of mental illness as a societal danger, re-educate mental health personnel to exercise more compassion and humane treatment, and to the greatest extent possible, help patients regain their connection to the world outside (Basaglia, 1964). As one observer explains, "The process for the reform of public psychiatric assistance which has taken place in Italy over the last 30 years has resulted in the transition from an asylum psychiatry based on exclusion and internment to a community mental health work-style based on inclusion and the restoration and construction of rights for persons affected with mental disorders" (Del Giudice, 1998).

Administratively, Law 180 establishes the essential levels of care for the mentally ill, and Italy's 21 provinces are responsible for translating and implementing the mental health guidelines. Drug and alcohol problems are managed outside of the mental health system. Community-based mental health services utilize multi-disciplinary teams (e.g., psychiatrists, psychologists, social workers, nurses) to assist the mentally ill.

A complete network of mental health service in Italy consists of the following components (de Girolamo, Basi, Neri, Ruggeri, Santone, & Picardi, 2007):

- Departments of Mental Health (DMHs) represent the core of the system and are responsible for planning and managing all medical and social resources related to prevention, treatment, and rehabilitation (Lora, 2009, p.7) in defined geographical areas across the country.
- Community Mental Health Centers (CMHCs) are the hub of the community care (Lora, 2009) and manage a large portion of the outpatient and non-residential care through a network of therapeutic and rehabilitative services. CMHCs "provide individual consultations and visits, organize a variety of daytime

and domiciliary care activities for the most severely and disabled patients, establish and maintain contacts with other health and social agencies, and provide emergency interventions" (de Girolamo et al., 2007, p. 87). CMHCs are open on a 24-hour, 7-days-a-week basis. Less than 10% of the CMHCs provide overnight care (Lurie, 2008).

- General Hospital Psychiatric Units (GHPUs) provide acute in-patient care and work closely with CMHCs to provide continuity of care. GHPUS are open on a 24-hour, 7-days-a-week basis. By law, hospital units include no more than 20 beds (Lurie, 2008).
- Day Facilities (DFs) provide a range of activities including milieu therapy, vocational skills training, and job placement assistance. DFs are open typically 8 hours a day, 6 days a week.
- Italy has Residential Facilities (RFs) for chronically disabled people who require long term intervention. Frequently, RFs become a second home to a number of patients and resident turnover is low. Residential care includes visits and team based interventions in people's homes (Lurie, 2008).

Italy's healthcare system includes coverage of the mentally ill. Access to mental health services is free including medication for major mental disorders. The public health system also covers inpatient psychiatric care but it does not cover outpatient private consultations (de Girolamo et al., 2007). In comparison to the high ratio of mental health spending of the United Kingdom and Luxembourg (12% and 13%, respectively) Italy's mental health spending, along with Portugal and Spain, is low at an estimated ratio of 3–5% (IHE Report, 2008).

Current estimates for personnel employed by public mental health services include nurses making up nearly one-half of the workforce with psychiatrists and psychologists representing approximately one-quarter of mental health personnel. Statistically, the mental health system is made up of: 14,760 nurses (48%); 5,561 psychiatrists (18%); 1,850 psychologists (6%); 1,551 social worker's assistants (5%); 2,095 rehabilitation personnel (6.8%). Official information on the large number of private psychiatrists and psychologists is not available (Lurie, 2008; de Girolamo et al., 2007).

According to the European Policy Information Research for Mental Disorders (EPREMED, 2008) the most common mental disorder in Italy is major depression (9.9% of the general population) followed by specific phobia (5.4%) and panic disorder (1.5%).

As a group, anxiety disorders were the most frequent category of mental disorders, particularly for individuals aged 35–64. Alcohol dependency

(0.3%) and conduct disorder (0.3%) were less frequent. Women report higher rates of mood and anxiety disorders than men.

A survey (2001–2003) conducted by European Study of Epidemiology of Mental Disorders (ESEMeD), based on a sample of 4,712 Italian citizens, found that "men were twice as likely as women to report an alcohol disorder" (Lora, 2009, p. 7). Reports on the rate of suicide in Italy are conflicting (Girolamo et al., 2007). According to EUROSTAT, for example, the suicide rate in Italy decreased from 7.1% per 100,000 persons in 1996 to 5.9% per 100,000 in 2003, while other data suggest that the rate of suicide in Italy has increased over the past twenty years. Researchers agree that several sociological and cultural factors may affect interpretation of trends in suicide. Perhaps the most significant observation is that worldwide, Italy has one of the lowest rates of suicide (de Girolamo et al., 2007).

Italy's revolutionary approach to psychiatric reform has resulted in a number of favorable outcomes. Italy has demonstrated that the community-based model of mental health can be successful, particularly in terms of creating access to patients "who in the past might have refrained from any contact with the old-fashioned asylum system" (de Girolamo et al., 2007, p. 88). Statistically, over the past thirty years, the mental health system shows significant growth in treatment capacity (+89%) and accessibility (+243%) for new cases (Lora, 2009). Three years before the reform in 1978, compulsory admissions declined by 50%; by 1994 the percentage of compulsory admissions dropped by an additional 30% (20% in 1984 and 11.8% 10 years later) (Lora, 2009).

Largely due to his belief in work as an important pathway to rehabilitation, Basaglia's visionary efforts in psychiatric reform led to the development of highly successful social cooperatives, employment situations designed to assist marginalized members of society (e.g., mental patients, the disabled, substance abusers) to transition to the community and the workforce. Passed in 1991, Law 381 provides the regulatory framework for social cooperatives and stipulates that, at a minimum, 30% of the workers must be disadvantaged (Borzaga & Santuari, 2000).

Social cooperatives support the ideal of the community as stakeholders in the rehabilitative process. "In mental health practice, value is increasingly given to diversity, the promotion of connections and exchanges and social co-op strategies" (Del Giudice, 1998). Social cooperatives operate in the public and private sectors and provide a variety of services such as industrial cleaning, laundering services for hospitals and nursing homes, bookbinding, and hotel management. "By demonstrating that some specific needs can be better satisfied by the production of services, rather than by monetary transfers, social co-ops have helped to transform the Italian welfare system, in that they are better able to create social cohesion. Moreover, many of the services supplied are for the benefit of particularly needy groups (drug addicts, former inmates, and so forth). These services, as well as volunteerism, have also enhanced political awareness of the problems connected with social exclusion" (Borzaga & Santuari, 2000, p. 26).

Innovative strategies, no matter how successful, often involve significant issues that require attention. From a research perspective, one of the most concerning issues raised in the literature is that over three decades there has been only limited monitoring of Italy's dramatic change to a community care model: "Despite this model's dissemination throughout Italy and other European and non-European countries, its effectiveness has never been properly assessed" (Monzani, Erlicher, Lora, Piergiorgio, & Vittadini, 2008). Several years of possible lessons and discoveries to improve psychiatric care were lost due to the lack of scientific inquiry.

By 1999 all 76 of Italy's public mental institutions were shut down (Lora, 2009; de Girolamo et al., 2007). However, the physical closing of mental health institutions should not be confused with success in operationalizing the concept of community-based care. Progress in this regard has been slow and uneven (Lora, 2009; de Girolamo et al., 2007). As observers of the early days of reform suggest, guidelines for deinstitutionalization were general (Lora, 2009) and financing regulations, aimed at efficient health spending and ensuring quality interventions, opened the door to a number of unanticipated issues: "First, it soon became apparent that operational standards were difficult to set in psychiatry, owing to lack of agreement in the definition of diagnostic paradigms and therapeutic approaches" (Piccinelli, Politi, & Barale, 2002, p. 541). As a result, accreditation standards for mental health were based more on organizational and structural criteria such as the number of facilities, and availability of personnel rather than evidence-based practice (Piccinelli et al., 2002). As a decentralized health system, the 21 regions exercise great autonomy in mental health planning and budgeting. Piccinelli et al. (2002) point out the implications of regional discretion and mental health service: "In the absence of operational criteria, each mental health department is not required (by law, at least) to implement a comprehensive set of effective interventions. Apart from drug treatments, which are widely available, psychotherapeutic, and rehabilitation interventions may be based more on the availability, training and cultural paradigms of the personnel than on evidence–based data." (p. 541).

Community focused care in Italy presents challenges related to the coordination of mental health services including continuity of care, quality of care (e.g., poor prescribing practices) and the availability of specialized mental health services (e.g., services for child and adolescent psychiatry). Similar to the delivery of health care in general, these issues are strongly tied to the persistent issue of regional differences in service delivery, "... especially between the more wealthy areas of Northern and Central Italy and the poorer Regions of the South and the islands (e.g., Sicily and Sardinia)" (de Girolamo et al., 2007 p. 89). As an example, when it does become necessary to hospitalize a patient, a shortage of public inpatient beds is noted as particularly severe in the south (de Girolamo et al., 2007) with the number of beds varying greatly from the south to the northeast by nearly a 1:2 ratio (Lora, 200). The bed shortage issue affects length of stay. Data reveal the average length of stay in the northeast region as being nearly twice that of the central and southern regions (Lora, 2009). "In regions where public beds are scarce (as in the South) compulsory admissions are almost twice as frequent as they are in other areas of the country, in order to "oblige" hospitals to accept acute patients, at least in some instances" (de Girolamo et al., 2007, p. 86). Italy is recorded as having the lowest rate of inpatient beds in Europe (0.78 public acute inpatient beds per 10,000 inhabitants) and falls below the official national standard of 1 bed per 10,000 inhabitants (Lora, 2009). The low inpatient bed rate raises concerns for patients in acute crisis. Critical attention must be given to expanding the capacity of GHPUs and CMHCs to address this issue (Lora, 2009). An interesting feature of Italy's bed situation is that Law 180 did not affect private psychiatric facilities which provide over one-half (54%) of the acute inpatient beds (de Girolamo, et al., 2007). "Unfortunately, no reliable systematic data concerning the type and quality of care provided by private psychiatric facilities is to date available" (de Girolamo, et al., 2007, p. 89).

Added concerns for Italy's mental health system include the need for more attention to family burden in caring for the mentally ill, in other words, providing more educational interventions to help families work through the stress of caring for their mentally ill family members (e.g., feelings of loss, depression, and financial issues). Fioritti (2010) offers perspective on family burden: "Generally speaking, Italian society still relies very much on family links. Some comparative studies (de Girolamo et al., 2007, Fioritti et al., 1997) have shown that over 70% of patients with psychosis live with their family in an accommodation they own and in which they have lived for about twenty years. Patients are usually protected from certain psychosocial stresses (e.g., housing and finance) but quite dependent on significant others, whose involvement in the care process is almost always required" (p. 69).

Additional questions associated with Italy's reform concern quality of life issues in residential care: the restrictive rules imposed on patient behavior; the high dropout rates among patients with non-psychotic disorders; discharge issues in day care treatment centers (e.g., some patients may be in treatment for three or more years); and the need for more evidence-based practice to improve the quality of mental health care (Girolamo et al., 2007).

Researchers suggest the need to clarify the role of primary care in the mental health system. Deinstitutionalization has increasingly placed the General Practitioner (GP) in the system of psychiatric care. CMHCs tend to focus on the care of the severely mentally ill (e.g., schizophrenia) (Girolamo et al., 2007) while people with common mental health disorders (e.g., depression, anxiety, phobias) are more likely to seek out the GP for help (Berardi, Bortolli,, Menchetti, Bombi, & Tarricone, 2007). In The United States and the United Kingdom, the GP is recognized as having a crucial role in referring patients to mental health services (Berardi et al., 2007). In Italy, however, the scenario is more complicated "since general practice is not organized in a formal primary healthcare service" (Berardi, et al., p.80) and GPs work mostly solo. Further, patients may go directly to a mental health service without a physician referral. Characterizing cooperation between primary care and mental health as an unresolved issue, Berardi et al. (2007) suggest that, "The lack of national health policies on the management of common psychiatric disorders in General Practice, along with the lack of a General Practice filter to CHMCs implies, in our experience, poorly coordinated pathways to care. In fact, these patients can be visited by either GPs or psychiatrists, regardless of the severity and prognosis of their disease" (p.81). While collaborations between the family doctor and the consulting psychiatrist have proven effective in terms of continuity of care and improved patient care, the collaborative model is not widely practiced and, in some cases, is restricted to the type of psychiatric issues that can be addressed (Berardi et al., 2007).

In spite of a seemingly endless list of issues, many of Italy's reform challenges could be addressed through more systematic collection of data (Lora, 2009; Monzani et al., 2008; de Girolamo et al., 2007). "The lack of a national mental health information system severely hampers not only planning and monitoring, but also any analysis of the mental health system" (Lora, 2009, p. 14). High quality information is viewed as a key strategic tool for strengthening Italy's new system. "From information to action: this is the virtuous circle that we should be implementing over the next decade, promoting high quality information and using it to improve mental health systems and clinical practice" (Lora, 2009, p.15).

PREVALENCE AND MANAGEMENT OF BEHAVIORAL HEALTH CARE IN DEVELOPING COUNTRIES

Behavioral and Mental Health in Brazil

The mental health policy of Brazil is inspired by the Caracas Declaration of 1990, issued at the Regional Conference for the Restructuring of Psychiatric Care in Latin America in Caracas, Venezuela (de Almeida & Horvitz-Lennon, 2010). "The Caracas Declaration was the culmination of a process set in motion by several developments. One of them was the recognition that traditional psychiatric hospitals failed to meet the complex needs of people with mental disorders and engaged in frequent violations of patients' human rights" (de Almeida & Horvitz-Lennon, 2010, p. 218). Federal Law 10,216, implemented in 1991, and later revised in 2001, establishes the legislative framework for a model of mental health care in Brazil that ensures the civil rights of people with mental health problems, and "defines hospitalization as the last resource in the treatment of mental disorders" (Goncalves, Vieira, & Delgado, 2012). Mental health care is supported by, and falls under, the governance of the Brazilian Ministry of Health.

The primary source of financing for mental health in Brazil is tax based (WHO Mental Health Atlas, 2005). Under Brazil's Unified Health System, all citizens have free access to medical care including essential medications for all mental health conditions. "The medications considered essential according to the National List of Essential Medications include: carbamazepine, clonazepam, diazepam, phenytoin, phenobarbital, valproic acid, amitriptyline, hydrochloride, clomipramine, fluoxetine, biperiden, chlorpromazine and nortriptyline, lithium, carbonate, haloperidol, and risperidone" (Kantorski, Jardim, Porto, Schek, Cortes, & Oliveira, 2011, p. 1476). The essential medications are available at the primary care level as well as pharmacy units under The Brazilian Popular Pharmacy Program instituted in 2004. High cost drugs for chronic conditions such as epilepsy, Alzheimer's disease, and schizophrenia, are also part of an essential list of medications and financed by the Ministry of Health.

Kantorski et al., 2011, suggest that among the factors affecting the choice of an appropriate treatment, the costs of medication is a "complicating factor" in gaining access to medication. While community-based mental health centers were created to improve the accessibility of medications, many users need to buy their prescribed drugs. The costs of antipsychotics for users are 5% of the minimum salary for one day at the lowest price available, and for antidepressant medication it is 6% of the minimum salary for one day for the most inexpensive drug available (WHO-AIMS, 2007). "These are rather high values for people receiving less than one minimum salary or in some cases, no income at all" (Kantorski et al., 2011, p. 1476). Approximately 51% of the population receive low income salaries or none at all. In 2007, Brazil enacted directives that place responsibility on the states of the Federation and the municipalities to manage the procurement and distribution of psychotropic drugs (Kantorski et al., 2011).

A study of federal expenditures on mental health from 2001–2009 revealed a 53.1% increase in the funding of Brazil's mental health program (Goncalves, et al., 2012). This growth in expenditures revealed a significant increase in expenditures for community-based services (from 8% to 15% in 2005) and a decrease in funds allocated to hospital expenses, (from 95.5% to 49.3 % in 2005) (de Almeida & Horvitz-Lennon, 2010). "From 2006 onwards, resource allocation was shifted towards community services. The funding component played a crucial role as the inducer of the change of the mental healthcare model. The challenge for the coming years is maintaining and increasing the resources for mental health in a context of underfunding of the National Health System" (Goncalves et al., & Delgado, 2012).

Although Brazil demonstrates more fully developed mental health reform processes than other countries in the Latin American region, the outlay of federal spending for mental health is extremely small (de Almeida & Horvitz-Lennon, 2010) ranging between 2.0% and 5% of the country's federal health budget (Goncalves et al., 2012; de Almeida & Horvitz-Lennon, 2010). Current data indicate mental health spending in Brazil estimated at 2.35% of the total health budget (Almeida & Horvitz-Lennon, 2010), an investment in mental health that falls below the expenditure of 5% recommended for the adequate development of mental health services (Kantorski et al., 2011).

According to the WHO Mental Health Atlas (WHO, 2005), Brazil's mental health personnel include 4.8 psychiatrists, and 31.8 psychologists per 100,000 population. Alternative data collected in 2005 indicate that there are 6,003 psychiatrists, 18,763 psychologists, 1,985 social workers, 3,119 nurses, and 3,589 occupational therapists working for Brazil's Unified Health System. At the primary care level there are 104,789 physicians, 184,437 nurses and nurse technicians, and 210, 887 health agents (Mateus et al., 2008). Regional variations in staffing are evident in Brazil's north-south divide. As compared to the wealthy, industrialized southeast region with approximately 5 psychiatrists per 100,000 inhabitants, the poverty-stricken northeast region has less than 1 psychiatrist per 100,000 inhabitants (Mateus et al., 2008).

The shortage of psychiatric nurses is a problem in all geographic areas of Brazil. The insufficient numbers of psychiatric nurses in many countries is attributed to the stigma of mental illness, low salaries, concerns about safety, the lack of teamwork, and the fact that mental health nursing has not been a priority for decisionmakers or education systems (WHO, 2007). "Psychologists outnumber psychiatrists in all regions of the country. The distribution between urban and rural areas is also disproportionate. The density of psychiatrists in or around the largest city (Metropolitan Sao Paulo) is 1.75 times greater than the national average" (Mateus et al., 2008).

National epidemiological data on mental illness in Brazil are scarce or not available (Schmidt et al., 2011). However, several local studies and surveys indicate that the psychiatric burden of diseases is significant, about 19% (Gadelha et al., 2002).

- In 2007, 72% of all deaths were attributable to NCDs (principally, cardiovascular disease, chronic respiratory diseases, cancer, and diabetes). NCDs are the main source of the disease burden in Brazil with neuropsychiatric disorders being the largest contributor (Schmidt et al., 2011). "Most of the burden from neuropsychiatric disorders is due to depression, psychoses, and disorders attributable to alcohol misuse" (Schmidt et al., p. 1950).
- The most prevalent disorders in Brazil include nicotine dependence, alcohol abuse, anxiety disorders, and somatoform disorders; depression is the most common mood disorder (WHO, 2005).
- Depression and anxiety disorders in Brazil are more prevalent in people who are unemployed, have low education and income (Schmidt et al., 2011). Fregni (2007) points out that while Brazil has the eighth largest economy in the world; it has one of the worst income distributions. "These statistics explain why Brazilians get depressed." The difficult economic situation finds many Brazilian children dropping out of school early to help out their families. Researchers estimate that about 95% of children have access to school in Brazil but only 59% finish the 8th grade (Tramontina et al., 2001); low educational status is one of the known determinants of poor mental health. Belfer and Rohde (2005) observe that "street children with overt mental health problems go totally unattended" (p. 359) in Brazil.
- According to WHO, in 2003 18.8% of Brazilians were diagnosed as having depression in the last 12 months (Schmidt et al., 2011).
- A survey of 8th grade students (average mean age 14 years) in Brazilian state capitals revealed 71% had experimented with alcohol, 27% had consumed alcohol in the past 30 days, and 25% had been drunk at least once in their lives (Instituto Brasilerio de Geografia e Estatistica, 2009).

- Findings from a Brazilian study of school students aged 7 to 14, in a medium sized city in the state of Sao Paulo, revealed the overall prevalence rate of psychiatric disorders as 12.7%. Disruptive behavior disorders were the most prevalent (7.0%) followed by anxiety disorders (5.2%). Lower prevalences were found for hyperkinetic disorders (1.8%) and depressive disorders (1.0%) (Fletlich-Bilyk & Goodman, 2004).
- In a systematic review of dementia among elderly Brazilians, Fagundes, Silva, Thees, & Pereira (2011) observed that dementia was most prevalent among poor, illiterate, female, and very elderly individuals. Between 1996 and 2007, age-standardized dementia increased from 1.8 per 100, 000 to 7.0 per 100, 000, (Schmidt et al., 2011, p. 1951).

An outstanding feature of mental health care in Brazil involves the significant and growing role of mental health in primary care. Under Brazil's healthcare system, patients can receive treatment for their physical and mental health problems. In the context of primary care and an active commitment to mental health reform aimed at community-based care, Brazil provides mental health services through an "interconnected Comprehensive Mental Health Network" (Lazarus & Freeman, 2009, p. 26) that consists of the following components (Mateus et al., 2008).

- Family Health Teams (FHTs) are the model of primary care for Brazil as a whole, (Lazarus & Freeman, 2009). FHTs provide service to geographically defined areas throughout Brazil including the rural areas. The core providers of mental health care in FHTs usually include a GP, at least one nurse or nurse technician, and a community health worker (Lazarus & Freeman, 2009). The Mental Health Network provides support to FHTs through Mental Health Teams (MHTs) staffed by psychiatrists, psychiatric nurses, psychologists, social workers, and occupational therapists. Mental health care under the primary care model emphasizes joint collaboration, i.e., collaborative or shared mental health care. "Rather than transferring care through up and down transfer referral, collaborative care facilitates care remaining at the primary care level but with shared responsibility for decisions. This approach ensures good quality mental health care while also building the competence and autonomy of primary care practitioners. Therapeutic groups are facilitated by mental health and primary care professionals, while community workers and lay participants, run support groups" (Lazarus & Freeman, 2009, p.26).

- Psychosocial Community Centers (CAPS) provide specialized outpatient day and limited in-patient care. CAPS treat moderate to severe mental disorders with an emphasis on the severe (Mateus et al., 2008). The mental health teams of CAPS typically include a psychiatrist, a registered nurse, and professionals in areas such as social work, occupational therapy, and nursing assistants. CAPS are organized according to three levels of care. CAPS I units are located in small towns (20,000–50,000 population) and are open 5 days a week. CAPS II units provide service to medium size cities (50,000–200,000 inhabitants). CAPS III units are large units targeted at large cities (more than 200,000 inhabitants) and are open 24 hours a day including 5-24 hour beds for admissions. There are 66 CAPS for children and adolescents, and 109 CAPS for alcohol and drug problems (de Almeida & Horvitz-Lennon, 2010). Mateus et al. (2008) observe that CAPS for alcohol and drug abuse are strategically placed in cities where the problem shows a high prevalence. However, these CAPS are unevenly distributed with lower numbers in the north and northeast regions than the south and southeast regions.
- The Return Home Program provides help to individuals with long histories of psychiatric hospitalization, to regain their footing in the community through a monthly stipend transferred to their bank accounts. In 2006, there were 2,519 people receiving this benefit in the country.
- Psychiatric Hospitals, of which Brazil has 228, are either public or private and provide services to the public system. The total number of beds in psychiatric hospitals is 50,045 (27.17 beds per 100,000 inhabitants). The average length of stay in mental hospitals is 65.29 days. There are 592 general hospitals offering some psychiatric beds in general wards (approximately 1,224 beds). Data on the number of beds available for the destitute, persons with mental retardation, or in detoxification inpatient facilities is not available (Mateus et al., 2008). Brazil has 25 hospitals for custody and psychiatric treatment of criminal patients that are suspected of having, or actually have, a mental illness. The forensic hospitals are run by the prison system.
- Residential Facilities numbered 418 in 2006. These community residential facilities are allowed a maximum of 8 residents (Mateus et al., 2008).

Over the past two decades, Brazil has demonstrated remarkable progress in an attempt to restructure its mental health system to reflect the community oriented aims of the Caracas Declaration. Several innovative programs, such as CAPS and the Return Home program, have replaced flagging outpatient services through a "mixed system of mental health outpatient services, day hospitals, and therapy workshops" (Mateus et al., 2008; Jacob et al., 2007). Additionally, Sobral, a city in Brazil's low-income northeast region, is frequently referred to as a successful example of fully integrated mental health care in primary health care (Lazarus & Freeman, 2009; WHO/WONCA, 2008). The Sobral model "demonstrates the value of a number of interlocking strategies: a strong system of family centered primary health care (particularly appropriate for mental health care) together with specialist mental health support delivered through collaborative care and a network of supporting mental health resources including both hospital and community" (Lazarus & Freeman, 2009, p. 27).

Despite Brazil's impressive gains in mental health reform, and in less than two decades, the country faces a number of challenges. Several factors create huge treatment gaps in the delivery of mental health care, i.e., the proportion of people who need care and do not receive it (Rodriguez, 2010, p. 339). The difficulties start with the uneven distribution of mental health services at nearly every level of care. Typically, inhabitants in the urban areas have greater access to mental health services than those living in rural areas. The greatest number of health professionals, psychiatric beds, and CAPS are located in the urban areas. The north and northeast have fewer CAPS than the south and southeast regions (Mateus et al., 2008). Fregni (2007) introduces a phenomenon known as the "inverse care law" to characterize the socioeconomic factors that negatively impact access to mental health care: "At the present time, lower income populations that suffer the most from depression receive less mental health care, compared to the more privileged population."

Primary care is a part of Brazil's mental health system but it is limited and not well integrated. As Lazarus and Freeman (2009) explain, "The approach was developed during a period of general health care reform in Brazil (and Sobral in particular) that provided a set of favorable circumstances that may not be present in other contexts. The failure of some municipalities to authorize prescribing rights for primary care practitioners suggests, however, that there has not been universal acceptance of the value of primary mental health care–whether by primary care practitioners themselves, or mental health specialists" (p.41). Primary care is in need of more health professionals, and there is a need to expand training of GPs and general health professionals in the area of mental health.

The efficiency of the system would be enhanced if Brazil's academic institutions helped with the development of key common mental disorders guidelines to be applied in primary health care (Mateus et al., 2008).

The mental healthcare system requires more psychiatric nurses, more beds in general hospitals, and more CAPS dedicated to address the mental health needs of children and adolescents.

Researchers consistently point to Brazil's "chronic" lack of clinical research in mental health. "Research conducted in Brazil does not necessarily address national health priorities because research grants are based only on scientific merits. Researchers usually choose topics likely to be published internationally such as clinical trials involving newer and more expensive drugs. Information generated from this research does not benefit the poor" (Fregni, 2007). Mateus et al. (2008) add that there is a need to develop standardized epidemiological tools to aid in the systematic collection of data concerning the prevalence and incidence of mental disorders.

In the global market of escalating drug prices, sometimes 30 times higher than traditional psychotropic medication, Brazil must identify alternatives that are tailored to its socioeconomic conditions. For example, there are studies which demonstrate that "old antidepressants can be as effective as newer antidepressants; therefore these old drugs need to be included and mandatory in the psychiatric training. This is especially important as physicians are more likely to prescribe and use drugs with which they have experience" (Fregni, 2007).

Similar to many countries, Brazil is facing the challenge of meeting the mental and physical needs of a rapidly aging population; this issue involves an inevitable burden on families. "Moreover, changes such as smaller families and more women in the paid workforce have reduced families' ability to provide support and health care for elderly people" (Schmidt et al., 2011, p. 1955). Finally, increasing the health budget to 5% will provide Brazil with a sounder financial basis for strengthening the mental health system and narrowing treatment gaps. Careful attention must be given to directing funds to community-based and ambulatory services rather than psychiatric hospitals.

Brazil is committed to creating a viable mental health system. In October 2009, nearly 20 years after the Caracas Declaration, the 49th Directing Council of the Pan American Health Organization (PAHO/WHO) approved the Strategy and Plan of Action on Mental Health for the Region of Americas. Brazil's Ministry of Health has adopted this plan. The Regional Strategy emphasizes the development of national mental health policies and laws, the psychosocial development of children, primary healthcare centered mental health services delivery, and capacity building in terms of human resources and strengthening the capacity to produce, assess, and use information on mental health (Rodriguez, 2010, p. 339).

Behavioral and Mental Health in Cuba

Cuba, considered a developing country by the World Bank standards, in regard to its healthcare system is more characteristic of a high income country. Cuba commits 50% of its total health budget to mental health. Similar to its general healthcare policies and provisions, mental health services are structured and provided at the primary care level, with direct care and services provided by primary healthcare physicians, psychiatrists, and psychiatric nurses based in the community. All primary care mental health professionals receive regular training. The Cuban structure of mental healthcare supports 1 medical doctor for every 200 persons, making the integration of mental health care and services almost seamless (WHO, 2005).

Although the emphasis is on community-based care and services, where 75% of mental health services are provided, there are 7.36 psychiatric beds per 10,000 in the population which equates to each of the 14 regions in Cuba having a 20–30 bed psychiatric unit. There are 10 psychiatrists per 100,000 in the population, 7.7 psychiatric nurses, and 1.9 psychologists (WHO, 2005).

The community-based mental healthcare stresses prevention, promotion, and intervention, especially in the home and residential facilities with family integrally involved. Comprehensive mental health services are provided as well as social rehabilitation that includes vocational and employment training and education (WHO, 2005).

Cuba has had a substance abuse policy since 2000 that has been 50%–75% implemented and a National Mental Health Program that was 85–90% implemented by regional and national authorities by 2000. Other legislation policies and initiatives include a substance abuse policy initially developed in 2000 that decentralizes mental health resources. Special populations include older adults and children, and there are special programs for victims of domestic violence, suicide, substance use, and social rehabilitation. The ICD-10 system is used for data collection purposes (WHO, 2005).

Using a representation sample of 1,140 persons over the age of 60 from two Cuban regions and using a two stage sampling technique, DSM-III-R and NINCDS-ADRDA criteria, Libre et al. (1999) reported the following findings:

- Dementia was found in 8.2% of the population, of which 5.1% was attributed to Alzheimer's Disease and vascular type dementia.

- Dementia was positively correlated with being female and without a spouse.
- Of the sample, 45.2% reportedly were drinkers, although the overall prevalence of alcohol dependence in the over 15 year old population is 8.8%.
- The eastern regions had higher prevalence rates of alcohol drinking.
- Smoking was highly correlated with heavy drinking.
- Suicide was higher in rural areas of Cuba among older adult men, although women had more suicide attempts than men.

Reynaldo et al. (2002) used a psychometric testing and structured interventions to assess the prevalence of psychiatric disorders in 150 patients with spinocerebellar ataxia type 2, and found that 88% manifested symptoms related to mental disease which included disorders involving adaptation, sleep, mood, and sexual disorders. Mental retardation and dementia were also diagnosed.

Cuba has a relatively high mental illness prevalence rate with an associated high incidence of violent acts. In fact, homicide, suicide, and violent events, considered external causes of death, account for the fourth leading cause of death in Cuba. Cuba's suicide rate is inordinately higher than other Caribbean countries of similar background and region (deGordon, nd). Annual suicide deaths per 100,000 in Cuba for 2003 – 2005 was 13.6, while the rate in the USA was 10.8 (PAHO, 2009). Many attribute the external causes of death in Cuba to the high rates of alcohol consumption or binge drinking, reported as 80% of the adult population (deGordon, nd).

Other areas of mental health concern in Cuba include the high abortion rate—although declined from 1999, it is still among the highest in Latin America (Sixto, 2002)—and a homicide rate of 7.0 per 100,000. Also, there seems to be a steady increase in posttraumatic stress disorders, dementia, and cognitive impairment. In 2000, The Pan American Health Organization (PAHO) reported that 4.38% of Cuba's population between ages 60 and 74 suffered from Alzheimer's dementia. This prevalence jumped to 22.6% for Cubans 75 years and older (PAHO, 2002).

Typically, the majority of Latin American countries devote less than 2% of their total health budget to mental health, perpetuating the problem of burden of diseases. Such problems as stress-related relationship violence and sociopolitical stressors go unaddressed. Latin America shows 10.5% of the world's total burden of disease due to neuropsychiatric disorders, among which unipolar depression represents 35.7% of the psychiatric problems, alcoholism represents 18.2%, schizophrenia 7.8%, bipolar affective disorder 6.6%, and substance abuse 5.6%.

Behavioral and Mental Health in India

Psychiatric epidemiology studies lag behind other branches of epidemiology. According to Math, Chandrashekar, and Bhugra (2007) epidemiological studies report "prevalence rates for psychiatric disorders in India from 9.5 to 370/1,000 in the population" (p. 183). These discrepancies can be attributed to, "difficulties encountered in conceptualizing, diagnosing, defining a case, sampling in selecting an instrument, lack of resources and stigma" (Kessler, 2000). These discrepancies, commonly seen in international studies, although not specific to India, could impact planning, funding, and healthcare delivery. Providing accurate data about the prevalence of mental disorders in the community would help to justify the allocation of scarce resources and planning of health services (Math et al., 2007).

Math et al. (2007) attempted to critically evaluate the overall prevalence rate of psychiatric disorders as reported in epidemiology studies from India. With the exception of one study, all the past epidemiological studies have surveyed a population of less than 6,000 raising questions about generalizing the findings to even one country like India. However, the findings of one study suggest that, "mental healthcare priorities need to be shifted from psychotic disorders to common mental disorders like depression, anxiety disorders, somatoform disorders, etc. which are also associated with high disability in all measures" (Patel et al., 1998).

Chandra et al. (2001) report that India has an estimated 5.8% prevalence rate of mental illness with the highest prevalence in females over 55 years old. Depression is reportedly the most common problem among individuals 60 years and older. The national suicide rate is 9.2 per 100, 000 in the population (males 10.6 and females 7.9). Suicide is highest among the 30- to 44-year-old age group. The most common method of suicide is by poisoning and hanging. Epilepsy and hysteria are significantly higher in rural India than in the urban areas (Chandra et al., 2001).

In a study assessing the prevalence of suicide, clinical depression, and anxiety disorders in a sample of 150 men who have sex with men (MSM) in Mumbai, India, Sivasubramanian et al. (2011) found that "the frequency of psychosocial and mental health problems among MSM in Mumbai was strikingly high suggesting a significant mental health burden exists among this population" (p. 458). Further, 45% reported current suicidal ideations, suggesting that there is a significant unmet need for mental health services for MSM in Mumbai (p. 458).

India has the greatest number of HIV infections of any nation in Asia and the third largest national HIV epidemic in the world (UNAIDS, 2008; UNAIDS & WHO, 2008). While the generalized heterosexual epidemic of HIV in India appears to be stabilized or declining (Arora, Kumar, Bhattacharya, Nagelkerke, & Jha, 2008) "MSM ...prevalence estimated to be 7.4% nationally, is 12.5% in Mumbai, India's largest city" (Kumta et al., 2010; National AIDS Control Organization, 2008). The role of mental health, although unclear, may be linked to the associated stress experienced by MSM.

India spends 2.05% of its total health budget on mental health. The primary funding sources financing mental health, in descending order, are taxes, out-of-pocket, private insurance, and social insurance (WHO, 2005). India has re-strategized its approach to mental health. It aims to provide a balanced mix of closely networked services with budgetary support for modernizing government-operated mental hospitals, strengthening its medical colleges, and departments of psychiatry, and implementing a 100 district mental health program. During the first phase of this program the focus will be on improving information, education, communication strategies, training, and research. This first district-wide mental program covers 24 districts; however the plans are to expand the program to 100 districts by 2020 (Chandra et al., 2001).

Mental health care in India is part of the primary healthcare system and is available in 22 of 660 districts in India. The plans are to eventually expand to 100 districts. India's Mental Health Act of 1987 simplified admissions and discharge procedures and provided facilities for children and drug abusers. This legislation also promoted human rights for the mentally ill. Other mental health legislative initiatives that seek to protect the rights of the mentally ill include the Juvenile Justice Act, The Persons with Disabilities Act, and the Narcotic Drugs and Psychotropic Substance Act last amended in 2001 (WHO, 2005). Services provided by the government health center are free. The country also has limited disability benefits for persons with mental illnesses.

There are 0.25 total psychiatric hospital beds in India per 10,000 in the population (0.2 in mental hospitals and 0.05 in general hospitals). One-third of the mental health beds are confined to one state (Maharashtra). Several states have no mental health hospitals at all. For the hospitals with beds, many of the beds are taken up by patients who have long term stays. During the past two decades, many mental hospitals have been reformed through the interventions of volunteer organizations such as Action Aid India and the National Human Rights Commission. However, mental hospitals still have shortages of drugs and other treatment. Also, there are very few mental health beds in rural areas, resulting in family being encouraged to stay with patients who were voluntarily admitted. Some beds are specifically designated for the care of patients who were admitted for drug treatment and some are designated for children.

There are 0.2 psychiatrists per 100,000 in the population, 0.05 psychiatric nurses, 0.03 psychologists and social workers. Keeping mental health professionals is a challenge for India. For example, in 2003 India lost more than 82 psychiatrists to the United Kingdom where they went for training sessions and never returned (WHO, 2005). Similar to other countries, NGOs are involved in mental health in a variety of ways. They assist with counseling, suicide prevention, training of lay counselors, and providing rehabilitation through day care, sheltered workshops, halfway houses, and providing hostels for recovering patients, and long-term care facilities as needed. They also support, advocate for, and operate family self-help programs. There is, however, no consistent data on evaluation of care outcomes or epidemiological studies on mental health for disaster affected populations and older adults, and there are no documented school-based programs (WHO, 2005).

Jorm (2000) suggests that mental disorders in India are, "highly stigmatized conditions that many people want to keep private because of their embarrassment or fear of discrimination" (p.187). According to Math et al. (2007), the problem with systematic underreporting continues to be a major challenge for the future of psychiatric epidemiology in India (p. 187).

Behavioral and Mental Health in the Russian Federation

Soviet psychiatry is the predecessor of modern day psychiatry in the Russian Federation (Polubinskaya, 2008). For several decades, including the Soviet era, mental illness was regarded as a biological disease. Soviet psychiatry operated from this disease perspective. In this context, mental illness was viewed as a sickness (Jenkins, et al., 2007) that required medical treatment, and in severe cases, institutionalization. The disease focus was not person-centered, psychodynamic, or introspective, and except for a few rehabilitative measures, such as work therapy, treatment of the mentally ill was largely somatic in nature (Roth, 1994). Polubinskaya, (2008) suggests that the predominantly biological nature of psychiatry in the Soviet era meant that the patient's psychology, problems, and rights, did not take first place with the psychiatrist.

The disease focus, along with other factors of Soviet society, set the stage for the abuse of psychiatry and "total neglect for the human rights" of the mentally ill (Polubinskaya, 2008). The Soviet abuse of psychiatry was associated with the practice of hospitalizing people who were not mentally ill for their dissident political or religious beliefs (Lavretsky, 1998, p. 537). "The lack of a democratic tradition in Russia, a totalitarian regime, and oppression and extermination of the best psychiatrists during the 1930-50 period, prepared the ground for the abuse of psychiatry and the Russian-Soviet concept of schizophrenia" (Lavretsky, 1998, p. 537). A complex array of causes has been attributed to the abuse of psychiatry in Soviet Russia, starting with the imprecision of the disease model and diagnostic criteria, particularly the classification of schizophrenia. "The interpretation of any deviation from the norm by a psychiatrist as a symptom of schizophrenia played an important role in the abuse of psychiatry in the Soviet Union (Polubinskaya, 2008). The problem of inadequate diagnostic criteria was fueled by Soviet psychiatry's isolation from different schools of thought regarding the etiology and treatment of mental illness, poor standards of clinical training and practice, and the absence of a legal infrastructure and a professional code of ethics.

Since the fall of the Soviet Union, the new Russia has attempted to address a Soviet legacy of difficult psychiatric practices including the political abuse of psychiatry. The Ministry of Health and Social Development provides the central policy for the delivery of mental health care in Russia. In keeping with the democratic aims of Glasnost (openness) the Russian Federation Mental Health Act was adopted (On Psychiatric Care and Guarantees of Citizens' Rights) in 1992. The Law of Psychiatric Care called for professional accountability through the creation of a code of ethics, a respect for patients' rights, and monitoring of psychiatric facilities to ensure the observance of patients' rights. The law established what was missing in Soviet psychiatry—a legal foundation for the delivery of psychiatric care. The law "became the first step in the reform of Russian psychiatry" (Polubinskaya, 2008). From a therapeutic perspective, the law was aimed at encouraging the development of the psychiatrist–patient relationship as a partnership rather than the dominant paternalistic relationship of Soviet psychiatry (Gurovich, 2007, Bartenev, 2004).

The Medico-Social Expert Commission (MSEC), established under the Ministry of Health and Social Development, plays a pivotal role in the Russian mental health system (Jenkins, et al., 2010) and "acts as a gatekeeper to social protection services, including pensions, rehabilitation, and employment services" (p. 222). Local branches of the MSEC assess the level of disability of individuals with physical or mental problems. The evaluations of MSEC staff can affect whether or not people are able to access rehabilitation and employment services. Jenkins, et al. (2010) identify a critical issue of access presented by MSECs: "In Russia, the emphasis remains on medical aspects of treatment, without adequate consideration of social and occupational rehabilitation. Links with local employment services are weak. To promote social inclusion, steps must be taken to encourage and facilitate cooperation and collaboration between the MSECs, employment services and medical services" (Jenkins, et al., 2010, p.222).

Russia's mental health services are financed through central taxation followed by the ministries of each oblast determining how funds will be allocated. The essential levels of care provide free medication to people who are hospitalized, disabled due to mental illness, and those affected by schizophrenia and epilepsy; medications for outpatients services are inexpensive (WHO 2005, p. 392). "The compulsory insurance scheme introduced in the 1990s and funded through central taxation does not include coverage for outpatient mental health counseling. Russian employers typically do not have private insurance that allows for third-party payments to cover mental health counseling or psychotherapy. This means counseling is available only to those who can afford private fees, or have access to an Employee Assistance Program (EAP)" (Sharar & Shtoulman, 2010).

Mental health spending is a low priority in most health systems across cultures. "Two-thirds of the world's population live in countries that spend less than 1% of their total budget on mental health services including 15 out of 19 countries in Africa for which data were reported" (Dixon, McDaid, Knapp and Curran, 2006, p.171). Russia is on record for having spent 0.2% of the GDP in the mid 1990s on mental health initiatives which eventually failed due to lack of funding (Jenkins et al., 2007; Polubinskaya, 2008). Data on the specific amount of the GDP budgeted for mental health spending in Russia is not available (WHO, 2005). "Despite the staggering social and economic impact there is little interest or priority given by public and private funders to the development of mental health services in Russia" (Fuchs, 2007, CCDS, 2007).

Russia's mental health infrastructure consists of the following services (Gurovich, 2007):

- Inpatient hospital care or psychiatric hospitals which provide specialized psychiatric care (e.g. suicidological, neuropsychiatric, sexological, adolescent, gerontological).
- Dispensary services or Psychoneurological Dispensaries (PNDs) are mental health institutions which focus on outpatient care and provide rehabilitation services, specialized psychiatric services, occupational therapy facilities, and hostels for individuals who have lost their social connection.

- Out-of-Dispensary Services also provide outpatient care, and emphasize service delivery in consulting rooms which are located within inpatient and outpatient facilities, institutions, and industrial work settings. Consulting rooms are a predominant form of mental health delivery in rural areas.
- Community Crisis Response Services, created in the 1990s under the Ministry of Emergency Situations, provide medical and psychological services related to wars, ecological disasters, homelessness, violence, emergencies, post-traumatic stress, psychosomatic disorders and forced migration (refugees).

There are reportedly up to 450,000 active NGOs in Russia (Flounders, 2006); however the number of NGOs providing service to the mentally ill is insufficient (Krasnov, Gurovich and Bobrov, 2010). According to WHO 2005, only 10 NGOs provided mental health services including social service support by religious organizations such as the Russian Orthodox Church (WHO, 2005). Treatment centers for drug and alcohol addiction operate outside of the mental health system. People who use the cost-free state services are put on the government's drug user registry. However, many prefer to pay for treatment and avoid the consequences of registration. "The drug user registration system keeps users away from substance abuse clinics by penalizing rather than rewarding treatment-seeking behavior" (Human Rights Watch, 2007, p. 56). In spite of confidentiality laws, drug users are concerned that registration will affect their ability to keep a job or seek employment opportunities, and restrict their ability to drive or own a car The continuous underfunding of treatment clinics, long wait lists, and the threat of the registry have led to the widespread practice of out-of-pocket payments. Patients who can afford to pay have access to higher quality service (Bobrova et al., 2007; Human Rights Watch, 2007). A qualitative study of Intrauterine Device (IUD) users in Russia identified three main barriers to treatment access: financial constraints, the fear of stigma, and the perceived low effectiveness of treatment procedures (Bobrova, Alcorn, Rhodes, Rughnikov, Neifeld, & Power, 2007).

In 2003, the number of mental health professionals included 14,439 psychiatrists, and 1,939 psychotherapists per 10,000 of the population. Recent data indicates that psychiatrists outnumber mental health specialists (e.g., psychologists, social workers) by a ratio of 4 to 1, and there are regional differences in the number of specialists throughout the country (Gurovich, 2007). According to Jenkins et al. (2010) "The shortage of social workers in Russia, which is exacerbated by the fact that many new social work graduates seek employment in the higher paid private sector, means that social work is severely constrained" (p.223). Gurovich (2007) emphasizes that low salaries are only part of the difficulty of attracting specialists to psychiatry and that "the initiative of mental health system administrators is insufficient" (p. 2).

Despite a significant decrease in psychiatric beds since 1990 (40,000 beds or one-fifth of its total bed capacity) (Gurovich, 2007), Russia has the highest number of psychiatric beds in the European Union with a reported 164,752 beds or 11.6 per 10,000 of the population in 2003 (Bartenev, 2004). Gurovich (2007) points out several issues related to Russia's bed capacity that raise questions for the development of community-based care: the high length of stay for all patients in general (77.4 days in 2006); the high rate of re- hospitalizations in hospitals more than one year; and the hospitalization of patients with non-psychotic disorders who could be receiving outpatient services. "In Russia, bed capacities are also highly centralized: more than 40% of beds belong to large hospitals of at least 1000 beds each. The question arises: With respect to reducing bed capacities, are we really achieving the goal of departing from relying on the hospital component of our mental health services?" (Gurovich, 2007).

Russia's mental health problems are as concerning as the health issues it is struggling to address. Dwindling social support services, unemployment, and an unstable economy following the collapse of the Soviet Union, are often cited as critical factors that account for Russia's poor mental health outcomes. However, certain culturally condoned norms (Oxford Analytica, 2009) as well as unhealthy life styles (e.g., poor nutrition) figure significantly in Russia's mental health challenges. For example, Russia's problems with alcohol and tobacco consumption are legendary. One million people die each year from alcohol and tobacco related illnesses in Russia (NBGH, 2011). As a country in the depths of a population crisis, what Russia regards as lamentable is that alcohol and tobacco consumption are among the leading causes of preventable deaths. With regard to the prevalence of smoking in Russia, approximately 60% of all adult men over age 18 smoke; more than half of teenagers smoke (approximately 60% males, and 40% females); and approximately 27.5% of 15-year-old males and 18.5% of 15-year-old females are current smokers of at least 6 cigarettes per day at least 17 days per month (NBGH, 2011).

The prevalence of alcohol consumption in Russia has been captured in banner headlines: "The Kremlin estimates that Russians consume 32 pints of pure alcohol per capita per year, more than double the World Health Organization's recommended maximum" (Osborn, 2011). The estimated percentage of disability-adjusted life years lost (DALYs) due to alcohol is 28% for men and 11 percent for women, much higher than in other large countries such as the United States, Brazil, Germany, or

China. (Oxford Analytica, 2009). Heavy drinking in Russia has exacted tremendous social costs in terms of reduced workplace productivity, high rates of absenteeism from work (as high as 75%), traffic accidents, violence, elevated crime levels, and the breakdown of family life (RIA Novosti, 2011; Sharar & Shtoulman, 2010; Oxford Analytica, 2009). According to the United Nations, Russia had the world's highest rate of divorce in 2010 (RIA Novosti, 2011). Russian government officials indicate that 75% of the 12,000 murders prosecuted in the country in 2010, were carried out under the influence of alcohol (Osborn, 2011).

The status of mental health in Russia is characterized by more dramatic statistics. News stories worldwide report that in the 20 years since the break-up of the Soviet Union, 800,000 people committed suicide, "more than one every 15 minutes in a country with a population of 142.9 million" (Amos, 2011). In 2002, Russia had the second highest rate of suicide for men in the world (McDaid et al., 2006) particularly in the middle-aged group. "The WHO Global Burden of Disease Study reported that in 2002, Russian men had the highest rate of suicide in the WHO European region with rates of 69.3 per 100,000 males and 97.2 per 100,000 in the 45-54 year old age group" (Fuchs, 2007). Current WHO data place Russia as having the sixth highest suicide rate in the world, with 23.5 per 100,000 people, while the country's Sebersky State Research Center indicates that Russia has the second highest suicide rate in the world, with Lithuania in the lead (Chaykovskaya, 2011). Suicide rates for Russian children are equally as gripping. Russia has the third highest rate of adolescent suicide in the world behind Kazakhstan and Belarus, (UNICEF, 2011). Approximately 1,500 teenagers between the ages of 15 and 19 commit suicide each year (UNICEF, 2011); similar to other countries, the suicide rate for this age group is higher for adolescent males--on average, 10.5% (Wasserman et al., 2005). "Poverty is not the leading cause of suicide. According to various research data, up to 92 per cent of suicides among children and adolescents are directly or indirectly rooted in their disadvantaged family situation (parental alcoholism, conflicts in the family, abusive treatment)" (UNICEF, 2011).

Approximately 10% of the Russian population, or at least 3 million Russians, (Levina & Lubov, 2007) suffer from a severe mental illness. Krasnov et al. (2010) report the prevalence of mental disorders registered in psychiatric institutions as 2,978.7 per 100,000 population. From the perspective of family burden, "More than 80% of these people are cared for by their family members. In total, considering the number of family caregivers, mental illness directly affects at least 10 million Russians, or one in every fifteen people. However, the mental health service system has an extreme deficit of personnel skilled in psychosocial support and intervention, resulting in little support for families" (Levina & Lubov, 2007). In 2002, 934,200 people were certified with disabilities because of mental illness (Bartenev, 2004). Sharar and Shtoulman (2010) indicate that this number has reached 1 million. "Mental health problems such as depression and bipolar illness account for 20% of all those registered as disabled" (p.3).

Similar to the country's healthcare system, primary care in Russia's mental health system is underdeveloped and offers little to people with psychological problems (Sorlie, Rezvy, Hoifodt, Yashkovich, & Proselkova, 2011). Krasnov et al. (2010) speak to the urgent need to develop and reform outpatient psychiatric services due to the increasing numbers of primary care patients (25–30%) that require a psychiatric consultation. In their look at the issue of primary care in post-communist countries, Jenkins, Klein, and Parker (2005) point out issues in contemporary Russia's mental health services that are reminiscent of issues in Soviet Russia: "Primary care services are not generally expected to manage common mental disorders, and most simply refer patients to specialist services. While access to essential medicines is usually possible, access to evidence based psychological interventions is still limited. This arises from isolation from the West, and poor awareness of the international evidence base on diagnosis, effective services, and interventions." (p. 173).

The new Russia has attempted to shed the narrow model of Soviet psychiatry in favor of mental health initiatives that emphasize community-based care. Under Russian mental health law, GPs with no specific specialization in psychiatry have been barred from diagnosing or treating mental health disorders. Recognizing the important role of mental health services in primary care, recent amendments in 2011 will "enable General Practitioners to treat depressive and psychosomatic disorders, diagnose serious mental disorders and follow up psychiatric patients after their treatment by the specialist health services" (Sorlie, et al., 2011, p. 1568). Over the past decade, interventions such as The Sverdlovsk Mental Health Reform Project, an action research project aimed at establishing an integrated approach to mental health reform (see Jenkins, et al., 2007) and the Canada-Russia Disability Program, an initiative aimed at improving social work practice in mental health settings (see Fuchs, 2007), provided Russia's health professionals with education and training on mental health issues, evidence-based technologies, curriculum development, and psychiatric consultation. The projects demonstrate the important role of knowledge development in creating community-based care (Fuchs, 2007) and that it is possible for Russia to forge sustainable links between mental health services and primary care (Jenkins, et al., 2007).

In spite of promising moves forward, changing the balance of mental health services in the Russian Federation will require attention to a number of challenges. "Addressing these barriers is necessary to shift away from hospital-centered mental health services emphasizing institutionalization, towards multisectoral approaches that foster community-based services supported by multidisciplinary teams that foster social inclusion of persons with mental health" (Fuchs, 2007).

An outstanding issue that limits access to mental health care and impacts all levels of service to the mentally ill involves funding. In particular, hospital dominated funding must change; economic incentives must be created to overcome undue delays in discharging individuals from inpatient care, and to discourage health professionals from opposing change (McDaid et al., 2006). "Downsizing the hospital sector and shifting to community based care requires reducing or redeploying staff. This is politically difficult to achieve and requires carefully designed human resource policies" (Fuchs, 2007).

Secondly, financing regulations prevent pooling of budgets from different service sectors, and shifting funds from health to social protection services (Fuchs, 2007). The restrictive funding mechanisms hamper timely, coordinated access to mental health care. Considerable attention must be given to building the capacity of social protection services and providing patients access to housing, social services, vocational rehabilitation, and jobs (McDaid et al., 2006). Federal law in Russia requires employers to ensure that 3% of their workforce includes persons with disabilities or they will be fined. However, individuals with mental problems are rarely placed. Jenkins et al. (2010) observes that while there was a remarkable increase in hiring the disabled in the Sverdlovsk Oblast (273 individuals in 1997 to 1,540 disabled in 2002) very few jobs went to people with mental health problems. "Not surprisingly, many employers would have opted to pay the meager fine of 2,000 rubles ($70) that the law prescribes rather than employ people with disabilities. In 2003, the Sverdlovsk Oblast government collected fines amounting to two million rubles ($70,000). This revenue has been allocated to rehabilitation and sheltered work placements for people with physical disabilities but not to services for people with mental illness" (Jenkins et al., 2010, p. 224).

Finally, achieving fully integrated mental health services in the Russian Federation will require policies that address the Russian *health system as a whole* including financial, structural, and legal issues (Fuchs, 2007). Commitment to mental health reform is evidenced in Russia's federal program for The Prevention of and Fighting Against Socially Significant Diseases 2007–2011. Under this program, improving mental health services in Russia will include more emphasis on building the multi-professional team approach to mental health care; increased collaboration between mental health and social services; more attention to providing comprehensive treatment that emphasizes psychosocial interventions at early stages of patient care; and strengthening the capacity of the primary care sector, particularly in identifying non-psychotic disorders (e.g., depression, psychosomatic disorders) for people who access primary care professionals (Gurovich, 2007).

Behavioral and Mental Health in Ghana

The lack of recent literature documenting healthcare initiatives, especially mental health, suggests that there have been very few changes in the healthcare system in Ghana for decades. Also, Ghana's epidemiological data are dated.

The WHO (2008, p. 9) estimates that, "of the 216 million people living in Ghana, 650,000 are suffering from a severe mental disorder and a further 2,166,000 are suffering from a moderate to mild mental disorder. The treatment gap is 98 percent of the total population expected to have a mental disorder." One of the reasons attributed to making it difficult for mental health practice in Ghana, is the traditional stigma attached to mental health. The traditional healing of mentally ill patients in Ghana gives rise to disturbing trends. For example, according to the WHO (2006, p.10), "in Ghana, the proliferation of spiritual churches, prayer camps and other unorthodox institutions have become threats to patient's rights and appropriate treatment."

In a 2006 Public Agenda report, Acting Medical Dr. Anna Dzadey of Pantang Psychiatric Hospital was quoted as saying that "more often, mental health patients are kept in police custody for a prolonged period of time without any legal reason, before being brought to the hospital for evaluation and treatment" (Public Agenda, 7 April 2006, p. 10). According to the Accra Office of the Commonwealth Human Rights Initiative (CHRI) human rights violations in prayer camps are widespread in Ghana, in the form of chaining, beating, insults, denial of food and lock-ups in crowded rooms". The report continues, Minister of Health Quashigah says that, "his outfit was preparing various health bills that included a bill on traditional, psychic and faith based healers. It is expected that the bill will become a law which would allow the country to regulate and monitor such practices" (Public Agenda, 15 August 2008, p. 10).

Affinnih (1999) found in a sample of 117 Ghanaians that heroin and cocaine were the most common drugs abused in Ghana. Prevalence of psychiatric disorders in 96 patients revealed that 50% of them suffered from affective, neurotic, and stress disorders. Behavioral disorders and drug use was common among adolescents. Depression, dementia, and paranoid disorders ranked highest in the over 60-year-old age group.

Although the first mental health asylum opened in Accra in 1906, Ghana did not formalize its mental health policy until many decades later. This is especially noteworthy because the asylum had housed more than 1,700 patients by 1960. Ghana enacted mental health legislation in 1961. However, it did not have a specific Mental Health Policy in place until 1994 to implement legislative mandates. The policy was later revised in 2000. The policy has the components of advocacy, promotion, prevention, treatment, and rehabilitation. The NRC Decree enacted in 1972 remains the current mental health law. There are also three legislative initiatives in Ghana that govern substance abuse. These are The Narcotic Drugs (Control, Enforcement and Sanctions) Law of 1990, PNDC Law 236, and the Pharmacy and Drug Act of 1961 (WHO, 2005).

The Ministry of Health is the core structure under which mental health services are provided. Ghana commits 0.5% of its total health budget to mental health that is supported by a tax-based source of financing. The WHO also contributes to Ghana's mental health budget. Mental health hospital admissions, medications, and tests are subsidized unless the patient is very poor, in which case care is free. Disability benefits are available to persons with mental disorders although they are primarily available to persons who are employed in the public sector (WHO, 2005).

Mental health in Ghana is part of the primary healthcare system. Trained psychiatrists and nurses are available in most regions to respond to the needs of patients. With Danish support, regular training of especially community psychiatric nurses and medical assistants is conducted in the northern regions of Ghana. WHO support provides much-needed training of volunteers and mental health professionals staffing facilities based in the community. Ghanaians utilize "healing churches" that help with community care. Although not in abundance, there are also half-way houses and charitable institutions that support community care for the mentally ill.

There are 1.03 psychiatric beds per 10,000 in the population of which one in 10,000 beds is specifically in what is designated as a mental hospital. In Ghana's three regional hospitals, there are approximately 10–20 beds designated as psychiatric, to which patients with mental illnesses may be admitted. There are no beds specifically designated as psychiatric in Ghana's Military or Police Hospitals.. Rather, if necessary these patients are transferred to the already overcrowded Accra Psychiatric Hospital. This hospital also lacks the necessary infrastructure to support the number of patients or sustain the facility. There is 0.08 psychiatrists per 100,000 in the population, 2.0 psychiatric nurses, and 0.04 psychologists. Similar to India, when professionals are sent abroad for training, some do not return, presenting a particular challenge as Ghana attempts to retain qualified mental health professionals (Who.int/country_ profiles, 2005).

SUMMARY

As this chapter on behavioral health suggests, providing true access to mental health care involves a number of challenges. Mental illness does not occur in a vacuum; emotional difficulties are often linked to employment issues, health problems, and family dynamics. Research on the psychological trauma experienced by those trying to adjust to a new way of life in post-communist countries, highlights the political, economic, and societal factors that can affect an individual's sense of well-being. Studies which focus on the psychological impact of natural disasters, such as the Tsunami in Japan, the Chernobyl nuclear disaster in Russia, or the stress of living in a war torn environment, provide added perspective on the enormity of problems a country may face in its attempts to help people regain mental stability.

Over the past three decades, and with Italy leading the way as the breakthrough model for deinstitutionalization and community-based care, mental health care has undergone significant change in the 11 countries studied in this text. The paradigm shift emphasizes a respect for the civil rights of the patient, more humane treatment of the mentally ill by healthcare providers, and social inclusion rather than social isolation. Approaches to treatment have moved from hospitalization as the sole response in dealing with a patient's needs to a variety of interventions such as milieu therapy, group therapy, and rehabilitation day treatment centers. Mental illness is viewed less as some type of demonic affliction that must be hidden or exorcised, and has become more broadly conceptualized along a continuum of mild stress disorders to severe psychiatric disease.

Increasingly, the mind–body connection to wellness is taking hold, i.e., good health refers to being sound physically, mentally, and socially. Countries such as Russia and Brazil are painfully aware of the interrelatedness of physical and mental health as they strive to create healthcare initiatives to address the phenomenal loss of their male population (adolescent and middle-aged) to violence, binge drinking, drunk driving, and preventable, non-communicable diseases. Deinstitutionalization has led to a dramatic decline in the use of psychiatric beds, and at the same time, called considerable attention to the important and much needed role of primary care in mental health.

The 11 countries under study share common challenges in their efforts to provide quality mental health care. The most obvious concern, particularly among the developing countries, is the low rate of mental health spending. In addition to inadequate financing, there are regional variations in gaining access to mental health services. Despite federal guidelines, states and municipalities provide mental health services based on their interpretation of need and economic capabilities. In terms of disparities, low socioeconomic groups are most likely to experience mental health distress than those with higher incomes, and urban dwellers have greater access to mental health services than those who live in rural areas. Even in situations where primary care is available, there are issues concerning the ability of healthcare professionals to help people with their mental health concerns. Mental health patients require a number of services. Providing well-coordinated, continuity of care is an ongoing challenge. Researchers suggest that service effectiveness and efficiency could be improved through more systematic collection of data, and critical attention to the development of management skills.

Finally, unlike other services, behavioral and mental health must contend with the negative perceptions steeped in centuries-old beliefs that are difficult to dispel. The stigma associated with mental illness finds employers, housing authorities, and other types of social systems, skirting the rules, and therefore confounding the ability of the system to effectively assist the mental health patient. Although these examples are difficult and persistent, it is important that countries recognize the issues and remain engaged in full scale strategic plans to deliver quality mental health care.

Discussion Questions

1. How were you raised to think about mental illness? In what ways, if any, did your upbringing influence your thoughts about mental illness?

2. Have you experienced psychological stress in your own life? How did you handle it? Did you seek out professional help? Was your family supportive? Is your behavioral problem something you would share at work? Why or why not?

3. Have you worked with someone with a behavioral disorder? How is mental illness among staff addressed in your workplace?

4. To what extent does religion play a role in helping families cope with mental illness in the population you serve?

5. If you do not have formal preparation and training to work with people with mental illness, would you feel equipped to work with them in a primary care setting? Would you be able to pick up on any signs of mental distress? For

example, would you be able to identify depression or suicidal tendencies in a patient?

6. What screening tools do you have to identify mental illness in your work setting? Are there certain protocols to follow if you find you are working with a mentally distressed patient?

7. Describe mental health services in your community? Are they effective? Is your workplace part of the network of community-based services for the mentally ill?

8. A frequent complaint of many city dwellers is dealing with the panhandling of the homeless who, in their estimation, require psychological assistance. Describe your experiences with displays of public behavior of the mentally ill. What should be done about the homeless and other types of individuals who seem to wander the streets? Is deinstitutionalization a good idea? Why or why not? In what way, if any, can deinstitutionalization efforts be more effectively addressed?

9. Families of the mentally ill experience significant stress psychologically and even financially. Have you observed this situation? How is this problem addressed in your community? Describe support programs to assist families of people with behavior disorders including your opinion of their effectiveness.

10. Community-based behavioral health involves multi-professional teams. Describe the advantages and drawbacks of this team approach to care.

11. Describe treatment programs for substance and alcohol abuse in your community (or work setting). Are these programs effective? Which programs are viewed positively? What accounts for their success? How would you "fix" less successful programs?

12. In your opinion, what types of education and training should be provided in the workplace regarding behavioral health?

13. What outstanding differences have you noticed among developing and developed (industrialized) countries regarding true access to mental health services?

14. When psychiatrists and other mental health professionals are sent abroad for training they often do not return. This presents a particular problem for developing countries such as Ghana and India that are experiencing difficulty retaining qualified mental health professionals. To what do you attribute this problem? In what way(s), if any, might this problem be effectively addressed?

15. Some people feel that work is one thing and politics are another. To what extent do you feel health practitioners should be involved in politics to improve mental health services in their community? In your opinion, is political activity something that falls outside of your work responsibilities? Explain your point of view.

Case Scenarios

Introducing the Scenarios:

The following scenarios are based on true events. The scenarios are purposefully generic and contain essential information for discussion. You will notice that identifying information such as names and locations are not included in an attempt to stimulate your thinking about how these events would play out in the 11 countries we have studied in this chapter.

Scenario 1: The Weekend

The son was at his wit's end. He was home from college for what he had hoped would be a fun weekend with his mother to celebrate the grandmother's 75th birthday. He was also looking forward to seeing his married older brother, his charming sister-in-law, and their new 6-month-old baby boy. But he had been home for less than 24 hours and things were unraveling. Since he had arrived Friday night, the mother had come up to him at least five times and asked: "Do you think I've been a good mother? Do you still love me?" No matter how he tried to reassure her, the mother kept pushing. Where were these questions coming from? When he pressed her for answers, she stared at him for a few seconds and then walked away.

Since his father had walked out on them five years ago, his mother had gone in and out of strange moods. It was clear she was bitter; being left for another woman was something she could not get over. The mother even watched from across the street, the apartment where the new woman lived just to see what she looked like. Last summer, the mother was hospitalized for "nervous exhaustion" and after one week, she was released with the doctor's advice to take things easy. Following this episode, the son made more of an effort to call his mother from school as frequently as possible. This wasn't always easy between classes and practice sessions required to keep his athletic scholarship.

Sometimes the mother sat up all night smoking; other times she would say very little and just curl up on the couch and sleep most of the day away—especially on weekends. Despite her dark periods, the mother was able to hold down her teaching job at the elementary school and was highly regarded as one of the best teachers in the system. But she worried about money constantly. Once the son overheard his mother say to her sister: "You know it's all on me now. I really can't depend on anyone else. My ex-husband hasn't got any money; I was always the stable breadwinner if you think about it, and I am not up to going to court to get blood out of a stone." The sister advised her to go for counseling or at least join a self-help group but the mother insisted she could work out things for herself—what did those doctors know anyway? Besides, she did not want anyone in her business—her faith would pull her through.

Saturday afternoon the son and the mother joined everyone for the party at his aunt's home. Surprisingly, his mother was less agitated today and she seemed to enjoy the grandmother's birthday celebration. Everyone remarked on how attractive the mother looked in her bright red sweater.

On Sunday morning the son decided to accompany his mother to church and then treat her to breakfast afterwards. He would meet up with friends later that afternoon and then catch the evening train back to school. He went to her room to discuss the plan. The door was half-way open. Calling her name, the son knocked briefly, opened the door, and found his mother drooping over the side of the bed with an empty pill bottle on the floor.

DISCUSSION POINTS

1. In what country are you most likely to experience this scenario and why?
2. In your opinion, which of the countries studied would provide the best support for addressing these issues, and why?
3. What family support is most needed to assist in addressing this situation?
4. Select one of the following endings and respond to the questions which follow:
   a. The son arrived in time—he called emergency services and the mother was saved. What happens now?
   b. The son found the mother too late. She is dead. What happens now?
5. How might either of these endings been averted? Replay the scenario for a more positive ending.
6. Do you think the family might worry about the possibility of the mother's problem transferring to younger members of the families?

Scenario 2: The Brother

No one was ever sure what to think about the brother. When he was born, one of his aunts noticed that he rocked back and forth while standing in the crib. Another aunt commented that the mother smoked while carrying him and that may have had something to do with his excessive rocking.

When he was about 8 years old, the parents were concerned about his capabilities and had him tested. The parents never explicitly shared the results of the testing with the rest of the family but the word was that the boy was "educable." At least, one relative observed, the boy was not "retarded."

The boy's mother went as far as to say she thought her son might be "emotionally immature."

As he grew older, it was noticeable that the brother did not seem to start conversations but only repeated what people said. Also, the family seemed to press him into housework activities. As educated people themselves, the parents wanted to make sure their son had a degree in something. They sent the brother to an electronics school but he never seemed to get a job in the field.

When the mother fell ill, the son took up her care with little assistance from the older sister. She was raising three children and in the middle of a divorce. Another brother lived 200 miles away and rarely kept up with the family.

One of the aunts had a fit when she learned that the brother was bathing his very ill mother. Why didn't they get a woman to help out with something that personal? She would do it but her arthritis made it hard for her to help anyone. Why couldn't the daughter at least help out with the mother's hygiene? The brother took care of his mother until her death.

Several years later, someone heard that a 50-year-old man was found dead on the street. Later, the family learned that the man was their brother. He had died of a heart attack. For approximately 5 ½ years after his mother's death, he had survived on cigarettes, beer, and ate only food that he liked—usually meat and potatoes. Since his mother's death, he had worked for the past six years in an entertainment hall, setting up chairs and buffet tables at minimum wage. The owner let him stay rent free in a room above the hall. His married sister had enough room for the brother but never invited him to stay with her. At his service, a family friend remarked. "It's a shame. If the parents would just have admitted their child needed special help in the first place, the brother might be alive today."

DISCUSSION POINTS

1. In what country are you most likely to experience this scenario and why?
2. In your opinion, which of the countries studied would provide the best support for addressing these issues, and why?
3. What family support is most needed to assist in addressing this situation?
4. In your opinion, what was wrong with the brother? Was it caused by something the mother did when she carried him? Do you think the family might worry about the possibility of this problem being passed down through generations?

REFERENCES

Prevalence and Management of Behavioral Health Care in Industrialized (Developed) Countries

United States

Bolson, MD. (2004). The Child Youth and Families Mental Health Program in New Mexico. Department of Community Services Section of Behavioral Heath. Retrieved December 10, 2011 from http://www.cyfd.org/pdf/providers/CBHSDM04rev.pdf

Burroughs, V. J., et al. (2002). Racial and ethnic differences in response to medicines: Towards individualized pharmaceutical treatment. *Journal of the National Medical Association,* 94:10, 1–26.

Centers for Disease Control and Prevention (CDC). (2007). Eliminate disparities in mental health. Fact sheet. Retrieved December 10, 2011 from http://www.cdc.gov/omhd/amh/factsheets/mental.htm

Centers for Disease Control and Prevention (CDC). (2010). Leading Causes of Death. Hyattsville, MD. Retrieved June 13, 2012 from www.cdc.gov/nchs/fastats/lcod.htm

Christian, S., Dower, C., & O'Neil, E. (2007). Overview of nurse practitioner scopes of practice in the United States. Retrieved from www.acnpweb.org/files/public/UCSF_Discussion_2007.pdf

Demyttenaere, K., Bruffaerts, R., Posasa-Villa, J., Gasquet, I., Kovess, V., & Lepine, J. P. (2004). Prevalence severity, and unmet need for treatment of mental disorders in the World Health Organization world mental health surveys. *Journal of the American Medical Association.* 291, 2581–90.

Exner, D. V., et al. (2001). Lesser response to angiotensin-converting-enzyme inhibitor therapy in black as compared with white patients with left ventricular dysfunction. *New England Journal of Medicine,* 344(18), 1351–1357.

Feldman, S., Bachman, J., Cuffel, B., Friesen, B., & McCabe, J. (2003). Advanced practice psychiatric nurses as a treatment resource: Survey and analysis. *Administration and Policy in Mental Health,* 30(6), 470–494.

Goroll, A. H. & Mulley, A. (2000). Primary Care Medicine: Office Evaluation and Management of the Adult Patient (4th ed.). Philadelphia: Lippincott, Williams & Wilkins.

Hanna, E. Z. (2000). Approach to the patient with alcohol abuse. In: Goroll, A. H. & Mulley, A. (2000). *Primary Care Medicine: Office Evaluation and Management of the Adult Patient* (4th ed.). (pp. 1169–1170). Philadelphia: Lippincott, Williams & Wilkins.

Herrman, H., Saxena, S., & Moodie, R. (2005). Positioning mental health: Concepts, emerging evidence and practice. A report of WHO, Department of Mental Health and Substance Abuse in Collaboration with The Victorian Health Province University of Melbourne. Retrieved December 10, 2011 from www.who.int/mental_health/evidence/mhpromotion_book.pdf

Kirby, M. J. L. (2006). Mental health, mental illness, and addiction: Interim report of the standing committee on social affairs, science and technology, Parliament, Canada. Report 1. Overview of policies and programs in Canada. Retrieved December 10, 2011 from http://www.parl/SEN/committee/381/soci/rep/parl.gc.ca/content/.pdf

Kleintjes, S., Lund, C., & Flisher, A. J. (2010, May). A situational analysis of child and adolescent mental health services in Ghana, Uganda. *African Journal of Psychiatry*. South Africa and Zambia. MHaPP Research Programme Consortium. *13*(2), 132–139.

Long, J. A., Chang, V. W., Ibrahim, S. A., & Asch, D. A. (2004). Update on the health disparities literature. *Annals of Internal Medicine, 141*(10), 805–812.

Parker, S. P. (2002). *McGraw-Hill dictionary of scientific and technical terms* (6th ed.). New York: The McGraw-Hill Companies.

National Institute of Health. (2009). The National Institute on Alcohol Abuse and Alcoholism (NIAAA) Report. Retrieved from www.everydayhealth.com/publicsite/news/new.aspx/id=64999

Ringold, S. (2005). Alcohol abuse and alcoholism. *JAMA*. Retrieved from www.jama.ama-assn.org/content/295/17/2100./all.pdf

Smedley, B. D., Stith, A. Y., & Nelson, A. R. (Eds.). (2002). *Unequal treatment: Confronting racial and ethnic disparities in health care*. Washington, DC: National Academies Press.

Smith, T. E. & Sederer, L. I. (2009). A new kind of homelessness for individuals with serious mental illness? The need for a "mental health home." *Psychiatric Services, 60*(4). 528–533.

United States Department of Health and Human Services. (2006, Dec.) *Healthy People 2010: Midcourse Review*. Washington, DC: Office of Disease Prevention & Health Promotion.

United States Department of Health and Human Services. (2007). *Healthy People 2010*. Retrieved from www.healthypeople.gov/2010/?=1

World Health Organization (WHO). (2004). Promoting mental health: Concepts, emerging evidence, practice. Summary Report. Retrieved December 28, 2011 from http://www.who.int/mental_health/evidence/en/promoting_mhh.pdf

World Health Organization (WHO). (2005). *Mental health atlas*. Retrieved December 10, 2011 from http://www.who.int/mental-health/evidence/mhatlas05/public/en/index.html

World Health Organization (WHO). (2001a). Fact sheet. No. 220. In: World Health Organization (WHO). (2004). Promoting mental health: Concepts, emerging evidence, practice. Summary Report. Retrieved December 28, 2011 from http://www.who.int/mental_health/evidence/en/promoting_mhh.pdf

World Health Organization (WHO). (2001b). Strengthening mental health promotion. Geneva.

World Health Organization (WHO). (2003). The mental health context: Mental health policy and service guidance package. Retrieved from who.int/mental_health/policy/services/3_context_WEB_07.pdf

World Health Organization (WHO). (2004). The global burden of mental disorders and the need for a comprehensive, coordinated response from health and social sectors at the country level. Retrieved from who.int/gb/ebuwh/pdf_ files /EB130/B130_r8.en.pdf

World Health Organization (WHO). (2010, September). Mental health: strengthening our response. Fact sheet. Retrieved December 10, 2011 from http://www .who.int/mediacentre/factsheets/fs220/en

Worthington, J. J. & Rauch, S. L. (2000a). Approach to the patient with depression. In: Goroll, A. H. & Mulley, A. G. (2000). Primary Care Medicine: Office Evaluation and Management of the Adult Patient (4th ed.). (pp. 1147-1168). Philadelphia: Lippincott, Williams & Wilkins.

Worthington, J. J. & Rauch, S. L. (2000b). Psychiatric and behavioral problems: Approach to the patient with anxiety. In: Goroll, A. H. & Mulley, A. G. (2000). Primary Care Medicine: Office Evaluation and Management of the Adult Patient (4th ed.). (p. 1147). Philadelphia: Lippincott, Williams & Wilkins.

Canada

Adlaf, E. M., Begin, P., & Sawka, E. (2005). Canadian addiction survey (CAS): A national survey of Canadians' use of alcohol and other drugs. Prevalence of use and related harms. Detailed report, Canadian Centre of Substance Abuse. 20-35.

Clayton, D. & Barcel, A. (1999). The cost of suicide mortality in New Brunswick, 1996. *Chronic Diseases in Canada, 20*(2), 89-95.

Donnelly, T. T., Hwang, J. J., Este, D., Ewashen, C., Adair, C., & Clinton, M. (2011). If I was going to kill myself, I wouldn't be calling you. I am asking for help: Challenges influencing immigrant and refugee women's mental health. In: *Issues in Mental Health Nursing, 32*(5), 279-290.

Global Business and Economic Roundtable on Addiction and Mental Health. (2004). Roundtable roadmap to mental disability management in 2004–2005.

Health Canada. (2002). Economic burden of illness in Canada, 1998 & 2002. Ottawa. HealthCanada, Population and Public Health Branch.

IHE Report: Institute of Health Economics. (September, 2008). How much should we spend on mental health? Retrieved December 12, 2011 from www.ihe.ca /documents/spending%20on%20mental%20health%20final.pdf

Jacobs, P., Ohinmaa, A., Eng, K., Yim, R., Dewa, C. S, Bland, R., et al. (2008). Expenditures on mental health and addictions for Canadian provinces from 2003-2004. *The Canadian Journal of Psychiatry, 53*(5), 33-40.

Kirby, M. J. L. (November, 2004). Mental health, mental illness, and addiction: Interim report of the standing committee on social affairs, science and technology, Parliament, Canada. Report 1. Overview of policies and programs in Canada. Retrieved December 10, 2011 from http://www.parl/SEN/committee /381/ soci/rep/ parl.gc.ca/content/.pdf

Kirby, M. J. L. (May, 2006). Final report: Out of the shadows at last, highlights and recommendations. Ottawa, Ontario. The Standing Senate Committee on Social Affairs, Science and Technology.

Langlois, S. & Morrison, P. (2002). Suicide deaths and suicide attempts. *Health Reports, 13*(2), 9–22.

Lim, K. L., Jacobs, P., Ohinmaa, A., Schopflocher, D., & Dewa, C. S. (2008). A new population based measure of the economic burden of mental illness in Canada. *Chronic Diseases in Canada, 28*(3), p. 94.

Mathers, C. D. & Loncar, D. (2006). Projections of global mortality and burden of disease from 2002–2030. *PLos Medicine* 3(11): e442.

Public Health Agency of Canada. A report on mental illness in Canada. Mental health in Canada: An overview. Retrieved November 28, 2011 from phac-aspc.gc.ca /publicat/miic-mmac/chap_1-eng.php

Romanow, R. J. (2002). Commission on the Future of Health Care in Canada. Building on values: The future of health care in Canada–final report. Saskatoon (SK). 1–392.

Toronto-Peel Mental Health Implementation Task Force. (2002). The time has come: Make it happen—A mental health action plan for Toronto and Peel: Companion document. Ottawa, Ontario Ministry of Health and Long-Term Care. 1–19.

Wilkerson, B. (2006). Business and economic plan for mental health and productivity. Toronto. *Global Business & Economic Roundtable on Addiction and Mental Health. The global burden of disease: A comprehensive assessment of mortality and disability from diseases, injuries, and risk factors in 1990 and projected to 2020.* Cambridge (MA): Harvard University Press, 1996.

World Health Organization (WHO). (2005). *Mental health atlas.* Retrieved December 10, 2011 from http://www.who.int/mental-health/evidence/mhatlas05/public/en /index.html

World Health Organization (WHO). (2001). Fact sheet. No. 220. In: World Health Organization (WHO). (2004). Promoting mental health: Concepts, emerging evidence, practice. Summary Report. Retrieved December 28, 2011 from http:// www.who.int/mental_health/ evidence/en/promoting_mhh.pdf

World Health Organization (WHO). (2002). In: IHE Report: Institute of Health Economics. (September, 2008). How much should we spend on mental health? Retrieved December 12, 2011 from www.ihe.ca/documents/spending%20 on%20mental%20health%20final.pdf

Japan

Hamid, H., Abanilla, K., Bauta, B., & Haung, K. Y. (2008). Evaluating the WHO assessment instrument for mental health systems by comparing mental health policies in four countries. *Bulletin of the World Health Organization. 86*(6), 467–473.

Ito, H. & Sederer, L. I. (1999). Mental health services reform in Japan. *Harvard Review Psychiatry, 7*:2008–2015. PMID: 10579100 doi:10.1093/hrp/7.4.208

Kennedy, R. & Luthra, K. (April 12, 2011). Health implications in the aftermath of Japan's crisis: Mental health, radiation risks, and the importance of continued surveillance. An interview with Dr. Francesco Cheechi (Department of Disease Control, London School of Hygiene & Tropical Medicine). The National Bureau of Asian Research, Center for Health and Aging.

Nakatani, Y. (2000). Psychiatry and the law in Japan: History and current topics. *International Journal of Law Psychiatry, 2000*: 23:589–604. PMID: 11143956 doi:10.1016/SO 1602527 900) 00061-3.

OECD. (2008, November). Mental Health in OECD Countries: Policy Brief. *OECD Observer*, 1–7.

Tsuchiya, K. J. & Takei, N. (2004). Focus on psychiatry in Japan. *British Journal of Psychiatry, 184*:88–92. PMID:14719534 doi:10.1192/bjp.184.1.88

Wilkinson, R. G. & Pickett, K. E. (2007). The problems of relative deprivation: Why some societies do better than others. *Social Science & Medicine, 65*(9), 1965–1978.

World Health Organization (WHO). (2005). Mental health atlas. Retrieved, 12/10/11 from http://www.who.int/mental-health/evidence/mhatlas05/public/en/index.html

United Kingdom

Boyle, S. (February, 2008). The UK health care system. Retrieved December 11, 2011 from www.commonwealthfund.org/usr_doc/uk_country_profile_2008.pdf?section=4061

Boyle, S. (2011). The United Kingdom (England): Health systems in transition. London: 13:1, 1-486. Retrieved June 13, 2012 from http://www.euro.who.int/_data/assets/pdf_file_/ 0004/135148/e94836.pdf

London Health Observatory (LHO). (n.d.). Mental health prevalence. http://www.lho.org.uk/LHO_Topics/Health_Topics/Diseases/MentalHealth.aspx

McManus, S., Meltzer, H., Brugha, T., Bebbington, P., & Jenkins, R. (eds.). (2009). *Adult psychiatric morbidity in England, 2007*. Leeds: NHS Information Centre. Retrieved October 2011 from http://www.mental health.org.uk/about-us/wales/

Mental Health Foundation (2012). Our work in Wales. Retrieved October 15, 2011 from www.mentalhealth.org.uk/about-us/Wales/

Sainsbury Centre for Mental Health. (2003a). The economic and social costs of mental illness: Policy paper 3. London: Salisbury Center for Mental Health. Retrieved November 11, 2010 from http://www.centreformentalhealth.org

Sainsbury Centre for Mental Health. (2003b). A window of opportunity: A practical guide for developing early intervention in psychosis services - Brief 23. London: Retrieved November 11, 2010 from http://www.centreformentalhealth.org.uk/pdfs/briefing_23.pdf

Singleton, N., Bumpstead, R., O'Brien, M., Lee, A., & Meltzer, H. (2001). *Psychiatric morbidity among adults living in private households, 2000*. London: TSO.

World Health Organization (WHO). (2005). *Mental health atlas*. Retrieved December 10, 2011 from http://www.who.int/mental-health/evidence/mhatlas05/public /en/index.html

France

Alonso, J., Angermeyer, M. C., Bernert, S., Bruffaerts, R., Brugha, T. S, Bryson, H., et al. (2004). Use of mental health services in Europe: Results from the European Study of epidemiology of mental disorders (ESEMeD) project. *Acta Psychiatrica Scandinavica, 109*(suppl) 420, 47–54.

Jaeger, M. (1995). Inflection in France's mental health policy. *Sante Mentale an Quebec*, 20, 77–87.

Provost, D. & Bauer, A. (2001). Trends and developments in public psychiatry in France since 1975. *Asta Psychiatrica Scandinavica, 104*(suppl), 410, 63–68.

Verdoux, H. (2003). Psychiatry in France. *International Journal of Social Psychiatry*, 49, 83–86.

World Health Organization (WHO). (2005). *Mental health atlas*. Retrieved December 10, 2011 from http://www.who.int/mental-health/evidence/mhatlas05/public /en/index.html

Italy

Basaglia, F. (1964). The destruction of the mental hospital as a place of institutionalization. Thoughts caused by personal experience with the open door system and part time service. First International Congress of Social Psychiatry, London 1964. Retreived from http://www.triestesalutementale.it/english/doc /basaglia_1964_destruction-mhh.pdf

Berardi, D., Bortolli, B., Menchetti, M., Bombi, A., & Tarricone, I. (2007). Models of collaboration between general practice and mental health services in Italy. *European Journal of Psychiatry, 21*(1), 79–84.

Borzaga, C. & Santuari, A. (July 2000) Social enterprises in Italy: The experience of social co-operatives. Working paper n.15. Retrieved from http://www.issan .gelso/unitn.it

de Girolamo, G., Basi, M., Neri, G., Ruggeri, M., Santone, G., & Picardi, A. (2007). The current state of mental health care in Italy: Problems, perspectives, and lessons to learn. *European Archive of Psychiatry and Clinical Neurosciences, 257*(2), 83–91.

Del Giudice, G. (1998). Psychiatric Reform in Italy. Retrieved from http://www .triestesalutementale.it/english/doc/delgiudice_1998_psychiatric-reform-italy .pdf

European Policy Information Research for Mental Disorders (EPREMED). (2008). Final Report. Retrieved from http://www.epremed.org/

Fioritti, A. (2010). Development of Community Mental Health Services: The Case of Emilia-Romagna Italian Region. *Psylogos,* 67–76. Retrieved from http://www.psilogos.com/Revista/Vol6N1/Indice9_ficheiros/Fioritti%20_%20%20P67-76.pdf

Foritti, A., Lo Russo, L., & Melega, V. (1997). Reform said or done? The case of Emilia-Romagna within the Italian psychiatric context. *American Journal of Psychiatry,* 154, 94–98. In Fioritti, A. (2010). Development of Community Mental Health Services: The Case of Emilia-Romagna Italian Region. *Psylogos,* 67–76. Retrieved from http://www.psilogos.com/Revista/Vol6N1/Indice9_ficheiros/Fioritti%20_%20%20P67-76.pdf

IHE Report: Institute of Health Economics. (June, 2008). Retrieved from http://www.ihe.ca/documents/Spending%20on%20Mental%20Health%20Final.pdf

Lora, A. (2009). An overview of the mental health system in Italy. *Ann 1st Super Sanita,* 45 (1), 5-16. Retrieved from www.iss.it/publ/anna/2009/1/4515.pdf

Lurie, S. (2008). Arrividerci Trieste: Reflections and Observations about Mental Health Services in Italy. Retrieved from www.toronto.cnha.ca/ct_general/articles.asp

Monzani, E., Erlicher, A., Lora, A., Piergiorgio, L., & Vittadini, G. (2008). Does community care work? A model to evaluate the effectiveness of mental health services. *International Journal of Mental Health Systems, 2*:10. Retrieved from www.ijmhs.com/content/2/1/10. doi: 10.1186/1752-4458-2-10

Piccinelli, M., Politi, P., & Barale, F. (2002). Focus on Psychiatry in Italy. *British Journal of Psychiatry,* 181, 538–544.

Brazil

Belfer, M. L. & Rohde, L. A. (2005). Child and adolescent mental health in Latin America and the Caribbean: Problems, progress, and policy research. *Rev Panam Salud Publica /Pan American Journal of Public Health, 18*(4/5), 359–365.

de Almeida, J. M. C. & Horvitz-Lennon, M. (2010). An overview of mental health care reforms in Latin America and the Caribbean. *Psychiatric Services, 61*(3), 218–221. Retrieved from ps.psychiatryonline.org

Fagundes, S. D., Silva, M. T., Thees, M. F. R. S., & Pereira, M. G. (2011). Prevalence of dementia among elderly Brazilians: a systematic review. *Sao Paulo Medical Journal.* [online]. 2011, vol.129, n.1 [cited 2012-02-23], pp. 46–50. Retrieved from: http://www.scielo.br/scielo.php?script=sci_arttext&pid=S1516-31802011000100009&lng=en&nrm=iso. ISSN 1516-3180. http://dx.doi.org/10.1590/S1516-31802011000100009

Fletlich-Bilyk, B. & Goodman, R. (2004). Prevalence of child and adolescent psychiatric disorders in southeast Brazil. *Journal of the American Academy of Child and Adolescent Psychiatry,* 43, 727–734. In Belfer, M. L. & Rohde, L. A. (2005). Child and adolescent mental health in Latin America and the Caribbean: problems, progress, and policy research. *Rev Panam Salud Publica /Pan American Journal of Public Health, 18*(4/5), 359–365.

Fregni, F. (2007). Implications of globalization for mental health care in Brazil: Negative consequences for the treatment of depression. *ReVista Harvard Review of Latin America.* Retrieved from www.drclas.harvard.edu/revista/articles /view/940

Gadelha, A. M. J., Leite, I. C., Valente, J. G., Schramm, J. M. A., Portela, M. C., Campos, M. R. (2002). Relatorio Final do Projecto Estimativa da Carga de Doenca do Brasil-1988. Rio de Janeiro: ENSP/FIOCRUZ. In Kantorski, L. P., Jardim, V. M. R., Porto, A. R., Schek, G., Cortes, J. M., & Oliveira, M. M. (2011). *The supply and use of psychotropic drugs in psychosocial care centers in Southern Brazil.* Retrieved from www.scielo.br/pdf/reeusp/v45n6/en_v45n6a29.pdf

Goncalves, R. W., Vieira, F. S., & Delgado, P. G. (2012, Epub 2011, Dec 20). Mental Health Policy in Brazil: federal expenditure evolution between 2001 and 2009. *Rev Saude Public, 46*(1), 51–58. Retrieved from: http://www.ncbi.nlm.nih.gov /pubmed/22183515

Instituto Brasilerio de Geografia e Estatistica. (2009). Pesquisa Nacionale de Saude do Escolar 2009. Rio de Janeiro: Instituto Brasilerio de Geografia e Estatistica, 2009. In Schmidt, M. I., Duncan, B. B., Silva, G. A., Menezes, A. M., Monteiro, C. A., Barret, S. M., Chor, D., Menezes, P.R. (2011). Chronic non-communicable diseases in Brazil: burden and current challenges. *Lancet,* 377, 1949–1961. Retrieved from: www.thelancet.com. Doi: 10:1016/50140-6736(11)60135-9.

Jacob, K., Sharan, P., Mirza, I., Garrido-Cumbrera, M., Seeda, S., Mari, J. J., et al. (2007). Mental health systems in countries: where are we now? *Lancet, 370*(9592), 1061–1077. In Mateus, M. D., Mari, J. J., Delgado, P. G. G., Almeida-Filho, N., Barrett, T., Gerolin, J. et al. (2008). The mental health system in Brazil: Policies and future challenges. *International Journal of Mental Health Systems,* 2(12), doi: 10.1186/1752-4458-2-12. Retrieved from http://www.ijmhs.com /content/2/1/12

Kantorski, L. P., Jardim, V. M. R., Porto, A. R., Schek, G., Cortes, J. M., & Oliveira, M. M. (2011). The supply and use of psychotropic drugs in psychosocial care centers in Southern Brazil. Retrieved from www.scielo.br/pdf/reeusp/v45n6/en_v45n6a29 .pdf

Lazarus R. & Freeman M. (2009). Primary-Level Mental Health Care for Common Mental Disorder in Resource-Poor Settings: Models & Practice—A Literature Review. Sexual Violence Research Initiative, Medical Research Council, Pretoria, South Africa.

Mateus, M. D., Mari, J. J., Delgado, P. G. G., Almeida-Filho, N., Barrett, T., Gerolin, J. et al. (2008). The mental health system in Brazil: Policies and future challenges. *International Journal of Mental Health Systems, 2*(12), doi: 10.1186/1752-4458-2-12. Retrieved from http://www.ijmhs.com/content/2/1/12

Rodriguez, J. J. (2010). Editorial. Strategy and plan of action on mental health for the Region of Americas. *Revista Brasiliera de Psiquiatria, 32*(4), 3399–3340.

Schmidt, M. I., Duncan, B. B., Silva, G. A., Menezes, A. M., Monteiro, C. A., Barret, S. M., et al. (2011). Chronic non-communicable diseases in Brazil: burden and current challenges. *Lancet*, 377, 1949–1961. Retrieved from www.thelancet .com. Doi: 10:1016/50140-6736(11)60135-9.

Tramontina, S., Martins, S., Michalowski, M. B., Ketzer, C. R., Eizirik, M., Biederman, J. et al. (2001). *Canadian Journal of Psychiatry*, 46, 941–947. Retrieved from www.ncbi.nlm.nih.gov/pubmed/11816315

World Health Organization (WHO). (2005). *Mental Health Atlas*. Retrieved from http://www.who.int/mental_health/evidence/mhatlas05/en/index.html

World Health Organization (WHO). (2007). World Health Organization 2007 Atlas: Nurses in Mental Health. Retrieved from http://www.who.int/mental_health /evidence/en/

WHO-AIMS. (2007). World Health Organization. A report of the assessment of the mental health in Brazil using the World Health Organization Assessment Instrument for Mental Health System (WHO-AIMS). Brasilia: 2007. In Kantorski, L. P., Jardim, V. M. R., Porto, A. R., Schek, G., Cortes, J. M., Oliveira, M. M. (2011). The supply and use of psychotropic drugs in psychosocial care centers in Southern Brazil. Retrieved from www.scielo.br/pdf/reeusp/v45n6/en_v45n6a29.pdf

WHO/WONCA. World Health Organization/World Organization of Family Doctors. (2008). Integrating mental health care into primary care: A global perspective. Retrieved December 11, 2011 from www.who.int/mental_health /policy/services/mentalhealthintoprimarycare/en/

Cuba

de Gordon, A. M. (n.d.). Health and health care in Cuba: The transition from social-ism to the future. Finlay Albarran Medical Institute. www.finlay-online.com /finlayinsitute/healthandhealth

Libre, J. J., Guerra, M. A., Perez-Cruz, H. et al. (1999). Dementia syndrome and risk factors in adults aged over 60 residing in La Habana. *Revista de Neurologia*, 29, 908–990.

PAHO. (2002). *Health in the Americas*. Washington, DC. 2000. vol. 2, p.198.

Reynaldo, A., Reynaldo-Hernandez, R., Paneque-Herrera, M., et al. (2002). Mental disorders in patients with spinocerebellar ataxia type 2. *Cuba Revista of Neurologia*, 35, 818–820.

World Health Organization (WHO). (2005). *Mental health atlas*. Retrieved December 10, 2011 from http://www.who.int/mental-health/evidence/mhatlas05/public /en/index.html

India

Arora, P., Kumar, R., Bhattacharya, M., Nagelkerke, N. J., & Jha, P. (2008). Trends in HIV incidence in India from 2000 to 2007. *Lancet*, 372(9635), 289–290.

Chandrashekar, C. R. & Math, S. B. (2006). Psychosomatic disorders in developing countries: Current issues and future challenges. *Current Opinions in Psychiatry,* 19, 201–206.

Jorm, F. (2000). Mental health literacy: Public knowledge and beliefs about mental disorders. *British Journal of Psychiatry,* 177, 396–401.

Kessler, R. C. (2000). Psychiatric epidemiology: Selected recent advances and future directions. *Bull World Organization,* 78:464–474.

Kumta, S., Lurie, M., Weitzen, S., Jerajani, H., Gogate, A., Row-kavi, A., et al. (2010). Bisexuality, sexual risk taking, and HIV prevalence among men who have sex with men accessing voluntary counseling and testing services in Mumbai, India. *Journal of Acquired Immune Deficiency Syndrome, 53*(2), 227–233.

Math, S. B., Chandrashekar, C. R., & Bhugra, D. (2007). Psychiatric epidemiology in India. *Indian Journal of Medical Research,* 183–192.

National AIDS Control Organization. (2008). *HIV sentinel surveillance and HIV estimation in India 2007: A technical brief.* Retrieved from http://www.nacoonline.org

Patel, V., Pereira, J., Coutinho, L., Fernandes, R., Fernandes, J. & Mann, A. (1998). Poverty, psychological disorder and disability in primary care attenders in Goa, India. *British Journal of Psychiatry,* 172, 533–536.

Sivasubramanian, M., Mimiaga, M. J., Mayer, K. H., Anand, V. R., Johnson, C. V., Prabhugate, P., et al. (2011, August). Suicidality, clinical depression, and anxiety disorders are highly prevalent in men who have sex with men in Mumbai, India: Findings from a community-recruited sample. *Psychology, Health & Medicine, 16*(4), 450–462.

UNAIDS. (2008). Report on the global AIDS epidemic 2008. (USAIDS Publications No. USAIDS/08.25E/JC1510E). Geneva, Switzerland: UNAIDS.

UNAIDS & WHO. (2008). Asia: AIDS epidemic update regional summary. (USAIDS Publications No. USAIDS/08.09E/JC1527E). Geneva, Switzerland: UNAIDS.

World Health Organization (WHO). (2005). *Mental health atlas.* Retrieved December 10, 2011 from http://www.who.int/mental-health/evidence/mhatlas05/public/en/index.html

Russian Federation

Amos, H. (2011, October 21). *The Telegraph.* 800,000 Russians committed suicide since Soviet Union Collapsed. Retrieved from http://www.telegraph.co.uk/news/worldnews/europe/russia/8841619/800000-Russians-committed-suicide-since-Soviet-Union-collapsed.html

Bartenev, D. (2004). International Policy Fellow 2004–2005. Research Paper. Potential of human rights standards for deinstitutionalization of mental health services in Russia: A comparative legal analysis. Retrieved from www.policy.hu/bartenev. Center for Policy Studies, Open Society Institute, Budapest (Hungary).

Bobrova, N., Alcorn, R., Rhodes, T., Rughnikov, I., Neifeld, E., & Power, R. (2007). Injection drug users' perceptions of drug treatment services and attitudes toward substitution therapy: A qualitative study in three Russian cities (Abstract). *Journal of Substance Abuse Treatment, 33*(4), 373–378.

Canadian Centre on Disability Studies (CCDS). (2007). Canada-Russia Disability Program Final Monograph, Winnipeg: Author. In Fuchs, D. M. (2007). Social work and mental health reform in the Russian Federaton: synergies for social inclusion and recovery. *International Journal of Disability, Community & Rehabilitation, 6*(2). Retrieved from www.ijdcr.ca

Chaykovskaya, E. (2011). *The Moscow News.* Russia has the second worst suicide rate in the world. Retrieved from themoscownews.com/society/20111011/189114308.html

Dixon, A., McDaid, D., Knapp, M., & Curran, C. (2006). Financing mental health services in low- and middle-income countries. *Health Policy Plan, 21*(3), 171–182. doi:10.1093/heapol/czl004. Retrieved from *heapol.oxfordjournals.org/content/21/3/171.short*

Flounders, S. (2006). 450,000 NGOs in Russia: U.S. finances opposition. *Workers World.* Retrieved from http://www.workers.org/2006/world/ngos-0216/

Fuchs, D. M. (2007). Social work and mental health reform in the Russian Federaton: synergies for social inclusion and recovery. *International Journal of Disability, Community & Rehabilitation, 6*(2). Retrieved from www.ijdcr.ca

Gurovich, I. Y. (2007). The current status of psychiatric services in Russia: Moving towards community-based psychiatry. *International Journal of Disability, Community & Rehabilitation, 6*(2). Retrieved from www.ijdcr.ca

Human Rights Watch. (2007). Rehabilitation required: Russia's human rights obligation to provide evidence-based drug dependence treatment. *Human Rights Watch, 19*(7D), 1–114.

Jenkins, R., Klein, J., & Parker, C. (2005). Editorial. Mental health in post-communist countries. *British Medical Journal*, 331, 173–174. Retrieved from www.eldis.org/id21ext/h3dm6g1.html

Jenkins, R. et al. (2007). *Bull World Health Organ., 8*(11), 858–866. http://dx.doi.org/10.1590/S0042-96862007001100012. Retrieved from http://www.scielosp.ort/scielo.php?script=sci_arttext&pid-S0042-96862997991100012&1ng=en&nrm=iso

Jenkins, R. et al. (2010). Rehabilitation and social inclusion of people with mental illness in Russia. *Psychiatric Services, 62*(3), 222–224.

Krasnov, V., Gurovich, I., & Bobrov, A. (2010). Russian Federation: mental health care and reform. *International Psychiatry, 7*(2), 39–41.

Lavretsky, H. (1998). The Russian concept of schizophrenia: a review of the literature. *Schizoprhenia Bulletin, 24*(4), 537–539.

Levina, N. & Lubov, Y. (2007). The organization of self-help movement in the context of mental health system reform towards community based psychiatry. *International Journal of Disability, Community & Rehabilitation, 6*(2). Retrieved from www.ijdcr.ca

McDaid, D., Samyshkin, Y., Jenkins, R., Potasheva, A., Nikiforov, A., & Atun, R. (2006). Health system factors impacting on delivery of mental health services in Russia: multi-methods study. *Health Policy, 79*(2), 144–152. Retrieved from Department of International Development, Institute of Development Studies. www.eldis.org/id21ext/h3dm6g1.html

National Business Group on Health (NBGH). (2011). Retrieved from http://www .businessgrouphealth.org/tobacco/global/russia.cfm

Osborn, A. (2011, February 23). Russia's alcohol and tobacco consumption by numbers. *The Telegraph*. Retrieved from www.telegraph.co.uk/news/worldnews /europe/russia/8343090/Russias-alcohol-and-tobacco-consumption-by -numbers.html

Oxford Analytica. (2009, July 28). Alcoholism presents health crisis in Russia. Retrieved from http://www.forbes.com?2009/07/27/russia-alcohol-health -business-oxford-analytica.html

Polubinskaya, S. (2008). The Russian Federation Law on Psychiatric Care as a tool for reform of Russian Psychiatry. *Justitias Welt*. Retreived from http://justitias welt.com/Aufsaetze/AS07_200806_SP.html

RIA Novosti. (Moscow: 2011, July 8). Divorce-prone Russia marks Family Day. Retrieved from http://en.rian.ru/russia/20110708/165084698.html

Roth, L. H. (1994). Introduction. Access to and utilization of mental health services in the former Soviet Union. *Journal of Russian and East Europepan Psychiatry, 27*(2). 9. In Polubinskaya, S. (2008). The Russian Federation Law on Psychiatric Care as a tool for reform of Russian Psychiatry. *Justitias Welt*. Retrieved from http://justitias welt.com/Aufsaetze/AS07_200806_SP.html

Sharar, D. A. & Shtoulman, A. (2010, February 10). Moscow, Russia: Urgent need for EAP. Retrieved from www.globalhrnews.com

Sorlie, T., Rezvy, G., Hoifodt, T. S., Yashkovich, V., & Proselkova, E. (2011). Collaboration in psychiatry between Archangelsk and Northern Norway. *Tidskr Nor Legeforen nr.* 16, 1568–1570. Retrieved from *www.ncbi.nlm.nih.gov /pubmed/218662001568*

United Nations International Children's Emergency Fund (UNICEF). (2011, November). Adolescent deaths from suicide in Russia. *UNICEF Research*. Retrieved from: http:// www.unicef.org/ceecis/media_18672.html

Wasserman, D., Cheng, Q., & Jiang, G. X. (2005). Global suicide rates among young people aged 15-19. *World Psychiatry*, 4 (2), 114–120.

World Health Organization (WHO). (2005). *Mental Health Atlas*. Retrieved December 10, 2011 from http://www.who.int/mental_health/evidence/mhatlas05/en /index.html

Ghana

Affinnih, Y. H. (1999). Drug use in greater Accra, Ghana: Pilot study *Substance Use and Misuse, 34,* 157–169.

Ewusi-Mensah. (2001). Post colonial psychiatric care in Ghana. *Psychiatric Bulletin, 25,* 228–229.

Public Agenda. (2006, 7 April). In: Health care in Ghana March 2009. Austrian Red Cross, ACCORD, UNHCR & Austrian Federal Minster of the Interior 9-10.

Public Agenda. (2008, 15 August). In: Health care in Ghana March 2009. Austrian Red Cross, ACCORD, UNHCR & Austrian Federal Minster of the Interior 9–10.

Robits, H. (2001). A way forward for mental health care in Ghana? *Lancet*, 357, 1859.

Turkson, S. N. (1998). Psychiatric diagnosis among referred patients in Ghana. *East African Medical Journal*, 5, 336–338.

World Health Organization (WHO). (2005). *Mental health atlas*. Retrieved December 10, 2011 from http://www.who.int/mental-health/evidence/mhatlas05/public/en/index.html

World Health Organization (WHO). (2006). In: Health care in Ghana March 2009. Austrian Red Cross, ACCORD, UNHCR & Austrian Federal Minster of the Interior 9–10.

World Health Organization (WHO). (2008). In: Health care in Ghana March 2009. Austrian Red Cross, ACCORD, UNHCR & Austrian Federal Minster of the Interior 9–10.

CHAPTER **16**

Comparative Health Systems

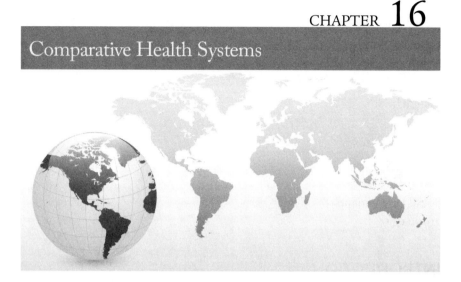

No two days are the same in one garden.

–Author Unknown

BEHAVIORAL OBJECTIVES

At the end of this chapter the learner will be able to:

1. Discuss similarities and differences of incidence and prevalence of disease among selected countries.
2. Identify common funding initiatives and challenges in developed and developing countries.
3. Describe the global inequities in health care.
4. Explain how social determinants affect health-seeking beliefs and practices in a global society.
5. Discuss ways in which one culture might learn from another.

KEY CONCEPTS

Behavioral health
Crude death rate
Decentralization
Developed country

Developing country

Epidemic

Health development index

Incidence

Mental health

Pandemic

Population density

Prevalence

Years of life lost

Social determinants

10/90 Gap

INTRODUCTION

The World Health Organization (WHO) (2001) defines health as a state of complete physical, mental, and social well-being and not merely the absence of disease or infirmity. A society is known for where it stands globally in regard to the health and wealth of its people. It is also known for where it fits in regard to the rest of the world in other measures of significance. A brief review of selected global comparisons is provided in order to lay the foundation for the discussion of 11 countries presented in Chapters 4–14.

DETERMINING A COUNTRY'S HEALTH STATUS

As the learner begins assessing health outcomes of specific countries, it is important to consider how the country covers the cost of health. **Table 16-1** presents the total health expenditures for selective high income countries. Also important is the information provided on population density. *Population density* is often reported along with other statistics when discussing healthcare accomplishments and challenges experienced by countries. Population density represents the number of people per square mile, or square kilometer (km) derived by dividing the total population per land area by square miles or square km. For example, Canada's population is 33 million divided by its land area of 3,559,294 square miles yielding a population density of 9.27 people per square mile. It is important to note, however, that because some areas are more densely populated than others, population density is a raw, rather than absolute estimate.

Infant mortality is widely considered one of the most important indicators of a nation's health status because it reflects such things as maternal

Table 16-1 Total healthcare expenditure in 2007 for selective high income countries.

Country	Percentage of GDP
United States	16.0
France	11.0
Germany	10.4
Canada	10.1
Italy	8.7
United Kingdom	8.4
Japan	8.1*

Data From: Gauthier-Villars, David. *France Fights Universal Health Care's High Cost*. The Wall Street Journal, April 7, 2009. http://online.wsj.com/article /SB124958049241511735.html. OECD Health Data 2008. *2006 data reported for Japan

health, quality of, and access to, medical care, socioeconomic conditions, and public health practices (MacDorman & Mathews, 2008). It is often one of the first considerations given when evaluating a country's overall health outcomes.

In a report on social determinants of health, Marmot (n.d.) indicates that:

> In general, the poor suffer much higher child mortality than the better-off. For example, in India, Indonesia, the Philippines and Vietnam, the under-five mortality rate among the poorest quintile of the population is three times higher compared to the richest quintile. Rural populations usually have worse access to clean water and sanitation facilities, greater risk of malnutrition, and lack educational opportunities. Urban populations however, are plagued with major sanitation problems, overcrowded, unsanitary housing, polluted air, slum and shantytown settlements, that are prevalent throughout the developing world (p. 12).

Clearly health is predicated on so many complex factors that good health outcomes become difficult, if not impossible for many countries to achieve. Further, says Marmot:

> Health is a universal human aspiration and a basic human need. The development of society, rich or poor, can be judged by the quality of its population's health, how fairly health is distributed across the social spectrum, and the degree of protection provided from disadvantage due to ill-health. Health equity is central to this premise. Strengthening health equity—globally and within countries—means going beyond

contemporary concentration on the immediate causes of diseases to the 'causes of the causes'—the fundamental structures of social hierarchy and the socially determined conditions these create in which people grow, live, work, and age. The time for action is now, not just because better health makes economic sense, but because it is right and just (p. 174).

From a global perspective there is great system emphasis on funding acute care initiatives and supporting highly technological infrastructures that seek to cure problems. On the other hand, there is relatively little emphasis on maintaining health and preventing disease. Funding healthcare initiatives in developing and developed countries vary greatly. Decentralization, a term used to describe government control over fiscal and political healthcare decisions at the lowest levels, is often viewed as a positive way to improve service delivery, equity, and quality (WHO, 2008). However, this is not always the case, as is evidenced by the United State's federaly funded, state mandated Medicare and Medicaid programs and a current trend toward health reform globally.

GENERAL TRENDS, SIMILARITIES, AND DIFFERENCES

Healthcare systems everywhere, whether they are centralized or decentralized, should be equitable, that is fair, just, and impartial in the treatment of those in need of services. Throughout the industrialized world, health care is universally government provided and controlled. Four examples of this are Canada, Italy, Japan, and the United Kingdom. Each has government provided, fully funded single payer systems that, with the exception of co-pays and or coinsurance, covers the care for all residents. Consequently, the playing field is leveled between the impoverished and the affluent.

A striking healthcare similarity globally is seen in how countries provide for individuals in need of behavioral/mental health care. The WHO has two programs geared toward achieving better outcomes in mental health care. These are the Mental Health Gap Action Program (mhGAP) and the Mental Health Policy and Service Guidance Package. Countries that utilize these tools are likely to improve their behavioral health and mental health outcomes.

The mhGAP Program aims to scale up services for mental, neurological, and substance use disorders for countries with low and middle incomes. This is a comprehensive program that includes the treatment of psychiatric and mental health problems. The intent is that, when adopted and implemented, tens of millions can be treated for depression, schizophrenia, and epilepsy, prevented from suicide and can begin to lead normal lives—even where resources are scarce (WHO, 2010, p.11). The combined Mental Health Policy and Service Guidance Package is a compilation of 14 user friendly modules with full instructions on how to use them. This package is designed to assist policymakers and planners to accomplish four things: 1) to develop policies and comprehensive strategies for improving the mental health of populations; 2) use existing resources to achieve the greatest possible benefits; 3) provide effective services to those in need, and 4) to assist with the reintegration of persons with mental disorders into all aspects of community life. It is believed that if this is accomplished, the individual's overall quality of life will be improved (WHO, 2003, p. 1).

Although disease incidence and prevalence varies widely from nation to nation and coast to coast, there are also similarities among countries in that the top ten diseases plaguing countries are usually preventable. In addition, these diseases are costly to treat, recovery is generally slow, there are many years of life lost, and millions of dollars are lost in earned income and productivity (Life Science, Intelligence, n.d.). The United States outranks other industrialized countries in potential years of life lost due to circulatory problems (773/100,000) and diabetes (99/100,000). Interestingly, for Cuba and the United States, the top three causes of death are identical (see **Table 16-2**). For many countries, industrialized and developing, similar patterns exist. When a person becomes ill in the *industrialized world* (developed countries), the responses by the more affluent among them might be to simply seek the assistance of a physician or visit the closest hospital, get the appropriate care needed to recover, then proceed with business as usual. For people in the *developing world* (non-industrialized countries), the situation is not so automatic or simple. Nor is it automatic for many in the industrialized world who are living in poverty, sometimes within the same geographic reach of the affluent, yet far removed from their radar screens.

Although the United States leads the industrialized world in pharmaceutical spending, and healthcare spending per capita, its health outcomes are anything but astounding. In 2006 the United States spent $843 per capita on pharmaceuticals, Canada spent $639, France $564, Germany $500, and all other industrialized countries spent well under $500. The United States' per capita spending on health care was $6,714 as compared to Canada's $3,678, France's $3,449, and the United Kingdom's $2,760 (OECD, 2008). Healthcare spending in the United States increased from $1.3 trillion in 2000 to $2.4 trillion in 2008. Projections suggest that by 2017, the cost of health care in the United States will reach $4.3 trillion and consume 20% of the GDP (National Coalition on Health Care, 2009). However, despite the disparity in healthcare spending, the United States has poorer outcomes. The World Health Organization's ratings of healthcare performance among

Table 16-2 Health indicators: a comparison between Cuba and the United States.

Indicator	Cuba	United States
Life Expectancy	77.6	77.8
Physicians per 10,000 population	62.7	26.3
Nurses per 10,000 population	78.9	79.5
Percent Births attended by a skilled health professional	99.9	99.0
Infant Mortality Rate	5.3	6.8
Maternal Mortality Rate	49.4	13.1
Percent of 1 year Immunization to DPT3	99	96
HIV Prevalence Among Adults		
15+/100,000 population	52	508
Top Three Cases of Death	Heart Disease	Heart Disease
	Malignant Tumors	Malignant Tumors
	CVA	CVA

Sources: Cuban Annual Health Indicators of Health. US, 2006. National Statistics Bureau, Havana

United States Statistics Yearbook, 2006. National Center for Health Statistics, Hyattsville, MD. WHOSIS

191 member nations, published in 2000, ranked Canada 30th, and the United States 37th, and the overall health of Canadians 35th and Americans 72nd.

The United States leads the world in the number of persons receiving dialysis, total knee replacements, and Percutaneous Transluminal Coronary Angioplasty (PTCA). It also experiences the most deaths from respiratory diseases such as bronchitis, asthma, and emphysema; and it has the highest incidence of adult obesity (defined as individuals with BMI >30) (OECD, 2008). **Table 16-3** presents the international obesity comparisons for eight countries of which the United States is highest. Mexico, not reflected in the table, ranks second highest and the United Kingdom ranks third highest. Japan is among the lowest obesity ranked countries in the world at 3.2 which is equivalent with Korea, a country also not represented on the table.

Years of life lost, as calculated by the number of deaths multiplied by a standard life expectancy at the age at which death occurs, is also used for

Table 16-3 Percent of adult obesity by country (weighted averages).

Country	Percent	Ranking
United States	30.6	#1
United Kingdom	23.0	#3
Canada	14.3	#11
Germany	12.9	#14
Netherlands	10.0	#20
France	9.4	#23
Italy	8.5	#25
Japan	3.2	#28

Data from: OECD Health Data, 2005 Retrieved from: www.nation master.com /graph/hea_obe-health-obesity

determining years of life lost due to disability. For example, the younger the individual at the time of death, the greater the number of life lost in years. This calculation is used sometimes to settle litigated financial settlements. In comparing the years of life lost due to communicable diseases as opposed to non-communicable diseases, the percentages of deaths are more than eight times higher for low income countries. Although the trend in some countries appears to be reversing to non-communicable diseases as the top ranked cause of death, worldwide infection still leads the world as the number one cause of death. One death in three is from an infectious or communicable disease, such as HIV/AIDS, and almost all the diseases and deaths occur in developing (non-industrialized) countries. **Table 16-4** highlights years of life lost to communicable and non-communicable diseases.

People worldwide are dying from infections that have all but been eradicated in industrialized countries. They are also dying from highly

Table 16-4 Distribution of years of life lost by cause, 2004.

Country or Place	Communicable %	Non-Communicable %	Injuries %
Cuba	09	75	16
Worldwide	51	34	14
High Income Countries	08	77	15
United States	09	73	18
Low Income Countries	68	21	10

Data From: World Health Organization. World Health Statistics 2009, Table 2, "Cause-specific mortality and morbidity." http://www.who.int/whosis/whostat/EN _WHS09_Full.pdf treatable infections because some countries do not have access to appropriate antibiotics to treat those in need. For example, pneumonia slightly outranks diarrheal illnesses as a deadly killer of children under 5 years old, worldwide. In the words of Rudan and colleagues "it is the forgotten pandemic, killing more children than any other illness—more than AIDS, malaria, and measles combined—more than 2 million children die from pneumonia in developing countries each year, accounting for almost 1 in 5 deaths of children under five worldwide. Yet, little attention is paid to the disease" (Rudan, Tomaskovic, Boschi-Pinto, & Campbell, 2004, p. 895).

In contrast, while many developing countries lack the necessary antibiotics to treat infections, health providers in the United States have for years overprescribed antibiotics to the extent that today, many infections have become resistant to antibiotic treatment. Topical triple antibiotics can also be purchased over the counter by anyone wishing to purchase them, including teens. Infectious and parasitic diseases remain the major killers of children in the developing world, partly as a result of the HIV/AIDS epidemic (WHO, 2003). Infectious diseases disproportionately affect children and consequently childhood death rates. A baby girl born in Sub-Saharan Africa faces a 22% risk of death before age 15. Whereas, in China the risk is less than 5%, and in industrialized countries the risk is much lower, just 1.1%. The vast majority of these deaths are preventable with the right interventions (UC Atlas of Global Inequality, 2000).

Once a disease exceeds epidemic levels and reaches *pandemic* proportions, affecting an exceptional number of the population like malaria has in many tropical countries, it is so widespread that it becomes almost impossible to control. Notably, health–illness trending patterns in Japan are shifting. Although still considerably lower than the United States and the rest of the western world, the prevalence of coronary disease is increasing in Japan. In fact, the prevalence of lipid risk factors in younger Japanese people is now similar to that in the U.S. population. There is also some evidence of a continuous increase in the frequency of diabetes in Japan (Kita, 2002). Although, India and China have made some progress in the declining numbers of child deaths by approximately 30 percent over a twelve year span, the cause-of-death pattern has remained fairly stable, with the exception of perinatal conditions whose proportions have notably increased (WHO, 2003).

Persons living in high mortality countries die of communicable diseases, while those in low-mortality countries die of non-communicable diseases (UC Atlas of Global Inequality, 2000) such as heart disease and stroke. **Table 16-5** presents selected causes of death as percentages of all causes of

Table 16-5 Selected causes of death as percentage of all causes of death in selective high income countries, 2004.

Cause	High Income Country	Australia	Germany	United Kingdom	United States
HIV	0.3	0.1	—	0.1	0.7
Diabetes Mellitus	3.0	2.7	2.9	1.1	3.1
Chronic Lower Respiratory Disease	6.4	4.4	0.6	4.5	5.1
Cerebrovascular Disease (stroke)	9.5	9.1	8.4	10.3	6.3
Ischemic Heart Disease	17.0	18.5	18.7	18.0	27.2
Malignant Neoplasm	26.2	28.7	25.6	26.2	23.1

Note: The UK statistics includes only England and Wales

Source: Anderson, GF, Frogner, BK and Reinhardt, UE. Health spending in OECD countries in 2004: An update. *Health Affairs.* (2007, September/October26 (5) 1481 – 89. http://www.commonwealthfund.org/Publications/In-the-Literature/2008/Jul /Health-Spending-in-OECD-Countries-in-2004--An-Update.aspx

Table 16-6 Ranked causes of mortality in developing countries in 2004 and 2030 baseline projections.

Disease	2004 Ranking	Projected 2030	Ranking Change
Ischemic Heart Disease	1	1	0
Cerebrovascular Disease (stroke)	2	2	0
Lower Respiratory Infection	3	4	−1
COPD	4	3	+1
Diarrheal Diseases	5	17	−12
HIV/AIDS	6	9	−3
Tuberculosis (TB)	7	19	−12
Prematurity & Low Birth Weight	8	20	−12
Road Traffic Accidents	9	5	+2

Source: (WHO, 2008a), In Nugent, RA and Feigl, AB. Where have all the donors gone? Scarce donor funding for non-communicable diseases. Working paper 228, November 2010. Retrieved from: www.cdev.org/files/1424546_file_Nugent_ Feigl_ NCD_final.pdf.

death in high income countries for 2004. **Table 16-6** lists ranked changes in death rate for diseases and injuries in developing countries for 2004 with baseline projections for 2030. It is predicted that, "if these projections are realized, lower respiratory infections and HIV will be the only infectious diseases remaining among the top ten causes of death two decades from now" (Nugent and Feigl, 2010 p.3).

Crude death rate is the number of deaths that occur in a particular population during a given period of time, such as from April through March. Crude death rates below ten per 1,000 persons in the population are considered low and over 20 per 1,000 are considered high (Rosenberg, n.d.). In July 2011, the crude death rate per 1,000 persons in the population worldwide was estimated to be 8.78. The U.S. fell slightly below, at 8.39 per 1,000 (CIA World Fact Book, 2011). Crude death rates below ten are considered low and over 20 per 1,000 are considered high (Rosenberg, n.d.). The July 2011 crude death rate was 17.23 per 1,000 persons in the population for South Africa, 16.03 for the Russian Federation, 11.49 for Sierra Leone, 8.57 for Ghana, and 6.38 for Brazil. In contrast, the crude death rate was 9.93 for Italy, 9.15 for Japan, 8.85 for France, and Canada 8.09 per 1,000 persons in the population (CIA World Fact Book, 2011). Typically, crude death rates in developing countries are unusually high (Rosenberg, n.d.).

Many developing countries, such as India and Ghana, are severely challenged by depressed economies and poor infrastructures, leaving them defenseless against such conditions as poor sanitation, cross contamination of crops from inadequate sewage systems, unstable electricity, contaminated drinking water, environmental noise, and a multiplicity of other problems threatening public health and decreasing their quality of life. While in developed countries, much focus is placed on protecting the ozone layer and cleaning up the environment by "going green," recycling, finding new and cleaner natural sources of fuel and energy, and installing barriers along highways protecting residents in neighboring communities from disruptive traffic noise.

GLOBAL INEQUITIES IN HEALTH

Global inequalities in health, within and among countries worldwide, send a serious message to consumers. *Social determinants* of health, defined by the WHO as "the social and economic conditions under which people live that determines their health" (p. 9) are major factors in health inequities. The conditions under which people are born, grow up, and work, and their cultural backgrounds, race, ethnicity, age, and gender, greatly influences their health-seeking behaviors. These things also determine how people define health/wellness and illness, and whether they are likely to self-treat or utilize the formal healthcare system when ill.

Another particular trend that results in a workforce disparity is candidly described by the WHO (2006), "health workers are migrating at unprecedented rates—increasingly from low-income countries with a low supply of health workers—to take up positions in the US and other affluent countries' long-term care sectors, leaving in their wake workforce shortages and what some call a global 'crisis in health.' Abandoning positions in countries already experiencing major staffing shortages of especially physicians and nurses leaves a deleterious void in the home country."

There is a major problem when documented evidence supports a widened gap in life expectancy and infant mortality among and within countries based on their wealth. Healthcare systems, irrespective of where they exist geographically, should be about the business of promoting health and preventing disease for all its residents. Some are better able to do this than others. The disparities seen in access to healthcare services, treatment options, life expectancy, infant mortality, and communicable diseases, vary among countries. Much can be learned if countries would embrace one another, drawing on unique strengths through interdisciplinary collaboration. Discussing strategies in this way might make a difference. The issues, trends, and influences of social determinants such as health literacy and illiteracy, living in poverty, culture, ethnicity/race and even gender are critical challenges that 21st century health policymakers, administrators, and practitioners must be prepared to address.

Health research and development is essential in order for healthcare organizations to remain viable. However, there is underinvestment in health research relevant to the needs of low and middle income countries, with a mere 10% of the worldwide expenditure on health research and development devoted to the problems that affect 90% of the world population. This is referred to as the *"10/90 Gap"* (GlobalForumHealth, 2005).

SUMMARY

There are a variety of differences among countries in the ability to finance and implement healthcare programs. Treatment priorities, availability of medicines, equipment and supplies, inequities in healthcare access and disparities are important considerations when determining overall health outcomes. Some countries are better able to address their health challenges than others. A careful review of the eight factors by country summarized in **Table 16-7**, and the 11 healthcare systems discussed in Part II of this book should be helpful in assisting the learner to determine whether a country has true access.

Table 16-7 The Eight Factor Model for true access.

Eight Factor Model for True Access

1	2	3	4
5	6	7	8

	United States	Canada	Japan	United Kingdom	France	Cuba	India	Ghana
HISTORICAL	Poor Access Many barriers	Open Access Barriers	Open Access Few barriers	Open Access Few barriers	Open Access Few barriers	Open Access Few barriers	Poor Access Many barriers	Poor Access Many barriers
STRUCTURE (Infrastructure, policies, staff needs roles & responsibilities)	Private run Physician shortage Cyclical nursing shortage	Govt. run Large migration of physicians and nurses	Govt. run	Govt. run	Govt. run	Govt. run Good supply of healthcare professionals and healthcare facilities	Govt. run Insufficient treatment facilities Major migration of physicians and nurses	Govt. run Insufficient treatment facilities Poorly staffed and ill equipped polyclinics Major migration of physicians and nurses
FINANCING (Cost & priorities)	Costly Unfunded Long term care (LTC)	Govt. funded Fragmented eldercare	Govt. funded	Govt. funded Regional financing disparity	Govt. and private funded Costly	Govt. funded Costly	Govt. funded Grossly inadequate and underfunded	Govt. funded Underfunded Priority maternal child health
INTERVENTIONAL (Care: primary, acute, restorative)	Acute, high technological focus Overuse of ED	Disparity among provinces and urban: rural	Good outcomes Balance between traditional and allopathic medicine	Rationing→Long waiting times Good advances in stroke care	Good outcomes No waiting time	Good outcomes Strong community-based care focus	Lack of dental care Good long term care Good health tourism	Acute and Maternal child focused

PREVENTIVE (Promoting health, preventing disease)	Emphasized but underfunded	Encouraged and financed / High literacy	Encouraged and financed / High literacy	Encouraged and financed	A leader in prevention / Encouraged and Financed	Actively promoted and financed	Not emphasized / Severely over populated	Not emphasized / Low obesity
PREVENTIVE (Promoting health, preventing disease)	Emphasized but, lacks funding	Encouraged and financed	Encouraged and financed	Encouraged and financed	Encouraged and financed	Actively promoted and financed	Not emphasized	Not emphasized
RESOURCES (Human & fiscal)	Insufficient human & fiscal							
MAJOR ISSUES (Top 10 diseases)								
DISPARITIES (Race/ethnicity, age, income)								

Discussion Questions

1. Explain how health is defined by the World Health Organization (WHO). Does this definition fit your view of health? Based on your observations as a health provider, would you say that patients subscribe to the WHO definition of health? In your opinion, do patients have an inclusive view of health or do they perceive health more narrowly, i.e., as absence of disease.

2. What is the connection between health and health equity? How does Marmot's notion of "strengthening health equity" affect your view of what it means to be an effective health provider?

3. In your opinion, what aspect(s) of health care does your health facility emphasize? Is the emphasis even handed or does one area receive more attention than the other? How does the health facility's emphasis impact access and the quality of health care?

4. Specifically, describe your healthcare facility's emphasis on each of the following:

   a) Funding acute care initiatives

   b) Supporting high technology to cure problems

   c) Maintaining health and preventing disease

5. Identify three issues that make it difficult to reduce the incidence of a preventable disease. Explain why these issues are experienced in countries worldwide.

6. What are health disparities? Identify health disparities that predominate your work setting. How do these disparities affect your ability to provide access and quality health care?

References

CIA World Fact Book (2009). Central Intelligence Agency (CIA). (n.d.). Retrieved February 23, 2011 from https://www.cia.gov/library/publications/the-world-factbook/rankorder/2066rank.html

Kita, T. (2002). Coronary heart disease risk in Japan – an East/West divide. *Oxford Journal of Medicine, European Heart Journal Supplement*, 6:supplA, A8–A11. Retrieved on December 10, 2010 from http://eurheartjsupp.oxfordjournals.org/content/6/suppl_ A/A8.full

Life Science Intelligence. (n.d.). *Disease incidence and prevalence: Europe, Japan, Russian Federation and Australia*. Retrieved February 17, 2011 from life sciencesintelligence.com/market.reports.page.php?id

MacDorman, M. F. & Mathews, T. J. (2008). Recent trends in infant mortality in the United States. Centers for Disease Control and Prevention. (9). Retrieved February 17, 2011 from http://www.cdc.gov/nchs/data/databriefs/db09.htm

Matlin, S. C. (2005). Global forum of health research: Helping to correct the 10/90 gap. Global forum update on research for health, Vol. 2. Poverty, equity, and health research.

Marmot, M., Bobak, M., & Smith, G. D. (n.d.). Explanations for social inequalities in health. 174.

National Coalition on Health Care. (2009). Health insurance costs. Retrieved from www.nchc.org/facts/cost.shtml

Nugent, R. A. & Feigl, A. B. (2010, November). Where have all the donors gone? Scarce donor funding for non-communicable diseases. Working paper 228. Center for Global Development. Retrieved from www.Cgdev.org/files/1424546 _file_Nugent_Feigl_NCD_final.pdf

O'Brien, P. & Gostin, L. O. (Fall 2008/Spring 2009). Health worker shortage and inequalities: The reform of United States policy. *Global Health Governance*. 2:2, 1–29.

Rosenberg, M. (n.d.). Migration of health workers. Retrieved December 11, 2011 from http://www.geography.about.com/od/populationgeography/a/cbrcdr_2.htm

Rudan, I., Tomaskovic, L., Boschi-Pinto, C., & Campbell, H. (2004). Global estimates of the incidence of clinical pneumonia among children under five years of age. *Bulletin of the World Health Organization*, 82(12), 895–903.

UC Atlas of Global Inequality. (2000). Infectious diseases kill 1/3 worldwide; AIDS is top cause of death in developing region. Retrieved November 10, 2010 from http://ucatlas.ucsc.edu/cause.php

World Health Organization (WHO). (2001). Strengthening mental health promotion. In: World Health Organization (WHO). (2004). Promoting mental health: Concepts, emerging evidence, practice. Summary Report. Retrieved December 28, 2011 from http://www.who.int/mental_health/evidence/en /promoting_mhh.pdf

World Health Organization (WHO). (2003). Global health: Today's challenges. *The World Health Report*. Retrieved November 26, 2010 from http://www.who.int /whr/2003/chapter1/en/index2.html

World Health Organization (WHO). (2006). Working together for health: The WHO Report. Health workers, Chapter 1. Retrieved December 10, 2011 from who.int/whr/2006/en/

World Health Organization (WHO). (2008). Decentralized health systems in transition. Based on a presentation to the 14th Annual Conference of the RHN in 2006 by Vaida Bankauskaite, Scientific Project Officer, Public Health Executive Agency, European Commission.

World Health Organization (WHO). (2010). Mental health: Strengthening our response. Fact sheet. Retrieved from http://www.who.int/mediacentre/factsheets /fs220/en

CHAPTER **17**

Conclusions and Future Leadership

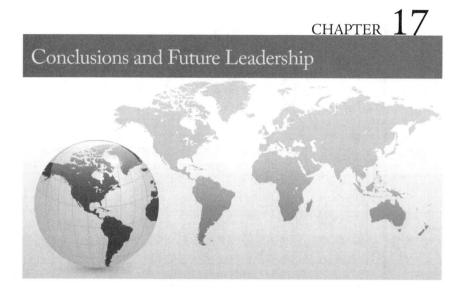

Alone we can do so little, together we can do so much.

–Helen Keller

INTRODUCTION AND EVALUATION OF THE EIGHT FACTOR MODEL

This discussion brings us to the end of our book journey. It summarizes the importance of the information included in the book and offers concluding remarks about what one country might learn from another. It also explores future leadership considerations that might prove beneficial in moving healthcare delivery toward a brighter future, worldwide. The Eight Factor Model was introduced for the first time in Chapter 3 to familiarize the reader with all aspects of it. The learner is encouraged to review it in greater detail. This table highlights a few of the most striking observations made about the countries included in Chapters 4–14 of the book. The observations may be useful in evaluating the extent to which true access is being provided. Healthcare delivery activities, positive and negative, are important considerations in determining true access. For example, although France and Italy are considered to be among the best systems in the world and they are progressively moving in the direction of providing full health care to all its citizens, one might conclude that neither is providing *true access*. Health care in both countries is costly, there is no consistent plan to

Table 17-1 Eight Factor Model for true access.

	United States	Canada	Japan	United Kingdom	France	Cuba	India	Ghana
HISTORICAL	Poor access / Many barriers	Open access / Barriers	Open access / Few barriers	Open access / Few barriers	Open access / Few barriers	Open access / Few barriers	Poor access / Many barriers	Poor access / Many barriers
STRUCTURE (Infrastructure, policies, staff needs roles & responsibilities)	Private run / Physician shortage / Cyclical nursing shortage	Govt. run / Large migration of physicians and nurses	Govt. run	Govt. run	Govt. run	Govt. run / Good supply of healthcare professionals and healthcare facilities	Govt. run / Insufficient treatment facilities / Major migration of physicians and nurses	Govt. run / Insufficient treatment facilities / Poorly staffed and ill equipped polyclinics / Major migration of physicians and nurses
FINANCING (Cost & priorities)	Costly / Unfunded long term care (LTC)	Govt. funded / Fragmented eldercare	Govt. funded	Govt. funded / Regional financing disparity	Govt. and private funded / Costly	Govt. funded / Costly	Govt. funded / Grossly inadequate and underfunded	Govt. funded / Underfunded
INTERVENTIONAL (Care: primary, acute, restorative)	Acute, high technological focus overuse of ED	Disparity among provinces and urban: rural	Good outcomes / Balance between traditional and allopathic medicine	Rationing→Long waiting times / Good advances in stroke care	Good outcomes / No waiting time	Good outcomes / Strong community-based care focus	Lack of dental care / Good long term care / Good health tourism	Priority maternal child health / Acute and Maternal child focused

PREVENTIVE (Promoting health, preventing disease)	Not emphasized; Low obesity	Not emphasized; Severely over populated	Actively promoted and financed	A leader in prevention; Encouraged and financed; Strong focus on healthy children, prenatal and maternal outcomes; Great palliative care efforts	Encouraged and financed; Programs directed at preventing exploitation of children; Protection of the mentally ill	Encouraged and financed; High literacy	Encouraged and financed; High literacy	Emphasized but underfunded
RESOURCES (Human)	Strong Kinship & family support; WE-ISM; Faith-based support	Strong respect for parents and grand parents; Faith-based support	High divorce rate; Large number of working women	Strong women's role in care of the ill; Faith-based support	Strength of family nuclear & extended	Global loss of physicians and nurses	Use of Level 2 nurses; Comparatively lower salaried physicians	Diverse cultures; Unprepared for eldercare; Lack of cultural competence in practice
MAJOR ISSUES (Top 10 diseases)	Physician attrition; Limited ED care; Cash 'n Carry; Physician's Bill of Rights	Over crowding, poor sanitation, slums; Water borne diseases; Castes	Illicit drug traffic				Younger Japanese lifestyle changes → evidencing Western health problems; High suicide	High uninsured population; Adult & child obesity; Lack of cultural competence in practice
DISPARITIES (Race/ethnicity, age, income)	Rural/urban divide; Lack of older adult care	Urban/rural divide; Wealthy/poor divide	Poorly coordinated eldercare	Rural/urban divide; Northern Ireland fewer disparities		Higher fertility in lower educated women; High regional HS drop-out rates; Rural/urban divide	Lack of professional accountability → high absenteeism; Over prescribing of medications	High uninsured population; Language barriers; Race-based challenges

care for non-citizens, and Italy has regional disparities. Similarly, countries such as Canada, Ghana, and India are challenged by a greater demand for services than can be provided because of a loss of physicians and nurses to other countries with better compensation packages. Planning and execution of interventions vary widely among countries as does funding for health care. Both affect the extent to which patients get their healthcare needs met even if they experience no difficulty accessing care.

LESSONS LEARNED

In regard to what lessons can be learned from the information discussed throughout the book, much can be said about embracing change with a new mindset. It is apparent that most healthcare systems would benefit from better collaboration and planning about how to maximize their current workforces. They would also benefit from planning new and creative ways to balance the supply of health professionals according to the demand for services. Another consideration is that a strengthbased approach to administering health care might prove beneficial. The obvious response from a larger, more powerful country might be, what can we learn from a developing country? However, by closely examining the strengths of even a relatively poor country, much can be learned. Replicating the country's successful practices will likely result in better outcomes despite the size or characteristics of the country.

France, a developed nation, is admired as a healthcare leader. Yet, it is looking to other countries for answers in reducing their healthcare costs. In considering the success of France's health system, lessons might be learned from the less costly United Kingdom system that achieves good outcomes without the extraordinarily higher expenditures.

Interestingly, the United States and Cuba demonstrate the same top three causes of death. A closer examination of the reasons for this might be helpful. The value of international collaboration on healthcare issues could provide insightful information on preventing future illness, and significantly improving health outcomes. Government officials must be transparent about the issues. They must also keep an open mind, and willingly negotiate for practice innovations that first and foremost address the needs of the people. Initiatives must include due diligence toward reforming what is clearly in need of changing in current systems, while retaining the best of what a system has to offer. It is also essential that there be more closely scrutinized bottom lines. That is, the sustainability of government financing of health care can only be made possible if there are serious efforts made to achieve system efficiency and effectiveness.

Another lesson learned is the importance of healthcare systems placing more attention on balancing health promotion, disease prevention, and interventions. Maximizing efforts at boosting preventive measures to keep people healthy, active, and more fully functioning while introducing interventions as early as possible to prevent complications, is essential. The ability to replicate the Cuban model where physician–nurse primary care partnerships are strategically entrenched in communities among the population masses could prove beneficial in that it assists people to remain in their homes and out of the hospitals. Joint crossdisciplinary efforts at improving *true access* is consistent with a major Healthy People 2010 goal. Providing access to quality services and service equality is of paramount importance in achieving the goal of eliminating healthcare disparities.

IMPLICATIONS FOR THE 21ST CENTURY LEADER

If healthcare delivery systems are to be transformed, it will require an entrepreneurial type leadership that is unapologetically refreshing, risk-taking, motivating, cutting edge, embracing of new ideas and strategies for accomplishing goals, and pro inter-collaboration. The 21st century leader working in health care could emphasize the following seven strategic elements:

- The importance of planning for a stabilized workforce reflecting adequate numbers of well-educated health professionals at every level needed requires some level of risk-taking. We need to ask, are we inviting people who think differently? Are we creating learning organizations in which people feel comfortable expressing their ideas although different from others'? Do we reward people for thinking differently?
- Planning for creating and maintaining a retention oriented environment that thrives for high patient and staff satisfaction. Do we promote a fair and equitable distribution of the workload? Do we promote transparency in the data that are reported? Is the mission of the organization clearly communicated at every level of the organization?
- The need to identify and eliminate unnecessary costs. We need to determine the redundancy in our practices and ask what are the essential services to provide quality outcomes? We also need to ask, what strategies do we have to evaluate our efficiency and effectiveness?
- Ways in which opportunities for continuing education and training can be expanded. We need to ask how we can utilize research to enhance the quality of care through evidence based practice.

- Improving strategies to maximize efforts in providing *true access* to care. In what way do we continuously assess progress toward the achievement of organizational goals?
- Opportunities to engage in collaborative decision-making. Are industrialized countries open to best practices of developing and vice versa?
- Striving for improved standards. Are our ways of thinking outdated? Or do we look for new ways to improve the delivery of health care?

Each of these elements is important for the effective leader who is focused on moving the healthcare organization well into the 21st century. In the words of Patton (2001), "good practices are only as good as the evidence that supports them and their definition and applicability typically evolves in time and space" (p. ii12).

SUMMARY

There is a strong argument in support of needing future healthcare leaders with vision. These leaders must be prepared to change environments. They must also establish better ways to improve effectiveness in approaches to preventing, diagnosing, and treating diseases. With increasing diversity more attention must be given to how we engage patients in their treatment and care. The effects of an aging society and the chronicity of illness and disability make strategic planning a priority. Heightened consumer expectations and demands, including their increased interest in using complementary/alternative medicine (CAM) require that providers be more sensitive to patient needs. Escalation in healthcare costs and budgetary pressures creates new challenges for providing coordinated high quality care.

REFERENCES

Patton, M. Q. (2001). Evaluation knowledge, management, best practices and high quality lessons learned. Retrieved from http://heapol.oxfordjournals.org/content/26/suppl_2/ii5.full.pdf+html

Appendix

WEBSITES ON HEALTH-RELATED INFORMATION AND CURRENT ISSUES IN HEALTH CARE:

Administration on Aging: http:www.aoa.dhhs.gov/
Agency of Healthcare Research and Quality: http://www.ahrq.gov/
American College of Preventive Medicine: http://www.acpm.org
American Public Health Association: http://www.apha.org
Association for Health Research Quality (AHRQ): www.ahrq.gov
Centers for Disease Control and Prevention: http://www.cdc.gov/
CultureMed: http://culturemed.sunyit.edu
Department of Health and Human Services (DHHS): www.hhs.gov
Global Health Office: http://www.cdc.gov/nceh/division/global.htm
Health Care Financing Administration: http://www.hcfa.gov
Health Care Information and Management Systems Society (HIMSS): www.himss.org/ASP/index.asp
Health Care without harm (publications list and library link to brochures): www.noharm.org
Healthy People 2010: www.health.gov/healthypeople/
Institute for Healthcare Improvement: www.ihi.org
Johnson & Johnson Campaign for Nursing's Future: www.discoveringnursing.com/
Medicaid: http://www.hcfa.hhs.gov/medicaid/medicaid.htm
Medicare: http://www.hcfa.hhs.gov/medicare/medicare.htm
National Academies of Sciences (IOM reports): www.nap.edu
National Association for Health Care Quality (NAHCQ): www.nahq.org
National Center for Chronic Disease Prevention and Health Promotion: http://www.cdc.gov/nccdphp/nccdhome.htm
National Center for Environmental Health: http://www.cdc.gov/nceh/info/programs.htm
National Center for Health Promotion and Disease Prevention: http://www.va.gov/NCHP/

National Healthcare Quality Reports: www.ahrq.gov/qual/measurix.htm

National Institute of Health: http://www.nih.gov/

National Institute of Occupational Safety and Health (databases and information resources): www.cdc.gov/niosh/database.html

National Patient Safety Foundation: www.npsf.org

Practice Greenhealth: http://practicegreenhealth.org/

Resources in Cultural Competence Education for Health Care Professionals: www.calendow.org/uploadedFiles/resources_in_cultural_competence.pdf

The Commonwealth Fund: http://www.cmwf.org

The Institute for Safe Medication Practices: www.ismp.org

The Joint Commission: www.jointcommission.org

The Office of Minority Health, U.S. Department of Health and Human Services, Culturally Competent Nursing Modules: www.thinkculturalhealth .org

Transcultural Nursing Society: www.tcns.org

U.S. Department Health and Human Services (DHHS), Health information technology (HIT): http://www.healthit.hhs.gov

Glossary

Access: Gaining entry into a system; reference in this book is to the health-care system.

Acupressure: Similar technique and effect as acupuncture, except the fingertips rather than needles are used to apply pressure.

Acupuncture: An ancient Chinese method of restoring balance between the yin and yang by inserting hair thin needles at specific anatomical points, altering blockage of energy flow patterns along meridians producing pain-relieving and mood-lifting chemicals (anti-inflammatory substances).

Advanced Practice Nurse: A registered professional nurse who has earned a master's degree or higher in a particular specialty area.

Allopathic: Health beliefs and practices derived from modern scientific models of treatment, diagnosis, early intervention, and prevention, and which use up-to-date technology.

Amenable mortality: Deaths that could have been prevented had the persons enjoyed good health.

Ayurveda: Traditional East Indian medicine that prevents disease causing imbalances (dosnas) within the body by emphasizing the use of diet, exercise, and herbal and natural remedies that strengthen the mind-body connection and add longevity and quality to life.

Capitation: A method whereby insurance companies reimburse providers, such as physicians and nurse practitioners, a pre-set amount for services given to the patients enrolled in their practices.

Cash 'n carry: Patients must pay for services up front in order to get care particularly, medications.

Centers of Excellence: Neighborhood polyclinics in Cuba.

Cholera: Acute bacterial infectious disease that causes excessive, uncontrolled diarrhea.

Chronic underfunding: A persistent gap between what the government guarantees for health care and what it can actually deliver.

Communicable disease: An infectious disease that can be transmitted either directly or indirectly from one individual or animal to another who is susceptible.

Community: A group of people living in a specific geographic locale who share a common interest.

Co-payment: The third party payer, such as an insurance company, pays the major portion of the medical bill, and the patient pays a significantly lower portion of the bill. For example, if the visit to the physician or specialist is $150, the patient may be responsible for a co-payment of $20–$40.

Crude death rate: The number of deaths occurring in a specific population, during a particular period of time.

Cultural competence: Striving to incorporate treatment and care plans embracing the patient's culture to ensure that the care and services are congruent with the patient's culture.

Datura: A narcosis-eliciting genus of plants that contains constituents of hyoscyamine and scopolamine which have anticholinergic properties.

Decentralization: The lowest level of government control over fiscal and political healthcare decisions.

Deductible: A fee that must be paid in advance before the third party payer will pay its portion.

Dengue Fever: An acute illness presenting with severe fever and muscle and skeletal pain caused by one of four different viruses transmitted to humans by a bite from the *Aedes aegypti* mosquito.

Developed countries: Countries which are industrialized, major exporters of commodities, and more economically stable.

Developing countries: Non-industrialized countries, once referred to as under-developed, Third World countries.

Diagnostic related groupings (DRGs): Predetermined fees set by grouping similar problems under 468 different categories; a negotiated fee-for-service, per diem, and capitation.

Disparities in health: Non-access related racial or ethnic differences in the quality of health care.

Docteurs: Physicians in general practice.

Dokudami: A creeping, low growing plant used to treat heart problems and counteract the effects of poisons.

Emic: An insider's view of an event or phenomenon.

Endemic: Something that is found in a specific population or a part of the world, such as in the case of malaria, that is a stable, expected, and continuous disease.

Epidemic: An outbreak of a disease that affects a large number of people in a geographic area.

Epidemiological transition: A change in the causes of mortality from communicable diseases to non-communicable diseases such as premature death due to violence and traffic accidents.

Ethnic: A group of people who, although they belong to a dominant group, have different experiences from the dominant group setting them apart; such as the case of members of the same dominant group who have vastly different religious affiliations.

Ethnicity: Defines the person by racial or cultural background or identity.

Etic: An outsider's view of an event or phenomenon.

Evil eye: A strong belief that someone can cause harm to befall another person, or bring harm to the person's property, by intensely staring at the person or the property.

Exclusions (limitations): Services not covered by the health plan.

Experience insurance rating: Reflects how often individual persons utilize the system and the complexity of their health problems.

Family Health Program: The main portal of basic health care in Brazil.

Fatalistic: Accepting that occurrences are predestined and cannot be humanly changed.

Feverfew: A herbal medicine used to treat migraine headaches; also commonly referred to as *bachelor's button* or *natsushirogiku*.

Filipino: Preferred term of reference to Philippine-born individuals.

Francophone: Canadians who have French as their first language.

Guaranteed Package Program: Identifies Russia's basic package of free healthcare benefits and services promised to all citizens by the government, as well as a description of some health services excluded from coverage, such as cosmetic surgery.

Gennoshoko: A traditional Japanese herbal medicine that treats diarrhea and infections of the gastrointestinal tract.

Global: Worldwide integration of cultures without geographic boundaries.

Group Insurance Ratings: Based on an overall rating of an aggregate group of people such as a particular workforce community.

Healthcare provider: Typically the physician, nurse practitioner, physician's assistant, and other clinical specialists, or a service institution etc. or a service institution, such as a hospital or nursing home, who receives payment out-of-pocket or by reimbursement.

Healthcare Development Concept 2020: A healthcare initiative drafted in 2009 aimed at improving Russia's healthcare facilities, updating medical technology, raising salaries of medical personnel, and transitioning to an insurance-based system to enhance patient choices and induce competition among providers for customers.

Health disparities: Racial or ethnic differences in the quality of healthcare that are not due to access-related factors such as insurance coverage, or clinical needs, preferences, and appropriateness of interventions.

Health Maintenance Organization (HMO): A form of managed care where individuals receive all their care from participating providers. Referrals are usually required to see specialists.

Health promotion: Placing emphasis on maximizing wellness and preventing illness.

Incidence: Number of occurrences of a specific condition or event.

Institutional core: Having the essential systems, processes, and updated technology in place to maximize efficiency and effectiveness.

Integrated delivery system: The merging of more than one health delivery system, therefore creating a larger system incorporating all the essential, existing services and processes; such as when smaller, more financially vulnerable healthcare systems merge with larger more financially stable ones.

Leptospirosis: A rare, but severe, spiral shaped (spirochete) bacterial infection in certain environments that results in high fever, headache, muscle aches, vomiting, diarrhea, and jaundice.

Long-term care insurance: Coverage that pays for all or part of the cost of home healthcare services, or care in a nursing home or assisted living.

Magico-religious: Use of charms, spiritual words, and actions to prevent and cure illness. Sometimes uses herbs and rituals in combination with prayer to prevent or cure illness.

Magnet hospital: A hospital that is held to very high standards. It engages in extensive review and systematic evaluation of its nursing practice to ensure the highest quality of nursing practice and patient care.

Mal ojo (evil eye): Spanish for excessively staring at an individual to cause a hex.

Managed care: An organized system of healthcare delivery that is linked to networks of participating physicians, hospitals, and other providers in the plan to keep costs down. Some plans require individuals to see in-network providers, some plans allow covered individuals to see providers outside the network but they will likely pay a larger share of the cost of care. The Health Maintenance Organization (HMO) is an example of managed care.

Medicaid: A state-operated healthcare insurance program that provides health coverage for the poor and those unable to pay for their health care. It is partially funded by the federal government under the Federal Social Security Act of 1966.

Medicare: Health coverage for those 65 and older in 4 parts (A, B, C, and D), and disability coverage for those who qualify for Social Security benefits.

Medigap: Supplemental insurance coverage to compensate for what Medicare does not pay.

Metis: Diverse ethnic groups in Canada with a mixture of French, Native American, and other cultural groups.

Metabolic syndrome: A combination of health related factors such as, being overweight, sedentary lifestyles, and genetics, placing individuals at risk for developing heart disease, diabetes, and stroke.

Midwife: A trained individual who assists during childbirth with labor and delivery. A lay midwife lacks formal training and a certified nurse midwife is a registered nurse who received additional training and passed a qualifying examination.

Non-communicable disease: A disease that is non-infectious and therefore cannot be transmitted.

Overcapacity: Exceeding the maximum number of patients a facility has the ability to care for.

Palliative: Care management directed at or near the end of life that provides pain relief and comfort and improves the quality of life of patients and their families.

Pandemic: A widespread epidemic affecting a very high proportion of a population, such as malaria in tropical countries.

Physician's Bill of Rights: A document that realizes the physician as the most important, most highly respected person in the healthcare system. Ghana operates on a system such as this.

Preferred Provider Organization (PPO): Patient-chosen physician or specialist from a network list. Out-of-pocket expenses are lower when individuals see providers who participate in the plan.

Polyclinic: Many community health centers or clinics strategically placed in areas of need.

Population density: The number of persons per square mile, or square kilometer, in a particular area (total population per land area divided by the square miles or square km of the area).

Portable: Insurance coverage that can be taken with individuals from one province to another.

Prevalence: The number of cases of a disease in a specified population present at given time.

Prevention: Maintaining and preserving physical, emotional/mental, and social health.

Primary care: The Institute of Medicine defines primary care as the provision of integrated, accessible health services by clinicians who are accountable for addressing a large majority of personal healthcare needs, developing a sustained partnership with patients, and practicing in the context of family and community.

Primary health care: The tenets of primary care that have been incorporated into the healthcare delivery system at all care levels, acute, minor, major, chronic, and well child and adult care, as well as in tertiary care especially as individuals with serious illnesses also need primary care.

Race: Connecting people together based on genetic similarities, skin color, and other physical characteristics.

Reflexology: A natural science that uses manipulation of reflex points in the hands and feet that correspond with organs in the body in order to clear the energy pathways and the flow of energy through the body.

Respite: A period of rest or relief, in regard to caring for the ill; primary care-givers are provided a temporary relief from their care-giving responsibilities.

Restorative: Assisting in effectively regaining health and strength.

Samu: France's emergency medical services.

San-epid network: An abbreviated term used to describe Russia's Sanitation Epidemiological System which focuses on the control of epidemics and infectious diseases.

Semashko model: Developed by Nikolai Semashko, People's Commissar of Public Health (1918–1930); under this model, the Soviet Russian health-care system was highly centralized and regulated, including state-hired medical personnel, and government owned medical facilities.

Simpatias: Medicinal animal concoction containing secret ingredients used to treat illness.

Single payer: A method of reimbursing health care where one payer, usually the government, pays for all the healthcare costs for its citizens; typically funded by taxes.

Social determinant: The social and economic conditions under which people live that determine their health and health status, how they view health, and their health-seeking beliefs and practices. Examples include, but are not limited to, poverty, illiteracy, race, culture, and gender.

Telemedicine: An approach to practicing medicine that allows for the diagnosis and treatment of diseases remotely over long distances by use of videoconferencing, cabled networks, and the Internet.

Tertiary: A level of health care available only in large care institutions and that includes techniques and methods of therapy and diagnosis involving equipment and personnel not economically feasible in smaller institutions.

The Bolsa Familia Program: A program in Brazil that provides monthly cash incentives to families who comply with government conditions such as ensuring their children attend school and are immunized.

Third party payer: An entity other than the patient or the healthcare provider pays for the health services, typically an insurance company.

Traditional birth attendant (TBA): An individual trained to assist with uncomplicated childbirth, in similar roles as midwives without the extensive educational preparation.

Traditional healer: Folk healer; one who uses herbal and magico-religious remedies to treat, heal, and prevent health problems.

True Access: Being able to get to and from healthcare services, having the ability to pay for the services, and getting your needs met once you enter the system.

Unani: Medicine based on the humoral theory that presupposes the presence of four humors; Dum (blood), Balgham (phlegm), Safra (yellow bile), and Sauda (black bile).

Unified Health System: National Health System or *Sistemia Unico de Saude*.

Universal health: Similar to single payer, and often used interchangeably in that health care for all citizens is paid for by the government; however, in the case of universal health it may be administered by different payer groups.

Ukon: Turmeric, an herbal remedy that boosts liver functioning and fights against infection.

We-ism: A strong concept of kinship that says, "I am because we are, and we are because I am;" in other words, we are all interdependent on each other. This concept is widely embraced in Ghanaian culture.

Years of life lost: The number of deaths multiplied by the standard life expectancy at the age at which death occurs. Deaths occurring at a younger age carry a higher weight than deaths occurring at an older age. In other words, the younger the person at the time of death the greater the number of years of life lost.

Index

A

Abortion, in Russian Federation, 183
Absenteeism, 81
  in Russian Federation, 258
Access, to health care, 6, 13–16
  barriers to, 65
  denied, 17
  Eight Factor Model for, 6, 8, 31–39
  lack of, 16–17
  lack of true, 14
  redefining, 15
  true, 6, 8, 32
Action for Global Health, 130
Acute care hospitals, 51
Addiction, 220
Administrative costs, lowering, 47
Advanced Practice Nurses
  (nurse practitioners), 106
Advanced practice nurses (APN), 54
  guidelines for, 55
Affordable Care Act, 46–50
African Americans
  in Canada, 83
  cardiovascular disease in, 12
  case study on, 23, 24–25
  compliance with medications, 20
  denial of access, 17–18
  distrust of healthcare system, 15
  heart disease in, 68
  hospitalization rates, 18
  hypertension in, 18
  life expectancy for, 45
  medical procedures and, 13
  mental health and, 220
  metabolic syndrome in, 14
  shortage of nurses, 51
  women, 13
Age disparities, 15
AIDS, 289, 290
  in Brazil, 149
  in Cuba, 162

  in France, 122
  in Russian Federation, 183, 184, 192
Alcohol dependency
  in Brazil, 245
  in Italy, 134
  mental illness and, 227
  in Russian Federation, 183, 194, 257
  in United States, 222
Allopathic, 203, 209
Alzheimer's disease, 227
Ambulance services, in United Kingdom, 109
Amenable mortality, 121
American Association for Colleges of
    Nursing (AACN)
  APN guidelines, 55
American Association of Colleges of
    Nursing (AACN), 51
American Association of Retired People
    (AARP), 60
American Health Benefit Exchanges, 48
  benefits offered through, 49
American Medical Association (AMA), 57
American Nurses Association (ANA), 51,
    52
ANAES (Agence Nationale d'Accréditation
    et d'Evaluation en Santé), 121
Annual cap, 49
Anxiety disorders, 226, 237–238
Asian Americans
  case study on, 26
  shortage of nurses, 51
Asthma, 19
  treating in Japan, 95
Ayurvedic medicine, 168

B

Baby boomer nurses, retirement of, 52
Basaglia Law, 236
Basic Health Units (UBS), 148, 149
Behavioral, definition of, 9

Art Credits

Chapter 1, 2, 3, 15, 16, and 17 Opener
© cobalt88/ShutterStock, Inc.

Chapter 4 Opener
map: © magicinfoto/ShutterStock, Inc.; **flag:** © Photos.com

Chapter 5 Opener
map: © Volina/ShutterStock, Inc.; **flag:** © VikaSuh/ShutterStock, Inc.

Chapter 6 Opener
map: © Irina Solatges/ShutterStock, Inc.; **flag:** © Dusan Po/ShutterStock, Inc.

Chapter 7 Opener
map: © skvoor/ShutterStock, Inc.; **flag:** © somchaij/ShutterStock, Inc.

Chapter 8 Opener
map: © Andrei Marincas/ShutterStock, Inc.; **flag:** © argus/ShutterStock, Inc.

Chapter 9 Opener
map: © fzd.it/ShutterStock, Inc.; **flag:** © Fenton/ShutterStock, Inc.

Chapter 10 Opener
map: © skvoor/ShutterStock, Inc.; **flag:** © Michael Roeder/ShutterStock, Inc.

Chapter 11 Opener
map: © Tshooter/ShutterStock, Inc.; **flag:** © Hemera/Thinkstock

Chapter 12 Opener
map: © Arunas Gabalis/ShutterStock, Inc.; **flag:** © yui/ShutterStock, Inc.

Chapter 13 Opener
map: © Andrei Marincas/ShutterStock, Inc.; **flag:** © PavleMarjanovic/ShutterStock, Inc.

Chapter 14 Opener
map: © Tshooter/ShutterStock, Inc.; **flag:** © Rene Grycner/ShutterStock, Inc.